W9-BBZ-448

"ABSORBING."
San Francisco Chronicle

"Morbidly fascinating . . . There was nobody even remotely like her."

New York Post

"Vividly evokes Lenya's striking personality . . . Well written."

Newsday

"The extraordinary tale of the Viennese prostitute who became the flame of Weimar Berlin."

Vanity Fair

Also by Donald Spoto:

FALLING IN LOVE AGAIN   *Marlene Dietrich*
THE KINDNESS OF STRANGERS   *The Life of Tennessee Williams**
THE DARK SIDE OF GENIUS   *The Life of Alfred Hitchcock**
CAMERADO   *Hollywood and the American Man*
STANLEY KRAMER   *Film Maker*
THE ART OF ALFRED HITCHCOCK   *Fifty Years of His Motion Pictures*

**Published by Ballantine Books*

LENYA
A Life

Donald Spoto

BALLANTINE BOOKS • NEW YORK

Copyright © 1989 by Donald Spoto

Documentary and archival material copyright © 1989 by the Kurt
Weill Foundation for Music

All rights reserved under International and Pan-American Copyright Conventions. Published in the United States of America by
Ballantine Books, a division of Random House, Inc., New York,
and simultaneously in Canada by Random House of Canada Limited, Toronto.

No part of this book may be reproduced in any form or by any
electronic or mechanical means, including information storage and
retrieval systems, without permission in writing from the publisher,
except by a reviewer who may quote brief passages in a review.

Library of Congress Catalog Card Number: 88-31421

ISBN 0-345-36542-9

This edition reprinted by arrangement with Little, Brown and Company, (Inc.)

Manufactured in the United States of America

First Ballantine Books Edition: June 1990

for Bill Phillips,
gifted editor and devoted friend

Forsan et haec olim meminisse juvabit.

Vergil, *Aeneid*, I, 203.

CONTENTS

ACKNOWLEDGMENTS

The following individuals generously granted interviews, volunteered special information and materials, or provided other assistances during the course of my research: Maurice Abravanel, Alan Anderson, Hesper Anderson, Quentin Anderson, Robert Anderson, Ken Andorn, Margot Aufricht, David Beams, Joy Bogen, John Canemaker, Milton Caniff, Carmen Capalbo, Stanley Chase, Linder Chlarson, Milton Coleman, Chandler Cowles, Cheryl Crawford, Hans Dudelheim, Fred Ebb, Richard Ely, Lewis Falb, Elfriede Fischinger, Ronald Freed, Neil Fujita, Amri Galli-Campi, Gigi Gilpin, Milton Goldman, Eric Gordon, Victor Carl Guarneri, Dolly Haas, Hilde Halpern, Margo Harris, Helen Harvey, Lucille Hauser, Helen Hayes, Hans Heinsheimer, Ernest Hood, George Jenkins, John Kander, Joseph Kennedy, Maurice Levine, Pearl London, Henry Marx, Joe Masteroff, Goetz Mayer, Burgess Meredith, Jonathan Meredith, Tala Meredith, Ted Mitchell, Paul Moor, Harriet Pinover, Maria Ley Piscator, Richard Plant, Harold Prince, Alan Rich, Ned Rorem, Julius Rudel, Victor Samrock, Albert Samuelson, Tonio Selwart, Dwayne Stiller, Erika Stone, Dolores Sutton, Jenny Torrell, Paul Violi, Lothar Wolff and Marguerite Young.

The Weill/Lenya Archive of the Yale University Music Library (established by Lotte Lenya and the Kurt Weill Foundation for Music, Inc., which is currently housed at Yale's Beinecke Rare Book Library) is one of two principal repositories for the archives of Kurt Weill and Lotte Lenya. My research there was much facilitated by the assistance of Helen Bartlett and Harold Samuel.

The other principal repository is the Weill-Lenya Research Center of the Kurt Weill Foundation for Music, Inc. at 7 East

20th Street, New York, N.Y. 10003. The Foundation granted permission to quote the correspondence of Weill and Lenya held by both institutions.

The staff in the Special Collections Division at Columbia University Library was also cordially helpful when I needed access to the Max Lincoln Schuster papers.

At the Austrian Press and Information Service, New York, special historical information was provided by Sylvia Gardner-Wittgenstein.

James Edward Fall kindly made available to me the correspondence between Lenya and his mother, Ann Fall.

Complex documents and historic papers in German were carefully rendered into English by Dr. Marlies Danziger, Professor of English at Hunter College of the City University of New York, by Ute Claus and by Dr. Jon Zimmermann, Professor of German Linguistics at the California State University at Fullerton. Likewise, important questions regarding theater history were answered by Dr. Gerald Pinciss, Professor of English at Hunter College, City University of New York.

Kirtley Thiesmeyer, my attorney, offered not only his wise counsel during some especially trying times but also his abiding concern for and dedication to every aspect of my career. His constancy, good humor and loyal friendship evoke my very deep gratitude.

Elaine Markson is the most attentive and patient literary agent, and throughout the various phases of this book she has always been a serene and constant friend. I cherish her affectionate support as much as her professional guidance and her unflinching integrity.

This is my fourth book published by the careful and caring Little, Brown and Company—a relationship that always makes me glad and grateful. At Little, Brown, Roger Donald—who years ago knew Lenya and encouraged her to write a book—first endorsed this project. Perdita Burlingame read the manuscript and offered prudent, cogent suggestions. Colleen Mohyde and Karen Dane were endlessly cheerful and efficient in managing daily details. And Mike Mattil brought to the manuscript his considerable gifts as copy editor—a talent which evokes both admiration and thankfulness.

But I save the best for last mention. My editor for the decade and quartet of books has been William Phillips, now Little, Brown's Editor-in-Chief, and he has guided me with a gentle sagacity and keen perception that I never take for granted—thus the dedication of this book. No doubt about it: Bill has been the single most important and effective presence in my career, and in spite of my occasional bouts of authorial hysteria he has remained a close and true friend. Individually and jointly, we endured many dark, anxious hours preparing this book, and it is a testament to his generous spirit that our trust and our amity survive not merely intact but enhanced.

Indeed, to all my dear friends I have a debt of loving gratitude that defies articulation. Their faith and devotion sustained me even when my own hope was dim; no words can adequately express what I owe them.

D.S.
22 July 1988
The Feast of Mary Magdalene

One

Premiere

AUTUMN 1966

AT BOSTON'S VENERABLE SHUBERT THEATRE ON THE evening of Monday, October 10, 1966, a new show opens prior to its Broadway premiere, and next morning the review in the *Globe* bears the headline: "*Cabaret* Has the Makings of a Rare Musical."

Based on stories by Christopher Isherwood, Harold Prince's production contrasts the frivolous frenzy of 1930 Berlin nightlife with the imminent horror of the Third Reich. Theatergoers enter to see themselves reflected in an enormous mirror suspended over the darkened stage. A sign blinks the letters of the play's title—the first setting of the action—and then, with a clash of drums and cymbals, a bizarre Master of Ceremonies enters, bidding the audience "Willkommen!" His hair is slick and center-parted, his face clown-white, his lips rouged, his eyes dark with mascara. Everything in the Kit Kat Klub onstage is wonderful, he insists, and then a black-gartered female jazz band appears, wearing neither brassieres nor expressions.

Soon the stage is filled with the cabaret's customers, entertainers, waiters, bartenders, boys and girls for rent—all of them welcoming the audience to the grim glamour of Weimar Germany. But as the story unfolds, the atmosphere shifts from desperate gaiety to impending doom. Recalling the era of *The Blue Angel* and of Kurt Weill and Bertolt Brecht's *The Threepenny Opera*, John Kander's music and Fred Ebb's lyrics for *Cabaret* combine alternately jaunty and poignant songs with the undertaste of despair in Joe Masteroff's seriocomic dialogue.

1

From the smoky tawdriness of the cabaret the story moves to Clifford Bradshaw, a struggling young American novelist. He finds lodging in the rooming house of Fraülein Schneider, whose fee is twice what he can afford. At the Kit Kat Klub, Cliff later sees Sally Bowles, a performer he hopes to date. They do not meet again, however, until she comes to Cliff for comfort at the end of her affair with a jealous lover.

Soon the audience learns more about the private life of Fraülein Schneider. Her admirer is Herr Schultz, a Jewish grocer who brings her gifts of fruit. They plan to marry, and Sally and Cliff offer an engagement party for them. But soon the danger to Schultz—and potentially to Fraülein Schneider as well—becomes clear when a rock is thrown through his shop window: Nazi anti-Semitism is now violent, deadly. Schneider realizes she cannot marry Schultz; she would lose her license to rent rooms as well as any security for her future. She has seen too much of life and cannot risk what remains. Marriage to a Jew is out of the question.

As the political and social storm gathers, Cliff wants Sally (now pregnant) to quit Berlin with him. But she insists on staying where life is simply fun; politics and moralizing bore her—"Life is a cabaret . . ." She then trades in her fur coat to pay for an abortion, and Cliff departs. The Jewish grocer moves away, and the landlady endures alone. On a train to Paris, Cliff begins writing the story of this recent time.

In the role of Fraülein Schneider is the oldest member of the company, a small, thin woman who a few days hence will begin her sixty-ninth year. Everyone connected with *Cabaret* believes she is years younger—an innocent ruse readily supported by her unremitting energy and lusty humor. At one hundred pounds and just over five feet tall, she has angular features, an appealing Viennese accent and a sinewy humor. Onstage, a red wig covers her own short hair of the same defiant color, which dramatizes her otherwise unimposing appearance.

The actress fascinates other cast members as she recalls her early professional life in cosmopolitan Zurich during World War I and her fame as performer and recording star in Berlin in the 1920s, with that city's antic libertinism and its great rush of artistic achievement, both coexisting on the eve of Hitler's accession to power. She describes—and colorfully embellishes—

her deadline-escape from Nazi storm troopers. She tells of her sojourns in Paris and London in the 1930s, with their music halls and elegant salons, where her career progressed and her fame expanded along with her list of lovers. She remembers New York and Hollywood in the 1940s and 1950s, and her eventually triumphant ascent to international stardom in middle age under the tutelage of her second husband. She speaks of her return to Europe after the war, where her status as legend was both endorsed and challenged.

Her name is Lotte Lenya, and she is a living symbol of the Germany depicted onstage in *Cabaret*. To fans, critics, friends, lovers and husbands, she is always simply "Lenya," and thus she always signs even the most intimate correspondence.

Some young members in the cast and audience know Lenya from her appearance two years earlier in a James Bond movie, *From Russia with Love*. In it, she sports a clever pair of brogans from which deadly daggers jab at Sean Connery. And two years before that, thousands of American college students had seen her in person during a campus tour, reading and singing selections from Brecht, Weill and others.

Lenya's first husband had been the composer Kurt Weill, who collaborated with Brecht and wrote the scores for (among other works) *The Threepenny Opera, Rise and Fall of the City of Mahagonny* and *The Seven Deadly Sins*, in all of which she had appeared decades earlier in European productions. Years later— after Weill's sudden, early death—a new generation of playgoers discovered her in a famous Greenwich Village revival of *The Threepenny Opera*, after which she augmented her coterie of fans with recordings of Berlin theater songs, her frequent recitals and concerts, and her memorable appearances in a few films.

Onstage in *Cabaret*, Lenya performs four songs. In "So What?" she accepts half the amount of rent she had expected from her new boarder. The "Pineapple Song" ("It Couldn't Please Me More") is a duet with the grocer who brings what northern Europeans consider the most exotic fruit and a symbol of hospitality, and their second duet celebrates a sudden decision to be "Married." But when she realizes that she cannot do this, she sings "What Would You Do?"

Lenya's voice in 1966 (forever preserved on the *Cabaret* cast recording) is full of character and energy—not a gentle, pleasant instrument but "an octave below laryngitis," as she calls it.

Sometimes she is cavalierly off-key, but no one seems to care: there is so much candor and humanity in the voice, such sympathy and simple wisdom, that her delivery cannot be assessed by a narrow standard of tonal accuracy. One moment you can hear a smoky vibrato, then something like a thin, baritonic complaint—and just as suddenly there is a suppressed sob, and a single phrase full of a lifetime's memories.

But there is also her face, a boon to caricaturists with its somewhat equine features and a gash of red lipstick, her gaze enigmatic and insouciant one second and then—with a flash of apparently enormous teeth—fearless, inviting, bawdy.

"The central acting honors of the evening belong to Lotte Lenya as Fraülein Schneider," writes Kevin Kelly in the *Boston Globe* the morning after the premiere.

> Miss Lenya, the sad, homely, indomitable German woman of the period, is unforgettable [with her] heartbreaking dignity . . . [she] is delightful, too, in the easier, happier episodes.

Kelly's colleague Elliot Norton, in the *Record American*, comments that Lenya and Jack Gilford (who plays the grocer)

> are gifted performers of ineffable personal appeal. They give "Cabaret" its biggest lift towards ultimate success; they give it both heart and humor . . . she with her quizzical, shrewd manner which can collapse in a gust of laughter.

And critic Samuel Hirsch, in the *Herald*, describes Lenya as

> an acute and miraculous joy to watch and listen to. Although her voice is husky, she reaches out with absolute artistry to catch at your throat with her honesty and you marvel at her pure talent. Hers is the voice of Germany.

Columnist Alta Maloney states the matter simply in the *Boston Traveler*:

> Lotte Lenya holds the audience in the palm of her hand. . . . There's not a doubt in the world about [her] arousing the bravos on Broadway.

Everyone in *Cabaret*'s cast likes Lenya, and they all congratulate her on her unanimous raves.

But no one in the cast knows that Lenya's private life is not nearly so successful or fulfilled. Her third husband is Russell Detwiler, an unsuccessful artist and a self-destructive alcoholic. He is twenty-seven years her junior, and he is penniless and very much aware of his dependence on her. He often sarcastically calls himself "Mr. Lenya."

Cabaret moves from Boston to New York on November 20, where it begins a three-year run of over eleven hundred fifty performances, most of them with Lenya. On opening night, she asks her old friend Gigi Gilpin to accompany Russell Detwiler to the Broadhurst Theatre and to stay with him all evening, to keep him sober and Lenya free from embarrassment.

Gilpin and Detwiler go to a restaurant for a light supper before the show, but she cannot deter him from ordering a double martini, and then a second double. Later, during the first intermission at the theater, Detwiler slips away and returns to his seat after several more drinks. At the celebration following the premiere, he becomes so drunk he cannot talk or stand, and Lenya and her friend bundle him back to the apartment.

Before dawn, the first New York review arrives, the commercially critical assessment by the *New York Times*. "Miss Lenya has never been better," Walter Kerr writes, and he rates the musical "stunning." The subheadline of the review is, "Lotte Lenya Stars," and the accompanying photo features Lenya and Jack Gilford. For Richard Watts, Jr., in the *New York Post*,

> Lotte Lenya's dramatic presence and the hint of long experience of sorrow in her voice make her characterization of the landlady in love with the Jew genuinely moving. . . .

And Julius Novick, in the *Village Voice*, praises Lenya's "patented brand of angry pathos." Her success in the show is capped when her performance earns her a Tony nomination as best actress in a musical the following spring, and although another eventually receives that award, Lenya is quite happy with the nomination—which, she feels, is as good as a win. Her attitude with colleagues is uniformly generous, her manner unselfconscious.

Lenya's pleasure in her star status is evident from each beguiling performance she gives in *Cabaret*. She is always attentive and friendly toward others in the cast and gracious with her admirers. She never gives a hint of the awfulness at home, of the ugliness every evening when she finds her husband incoherent or unconscious, often bleeding after a fall during an alcoholic seizure.

But this is not the first time she has coped simultaneously with triumph and disaster, nor the first time Lenya has put a public smile over private anguish. From childhood she has known about violence and the painful cycles of the addictive personality. She has made a lifelong series of formidable decisions to overcome all obstacles—often at terrible cost—and even now she connects survival with role-playing. Because there is so much in her past that is shocking and in her present that seems futile, she clings tenaciously to the image of Fraülein Schneider, a woman compromised by events around her but buoyed by her own canniness and will to survive. Just so Lenya.

Her songs in *Cabaret* are eerily accurate stencils of her life story. With brittle courage Lenya endures by saying "So What?" to almost every human experience. She wants always to be "Married," and she weds four times; in none of the marriages is she fulfilled. To many offers of attention and devotion—even obsessive attention and stifling devotion—her reaction is "It Couldn't Please Me More."

Beneath the surface appeal, behind the image of grainy humor and tough resilience, is a fusion of contradictions—a fiercely independent person who hates to be alone, a gifted performer plagued with lifelong insecurities and stage fright who only rarely takes steps to advance her own career, a woman with a legion of lovers but perhaps no love. When there is conflict and trauma in her private life—as usually there is—she asks people close to her what she asks audiences in her final *Cabaret* number: "What Would You Do?" Then, with tragic irony but great spirit, she makes wrong choices for poignant reasons—and she sings about those choices, dramatizing them and documenting herself on stage, screen and recordings. And that is the secret of her allure, her charm, her wit, her sadness and her genius.

Two

The Coachman's Daughter

1898–1920

FOR A THOUSAND YEARS, VIENNA HAS BEEN ONE OF the great gateways between the Eastern and Western worlds. Extending over one hundred sixty square miles—from east of the Danube River to the lush Vienna Woods far west—its position in northeast Austria has remained as crucial for international politics as for trade. From 1558 the city was the seat of the Holy Roman Empire, and by the end of the eighteenth century the essential structure of the Austrian Empire had been formed by Empress Maria Theresa and her son Joseph. A strong and conservative Catholic monarchy supervised an efficient and highly detailed bureaucracy.

But in the nineteenth century it became clear that the national devotion to order and duty could not prevent the emergence of complex political problems. The vast empire, for one thing, embraced millions of Hungarians and Slovaks who had resisted Joseph's efforts to impose German as the language of the realm. The forays of Napoleon were followed by the weakness of the Hapsburg heirs, and the revolutions of 1848 brought into being an aggressive new middle class. That same year, eighteen-year-old Franz Joseph I took the throne, beginning a rule of almost seven decades.

The emperor's reign began auspiciously. Autocratic and severe, he was also a devoted family man and, in spite of serious intellectual limitations and a bland humorlessness, he gave new meaning to the concept of public servant. A national health insurance and social security were available to all citizens by

7

1888—and a good thing, too, for the empire then numbered fifty-four million, and most of Vienna's two million were poor peasant immigrants.

The emperor's vast construction projects were the talk of Europe. In 1857, he had ordered the razing of the ancient city walls at the start of a dazzling new master plan. For over thirty years, there followed the construction of the Ringstrasse. This grand boulevard of trees, parks and gardens stretched almost three miles long and two hundred feet wide, a ring encircling the entire central district near the Danube. Inspired by Baron Haussmann's great designs for Paris under Napoleon III, there was a notable difference in this enormous scheme for public buildings and public space, both on the grand scale. Where unity had been the French hallmark, an astonishing variety of styles emerged along the Ring. The Parliament was built in the neo-Greek style, recalling Athenian democracy. The neo-Gothic City Hall was thought appropriate to the medieval time of burgher civic rule. The buildings of the University of Vienna rose in Renaissance splendor, suggesting the humanities in full bloom, and the national theater and museums, the State Opera and a concert hall each had its own idiosyncratic personality. Even the apartment complexes on and near the Ring conformed to nothing adjacent. Erected in baroque imitation of Italian palazzos, they housed those whose new wealth resulted from new industries.

The spirit of the empire was no more unified than the architecture of its capital: the people lacked any collective identity determined by geography or tradition. Germanic and Slavic factions had fought so bitterly over law and language that the emperor had been forced to dissolve the national assembly and govern by decree. Parliament was torn with dissension, and the emperor rearranged his prime ministerial and cabinet appointments with alarming rapidity. Within the city itself, Franz Joseph resisted pressures for greater democracy as long as he could, denying the cry for universal voting rights until 1907. But he could not ignore the Viennese demand for a popular mayor, and after three refusals to confirm the election of the demagogic, virulently anti-Semitic Karl Lueger, Franz Joseph was forced to accede.

The paternalistic authoritarianism of the emperor was, by the end of the century, irredeemably distant from the rapid changes of a fragmented society, and by the 1890s the gap separating the extravagant wealthy from the grindingly poor was everywhere evident in Vienna, as in most European and American cities. Near the more elegant neighborhoods, however, some of the public benefits of the emperor's programs served rich and poor alike. Just off the Ringstrasse, there was the fragrance of chestnut blossoms, and tunes from hurdy-gurdies, calliopes and music boxes seemed to fill the city. Uniformed young soldiers and beribboned veterans strolled on Sunday afternoons with their wives or girlfriends, each woman wearing the garment that indicated her provincial origins.

In the Prater—the city's verdant public park—there were hundreds of shooting galleries for the young men's amusement, and Punch and Judy shows for the children, as well as chalk-faced clowns, trained dogs, magicians, knife-throwers, sword- and fire-swallowers, weight lifters and various sideshows. Candy and chocolate stalls were only a few feet apart, and everywhere could be heard the terms of formal address, the click of military boots, the rustle of starched linen as a young lady bowed to a gentleman tipping a plumed hat. It was difficult to find a hand on man, woman, child or vendor that was not white-gloved. On the face of it, the casual amusements of the wealthy were formal, restrained and wholesome.

But if the roads to the city outskirts were followed, the atmosphere changed sharply. The uniforms of the Lichtenstein Dragoons, glimpsed in regular springtime processions, gave way to the tattered coveralls of the peasants hovering near tenement doorways. Carts with fancy desserts were seen no more, replaced by wagons of cold meat and stale vegetables. The homeless routinely slept in doorways, and even the sewers were occupied at night by hundreds of women and children. The Archduchess Marie Valerie's favorite charity could provide rooms, one piece of bread and two spoonsful of soup each night for only 368,000 men, 228,000 women and 583,000 children in 1898.

But alongside social fragmentation, civic unrest and economic disparity, there was a mysterious burst of creative energy. A new surge of life released new energies, and this was naturally accompanied by anxiety, disorder and uncertainty—everything associated with a culture in crisis. By the turn of the century, there was a climate in which anything was possible, and social resistance to previously unacceptable forms of art was significantly muted.

In music, a striking modernism was imminent, and Alban Berg, Arnold Schönberg and Anton von Webern were already experimenting with musical phrases and ideas that would challenge the expectations of traditional concertgoers.

In literature, the poet Hugo von Hofmannsthal was developing verse forms to express fresh psychological observations in his plays, and Ludwig Wittgenstein was working toward a new philosophy of language itself. Playwright Arthur Schnitzler caught a mood of confused languor in the Viennese air; his *Liebelei, Anatol, Komtesse Mizzi* and *Reigen* characterized the casual amours of city life as detached, melancholy, lifeless affairs.

In the visual arts, the so-called Secession movement of 1898— led by the painter Gustav Klimt, the architects Josef Hoffmann and Joseph Maria Olbrich and the designer Koloman Moser— broke away from the conservative exhibition society that ruled art in Vienna. They vowed to display the most modern Austrian works in regular shows, and to aspire to unity among all the arts through collaborative effort. The inscription on the façade of their new hall announced their creed: *To the Age Its Art, To Art Its Freedom.*

Much was brilliant and innovative, much iconoclastic. Klimt's paintings celebrated sensuality, desire and sheer impressionistic luxuriance. Egon Schiele's hard, almost confrontational portraits, on the other hand, were a chronicle of idealism defeated. Whereas Klimt's paintings invite lingering, Schiele's have the cool cynicism of late adolescence, private, self-absorbed, devoutly narcissistic.

With tradition and iconoclasm, wealth and destitution, order and upheaval everywhere evident, it was perhaps inevitable—or at least appropriate—that the seminal contributions of Sigmund Freud to the new science of psychology took shape in fragmented Vienna. His *Studies in Hysteria* was written here, and from 1895 to 1900 he was working on his revolutionary book *The Interpretation of Dreams.* Freud's data came from the Emmas and Elizabeths who visited his office on the Berggasse. They were ordinary people afflicted with recurring nightmares, phobias, hysterical paralyses, sexual repressions and psychosomatic illnesses—all of them ailments unleashed by the increasing disruption in the social order. Among Freud's clients was the brilliant, tormented composer Gustav Mahler, obsessed with religion, death and decay. Frail but driven, he died of heart disease in 1911 at the age of fifty-one.

These trends and developments flourished in a city that suddenly had no prevailing worldview. For students and scientists and artists this was often exciting: new forms were at their doorsteps, and new ways of speaking and living. But the lack of social coherence provoked widespread anxiety and produced an elaborate cultural narcissism—thus the pursuit of bodily elegance and endless pleasure. The old forms of social protocol were still pervasive, but most people merely nodded and ignored them. Because they were not backed up by active involvement, lived practice and the dynamic of everyday life, the institutions of State and Church in Hapsburg Vienna became largely formal and empty rituals in a baroque world that placed a premium on appearances and on the cult of the body. Moral rectitude was preached everywhere, but it coexisted comfortably with a general public acceptance of child prostitution. Religious affiliation (preferably Roman Catholic) was affirmed on official identity papers, but a scorn for religion marked ordinary Viennese social discourse.

There was, indeed, very little external evidence that Catholic Vienna had heard the Christian gospel, and so extremes of wealth and poverty could flourish calmly in a climate where faith was mostly theoretical. Pious images adorned classrooms and public halls, but no one paid them much attention. Like the emperor's Jubilee celebrations or Mayor Lueger's civic pageants and masked balls, they were a matter of show.

Consistent with this tangled fabric of political, social and cultural life was a shift in public attitude about sensuality and sex. Just as in Victorian England—and at precisely the same time—there was a sudden emergence of the erotic in public life, a wild new celebration of the body and its freedoms. "Imperial Vienna," wrote author Salka Viertel, who arrived in the city from Galicia and was an actress for a time,

> exuded an intense erotic atmosphere. It was impossible for a young woman to walk alone without being followed. Alternating between the sentimental and the rudely obscene approach, men pursued one with undaunted persistence. On my

way home from the theater I had to take the Kärntnerstrasse, which at night was the domain of the prostitutes. Sometimes they chased me, sure that I was a novice intruding on their hunting grounds. . . . There were several other streets . . . [and] pimps used to wait there for their girls.

But the oldest profession was not restricted to the alleys or avenues of the crowded amusement centers. In Vienna, prostitutes were as plentiful as the cafés, of which there were three or four on every city block. Symptomatic of this open eroticism were the blatantly personal advertisements of *Die Zeit*, which seems to have inspired a tradition that still flourishes. A sampling of items from that journal in 1898:

The gentleman in uniform who sat at the opera in front of a young blond lady in a blue dress seated with an elderly couple would like to make her acquaintance. Please write to Rittmeister, 1 Maximilianstrasse, Poste Restante. . . .

Young lieutenant wishes to meet the girl in pink dress and grey hat waiting in front of the Hotel Erzherzog-Karl. . . .

Would like to meet the lovely fair lady at the Café Scheidl last week. . . . Please contact Baron F. . . .

Young lady, fifteen years old, very pretty indeed, wants to make the "honorable" [*sic*] acquaintance of officer of the cavalry or gentleman of high position. Write to Mitzi, 13579 Taborstrasse II, Poste Restante.

But along with this rush of libertinism was the Viennese sense of social propriety, which often became morbid. Streetcars offered passengers at least eighteen signs listing various actions that were legal or illegal. Stepping lightly on a public lawn could invite a citizen's arrest, and the merest show of impatience in a carriage summoned pedestrians who might beat the driver and damage the vehicle. "These," as one critic has observed, "were the same people who would offer you the kiss of the hand, serve you the nicest mug of draft beer you are ever likely to taste, tell you a sly joke and warmly wish you a good afternoon." The city, like its artists and art, combined "love and resentment, fear and arrogance, charm and virtriol—all cramped and congealed into a space uncomfortably small.'' Conductor George Szell has described Vienna as a rich dessert with an unsavory filling.

There was, then, a somewhat mad festival of contradictions in the twilight of the Hapsburgs. The tendency toward formality coexisted with an irrepressible urge for self-mockery. Squeamishness about using first names or entering a public place without proper attire paralleled an inability to take anything very seriously. Ordinary folk distrusted intellectualism and analysis, but rejected anything that had the merest hint of sentiment or of the romantic spirit.

"The people of Vienna," an Austrian writer remarked as early as 1843,

> seem to any serious observer to be revelling in an everlasting state of intoxication. Eat, drink and be merry are the three cardinal virtues and pleasures of the Viennese. It is always Sunday, always Carnival time for them. There is music everywhere. The innumerable inns are full of roisterers day and night. Everywhere there are droves of fops and fashionable dolls.

And so it prevailed to the turn of the century, when just as much stress was put on uniforms, ribbons, elaborate masques, military bands, court balls and the formulas of social life that had come to resemble a lovely lace thrown over a wizened and decaying body. By 1898 Vienna was famously referred to as ''a testing-lab for the end of the world,'' and in 1914 the Viennese writer and critic Robert Musil could write, ''What world? . . . There isn't any!''

But the apocalyptic testing-lab was not immediately evident in the autumn of 1898, the year of the emperor's Golden Jubilee. Pageants and festivals touched every square with festivity and every central park with music and gaiety. Even the old man's critics—those who saw that his dynastic rule was out of touch with racial and ethnic tensions and impending economic disaster—lowered their voices and tossed bouquets at Franz Joseph. His private life, after all, had been marred by tragedy and still he had borne his office with dignity and without wavering. On January 30, 1889, his only son, the heir apparent Crown Prince

Rudolf, had committed suicide in a death pact with his seventeen-year-old lover. The emperor's wife, Elizabeth of Bavaria—a great beauty with a prickly, unstable character—never recovered from that, and her love of travel had become a restless wandering. On September 10, 1898, as she was about to board a steamer in Geneva, the empress was assassinated by a mad Italian anarchist. The gala Jubilee celebrations that autumn—held only because of the emperor's devotion to public image and public duty—bore the tincture of official grief.

Civic piety honored the deaths as it did the Jubilee, but the colorful Viennese embellishments of religious and political spectacle could not disguise the fact that here was a regime spiritually bankrupt and socially shattered. Prolonged church services, exaggerated manners and extreme forms of courtesy could no longer mask a moribund culture.

In that Jubilee autumn of 1898, thousands of poor workers were living in close quarters in the Viennese district of Penzing. In the eighteenth century Penzing had been the cradle of the silk industry, and its location on the left bank of the river Wien, on the road to Linz, made it convenient for passing tradesmen. Since it was close to the Vienna Woods, it had once been a summer resort, but with the Industrial Revolution it became strictly working class. Biedermeier houses and factories—functional, squat and often grotesque—lined the streets of Penzing, and by 1898 there was also a proliferation of furniture shops and laundries. A tuberculosis sanatorium and a mental asylum completed the atmosphere of illness and deprivation in which the poor lived out a seven-day work week. Apart from the few declared holidays, only hospitalization assured warmth, rest and good food.

That year, Franz Paul Blamauer and his family were living in two small rooms in a tenement at 87 Linzerstrasse. His parents (Franz Paul Blamauer and Anna Maria Binderhofer) and their parents and grandparents had lived in greater Vienna for generations, all of them laborers and all of them nominally Roman Catholic.

On November 12, 1893, in the Catholic Church of St. Jakob, Penzing, the twenty-eight-year-old Franz Paul Blamauer married Johanna Teuschl, then twenty-five. Her family came from Ottenschlag, about fifty miles west of Vienna near Melk; her father, Johannes Teuschl, had been a tailor who married a local girl named Karolina Pastorfer. Johanna had worked as a tavern-girl in Ottenschlag before moving to Vienna and working as a laundress. This she continued even after her marriage to Bla-mauer, who earned only meager wages driving a carriage for a florist.

Franz Blamauer was a dashing figure, tall and slim, with a sharp nose and good teeth, reddish hair and a neatly clipped mustache and sideburns. His wife was short and pretty, with high cheekbones, fine skin, deep-set gray eyes and thick chest-nut hair. Before their first anniversary, she bore a baby girl they named Karoline, after Johanna's mother. The baby delighted her father, who particularly enjoyed the child's precociously cute singing and dancing. But then the child died of a fever just before her third birthday, and in his grief (and perhaps also from guilt at not being able to prevent his daughter's death) Franz Bla-mauer's tendency toward heavy social drinking became a chronic and brutal alcoholism.

A son was born on August 2, 1897; he was given his father's name. Then, on October 18, 1898, Johanna had a second girl. Franz insisted she be named after the dead first child, and next day the infant was christened Karoline Wilhelmine Charlotte, memorializing a sister she never knew and two aunts. She was known at home as Linnerl, the Viennese nickname for Karoline; much later, she would be called Lotte Lenya. By the time Jo-hanna gave birth to her last two children—Maximilian in 1900 and Maria in 1906—the family had twice relocated. In 1901 they took an apartment near the Linzerstrasse and soon after moved to 38 Ameisgasse.

A proletarian flat located near the railroad tracks, the Bla-mauer apartment on Ameisgasse could not really be called a slum. There were eight residences to a floor, each entered through a heavy oak door with cut-glass insets and wrought-iron designs. A wide staircase and handsome brass railing curved from story to story, the hallways were invariably tidy, the mosaic designs in the public corridors were swept daily and the common toilet off the central hall—for the use of the families on each floor—was kept clean by the residents and their concierge.

Linnerl and her family lived in two small rooms on the third floor—a kitchen-workroom and a bedroom—where they not only ate and slept but also where Johanna Blamauer washed, sorted, ironed and arranged the bundles of neighbors' laundry she took in to supplement her husband's erratic income. Physically, family life was extremely simple; Linnerl's plain wooden bed, she remembered, was really just "a wooden box used as an ironing board during the day, or for people to sit on, and Mother made noodles on it." The apartment seemed even more cramped when, as they frequently did, the Blamauers took in transient boarders who slept on a couch in the kitchen-workroom.

Holidays meant only the most rudimentary pleasures, but certain sense images remained with Karoline Blamauer forever. At Christmas her mother made a doll from assorted pieces of broken pottery, and Linnerl wept for hours when she accidentally broke it, slipping on the hall stairs only hours after she received it. Her mother consoled her with a sugar cube dipped in hot milk, a special treat that forever bore the memory of childhood Christmases.

Our knowledge of Lotte Lenya's earliest years is based largely on her own memories, both oral and written. In her fifties—with the help of her second husband, a writer and editor whose assistance was invaluable—she began the process of compiling a memoir. Never published, the notes and several drafts of this document contain sharp images of a bitter and brutalizing childhood, and her earliest recollections were of her father's beatings. In her memoir-notes, she described the abuse she endured:

It was always me who was dragged out of bed when he came home drunk—and drunk he was and stayed drunk until he died. I had to sing to him. And I stood there with my eyes full of sleep and tried to please him, tried to be as good as the first one was, tried desperately to turn my head the other way, so I wouldn't have to smell his sour breath until I was pushed back to bed. . . . The worst thing was the way he lifted me out of my bed. He placed his two big hands around my neck like a strangler and lifted me out—only to throw me back after a few minutes when I could not satisfy him with my singing the way the first Karoline had. Other nights he grabbed the kitchen knife, and sometimes I had to run downstairs. . . . One night he was dreadfully drunk and he got so furious at me for not remembering the lines to a song that he picked up the oil-lamp and threw it at me. The flame went out, but I could have been burnt to death from the explosion.

Even before school age, the child was regularly beaten when her father came home at night—beaten because she was still awake, or beaten because she was asleep and had not prepared him a drink or told him how she had helped her mother that day.

> On the corner of our street was a tavern [she wrote in her memoir-notes]. From it I had to bring beer in a stein for my father, and running across the street with the beer I sometimes spilled some of it. When I handed the stein to my father, I was fully prepared to be slapped in the face, which he did more often than not.

Her sister Maria, in a letter to Lenya in 1954, remembered that the violence was directed only at Linnerl. More than once, Maria wrote, the enraged father tore glassware and dishes from a cabinet and smashed them against a wall; she also recalled the incident of the hurled oil-lamp.

For the adult Lenya, the memory of the brutality was always connected to the older sister she never knew.

> She had been my father's darling. I was always unfavorably compared to her. The first Linnerl had been a fair, dimpled child with golden curls, who had always danced and sung for her adoring papa. For me, the second Linnerl who looked so different and only reminded him of his dead beloved, he had only a maniacal hatred. Too many nights, too often, he staggered home, dragged me from my bed, shook me awake and forced me to sing and dance, as if trying to revive his first-born. . . . Often the mere sight of me would drive him into a blind fury, and he pursued me with curses and slaps.

Whether other factors contributed to Franz Blamauer's alcoholism and brutality may never be known, for all we have of him is the testimony of the abused daughter (and a confirmation of this from her sister Maria). But it is significant that Lenya understood his brutality as expressing a resentment of her; and so, as the abused child typically does, she saw her own life as the cause of violence, the reason for the withholding of love. Her own existence, in other words, was perceived (however dimly) as the grounds for the awfulness. By good conduct, by quick obedience to his demands, by avoiding him, by cowering submissively, she hoped to pacify him, to win him, his approval, his love—but she never could. And so she had to face the dilemma that the man who was supposed to love and nurture her instead withdrew, resented and hurt her, and that her own repeated attempts to be perfect, to please, were futile and forever unrewarded by affection. "God, how [my father] must have hated & resented me," she scrawled in a marginal note to herself.

Her mother, however, she depicted (and always described to friends later) as a strong and protecting comforter in Linnerl's life.

My mother had wonderfully alive and searching eyes and a wide sensual mouth. Brutal drunkard, skirt-chaser and wretched provider my father turned out to be, but my mother wasn't the type to pop her head into the gas oven for such run-of-the-mill faults in a man. Her nature was basically gay, stalwart, intrepid, with a horror of all fake sentiment. She was also deeply and resourcefully female, with a quietly operating magnetism that attracted all men. Not that she had much time for lovers.

Although Johanna appears to have been a passive accomplice in her husband's abuse of their daughter, Lenya never wrote or spoke in any but admiring and affectionate terms of her mother. If she could not prevent the beatings, however, at least Johanna Blamauer encouraged her daughter:

Once in a while, when I helped her with the washing, she would look across where I was standing, and Mother would smile and say, "Linnerl, try to make a better life for yourself," and I would say, "Yes, Mother, I will." Once I asked my mother, "Tell me, am I pretty?" And I remember my mother standing back, looking at me with those incredibly alert eyes, saying, "No, Linnerl, you're not pretty—but men will like you."

Before she was of school age, Linnerl was doing more than helping her mother with the laundry. Hilde Halpern, her friend in later years, recalled her recurring description of polishing the banister of the apartment building for the landlady, for which she received the equivalent of five cents a week. "She said she did this so well," according to Halpern,

> that then she got to shine all the brass fittings in the building, and a few pennies were added. But half the time the landlady cheated her even out of that small sum, and when she had nothing to turn over to her father that night, his rage was increased.

According to another friend, Harriet Pinover, Lenya claimed she was often paid by the landlady with a stale piece of chocolate.

The autumn of 1904, when Linnerl first attended the local elementary school, was a brief and chilly season that ushered an early, fierce winter. The chestnut trees in the Prater glistened with ice every day from early November, and heavy snowfalls were frequent. Several times that season Linnerl was hospitalized at St. Roch's Clinic for fevers and for urticaria—massive and painful hives that afflicted her hands and feet, eyelids and lips. At the hospital she was warm and well fed, free of her father's brutality and comfortable in a real bed with more privacy than she had ever known.

But another hospital experience that season was more frightening, although she was not the patient. Her father's sister was confined to the local mental asylum after walking naked through the streets of Penzing. When the Blamauers went to visit her, they brought a cake. The aunt broke off a piece and handed it to Linnerl, but the child screamed and fled, afraid that she, too, might be sent to the prisonlike building if she ate a piece of cake touched by the woman.

Classes in the crowded elementary school were devoted to geography, arithmetic, German and French reading (with rudimentary English conversation) and the history of the Austro-Hungarian Empire. Karoline Blamauer's academic performance must have been impressive, for in 1908 she was transferred to a school for gifted children in the Hitzing district, a fashionable neighborhood near the Schönbrunn Palace. There, in classes especially designed for achievers, she flourished under the tutelage of a teacher named Miss Schwartz, a kind, humpbacked little lady whose skill and warmth impressed all her students, according to Lenya years later. Miss Schwartz taught her not only her first courses in appreciation of the arts, music and history; she also pointed out during afternoon walks the names of trees and flowers and plants.

During two summers of her childhood, Linnerl and her baby sister Maria were befriended by a family named Griesmeyer, who lived in two vans in a field near their home. In warm months, these neighbors operated a modest traveling circus on collapsible stages attached to the vans, and it was with them that Lotte Lenya's debut occurred. The Griesmeyers' young daughter fell sick one summer day, and because Linnerl was the same age and had often stood watching their antics, she was pressed into service, outfitted in a peasant dress and handed a tambourine. She then danced around a makeshift arena, singing and smiling at bystanders. Even her father, she recalled, approved her little performance; for a moment, perhaps she *was* the mourned first daughter.

In the spring of 1912, before her secondary education was complete, the thirteen-year-old Linnerl left school. Her mother knew a member of the Ita family, who owned a large and prestigious hat factory and retail store, and for a brief time the girl worked as an apprentice seamstress. She also ran errands, making deliveries to stores and customers.

The job did not last long, however. It was succeeded by one she had already undertaken earlier when, while still in school, she had joined the company of local girls earning money as prostitutes. When Karoline Blamauer became one of the "sweet young things," she was joining a well-established, highly visible and socially disreputable company in Vienna.

Some parts of her life aren't very pretty, but all of it was significant for the development of her unique personality. She was, as she admitted to me, on the streets before she was twelve years old. She gave the impression that she wasn't forced to do it, but that she had wanted to.

So said Margot Aufricht, the wife of the producer of the original *Die Dreigroschenoper (The Threepenny Opera)*, who was a friend and confidante during especially difficult times later. And Paul Moor, the American journalist who lived for many years in Germany and became a good friend to Lenya there, agreed: "This part of her past she admitted quite freely to anyone who cared to hear about it. She wasn't proud of it, and she wasn't ashamed of it. It happened."

A battered child is, of course, fair prey to this pathetic introduction to street life, and the picture of the schoolgirl Linnerl making herself available at a price in late afternoon and on weekends is not far different from the young prostitutes of other times and places. Vienna's streets and alleys during the early years of this century were literally crowded with prostitutes, many of them teenagers, some of them even younger. It is not surprising that Linnerl joined them, for in a home atmosphere of threats and violence she would naturally look elsewhere for affirmation from men. Selling herself at the age of eleven, Linnerl was catapulted into a grotesque parody of bartering for affection. And like many women who are belittled and reviled by their fathers—even without physical abuse—she sought constant reassurance of her merit in a long succession of new men. Often (as later with Lenya) even an adoring husband fails to fill the void.

Both her family situation and her culture, therefore, helped to form her as a vulnerable child-woman, shrewdly independent, street-smart and canny in making herself agreeable to men and dealing with them on a directly physical and emotionally unthreatening level. Like many abused children, she turned to prostitution early, trying to capitalize on the one element that she felt gave her a kind of temporary psychological affirmation and comparatively easy financial compensation. Apart from the obvious trauma from this time of her life—the child prostitute's quest for emotional satisfaction being invariably frustrated—there was the psychological leapfrog over key stages of adolescence. She never experienced the ordinary teenager's wonder, the doubt and hesitation about intimacy and its physical expression. And whatever might have been her parents' reactions to her street life, she remained with them, perhaps dissembling when she could, perhaps quietly sharing her profits without explanation.

Late in the summer of 1913, Johanna Blamauer's older sister Sophie came to Penzing for a visit. Linnerl had met her once before, during an earlier trip to Aunt Sophie's home in the Austrian countryside.

Aunt Sophie was my mother's older sister [Lenya wrote later in her memoir-notes], and looked much like her, except that you could tell Aunt Sophie was accustomed to a gentler, more prosperous life. She too had come first to Vienna as a servant-girl, then had married in fairly rapid succession three well-to-do but sickly men; after the death of the last one she had rather mysteriously landed up in Zurich, where she was now housekeeper for a retired doctor.

Sophie was childless, and now she lamented this fact to her sister. Embracing Linnerl, she repeated that the companionship of a daughter would have been a great comfort. Her niece seized the opportunity, as she recalled in her memoir.

I attached myself to her, ran to do her bidding, worked all my charm on her. And Aunt Sophie then announced that she yearned to take me back to Zurich with her. My father said, "She'll be a whore!" but I still remember my mother's smiling face at the train station, and her farewell: "Be smart, Linnerl, and don't come back if you can help it!"

And so, at her aunt's suggestion and with at least the complicity of her mother (if it was not indeed Johanna's own idea), Linnerl quit the gray atmosphere of proletarian Penzing and headed for the brighter slopes of Switzerland. Between them both mother and aunt were offering a clear lesson: take advantage of any helpful situation to correct an unprosperous life.

Karoline Blamauer may not have been pretty—her skin was pale, her hair mousy brown, her nose large, her mouth wide and her jaw concealed a pronounced overbite—but as Margot Aufricht said, "She knew how to make herself appealing." She also knew how to exploit that appeal for her own goals.

As the overnight train approached Zurich, Sophie became more and more agitated, wondering aloud what the doctor's reaction to a new resident might be. The decision was made to tell him Karoline had arrived for a brief visit. (From her arrival in Zurich, she was known to all outside her family—at least for the next few years—by her more formal Christian name.)

Surrounded by richly forested mountains and situated on the northwest end of the lake that bears its name, Zurich is Switzerland's largest city. In the fall of 1913 it housed a great number of transients from all over Europe, and the result of this was a colorful and cosmopolitan flavor. Solidly Protestant, the sober and frugal Swiss were an immediate contrast to the indulgent Viennese. But despite the Swiss reputation for austerity, the theatrical and musical life of Zurich had always welcomed experimentation, and there were new plays, symphonies, operas and pageants weekly through the year at the Stadttheater (the City Theater, where opera, ballet and spectacles were staged) and the Schauspielhaus (home of the theatrical repertory company). Albert Einstein, who had earned his doctorate at the Zurich Polytechnic in 1905, had already published his theory of relativity and was teaching at the university.

Aunt Sophie and Dr. Zaug lived in a modest part of town, near the seventeenth-century guildhouses that were part of the city's rich architectural legacy. As her aunt expected, however, the doctor was not pleased about the new arrival, whom he considered an invader of his privacy. For the first several days, the girl was kept out of sight in a servant's room, where she was told to amuse herself with a large straw trunk that held the remnants of Sophie's marriages—linen sheets, faded nightgowns, fur pieces. Her aunt prepared Karoline's meals and delivered them to this room, which was becoming a virtual cell. Only if Dr. Zaug was in good humor was she permitted to come to the kitchen or to sit in the parlor. The atmosphere, although not violent, was no more affectionate than in Penzing.

After several anxious weeks, it was arranged that Karoline would stay with friends of her aunt, a warm and welcoming elderly couple named Ehrenzweig who took to the girl at once and treated her like the child they never had. Ehrenzweig was a photographer specializing in group pictures of theater people in the typically artificial poses of the day, and one afternoon he showed his new boarder a photograph of a large-busted, dark-eyed beauty named Steffi Herzeg, who was then ballet mistress at the Stadttheater and a close friend to Ehrenzweig. When Karoline said she had once performed with a local circus troupe and had always wanted to be a dancer, he offered to speak to Herzeg on her behalf. Within a week, lessons were arranged, with the monthly charge of twenty-five francs to be shared by Aunt Sophie and Dr. Zaug, and by Karoline's new patrons, the Ehrenzweigs. In return, the girl was to make the Ehrenzweigs' breakfasts, clean the photographer's studio before class, come home to help with luncheon and then help prepare dinner. She had found a surrogate family.

Mrs. Ehrenzweig was busy on Karoline's behalf while the girl was at ballet class. She began to make a wardrobe of clothes for her, and soon there hung in her closet a new skirt and blouse, an overcoat, dresses, even handkerchiefs. When Sophie visited one day and saw her niece trying on the new clothes, she knew Karoline had won not only a place in ballet class, but also in the lives of her friends. "Aber das ist Eine!" she wrote to her sister Johanna soon after: "She's quite a little number, this girl!" Plain-faced but precocious and sparkling with energy, Karoline knew how to maneuver for herself; vulnerable but tough, she captivated men and women, and she knew how to migrate from one position of advantage to another.

Even more than Mrs. Ehrenzweig's new wardrobe for her, however, Karoline was delighted by the dancing slippers given to her by Steffi Herzeg. The ballet mistress was a temperamental Hungarian who worked Karoline to exhaustion, but the girl thrived on the classes—despite the early, solid evidence that classical ballet was not her forte.

Of the twelve girls in the class, I was and remained the least talented on point [she wrote in her memoir-notes years later]. My body, feet, face, entire nature were against it, against all the attitudes of formal ballet. Instinctively, I seized instead on pantomime, improvisation, free movement to give a sense of character. And in these I found myself.

By Christmas 1913, she had demonstrated sufficient stage presence to be assigned a walk-on role at the Stadttheater, as a flower girl in Gluck's opera *Orfeo*. Twenty years later, when she returned to Zurich as a star, Lenya recalled in a press interview the first rehearsal for her Zurich debut:

The rehearsal was scheduled for six o'clock, so I got up at five in the morning and was in front of the theater punctually at six. I rang the bell and awakened the night porter. "What the hell do you want?" he asked. "I have to begin rehearsing

at six," I said shyly. "Well, that means six in the evening!"
So I walked up and down for twelve hours outside, waiting!

The chorus rehearsals, she thus learned, were scheduled to accommodate girls who worked at legitimate full-time employment.

Her next role was also a nonspeaking one, as a farmer's boy in the opera *William Tell*. "I began putting on my make-up three hours before the performance, and I made up my eyes like [the later film appearances of] Greta Garbo. The director caught me just before I went on and made me wash my face."

In June 1914, as Steffi Herzeg's classes drew toward a summer hiatus and the theater season prepared to close, Aunt Sophie appeared at the Ehrenzweig home and announced that her niece would have to return to Vienna. Dr. Zaug had withdrawn his share of the financial support of Karoline, and there was talk of war; the girl, it was felt, ought to be with her mother.

Sophie and her niece appeared at the Austrian consulate in Zurich, where the aunt pleaded poverty and begged for train fare. When Karoline arrived in Vienna, however, there were unpleasant surprises. Her father had left home to live with another woman, and her mother had taken for her companion a kind man who (according to Maria later) might have become a good stepfather had he not soon died.

The summer of 1914 was tense—in Penzing as around the world, which was poised for war following the assassination of Archduke Franz Ferdinand at Sarajevo on June 28. Johanna Blamauer and the new man in her life were a welcome change from the brutal atmosphere caused by her husband, but the boarder-lover fell ill with tuberculosis and died. Soon there was a replacement, a man Johanna met when she was working at a military hospital later that year. His name was Ernest Hainisch, and he must have seemed a carbon copy of Franz Blamauer, for he was as cruel to Maria as their father had been to Karoline. The younger daughter often slept at neighbors' apartments to avoid Hainisch's beatings. Johanna, meanwhile, seemed content in yet another unhealthy and dependent relationship with an angry and violent man.

The war that was to have ended all wars was declared on August 3. Within days, young Franz Blamauer was sent to work in a bayonet factory and Max was heading east as an ambulance driver. Johanna's income as a laundress was drastically reduced, and Maria—who appeared pale and undernourished to her older sister—had to endure even severer rationing, for Hainisch contributed little if anything. Karoline, insisting she could send small sums and packages from Zurich and aware that each week's delay would make a return more difficult, wrote to the administration of the Stadttheater. Only a formal contract could, after the declaration of war, secure her a passport to leave Austria.

Finally, those two documents in hand, Johanna and Karoline together approached those who had regularly sent their laundry to the Blamauer apartment. Every customer sympathetically offered a few coins, and the fare to Zurich was quickly collected. Only later did the girl learn that her mother had not asked for charity, but had promised that the money would be an advance against future sacks of wash.

The journey by train that should have been a smooth overnight ride took four days, with the cars full of soldiers and refugees, frightened civilians, the usual number of students returning from summer holiday and hundreds of others on various war-related tasks. There were many unscheduled stops, inspections and delays before Karoline finally arrived and headed straight for the office of the Stadttheater's manager, Alfred Reucker. Kindly and protective toward young talent, he promised her understudy jobs and small roles. These assignments, however, would not be immediately forthcoming.

From Reucker's office she went to Aunt Sophie, who told her the Ehrenzweigs would welcome her back and that another friend (apparently one of Aunt Sophie's former beaux) had a part-time job for her.

He was a nice man named Emil [Lenya wrote in her memoir-notes years later], about fifty years old, but his great passion seemed to be catching flies. This he did, calmly seated with a big cigar in one hand and when he caught the flies he put them in a jar, blew cigar smoke in and watched them drop in stupor. Meanwhile, I sold postal cards in his souvenir shop. He was glad to have me there, since I was a friendly salesgirl and he could devote more time to his flies.

Before winter's first snow fell on Zurich, the war altered life dramatically. Tensions between the French-speaking minority and those who were sympathetic to the Germans were intensified by evidence that some major Swiss statesmen were passing secrets on to Germany, in defiance of Swiss neutrality. Political refugees poured into the country. That September, Lenin arrived from Russia and began working with other anti-imperialist socialists. Switzerland was forced to levy an income tax, food rationing was strictly observed, and the autumn sharpshooting contest was only one among many sporting and social events canceled in Zurich.

Saving money from her part-time job, Karoline sent packages of woolen mittens and Swiss chocolate home to her mother and sister, with letters of encouragement and news of life in the theater. By Christmas, she had also saved enough to take a further step toward independence by moving from the Ehrenzweigs' to the home of Grete Edelmann, a girl she had befriended in her dance class. The Edelmann family rented rooms in their large apartment to transient theater people.

Grete's father was a shy little man who worked as a printer. He wore thick glasses and rarely spoke, and when he was home generally took orders from his wife—a domestic situation that must have seemed astonishing to Karoline. Mrs. Edelmann, on the other hand, was a character straight from the pages of Arthur Schnitzler or Stefan Zweig, and years later Lenya recalled in her handwritten memoir:

> She [Mrs. Edelmann] had pretty blond hair but she was enormously fat, and a large golden cross dangling on a black velvet ribbon heaved up and down on her huge bosom like a landmark. She very often expressed the belief that if luck had been on her side she would have had a great career on the stage, and all her gestures were grand and histrionic. Every morning, for instance, she announced breakfast by running her fat fingers over the piano keys in a swooping glissando.

As for Grete, she had none of her mother's affectation, nor of her father's shyness. But she knew how to look demure—especially when her mother pointed out to friends, neighbors and boarders that the dangers of city life were no worry for Grete. Her virgin daughter, she proclaimed, was keeping her vir-

tue for some lucky man in marriage. The truth appears to be
quite another matter, for Lenya noted later in her memoir-notes
that Grete was in constant trouble and had one abortion after another. In fact both girls seem to have led a freewheeling life, for
Karoline herself had an abortion during her time in Zurich.

Grete's official fiancé was a "dreary Serb," Lenya wrote, but
at least the Serb and Grete invited Karoline to nightclubs with
them. At that time, such places were crowded with war profi-
teers and their girlfriends. Zurich realized an unprecedented
prosperity because of the war, as money, goods and art were
legally and illegally transferred into the city. ("In all my time
there I never saw a really poor Swiss," Lenya wrote. "Every
second house, it seemed, was a bank.")

The Serb was eventually replaced by another official fiancé—
this one a French jewelry dealer who provided Grete with new
clothes and a few pieces of his merchandise—"nothing really
good," Lenya wrote in her memoir, "but enough to keep her
mother happy and give her the illusion that Grete was going to
make a great marriage."

By the spring of 1915, Karoline was having a serious affair of
her own, with a young Swiss sculptor named Mario Perucci, of
whom nothing is known except his generosity toward her and
her family.

An important development in Karoline's professional life occurred during the second season in Zurich. She was interviewed
and prepared for new roles at the Schauspielhaus, the repertory
theater, by the actor, producer and director Richard Révy.

He was a pudgy, moon-faced man [Lenya noted in her
memoir-notes], highstrung, vital, with a profound knowledge
of theater and a growing reputation as a director of plays by
the German Expressionist playwright Georg Kaiser. Révy told
me that he had been watching me, that he was impressed,
that he was confident I had a talent for acting, and that he
was willing to take me as a private student, without payment.

Within days she was meeting Révy daily and learning roles
in plays by Shakespeare, Sophocles, Wedekind, Kaiser, Mae-
terlinck and Shaw. He gave his apprentice an informal but rich
education in literature as well as drama, urging her to read
Goethe, Tolstoy, Dostoevski and Gorky. Soon they were close

companions. Révy was considerably older—in his early for-
ties—but he was precisely the kind of gentle, affectionate pro-
tector she had never known, an attentive, generous and loving
man, and it is hard to imagine a needier recipient for those
qualities. Nor is it difficult to understand how the benevolent
Révy was simultaneously a kind of father figure. Senior, polished, educated and concerned, he was entirely different from
Franz Blamauer. At first Révy called Karoline "Grushenka,"
after Dmitri's beloved in Dostoevski's *The Brothers Karama-
zov*—the girl of doubtful reputation, playful and gentle sometimes, but often sly and wicked. But then Richard Révy and
Karoline Blamauer invented the name by which she would be
known for the rest of her life—they took the Viennese nickname
"Linnerl," created a Russian analog, and she became "Lenja."
When she returned to Zurich as a star twenty years later, however, she told an interviewer that a theater manager in Berlin
had changed her name from Blamauer because that name
"sounded too much like the old court theater." (For consistency
and simplicity, she will henceforth be referred to as Lenya, the
anglicized form she adopted later when she came to America.)

An important element in Zurich's social and cultural life was
the notorious Café Voltaire, and Lenya would certainly have
known of it—and perhaps even, with a few friends, have attended the café. Part fringe coffeehouse and part rowdy bar,
Hugo Ball's untidy spot was a haven for the bold, brave anarchic
poets, musicians and artists who rebelled against the butchery
of the war. It was also the place where the movement known as
Dada was virtually codified by 1916.

Precursor of Surrealism, Dada was a nihilistic movement in
the arts that denounced social and aesthetic restraint as well as
the nature of literature itself. The eponymous nonsense syllable
was a symbol of the madcap, childlike discarding of all the
traditions its founders associated with dying empires and mur-
derous, imperialist wars. Tristan Tzara, a poet, gave this movement its greatest energy, the artist Hans Arp contributed its early
graphics, and sculptor Marcel Duchamp—who once sent a toilet
bowl for exhibition at a Paris art show—became one of Dada's
most flamboyant members.

At various times during the war, Zurich hosted James Joyce,
Stefan Zweig, Romain Rolland and Lenin, among others. But
it was Hugo Ball and his mistress Emmy Hennings who gathered

the disparate refugees and local talents together. On a typical evening, German poet and psychiatrist Richard Hülsenbeck chanted his "Fantastic Prayers," swirling a riding crop over the heads of his audience and shouting lyrics which, when they were at all intelligible, described various acts of violence and warnings about the end of the world. Marcel Janco dressed in Cubist costume and sang nonsense syllables through megaphones. Ball appeared in a costume that gave him the look of a human obelisk, and while Emmy Hennings sang at the piano, young artists and poets from all over Europe surrounded them, took notes, joined in, drew inspiration. Ball's announcement, which appeared in Zurich's newspapers, stated his purpose:

> Cabaret Voltaire. Under this name a group of young artists and writers has formed with the object of becoming a centre for artistic entertainment. The Cabaret Voltaire will be run on the principle of daily meetings where visiting artists will perform their music and poetry. The young artists of Zurich are invited to bring along their ideas and contributions.

Boisterous but intimate, the Voltaire quickly shocked the staid Zurich burghers and sent warnings about immorality all over the city. They need not have worried. Neither spies nor anarchists nor addicts conducted business at the café; there were only experimental artists insulting the audience directly or by obfuscation.

An average program at the Voltaire was itself a wild, unsystematized collage: a balalaika orchestra played chords without rehearsal; a doll was auctioned; Artur Rubinstein played Saint-Saëns; Max Jacob read his latest poem; cowbells were rung while Janco and Tzara gave antiphonal readings of unconnected texts—and all the while spectators ate sausages, drank beer, told off-color stories, commented aloud on the proceedings, and sometimes raced the performance area and joined in.

Another kind of artistic energy was introduced to her in the presence of Ferruccio Busoni, the composer and pianist, son of an Italian musician and a mother of German descent. Born in Empoli in 1866, Busoni had been a child prodigy, had studied in Vienna and Leipzig and toured from Russia to America as pianist and teacher before he was thirty. One morning in 1917,

while Lenya was studying at the Stadttheater, she and her colleagues were summoned to a rehearsal of one of Busoni's compositions. When she arrived, he was sitting at the piano.

> His long, beautiful hands seemed to belong more to the key-
> board than to his body [she wrote in her later memoir-notes].
> He created a sort of stillness. . . . After his rehearsal was
> over, Busoni sat down on the floor and started talking about
> his opera. But he was talking to us, the girls, not to the wait-
> ing rehearsal pianist.

On September 27, 1917, the German playwright Frank Wedekind directed his *Franziska* at the Stadttheater. In the small role of
one of the barroom customers was "Caroline Blamauer" (the *k*
and *c* being interchangeable in printing German names). The program also listed, in an equally small role, Elisabeth Bergner.

> I was holding a champagne glass in my hand [Lenya noted],
> and my little finger was sticking way out—I thought this was
> an extremely elegant way of holding a glass. But then Bergner
> crossed the stage in front of me, pushed my finger back and
> said aloud, "Das macht man nicht in feiner Gesellschaft!—
> One just doesn't do that in elegant company!" Well, she got
> a big laugh with that improvised line, and she kept it in.

Later internationally famous on stage and screen, Bergner
wrote of Lenya in her autobiography:

> She was only a bit player with no lines, although sometimes
> she was also in the chorus. . . . She was often seen in the
> company of [military] officers, and she was very often met
> afterward at the theater by them—but each time it was a dif-
> ferent one. The rumors about her loose life were widespread.
> The nice thing about her was that she was always in good
> spirits, but there was around her an atmosphere of something
> forbidden—and, I should say, *very* interesting.

On February 14, 1918, Lenya appeared in the nonsinging role
of the assistant to the hairdresser (no more than a brief walk-on)
in a performance of Richard Strauss's opera *Der Rosenkavalier*,
conducted by the composer.

She then appeared at the Pfauen Theater, Zurich, as part of a dance program choreographed by Ingeborg Ruvina, a student of Emile Jaques-Dalcroze, the Swiss originator of a system called eurythmics. In this method, bodily movements represented musical rhythms and were designed to increase "communication" between the brain and the body. Note values were indicated by movements of the trunk and feet, and time values were indicated by arm motions. Teachers quickly adopted his methods across Europe, and dancers learned to give plastic expression to a variety of musical forms. On July 2, Caroline Blamauer—with Ruvina, Grete Edelmann, and Helene Clausen—offered an expressionistic, Dalcroze-inspired dance to music of a Johann Strauss waltz.

At the same theater, on September 1, Richard Révy directed her in a small role in Ludwig Fulda's comedy *Die Verlorene Tochter (The Prodigal Daughter)*. Three evenings later, Blamauer, Ruvina, Edelmann and Clausen danced the "Blue Danube Waltz" during a second-act interlude of *Die Fledermaus*. Similar evenings were repeated through January 1919, when, again under Révy's direction, Caroline Blamauer played the role of Lisiska in the premiere of Wedekind's *Tod und Teufel*, a musical "death-dance." Of these performances all that has survived is the programs; there is no mention of her individual performances in the press, but the smallness of the roles explains that. In any case, she was still an apprentice, one member of a large repertory company whose goal was neither to promote nor to advertise "stars." No matter how widespread their fame might or might not become, she and her colleagues were working members of a prestigious theater community, and they were constantly learning new aspects of a complex and demanding craft.

Zurich's general strike in 1918 was aggravated by the effects of the influenza epidemic that spread across Europe. Lenya was confined for a month late that year, but she recovered fully enough to join Grete Edelmann and her boyfriend at a nightclub premier in early spring. Across the room she saw a handsome man with dark glasses, surrounded by a noisy group who were clearly his guests. The star of the act ran to his table when she had finished her songs, and this increased Lenya's curiosity.

As it happened [she wrote in her memoir-notes], Grete's boy-friend knew him and later he left his table and joined us. He seemed bored with his company, and seemed to enjoy every remark I made about his drinking companions. He was very nice to me.

Nice enough, indeed, to send an elaborate and expensive bouquet of flowers to her at the repertory theater the following day. They met at the nightclub the following week, and then the man told more about himself. He was a Czech refugee, very rich, very influential and very lonely. He owned a villa on Lake Zurich, and soon Lenya was living with him and accepting his lavish gifts of jewelry, as she recorded in her memoir-notes.

It was just too tempting. I wanted to know how it feels to have everything, to be driven to the theater by a chauffeur, to have beautiful jewelry and not a care. His heavy dark glasses covered a condition [exophthalmia] that made his eyes stick out like two bubbles. But I got used to them the way I got used to the sudden wealth.

Life with the Czech (and with all the stereotypical trappings of the nineteenth-century ''kept woman'') was comfortable and convenient, but apparently neither emotionally satisfying nor socially stimulating, for before summer was over she departed— with the jewelry. In her memoir-notes, she claimed she missed the company of friends and the eccentricities of the Edelmann household.

By the end of the war, in 1919, Lenya had apparently resumed her affair with Mario Perucci, for when she returned to visit her family in Vienna, he accompanied her. She was shocked by the gaunt, care-ridden faces of the Viennese and by the dreadful conditions at home. The food she had sent, when it arrived, was taken by Hainisch; thirteen-year-old Maria was so frail she seemed tubercular, and Johanna was in a hospital following a terrific beating from Hainisch. Maria, as her sister found, brought scraps of food home for herself after visiting her mother at the hospital; it was virtually the only food the child had. ''Ernst knocked [Mother] around constantly, but she was infatuated with him and seemed not to notice,'' Lenya noted flatly and without interpretation in her memoir.

Perucci took the situation in hand. He arranged a passport for Maria to return to Zurich with them, took Johanna to rest with friends and gave them money to support her and to keep her away from Hainisch. Maria later remarked to a family friend that her sister looked that year like an elegant woman of the world; she remembered a red dress and matching hat and high heels. She also remembered Perucci's kindness and generosity toward the whole family.

In October and November 1919, Maria stayed in Zurich with her sister, sharing a room at the Pension Griese on the Dufourstrasse near Lake Zurich. Although the journey had further weakened her, Maria insisted on walking to the lake each day, much to the concern of Lenya who was terrified that she would faint and fall in.

When Maria was at last too ill to go out, Lenya sat and fed her, put her hair in curlers, sang to her. But with the arrival of winter it was clear that more professional help was needed, and she was taken to a rest home in the mountains, where nuns nursed her back to health. In the spring, a healthier Maria returned to Vienna, pleased to find her mother well and Ernst Hainisch in jail.

Lenya, meantime, grew restless,

> partly [as she noted in her memoir-notes] because Révy talked constantly about what wonderful new revolutionary things were happening in the Berlin theater. He urged me to put together a program and try to go to Berlin. . . .

Grete Edelmann joined Lenya in preparing an evening *à deux* of dance in a variety of styles and traditions. They worked feverishly in a small rehearsal hall, inventing their own choreography. In one number Lenya was a faun and Grete a nymph, in another she was Pierrot and Grete was Columbine; they were Scottish lasses in another. ''It was a corny mishmash of classic ballet, Dalcroze, Isadora Duncan—you name it: Hungarian *czardas*, country waltzes and so forth,'' she noted in her memoir. Throughout the summer and autumn of 1920, Lenya and Grete practiced their dance routines. Révy's wife, meanwhile, made costumes designed for the girls by her husband.

But classes and occasional small roles in the repertory company also occupied Lenya. On January 27, 1921, Richard Révy's production of Wedekind's *Lulu* was staged at the Pfauen Theater, with Caroline Blamauer in the very small role of the schoolboy Hugenberg. On April 26, Révy's amalgamation of the two parts of Shakespeare's *Henry IV* was presented at the same theater, with Caroline as a young boy. (In the English version, the character's name is Davy; in Révy's edited version the role was greatly reduced, but the character's mixture of premature cynicism and pathos must have appealed to Lenya when she read the play with her mentor.)

On May 11, the program for Révy's staging of *Henry V* listed Lotte Blamauer, again in the role of a nameless youth. The printed change of name was perhaps the most interesting thing about her appearance here, for once again the part was reduced to a small one. (Although the use of "Lenja" was inconsistent, she had by this time substituted the popular shortened form of her middle name, Charlotte, for her longer first name.)

By the summer of 1921, Lotte and Grete were ready to take their dance routine to Berlin. Grete's mother was not so convinced of the value of the girls' plans, and she was nervous about the move to Berlin. "She thought that if anything was stormed it would be Grete's virginity. She need not have worried," according to Lenya.

But where, Frau Edelmann wanted to know, would the train fare come from? And how could they afford to live in Berlin until they found work? Karoline had the answer: the jewels given to her by the rich Czech. "She told me," her friend Harriet Pinover recalled years later, "that he was a much older man, and that she left him, took the diamonds, and went off to Berlin."

And so, in early autumn 1921, with one suitcase apiece and a single large trunk full of costumes, Grete and Karoline boarded the train, convinced that brilliant careers awaited them as soon as they arrived in that most glittering city of the Weimar Republic.

Three

A Lover on the Lake

1920–1926

"WE THOUGHT WE'D TAKE BERLIN BY STORM, BUT NO agent was present to meet us and nothing happened," Lenya wryly told an interviewer years later. Nothing may have happened regarding their early Berlin careers, but around Karoline Blamauer and Grete Edelmann a great deal was happening.

Until 1870, Berlin had been the rather unworldly capital of the small, militaristic kingdom of Prussia, and the Hohenzollerns had not changed it much. Prussian discipline and Prussian-Victorian morals prevailed into the twentieth century. But then, at the end of World War I, when the last ruling family fled into Dutch exile, enormous changes occurred. Within the city limits there were soon chemical factories as well as thick forests, locomotive manufacturing plants near country lakes, blocks of new tenement apartments overlooking eighteenth-century castles. Only months before Lenya and Grete arrived, a legal act had expanded the city into Greater Berlin, a vast metropolitan center of four million people and three hundred fifty square miles.

In 1910, critic Karl Scheffler had called it a city doomed to a perpetual state of becoming, but never completed. The eternally inchoate atmosphere naturally attracted creative, argumentative minds, ready for mobility and constant change right up to the time of the Third Reich. And in February 1920, when playwright and poet Bertolt Brecht made his first trip to Berlin, he described it in a letter to designer Caspar Neher as "a wonderful

36

affair, overflowing with things in the most ghastly taste, but what a display!''

The display featured an astonishing variety of works in progress: new theaters, cinemas, swimming pools, racetracks, office buildings, factories, exhibition halls, luxury apartments and proletarian flats. There was variety in the languages heard, too: Polish, Slovakian, Hungarian, Danish, French, Dutch, English. The city was a major gateway, and citizens en route to and from their own countries often stayed, captured by the bedazzling life of the city. The air of Berlin, as music publisher Hans Heinsheimer wrote,

> swept in from the pine woods and the lakes and across the plains from the not-too-distant sea [and] changed slow-moving Austrians and sun-spoiled Italians, Russians and Poles, Frenchmen and Hungarians, and the Germans from all four corners of their land and made them into Berliners.

"There was a tremendous zest," Lenya commented years later in an interview. "All of a sudden a nation was unfolding and pouring out its talent."

If Zurich had been more exciting for her than Vienna, Berlin made both those cities seem like sleepy Alpine hamlets. The prolific activity in all the arts engaged her attention immediately, and later she recalled an impression that Berlin audiences were "the most acutely aware, the most perceptive theater public that has ever existed."

Things were happening quickly, reflecting the impact of the machine age and new developments in science. Everything was swift, agitated; life seemed like the high-speed "flickers" of the silent film era. Productivity had the highest priority in all fields—architecture, the arts, theater, cinema. Rapid advances in media were evident everywhere, and not dozens but literally hundreds of daily newspapers were available to a news-famished public.

In the theater, Max Reinhardt—an Austrian actor and manager who became Germany's preeminent producer and director—had brought startling innovations to stage and set design. His spectacular productions featured huge casts, mechanical devices and new approaches to lighting. Reinhardt aimed at freeing the theater from its literary base, and one of his methods was to project the stage into the audience, effecting intimacy and interconnection where before there had been only massive space and monumental separation between player and spectator.

Another theatrical genius, Erwin Piscator, brought new dramatic techniques to the Berlin stage, originating an epic style soon taken up by Brecht. Both men saw theater as an apt means for radical political instruction. A Piscator design might feature a single actor illuminated by a shaft of light against a black background, with limited scenery and symbolic props. Simultaneously there emerged a new style of writing with a frankly moral and political stance. Soon Piscator's stage techniques employed bold optical and architectural devices, mobile cantilevered bridges, flashing sirens and slide projections, and creative uses of mixed media (live music with mechanical sounds, radio with cinema, chanting performers with swirling lights).

The great designer Jo Mielziner had won a scholarship to study in Berlin at the time, and according to him the major concern of serious writers, artists, actors and composers was "what this new world of technology was *doing* to man." In Berlin, Mielziner learned the use of strong colors, surrealist staging, multimedia, lighting configurations and the simulation of natural occurrences (storms, for example) that he would later incorporate into a long list of creative and evocative designs for the American theater, including such classics as *The Glass Menagerie, A Streetcar Named Desire, Death of a Salesman, South Pacific* and *Gypsy*.

Experimentation proliferated in the cinema, too. Since the Weimar Republic abolished censorship, filmmakers were as free to explore new methods as stage designers and playwrights. Robert Wiene's *The Cabinet of Dr. Caligari* (1919) had exploited the full resources of theatrical expressionism. Although its cinematic style did not prevail in films afterward, its depiction of a mad world through deliberately artificial and distorted sets with violent angles heralded a new visual approach to the inner life. Similarly, the early films of Fritz Lang (*Destiny* [1921] and *Dr. Mabuse* [1922]) were dark thrillers with ominous implications about a society on the brink of anarchy. F. W. Murnau, Ernst Lubitsch and Robert Siodmak were also refining crafts they later took with them to their work as film directors elsewhere, and Billy Wilder, Fred Zinnemann and Alfred Hitchcock soon came to Berlin from Vienna and London to make films in the city's vast studio facilities.

Imports from America could be seen and heard everywhere, cross-fertilizing German cultural experimentation—in jazz rhythms and the films of Charlie Chaplin; in the verses of Walt Whitman and Carl Sandburg, and in the novels of Cooper, Poe, Melville, Twain and Sinclair—volumes which Berliners bought in the 1920s in as great quantities as the works of Kafka and Rilke.

Young German talent often emerged and flourished in un-likely places, and one of the most unlikely was a unique kind of supper-entertainment club. At its best it was a literary form of cabaret. The Kabaret der Komiker, for example, regularly of-fered satires by Kurt Tucholsky—''We say no to everything!'' was his piquant rallying cry—and by Erich Kästner, who freely used sophisticated literary allusions, classical references and razor-sharp comments on daily politics. It was, recalled com-poser and conductor Gershon Kingsley (who later worked with Lenya in America), ''a place like its time, pregnant with creative ideas. In this cabaret one was free to talk about and to perform anything. This unleashed all sorts of possibilities for good and for bad.''

The serious cultural life of Berlin engaged Lenya's interest from the first day of her arrival. Her instinct for the theater, her native intelligence, her spontaneity, openness and an eager will-ingness to learn (in art as in life) made her an apt pupil for the classroom that was Berlin society. Then, as for the rest of her life, her interests were wide-ranging, and she was keenly at-tracted to men and women whose education, professional train-ing or achievements excited her and complemented her own brief formal schooling. She craved the company of cultured peo-ple, those with both talent and perception, and she always learned from them.

Parallel with this was another side of her personality, the side that reveled in kitsch and loved what was tacky and perverse. The lustier turmoil of Berlin life—its animal energy and disre-gard for conventional morality—fascinated her.

In the bars and nightclubs of Berlin, for example, there flour-ished every possibility, every variant and experimentation of the Roaring Twenties. ''Boys—and not only professional prosti-tutes—paraded up and down [indoors as well as in the streets], wearing makeup and false waistlines,'' in the vivid account of writer Stefan Zweig.

> Every schoolboy was out to make money, while senior government officials and bankers were to be seen shamelessly flirting with drunken sailors. . . . Girls boasted about their perversions, and in every school in Berlin they would have been in disgrace if they were suspected of virginity at the age of sixteen.

On the Friedrichstrasse, in Berlin's center, bare-breasted prostitutes chatted with customers at the Café Nationale, and at the Apollo nude dancers of both sexes kicked and cavorted while customers found upstairs rooms for sex with offstage performers. At the White Mouse, on the Behrenstrasse, the cocaine addict Anita Berber, wearing chalk-white makeup, offered her Dances of Horror, Lust and Ecstasy, usually wearing nothing more than a crooked smile. She, like many of her patrons, died before the age of thirty.

The Kurfürstendamm, in the heart of the theater district, and its side alleys, were the locales of dozens of *Nuttenkneipen* (bars for whores) and *Schwulkneipen* (gay bars with singularly morbid atmospheres), like the Fuse, where an enormous lesbian smoked black cigars and decided which patrons to admit. At a once sober dance palace like the Carousel, girls and customers danced naked on the tables, shared drugs, exchanged addresses. At the Resi or the Femina, telephones at each table enabled customers to ring up a girl (or boy) at another table, and a pneumatic tube whisked handwritten messages to them if the noise interrupted phone conversation.

But life in Berlin was not simply a matter of high art or low life. In 1921 there was also record unemployment, and in spite of the building boom, a shortage of housing and food. Many workers could not afford minimal rents and became drifters. Families routinely fell apart. Crime and prostitution proliferated, and for the working class there were no luxuries. For them, it was in 1921 as it had been in 1910: Sunday afternoon meant a walk, a visit to a garden restaurant, cleaning one's clothes, perhaps attending a political party meeting.

Living conditions for laborers rivaled anything in Penzing,

and often surpassed it for sheer squalor. "Frequently six or more people live in the same room," the writer Julius Cohn commented at the time.

> Man and wife and one or two children inhabit the same bed. Bed linen is often missing, washing facilities consist of the kitchen sink and, despite all the housing misery, the kitchen is rented out as sleeping quarters for overnighters. . . . It had been decided, before the war, that attics and unhealthy cellar dwellings were not to be admitted as living quarters. But nowadays, countless families live in unheated attics without lavatories, in damp and deep cellars, in primitive woodsheds on garden allotments, insufficiently protected from winter storms, humidity and cold, and with sanitary installations that are a crying shame.

Two attitudes characterized the spirit of working Berliners in the 1920s: a bitter, ironic irreverence alternated with profound despair. Educated people cited texts from Schiller, Goethe or Heine in ordinary conversation, but laborers drew on a common legacy of jokes and tunes, advertising slogans and vulgar or obscene allusions. Everything was punctuated by a bitter humor and a casual refusal to take anything seriously.

"It was a completely negative world," the artist George Grosz wrote,

> with gaily colored froth on top that many people mistook for the true, the happy Germany before the eruption of the new barbarism. Foreigners who visited us at the time were easily fooled by the apparently light-hearted, whirring fun on the surface, by the nightlife and the so-called freedom and flowering of the arts.

But just beneath the surface, Grosz saw (and depicted in his caricatures) the "fratricide and general discord . . . the noise, rumors, shouting, political slogans."

Political demonstrations in fact regularly took a bloody turn, marches and meetings became street riots, and there were more than five hundred political assassinations in the streets of Berlin from the founding of the Weimar Republic in 1919 to the end of

1923. Men who signed the 1918 armistice were among the victims.

The economic situation after the war went from bad to worse. After a strike in the Ruhr Valley in January 1923, the great inflation surpassed everyone's worst expectations. In January 1919 an American dollar had been worth 8.9 marks; in January 1921 it was worth 64.9 marks. By January 1922 a dollar bought 191.8 marks, and in January 1923 one dollar was worth 17,972 marks. Before the end of 1923, a dollar equaled 4.2 trillion marks. Food riots in the streets of Berlin were daily events.

"In such an atmosphere," journalist Percy Knauth recalled, "reason itself, as well as currency, became debased." Wolfgang Roth, a stage designer working in Berlin at the time, remembered citizens living "in a strange mixture of absolute despair and enormous *joie de vivre*. The times were desperate and everybody knew it, and catastrophes were just around the corner, and everybody knew that, too." Also before the end of 1923, Adolf Hitler tried, prematurely, to seize power in the abortive Munich *Putsch*. Hermann Göring, to whom Hitler had given command of the storm troopers, was wounded in that attempt; he retreated to Austria where he became a morphine addict and, like Hitler, marked time until what he believed would be his vengeance.

For a year after her arrival in Berlin, Lenya was without regular or even irregular theatrical or dancing work, and she had been forced to live on the remnants of her sale of the jewelry— and perhaps as well on subsidies from lovers. At the same time she absorbed much of the city's rich and diverse life:

> I had a passion for The Scala [she wrote in her memoir-notes years later], the greatest variety theater in Berlin, where I saw Rastello, the great juggler, and Barbette swinging way out over the audience. It was my passion until I left Berlin in 1933. I saw my first wrestling matches in a beer garden, mostly Polish wrestlers walking in a long line accompanied by an incredible brass band playing the March of the Gladiators. I loved to walk on Saturdays up to the corner of the Tauentzienstrasse and K.D.W., a big department store where you could see girls in the strangest outfits standing at the corner, some with whips in their hands, some with high,

shiny boots on, indicating that they were equipped to fulfill every kind of human passion.

By early 1922—three or four months after the girls' arrival in Berlin—Grete and Lenya parted company.

Grete was a dancer only and not interested in anything else. I couldn't make her go and see plays, [and] she didn't care to walk around and get the smell of the city. When she finally got an offer as a choreographer in Elberfeld, a small German city, I didn't have to urge her to accept it. By that time, I had lost faith in our project too and was glad when she left. Now I didn't have to run daily from one stupid agent to another and I was free to go and see all the great actors of that time.

Soon Lenya contacted her mentor Richard Révy, who took her to a rooming house on the Lüzowstrasse. The dark, top-floor room with one dim overhead bulb was a stark contrast to the clean charm of the Pension Griese near Lake Zurich. But the neighborhood was not as squalid as some nearby. The building itself was gray stone, and at least she had a small balcony where she grew plants. From a magazine she cut a photo of Nijinsky, which she hung over her bed.

Her housemates were a motley crew, all of them (like her) subject to the daily dramatic fluctuations of currency. Next door was a Russian woman with a young daughter and a terrier that barked furiously at the slightest noise from Lenya's room. On the other side was another Russian, a piano student who committed suicide shortly after she arrived.

One meal was served daily to the boarders, and its identity was ordinarily a mystery. When she asked the landlady whether the dish were chicken, tripe or meat patties, she was told in a provincial dialect, "It ain't a cat you're eating, and don't forget, lady, we lost the war." From that day, Lenya presumed she was eating a kind of fishcake. The landlady turned out to be a good-hearted, hardworking woman who had lost her husband in the war and was trying to make a living for her fifteen-year-old daughter and her twelve-year-old son, a boy so thin and under-nourished he looked six. (The child eventually died of tuberculosis, as did fifteen thousand other Berlin children from 1921 to 1924. It was estimated that one-quarter of the population under fifteen was starving to death.) Except for a few boarders, the rooming-house register changed several times weekly, since few could afford to pay the rent the landlady had to collect daily because of the rapidly changing currency rates.

By early 1923, the money from her jewelry had run out. By happy coincidence, she then found that her landlady knew a producer named Otto Kirchner, who had a traveling troupe of actors trained especially in the comedies of Shakespeare. Like Révy, Kirchner was a gentle, cultivated man who was preparing a modest production of *Twelfth Night*. Perhaps recognizing that this short, feisty actress was very like the short, wisecracking Maria in that play, he asked Lenya to read the part and to return a few days later prepared for recitation. Soon she had a typed contract for the role. (From the time of *Twelfth Night* she was listed in theater programs only as Lotte Lenja.)

She was to receive the ridiculous sum of three million marks two weeks later, after opening night, and as she recalled in her memoir-notes she had to spend the money fast, since this was prior to the 1923 stabilization. A month later, the play was still running and by this time Lotte was paid in billions of marks. It had virtually no real value.

> You looked at that unreal paper money. It looked kind of pretty, and you never had to be afraid of losing it—it just wasn't worth anything. You just stuffed it in a drawer and tried somehow to get rid of it.

The part of Maria, lady-in-waiting to Olivia, was as short as the character's stature—''the youngest wren of nine,'' as Shakespeare has it—but it provided Lenya with some scope for her comic gifts, for Maria is a jokester. It is Maria's idea to forge the letter that sets up the duping of the smug Malvolio, and at the end of the comedy she marries Sir Toby Belch. No press review of her performance has survived, but Lenya loved the production and the role. She was working again, and in a part she liked. That was reward enough. At the same time, she resumed private lessons with Richard Révy, who coached her in more roles they both hoped would be helpful for her future.

One evening after a performance of *Twelfth Night*, Révy met her backstage and said the next evening she must give a particularly good performance. He was to bring Georg Kaiser, the leading German playwright of the day, to see her performance.

Then forty-three, Kaiser had turned from writing satiric comedies to expressionist depictions of the conflict of ideas. His concerns were the emptiness of modern life (in, for example, *Von Morgens bis Mitternachts* [*From Morn to Midnight*, 1916]) and the necessity of personal love and sacrifice (in *Der Brand im Opernhaus* [*The Fire in the Opera House*, 1918] and *Die Bürger von Calais* [*The Burgers of Calais*, 1914]).

When she met him, Lenya found Kaiser physically startling. Of medium build with thinning blond hair, his agate blue eyes held her attention. "I have never seen eyes of that color again," she wrote in her memoir-notes. "They showed no warmth, but neither were they harsh or cold. He seemed to see right through you."

Révy, Kaiser and Lenya took a late supper, and she learned that Kaiser was a kindly man, quietly supporting struggling young writers and drama students with unself-conscious generosity. He asked her to explain the plot of *Twelfth Night*, which she did with great enthusiasm until she came to the end and realized that of course he knew it already and was enjoying her recitation. Then, as Kaiser relaxed, she found he was also witty, and his slight lisp and staccato speech added a unique style even to the most casual comment. He also had a childlike faith in people, and she was soon to learn that his eagerness to aid those in distress often made him an easy prey to the unscrupulous. "He had no sense whatever of money," Lenya added in her memoir. "It ran like water through his fingers. Even after the mark was stabilized and money began to have some value again, he spent it as fast as he made it, and he was in deep debt until his death in exile [in Switzerland, in 1945]."

A fiscal stabilization program was instituted that very season, as Hjalmar Schacht (special currency commissioner in the finance ministry) ordained monetary reforms to restore the national economy. Money was no longer to be printed for free circulation, and all credit ceased. The Dawes Plan, set up by the United States, reduced Germany's enormous war debt. And finally the French withdrew from the Ruhr Valley, giving Germany title once again to their richest industrial area. Further, Gustav Stresemann, chancellor in 1923 and then foreign minister until his death in 1929, supervised the influx of American business capital into Germany. By 1924 and 1925, foreign investors were once again looking to Germany, confidence was restored and new factories were built. Unemployment fell sharply, wages rose, the arts flourished and optimism shone over faces begrimed with toil and heartache.

In Berlin's bars and restaurants, the economic stabilization freed people to enjoy themselves luxuriantly, as never before. According to its advertisements, the Opel factory near Frankfurt produced one car every five minutes, and the jobs this necessitated poured money into the pockets of thousands of laborers. By the time Hindenburg became president of the nation in early 1925, Germany seemed the center of a universal postwar return to order.

These measures signaled not only a change of international attitudes, of hopes for Germany's future. They also had immediate ramifications in the busy, ebullient world of the arts. By the time Stresemann was awarded the Nobel Peace Prize in 1926—which he received for his efforts for reconciliation and worldwide negotiation, and which he shared with French foreign minister Aristide Briand—the general restoration of a once dying economy had become a boon to artists and performers. There were investors now, patrons as well as spectators, students in apprenticeship as well as in master classes, and a generous apportionment of the national budget for every aspect of the creative arts.

But just as the situation was brightening over Berlin, Lenya's career—so hopefully rekindled by the production of *Twelfth Night*—again stalled. "I had thought that when I got to Berlin I'd be a star. No such luck. . . . From [the end of] 1923 to 1926, I had no career," she wrote in her memoir later. "Nothing."

Then, in early 1924, Georg Kaiser appeared unexpectedly at her door on the Lüzowstrasse. He invited Lenya to join his family at their country home that weekend, and he paid for her train fare. Several days later, there was another knock at the door. A tall, handsome, slightly gray-haired woman smiled and extended her hand. She was Margarethe Kaiser. Her husband had asked her to accompany Lenya on the hour-long train journey.

They arrived at Grünheide, an enchanting country spot outside the city center, and Frau Kaiser suggested they take the boat across the lake for the best view of the house. As the women approached the opposite shore, they were met by the Kaisers' son Anselm. The other Kaiser children were nearby—Sibylle, five, and Laurent, six. Lenya was shown to her own room, and then spent time with the children; before nightfall, Anselm had taken her for his best friend. He had learned she loved to ride bicycles as fast as he, and that she loved to play soccer.

The weekend was dedicated to the comfortable suburban life at the estate kept by the Kaisers as a refuge from town. The following week, she learned that Richard Révy had suggested Lenya as the Kaisers' guest. "I was depressed, since there were no [acting] jobs for me. Révy cheered me up and advised me to be patient." The Kaisers repeated the invitation for several more weekends and for several evenings at their apartment in town on the Luisenplatz.

Then, realizing that Lenya's financial situation was now desperate, the Kaisers extended their generosity further. They invited Lenya to move to Grünheide as an *au pair* who would help care for the children and perform light household duties in exchange for room and board with the family she was growing to love. For emotional security as well as for practical necessity, she accepted immediately, and by the summer of 1924 she was virtually a member of the Kaiser family. This was by far the most pleasant development in her life so far.

That same year, Georg Kaiser—seeking a collaborator for a new stage work—invited a young composer named Kurt Weill to Grünheide. Lenya had met Weill two years earlier, in the autumn of 1922—or more accurately, she had heard his voice:

> They were looking for a dancing actress for [Weill's] musical pantomime, *Zaubernacht* [she wrote in her unpublished memoir], and when I got onto the stage a very gentle voice came from the pit, "What do you want me to play for you?" And the director turned to me and said, "Oh, this is Mr. Weill, our composer." I hardly saw him, half-hidden down there, but I asked him if he could play the Blue Danube, and with a slightly amused tone he said, "I think so."

She neither played the role nor then met the composer in brighter light. That awaited Kaiser's invitation to Weill two years later.

Kurt Julian Weill stood only five feet three inches, his dark brown hair had (even in his twenties) yielded mostly to baldness, and he gave a first impression of intense shyness. He had delicate hands and a high speaking voice, and when he was amused there was a gently ironic lilt sometimes mistaken for arrogance; if he was angry (which was not often) his tone could be cold and flat. Meticulous to the point of obsession, he could remain absorbed in reflection or in his work for hours. It was not unusual for him to pace all that time, his right index finger tapping his nose.

"He exuded the unmistakable aura of a professional," music publisher Hans Heinsheimer wrote,

> a small, balding young man, squinting at the world through thick, professorial glasses . . . sucking a conservative pipe with the absent-minded absorption of an instructor in higher mathematics . . . quiet in his manner.

Weill was born March 2, 1900 in Dessau, a town thirty-five miles north of Leipzig in a region of meadows, woods and tree-shaded streets. His cultivated, genteel family was devoutly Jewish on both sides and the genealogy included a rabbi or cantor in every generation back to the fourteenth century. Kurt's father, Albert Weill (a cantor and composer of liturgical music), and his mother, Emma Ackermann (a pianist), were married in 1897. Their son Nathan was born in 1898 and became a doctor; Hanns was born in 1899 and became a metal technician; Ruth was born the year after Kurt.

Young Kurt began to compose music while still in school, and he studied theory and composition with Albert Bing in Dessau. From 1915 to 1918 he attended the local *Gymnasium* and continued his musical studies and performing on his own time.

At the age of seventeen he had become accompanist at the Dessau Opera, a position attained not only because of his talent but also because many other musicians were off in the war. In the spring of 1918 he went to Berlin to decide whether he wished to study at the university or at the Hochschule für Musik. He attended lectures at the university on philosophy and aesthetics by Max Dessoir and by Ernst Cassirer, and classes on music at the Hochschule by Engelbert Humperdinck (best known for his opera *Hansel und Gretel*) and by Rudolf Krasselt, a well-known conductor. That same autumn, he elected to study full-time at the Hochschule, where his teachers included Humperdinck, Krasselt and composer Friedrich Koch.

From Berlin he wrote to his brother Hanns in 1918:

> How wonderful it would be to marry as young as possible. . . . Those like us, suspended between two worlds, need this kind of support, or we run the risk of sinking in grief. Just once I'd like to fall madly in love and forget everything else. That would be a real blessing.

The "two worlds" are not entirely clear, but he may have meant the life of the German Jew (as other letters from this period suggest).

In the fall of 1919 Kurt was back in Dessau, on staff as rehearsal coach at the Hofoper, under Hans Knappertsbusch. Then in December he went to Lüdenscheid, where he worked for six months as a conductor at the municipal theater. From there he wrote to his sister Ruth (who in May had moved with the Weill family to Leipzig), asking a question that logically if humorously followed his earlier letter to Hanns:

> Is there among your girl-friends by any chance someone marriageable for me? Conditions: very pretty, very stupid, unmusical, with a ready dowry of one million marks.

But he also shared more serious thoughts with Ruth, in a letter from 1920, and in a tone suggesting a contemplative side to his character:

> I've been all alone in my apartment here for several days. . . . I seek out this solitude; it's the only satisfying thing, the only way to enjoy each minute and to listen to the slow rain of time. Life is short, and a minute is worth more than a thousand dollars. There is so much one has to clean up within oneself. One has to clarify matters no book can ever teach. So here I am, sitting in my half-darkened room, feeling an intimate bond with all those who ever sought, in the solitude of their little rooms, away from the rush of crowds, the better to take in the murmuring song of the stars. They hold out their hands to each other beyond all time. And they all pray for this frenzied humanity. . . .

In Lüdenscheid, he conducted operas by Johann Strauss *(Die Fledermaus)* and by Pietro Mascagni *(Cavalleria Rusticana)*, and to Humperdinck in Berlin he wrote: "Everyone assures me the musical theater [i.e., the first theater season in Lüdenscheid] has known a fresh impetus since my arrival." But there was only one uneven theater season there, and while Kurt profited from solitude he was no hermit. He missed the excitement of Berlin, and so in September 1920 he returned to the capital, intending to study with the highly respected composer and teacher Franz Schreker, who was moving there from Vienna. In the spring of 1921, Ferruccio Busoni began offering master classes to a small and elite group of students, and Weill was accepted.

The teacher's apartment on the Victoria-Luise Platz was just above a bar and restaurant that frequently provided beer for the students' intervals, and for Busoni's afternoon salons, which were open to a larger group. "There were two pianos in the living room," recalled Dimitri Mitropoulos in an interview years later. (He conducted at the Berlin State Opera from 1921 to 1924 and later conducted for the Minneapolis Symphony, the New York Philharmonic and the Metropolitan Opera.)

> We stretched out our scores [Mitropoulos continued] and listened to Busoni's comments. He was always very intellectual, very cold and objective. He always felt that music was an architecture of sounds, and as such had not to present any feeling. Any music can be adapted to any passion, he maintained. It has nothing definite to present. Busoni thought it must be judged as an abstract art. . . . Kurt Weill was Busoni's pet. He didn't like everything Weill wrote, but he knew Weill had to write it, and he had to give every artist his due—as he wanted for himself.

Weill had been supporting himself by playing organ at a Berlin synagogue and piano in a beer cellar. From 1923 to about 1926 he also taught students privately; at least two became internationally known. Chilean-born Claudio Arrau had studied since 1912 (at the age of nine) at the Stern Conservatory in Berlin, where he had been sent as a prodigy by his government. His brilliant debut as a concert pianist in Berlin in 1915 was followed by equally spectacular receptions all over the world and by a prize-winning career as a performing and recording artist. Greek-born Maurice Abravanel, the same age as Arrau, had studied in Switzerland and in 1924 began an international career as a concert and recording conductor of major orchestras in America, Europe and Australia; he also led the premieres of five works by Weill. Abravanel later headed the Utah Symphony Orchestra and was the recipient of numerous music awards around the world. He was one of Weill's closest associates and a shrewd observer of his marriage.

"Weill had a penetrating mind," according to Arrau.

He was also a wonderful teacher, eager to pass on what he knew—and he knew a great deal. Full of energy and vitality, he also had a strong personality and his interests extended to architecture, painting, modern dance—every aspect of the arts. He always stressed clear thinking.

Abravanel remembered that "the most important young composers at work were then Hindemith, Krenek and Weill, and everyone knew it. But Kurt had no air of superiority."

Kurt was still living on the edge of destitution by 1924, when he met the conductor Fritz Stiedry. Their friendship led Stiedry to conduct the premiere of Weill's first published composition, *Frauentanz*, in Berlin that same year. Set to seven medieval love songs translated from Latin to German, Weill's score bore the dedication "To Nelly Frank."

For about two years, until the summer of 1924, Kurt and Nelly were lovers. Three years older than he, she was married to a prosperous businessman and had two sons. She had met Kurt at the engagement of Hanns Weill to Rita Kisch, who was a cousin of her husband. It was easy for Kurt and Nelly to visit, since the Franks also lived in Berlin. The lovers were bold enough to travel together on a holiday to Switzerland and Italy in March 1924. On their return to Berlin in April she asked her husband for a divorce, but he took her at once on a trip to America. This had the desired effect, and the affair did not survive the summer of 1924.

Neither did Ferruccio Busoni, whose death at fifty-eight in July shook Weill deeply. "There had been a deep sympathy between them," Lenya said years later. To her death she kept two of Busoni's published scores, autographed "to dear Kurt Weill."

In May 1924, Weill moved to a small apartment on the Winterfeldstrasse and began work with Georg Kaiser on what they thought would be a three-act comic pantomime; what finally resulted, however, was very different—the one-act tragic opera *Der Protagonist*. That autumn, when the collaboration between Weill and Kaiser moved to Grünheide, Lenya was asked to meet him at the local train station and to escort him across the lake in a rowboat.

En route (as she noted in her memoir-notes) they spoke briefly of their quasi-meeting in 1922, and she commented on his wardrobe, for it was just as Kaiser had predicted, the obvious outfit of a composer: a dark suit, a bow tie and a wide-brimmed, Borsalino-musician's hat. Then, during their conversation, somehow Weill's eyeglasses were pitched into the lake. "Before we reached the other side, he asked me to marry him," Lenya claimed later in many interviews. "I accepted."

Her account, however charming, does not coincide with the well-established fact that Kurt Weill's marriage proposal to her came much later. And it was hardly typical of either her or him to leap from a rowboat to wedding plans. According to Margot Aufricht, Lenya confided that something more than conversation occurred, some rush of passionate kissing or amorous fumbling—although just how intimate they were is hard to gauge, since a rowboat is not, after all, the securest place for lovemaking.

Whatever happened, Weill and Lenya from that day met more and more often. An introverted intellectual from an ultra-conservative religious family, Kurt—who it seems had had but one love affair (with an older married woman, Nelly Frank)—now longed for intimacy and excitement with a girl. Surely some of Lenya's appeal must have been that he saw her as someone from the "real" world, just as many intellectuals seem always to regard the nonacademic or nonartistic life as "more real" than their own. Weill was fascinated by Lenya, full of raw energy and unspoiled by anything like a formal musical education, from which he forever dissuaded her.

The independent, feisty Lenya, with her uncomplicated attitude about sex, offered maximum contrast with what had earlier been Weill's rather stifling family environment. In an important way, then, she may have represented for him a counterpoint to his own serious personality. What Lenya's friend Gigi Gilpin said of her a dozen years later was always true:

> She had a tremendous sex appeal, which is amazing, since she also had none of the usual physical attributes we think of as attractive. But it was her charm, and although she didn't look sexy, she apparently just exuded sex, plain raw sex. And some women were attracted to her sexually the way some men were. And that was okay with her.

And according to Lys Symonette, who was Weill's rehearsal pianist for five years in America,

> There was no question: Lenya was ideal for him. She was bright without being educated or an intellectual. She was naturally musical without being a trained musician. And she was a highly erotic personality.

The Weill-Lenya relationship was, in summary, a complex symbiosis. His temperament enabled him to pursue the life of a creative artist with the solitude that requires, but his tendency for gravity needed the healthy kind of balance Lenya could provide. She drew out the playfulness in him, and the latent sensuousness. She could be impulsive and whimsical, and she loved to relax and enjoy herself—something he never did easily. He was a genuinely creative man, but she was a performer; his was the introverted personality, hers the extroverted. As time passed he would depend even more on her appreciation of his talent, as he always did on her ebullience.

For her part, she deeply respected his gifts. His respectable background, his education and refinement attracted her, compensating for what she admired but felt she lacked. Although a year and a half younger than she, Weill looked, spoke and acted much older than twenty-four, and his manner with her was as deferential as it was passionate. He seemed, then, everything she needed a man to be—generous and ardent, comforting and reassuring, protective and undemanding, and (like Richard Révy) with a great deal to offer her on an intellectual level. It must have been flattering, for a bright young woman who had left school so early, that a man like Kurt Weill would pursue her. He was also, in other words, a stark contrast to everything represented by Franz Paul Blamauer.

Weill and Kaiser worked on *Der Protagonist* throughout the autumn of 1924 and into late winter—on weekends at Grünheide, and sometimes in Weill's apartment in town. When he first invited Lenya to visit him there that winter, he extended the invitation to Margarethe Kaiser as well. His two small rooms were crowded with scores, music notes, papers and supplies—everything organized, everything tidily arranged—and the two women were offered coffee and cake. Weill was pleased he could offer them butter with the cake, since butter was rare in Berlin that year. But when he brought it from the window ledge, it was rancid. He ate it heartily, either because he took no notice or because he had known worse deprivation.

Soon Lenya was a regular visitor, making the trip from Grünheide to visit Kurt once or twice weekly. Often she arrived in early afternoon and played solitaire in the small bedroom while he finished lessons with his students. Then he and Lenya would go for a light meal and an evening at the theater or concert hall, and she would return with him to spend the night.

Their cultural life was rich and diverse. Erich Kleiber was upsetting tradition at the State Opera and preparing the world premiere of Alban Berg's *Wozzeck*. Wilhelm Furtwängler headed the Berlin Philharmonic (which by 1925 had performed three of Kurt Weill's works), and they frequently heard concerts there. Furtwängler was alternating with other notable conductors— Otto Klemperer, Bruno Walter, Thomas Beecham, Serge Koussevitzky, Ernest Ansermet. Composers routinely conducted their own works, and the programs for 1924 and 1925 list Stravinsky, Glazunov, Respighi and Ravel. Bartok, Prokofiev and Rachmaninoff appeared as soloists performing their own music. During one week of Austrian music, Alban Berg, Arnold Schönberg, Anton von Webern and Alexander von Zemlinsky alternated on the podium.

On January 22, 1925, the premiere of Weill's *Stundenbuch*, songs for baritone and orchestra set to poems by Rainer Maria Rilke, was offered at Philharmonic Hall. Weill and Lenya were in the audience, as she later recorded in her memoir-notes.

We had no money at all. After the concert we were about the last to leave and I found some paper money on the ground. It wasn't much at all, but we considered it a good omen for our future and spent it all the same night, having a wonderful dinner after the concert.

If they were separated for more than a few days, Weill wrote to Lenya—brief, warm notes at first, but then longer, passionate love-letters revealing the depth of his attachment to her. The earliest of these date from 1925:

You need a human being who belongs to you . . . this someone has to be me. How will you answer? . . . I think often of you and I hope you will come soon. Please!

His ardor was matched by his ingenuity in the affectionate nicknames he formulated. The letters and cards begin variously with a greeting to "Lilepe Lencha" (Saxonian dialect for Lenya, preceded by an invented nickname [February 13]); "Lenja-Benja" (March 12); and other terms, in letters through March and April, whose connotations were clear only to an ecstatic lover and his beloved recipient—"Tobili . . . Toby Angel . . . Muschelchen [literally, 'darling little mussel'] . . . Piepserich ['little pipsqueak'] . . . Tütchen ['little paper bag'] . . . Schwämmi ['little sponge'] . . . Spätzlein ['little sparrow']." In these he signs himself in equally personal, playful terms: "Dany . . . Didi . . . Buster," and even "Jesus," but never Kurt.

His longest letters are rhapsodic elaborations of commitment, explanations and defenses he must have thought she required and which were sometimes apparently offered after a lovers' quarrel—and which she obviously cherished, since she saved them for the rest of her life. Because either she did not write to him or her letters have not survived, it is impossible to know for certain if she was as ardent in her feelings toward him. But Weill's defensive tone suggests that in their meetings and conversations she might not have shared either his passion or his confidence that their relationship had a future.

For the practical, earthy Lenya (whose sexual life had begun at a very early age), Weill's diction must have been occasionally baffling, if not downright amusing. One typical letter—addressed to her as "Seelchen ['little soul']"—conveys his at-

tempts to convince her how crucial she is to his life. The language
of the letter is more than passionate, however, and even allowing
for the florid diction of a dizzy lover, some of the vocabulary
and syntax can only be called grotesquely unrealistic.

> Today I know who you are. You are beginning and end, rev-
> elation from above and a child's speech, sunrise and dusk of
> the evening. . . . White is your soul, as your body is white.
> All that you are is totally good. All the beauty of the clouds
> and the earth is upon you. . . . I have one destiny: to sink
> down into you, to disappear within your life, to drown in your
> blood and go to a new existence. I see myself in you, and for
> the first time I'm beginning to realize what I am, because I'm
> allowed to be inside you as a picture in a spring of water. As
> one expects death as an ineffable, mysterious gift, as the grace
> of a last immersion, I look forward to these days in May.
> They will bring a union that could only be longed for by
> others and which we can create because only you should ex-
> ist. My tenderness and my strength belong to you. I am glow-
> ing in your hands. Forge me according to your will. It's not
> Paradise we expect, but hot, burning life. . . . These words
> do not encompass what needs to be said. Let me reiterate it
> in another language in order to enlighten you better. You must
> be behind everything I complete, but no one shall recognize
> you because you are far removed from all of them.

His exaltation of her during these passionate months could
lead him to interpret a quarrel as a sign of his need, and of his
inferiority to her—and could even lead him to offer himself as
only a servant of her pleasure, if that in turn pleased her:

> The remembrance of your angry outburst today isn't painful.
> You were beautiful and you were right. The fault was mine.
> My opinion was still wrong. Now, at last, at last, I understood
> where you want to have me. Now I also know that that is not
> so difficult at all. A change, but not a weakening of my feel-
> ings, that's all. How glowingly I love you—today more than
> ever—and that is my very private affair. The expression of it
> mustn't be obvious, must be seen only by you—just like your
> love, which was evident to me even from today's outburst of
> your anger. For you were right in everything—except when

you said you never liked me. Too often you've proven to me the contrary and written to me that you were harder on me than on all the others, and that makes me happy because that is the strongest proof of your affection. . . . Our small arguments aren't the end, they're just the unimportant frictions of the beginning, caused only by my inexperience. That's all over now. Today at last I offer you a gift: me. You may simply accept this gift; it will only bring you good things. Let me simply be your pleasure-boy [or "lust-boy"—his German word: *Lustknabe*]—more than a friend and less than a husband. I live in this world only for you. . . .

In March 1925, Weill completed the score for *Der Protagonist*, which he dedicated "to Lotte Lenya." The collaboration with Kaiser had been cordial enough for Weill to ask about the use of the writer's Berlin apartment, at 3 Luisenplatz, which had a better piano than the tired upright Weill had been using on the Winterfeldplatz. Kaiser not only offered access to the instrument, he invited Weill to move in that May, since the Kaisers now lived almost exclusively in Grünheide and when in town could easily be accommodated at the apartment too. Lenya commuted more often to be with Kurt, and his dependence on her grew, as he wrote to her that spring:

I am so happy now that all the bad hours can now flow into the splendor of your closeness. That's the only thing that enables me to cope with difficult situations. And if I didn't know that I'd see you tomorrow, I'd be totally miserable. . . . Holy Linnerl, help! Come to me, but only if you're up to it. Otherwise I'll storm into your arms in the evening. To the very last artery, I'm your Didi.

But Kurt's parents were not members of the cabaret crowd, and they were not at all pleased about Kurt's attachment to a poor and uneducated gentile who (before the end of 1925) was living with him almost constantly. That must have outraged their sense of propriety at a time when prenuptial cohabitation was not so commonly accepted, just as the most cursory investigation of her past would have horrified them. Kurt wrote defensively to his parents:

I sometimes wish that I could share in your lives more than I do. But now I have reached the point in the life of an artist when he is continually perched on a powderkeg. Unused energies must discharge themselves explosively, and this hypercharged sensitivity produces a permanent state of excitement and stimulation. Only in this light can you understand some of the things about me that otherwise might seem incomprehensible. . . . I'm forging ahead toward ''myself,'' [and] my music is becoming much more confident, much freer, lighter—and simpler. . . . This is also linked to the fact that I have become noticeably more independent, more confident, happier and less tense. Of course, living with Lenja again accounts for much of this. That has helped me tremendously. It is the only way I could put up with living next to someone: coexistence of two differing artistic interests, without domestic ties, each one helping the other on his own course. How long will this last? I hope a long time.

In a civil ceremony at the City Hall of Charlottenburg, Greater Berlin, Kurt Julian Weill and Karoline Charlotte Blamauer were married on January 28, 1926, with neither rabbi, priest nor relatives present. Lenya's witnesses were two young women she had met on her rounds of the local theaters (something she still did from time to time). A modest luncheon at their apartment followed.

From the start, she was more realistic than he about the implications of this union. ''People have sometimes asked me,'' she said to interviewer Edwin Newman in 1970, ''was it love at first sight. I don't think so. . . . If you talk about love, that takes a little time.''

It remained to be seen, however, whether simple domesticity could satisfy her need for activity and for stimulation. The fact is that during her Berlin years, even after her marriage, Lenya's life was never characterized by sexual exclusivity.

Maurice Abravanel, for example, felt

uncomfortable to be with them both together. By this time Lenya was sleeping with quite a number of people, and I think there were more than one or two women in the group too. For me it seemed a rather strange arrangement all around. Another wife might have become very restless when the man was so totally involved in his music, and had no need for anybody. She did get nervous, she complained and got impatient and upset with him, but then she just went her own way. I suppose it was a very private and very practical arrangement for them. Once I came right out and told her that she really ought not to be cheating on Kurt so much. "But I *don't* cheat on Kurt," Lenya replied blankly. "He knows *exactly* what's going on!"

The marriage of Weill and Lenya was, from the start, far from traditional—so much even the Kaisers realized. Lenya insisted on the freedom to pursue her own path sexually, professionally and even geographically, for often she stayed at Grünheide while her husband worked in Berlin, closeted with his music. Her retreat from the city may have been occasioned by a recurring dialogue which, in various forms, characterized their life together at this time, and which she often quoted later to friends:

"Kurt," she would ask plaintively when he finally reemerged from days of solitude to take a meal with her, "don't you love me? Doesn't my presence in this house mean anything to you?"

"What do you mean, darling?" Weill replied, astonished at the question. "You know you come right after my music!"

Kurt Weill's temperament sometimes made him withdraw coolly, and the artist's frequent need for reflective solitude compounded a basically private personality. His ingenuous reply must have struck her deeply (she repeated it so often, so much later), and it may have stirred old embers within—the situation with her father, of whose love she felt deprived. To be sure, Kurt was never abusive or uncaring. But there was an element of emotional inaccessibility in her husband's character that her vulnerability caught and emphasized. Indeed, a vicious circle seems to have been drawn round them. Weill retreated obsessively to his work—not only because of his talent and ambition, but also perhaps partly to escape confronting Lenya's infidelities. She, meanwhile, indulged her sexual caprice to satisfy her own needs and, perhaps as well, to keep his interest in her aroused, to keep him enthralled, to make him jealous. In any case, his tolerance could have been only a rueful acceptance of something he could do nothing to change. Human psychology is never soap-opera simple, but it could be said that in the Weill-Lenya bond there was an interesting role-reversal of a relationship more typically found between an unfaithful husband and a long-suffering wife.

"While one was absorbed in conversation with him," Lenya remembered in her memoir-notes, "he would seem to be still listening, but he was listening to something else with an inner ear." If he was as gentle and supportive as a father figure could be, her need for reassurance was still as deep as her vulnerability, and she required constant reinforcement with an affection denied in childhood. This element in their relationship may account at least partially for her insistence on what has later come to be known as an "open marriage." Although, ironically—and at least partly because of her battered childhood—she relished expressions of passionate sex, she was not herself a romantic, and being "in love" was a state apparently foreign to her. In spite of her need for tenderness, she also seemed throughout her life to need relationships with men who would in some sense ignore or abuse her, as her father had; in this regard, she was very much like her own adored mother.

Meantime, an astonishingly prolific period in Weill's musical life had begun, and the Dresden premiere of *Der Protagonist* in March 1926 further marked the disparity in their professional lives. Over the next thirty-six months, Weill composed seven large stage works and more than a dozen concert pieces and incidental scores. His wife, on the other hand, was not a very widely known actress.

Inactivity irritated Lenya. Indeed, Kurt's writing to his parents about "unused energies" that must "discharge themselves explosively" could well have applied to her and her rather carefree approach to sexual encounters—which themselves may also be understood as a need for what Kurt was often unwilling to offer. "When he was at work composing," according to Maurice Abravanel, "Kurt had no need for [sex with] any woman." And so Lenya's infidelity—provoked by a complex of both emotional and physical needs—was something Weill endured.

Of a strong bond between them, however, there can be no doubt. She appreciated his intelligence, encouraged his work and enjoyed teasing him to relax when they were together. Prudently, he always asked her reactions to his music, for they were unschooled reactions musically but had a shrewd theatrical sensibility. With their independence of one another there was an abiding friendliness.

Toward the end of the year, Lenya took her first acting job since she had known Weill—as understudy to Grete Jacobson, then playing the lead in *Romeo and Juliet*. Georg Kaiser had prevailed on his friend Emil Lind, director of the play, and Lenya eventually played the role over sixty times at the Wallnertheater, near Alexanderplatz. Most evenings, Kurt delivered her to the stage door, left a bottle of May wine for Lenya to share with the others in the cast, and later returned to escort her safely home.

Four

Jessie and Jenny

1927–1935

IN EARLY 1927, KURT WEILL WAS COMMISSIONED TO create a work for the summer music festival at Baden-Baden, a gathering of composers, musicians and critics led by Paul Hindemith. He needed the right librettist for a short opera, and before the end of March, Weill had his writer. After reviewing a radio performance of Bertolt Brecht's play *Man Is Man* (which Weill termed "the most powerful and original play of our time"), Weill read some of Brecht's poems. Soon they met. "From that point on," according to Lenya, "Kurt and Brecht visited each other quite often and started discussing what they could do together."

A collaboration between the neat, taciturn, well-mannered and gentle Weill and the untidy, unwashed, cigar-smoking Brecht was hardly inevitable. Weill's god was music, and although he could be described as a liberal humanitarian he was bound to no political philosophy or ideology. Brecht, however, had been studying Marxism, and a genuine conversion to it would occur in 1929. Aware of his own genius, conceited and frequently a social embarrassment because of his crude and pugnacious manner, Brecht (who was Lenya's age) lived at the center of his own private universe, with mistresses, assistants, fiancées (and, eventually, a series of wives) revolving around him in complex and tense orbits.

Eugen Berthold (later Bertolt) Friedrich Brecht was born in Augsburg on February 2, 1898. Both parents were from peasant

families, and his father managed a paper mill. Raised as a Protestant, Brecht later acknowledged the early influence of Martin
Luther's plain, earthy translation of the Bible.

From his school days as coeditor of a literary magazine,
Brecht was a devoted reader of literature, drama and poetry, and
an Augsburg newspaper published his earliest verses. In 1917 he
began medical studies at the University of Munich, and when
he was called for war service the following year he was assigned
to a military hospital in his hometown. There, his work and the
suffering he saw contributed to his pacifist commitment and to
his later political philosophy.

A plainspoken man whose intelligence and wit could exert
great social charm, Brecht always had a core group of devoted
friends and admirers, among them the designer Caspar Neher,
who collaborated with Brecht on his first play, *Baal*, about the
moral decline of a young poet who becomes a wanderer and
then a murderer.

After the war, Brecht returned to Munich but abandoned his
medical studies for the theater. Following a month in 1919 as
drama critic for a left-wing newspaper, Brecht submitted his
play *Drums in the Night* to Lion Feuchtwanger, the literary adviser to the Kammerspiele Theater and later a famous novelist
and playwright. (Like Neher, Feuchtwanger became Brecht's
close friend.) That somber, cynical play concerned a German
soldier who returns from the war to find that his fiancée is pregnant by a black-marketeer. Disillusioned with personal relationships as well as social and political struggle, the man turns his
back on the German Communists working for a better future
and new freedom after the war and settles down with the faithless fiancée in a triumph of compromise. This play won for
Brecht the Kleist Prize as a promising young dramatist.

Although Brecht had sired an illegitimate son by Paula Ban-
holzer (a doctor's daughter), he married actress and singer Marianne Zoff in November 1922; their daughter Hanne was born
in March 1923. Two more plays, *In the Jungle of the Cities* and
a Brecht-Feuchtwanger adaptation of Christopher Marlowe's
Edward II followed, also in Munich productions. Then, in 1924,
Brecht settled in Berlin where he continued to rethink his politics and refine his art. He also worked for a time as dramaturg
(play reader and editorial assistant) at the Deutsches Theater.

In Berlin, Brecht was soon at the center of a group of leftist intellectuals and artists, and here he began an affair with actress Helene Weigel. She bore him a son, Stefan, in November 1924, but Brecht did not divorce Marianne Zoff until 1927 nor marry Weigel until 1929. (Brecht's marriages to Zoff and Weigel were paralleled by various long-term affairs with his collaborator and assistant Elisabeth Hauptmann and with the young actresses Margarete Steffin and Ruth Berlau, as well as by numerous brief liaisons.)

Few dramatists in the twentieth century have been as controversial as Brecht, and few have summoned students, performers and scholars to more complex study. Much is made of his theories of epic theater and alienation—theories which were codified only much later, after the facts of creation and performance. Briefly stated, his aim was didactic. Drama, he felt, must be a dialogue in which the audience participates, structured in such a way that the atmosphere of theater is always reinforced. To encourage a detachment from the familiar and to lead his audience to share what was eventually his Marxist defiance of conventional moralities and dead traditions, he delimited the normal flow of storytelling and sought to reform his hearers so they might join him in the reform of the world.

When Weill and Brecht met in the spring of 1927, Brecht was no legend, much less a commercial success. There had been only a few performances and mixed receptions accorded his plays *Baal* and *Edward II*, and only *Man Is Man* had won some real acclaim. But after reading a selection of satiric verses by Brecht (and after his favorable response to the last-named play), Weill suggested Brecht and Hauptmann's ''Mahagonny Songs'' as a basis for the commissioned work.

> When Brecht and I first met in spring 1927 [Weill wrote later] we were discussing the potentialities of opera, when the word ''Mahagonny'' was mentioned and with it the notion of a ''paradise city.'' The idea instantly seized me, and with a view to developing it and trying out the musical style I had in mind I set the five ''Mahagonny Songs'' from Brecht's *Devotions for the Home*, combining them in a small-scale dramatic form to make a ''Songspiel.''

The name Mahagonny (pronounced Ma-ha-*GUN*-nee)—a word heard on German recordings as early as 1922—became Brecht's and then Weill's catchword for a fantasyland, a modern Sodom and Gomorrah.

The Weill-Brecht work would describe life in an imaginary, quasi-American boomtown inspired by Jack London's Klondike and Chaplin's *The Gold Rush* (a film that had premiered in Germany in 1926). Like many young artists in Europe, both Weill and Brecht were fascinated by everything American, from fashion and jazz to movies, tabloid romances, Westerns, the tropical climate of Florida and California, and both the exuberance and the violence of the Roaring Twenties.

Weill began composing the music for the five "Mahagonny" poems for which Brecht himself had attempted various tunes. The words of three, in German, had come from Brecht, and two (the "Alabama" and "Benares" lyrics, in English) were written by Elisabeth Hauptmann. At Weill's urging, Brecht also wrote a concluding poem for what was becoming the *Mahagonny Songspiel*, later often called the "Little Mahagonny."

Time was short, however, and soon Brecht and Weill knew their submission for Baden-Baden would be only a preliminary sketch, a scenic cantata in preparation for the full-length opera they intended to write, *Aufstieg und Fall der Stadt Mahagonny (Rise and Fall of the City of Mahagonny)*.

Although rehearsals for the July performance did not begin until June in Baden-Baden, Brecht and Weill worked together—usually at Brecht's place, but occasionally in the Weills' furnished apartment on the Luisenplatz—with huge, dark paintings of hunting dogs glowering down and pitch-black wooden furniture in the living room, which Weill and Lenya nicknamed "Grieneisen," after a local funeral parlor.

Weill told Brecht that he had been working with Lenya on the "Alabama Song." His wife, he said, had an uncanny ear; in fact, she had a natural musical ability even without formal training, and when she had offered to learn to read music, he had stopped her: "God forbid, no! I'm so happy to have married a girl who can't!" Lenya's audition with Brecht was held one afternoon at the playwright's apartment.

Brecht looked very thin [Lenya wrote later in her memoir-notes], like a herring with very sensitive hands. He was already in his uniform, with that cap and that Russian blouse and leather jacket. It was a real collaboration. They were very good together, always changing things for one another. Brecht was not jealous, either—he was much too conceited for that.

And so Lenya sang the "Alabama Song," in a voice that was high-pitched, light and somewhat breathy and tentative. She walked around the room to the rhythm, and she crooned the daffy English lyrics for Weill's music: "Oh show us the way to the next whiskey bar . . . Oh moon of Alabama, we now must say good-bye. We've lost our dear old mama . . ."

I didn't realize it then [she continued], because it sounds so beautiful to sing, but of course it has nothing to do with Alabama. They were fascinated with America, that's all. We saw all the American movies. They had a map, and they just closed their eyes and chose Alabama just for the sound and the rhyme with "mama." Accuracy had nothing to do with it, because of course none of it fits together.

Lenya's voice was nonoperatic but oddly sensuous. It could be smoky and inviting or full of a childish innocence, alive with reedy anxiety or strident with expectation. And when she was finished singing, Brecht rose from his seat. "Now let's really work on it," he said. He encouraged simplicity above all.

Brecht then showed her how to take in the entire audience— "by forgetting them," she said later. "He told me to reach out my hands to the moon and to an invisible mama." But grand theatrical gestures and all the mechanisms of the acting studio had to be dismissed. Lenya needed only to be herself, Brecht insisted, not a conscious performer. Ironically, soon Lenya's technique seemed to be that there was no technique but herself. "Here I am, just what you see—that's all there is," she seemed to say.

Her lack of pretense, her apparent vulnerability as well as her nervousness—she fought stage fright all during her life—were a refreshing contrast to a great deal in the tradition of florid and elaborate "stage presence." Her contributions to the enduring popularity of the Weill-Brecht works were not in terms of the size of the roles nor of any great dimension she bestowed, but in terms of a stylistic focus she gave them. She always gripped spectators—then in Germany and later in America—by bringing them back to clear confrontations with elemental human feelings and experiences. Such confrontations were not presented as hysterical outpourings, but as quiet and almost inevitable statements of emotional and psychological experiences and needs.

Mahagonny Songspiel, a stylistic test for the full-length opera to come, was ready by early June for the summer festival. In a brief prologue, four men (Charlie, Billy, Bobby and Jimmy) enter with suitcases and announce their plan to go to Mahagonny, which is supposed to be a new utopia. They are joined by two slightly tarnished, blowsy girls, Jessie and Bessie, who come along in hope of good fortune. The action then shifts to the mythic city, where the men are drinking, smoking and card-playing but also complaining about the high cost of living. They and the girls agree that Mahagonny is a disappointment, and they decide to move on to a place called Benares—which they learn has been destroyed. As a symbol of human authority, one of the men now assumes the voice of an institutional "God," questioning the citizens of Mahagonny and ordering them to hell—a directive they cannot follow, they say, because they are already living there.

Brecht and designer Caspar Neher had prepared for Baden-Baden an unorthodox visual presentation for a staged cantata. The entire action took place in a boxing ring and the only backgrounds were images flashed on the rear wall in slide projections created by Neher.

George Grosz had already exploited boxing imagery as part of his cult of toughness and hard-boiled Americanism in his illustrations and drawings, and his 1926 painting of fighter Max Schmeling was popular everywhere. The intellectual vogue connected to boxing had also attracted composer Ernst Krenek, stage director Erwin Piscator and artist Karl Gunther. Very soon after returning from his apprenticeship in Germany, Alfred Hitchcock directed an English film (*The Ring*, 1927) in which a boxer's life is metaphorically linked with all his relationships, from boxing ring to wedding ring.

But for Brecht the ring, a frequent motif in his poems and plays, marked an increasing obsession with social and political conflict. Closer now to his articulated political ideology, he was beginning to see class conflict as an image of the inevitable dialectic: the decadence of Mahagonny and the final confrontation was for him only one stage in the progress of that dialectic. To the scenes of greed, sensuality and violence, Brecht had wanted to shock his audience even further by having Lenya appear totally nude throughout the action. Her husband and the festival management forbade that.

The premiere date was Sunday, July 17, on the last program of a three-day summer festival. Other new short works were also offered: Ernst Toch's *The Princess and the Pea*, Darius Milhaud's satire on *The Rape of Europa*, and Paul Hindemith's *Forward and Back*, a musical palindrome that proceeds in score and text to its exact middle and then reverses to its opening bar. The thirty-five-minute-long *Songspiel* concluded the evening. Lenya sang the role of Jessie (not Jenny, as she frequently said later); opera singer Irene Eden sang Bessie. The conductor was Ernst Mehlich, the director Walter Brügmann.

Some in the crowd at Baden-Baden booed and whistled their disapproval, while others applauded loudly. Success was not long in coming, however; in fact it was assured at a reception right after the performance. Most of the spectators were soon joining in the jaunty tunes and crowing the lyrics. The authors were hailed and toasted, and a roar went up for Lenya. She was most recognized of all, for while the cast members had appeared in the last scene carrying placards with political slogans— "Against war" and "Down with tyranny" and "For universal freedom," among others—Lenya's sign was clear to everyone: "For Weill!"

Following the festival, Weill returned to Berlin to work with Georg Kaiser on a one-act opera, *Der Zar lässt sich photographieren (The Czar Has His Photograph Taken)*. Lenya went for a summer holiday at Prerow, on the Baltic Sea, and Weill joined her on August 19. Shortly thereafter they returned together to Berlin, where by early the following year Kurt was working full-time with Brecht on the long opera *Rise and Fall of the City of Mahagonny*, with brief interruptions for work on incidental music for two plays.

By this time, there seemed no doubt that Lenya and Kurt would not have children; parenthood did not appeal to either of them. "It's just as well," Kurt's niece Hanne Weill Holesovsky said later. "She wasn't the motherly type. If they'd had a child it would have been a disaster for the poor kid." This judgment may seem somewhat harsh in light of Lenya's kindnesses to some of her friends' children, but it is certainly true that the professional lives of both Kurt and Lenya and the travel and independence that marked their marriage would have made the duties of parenthood difficult to fulfill.

In addition, Lenya's sexual life was still of the free-lance type; she had, for example, affairs with the writer (and sometime Piscator collaborator) Leo Lania—who later contributed to the screenplay for *The Threepenny Opera*—and with Rudolf Leonhard, one of the founders of a proletarian theater in Berlin in 1919, who also had an apartment at 3 Luisenplatz. Only the fact of these relationships is known (by Lenya's admission to friends in America later); we have no chronicle of them.

In early spring 1928, a twenty-seven-year-old actor and aspiring producer named Ernst-Josef Aufricht, hoping to extend his career by becoming a theatrical manager and impresario, took a lease on the Schiffbauerdamm. Situated in the heart of the theater district just off the Friedrichstrasse, the Schiffbauerdamm had less than eight hundred seats and was not designed for spectacles. Aufricht engaged Erich Engel, a successful stage director of the time, and Caspar Neher as resident designer. He then realized he also needed a play, and he contacted Bertolt Brecht.

Brecht's assistant Elisabeth Hauptmann, always on the alert for something Brecht could adapt, sent Aufricht a German translation she had prepared of John Gay's eighteenth-century English play *The Beggar's Opera*, which used popular songs by John Pepusch. That year was the two hundredth anniversary of the play, and its 1920 London revival had been followed by several others. This was an aggressively satirical work, ridiculing not only social and moral degradation but political ineptitude as well.

Aufricht read the incomplete draft of the adaptation and relayed his interest to Hauptmann. The Pepusch music, Brecht then said, was to be dropped in favor of a new score by Weill—an idea readily accepted by Weill, since he believed (with Brecht) that this would be an easy task—a simple, interim work to help them both financially while they worked on *Mahagonny*.

While Brecht continued to edit Hauptmann's adaptation—adding, subtracting and borrowing from poems by Kipling and Villon (and cribbing others' German translations of them without permission or payment)—Weill worked steadily, and Lenya was often present when the two worked together. Brecht's studio, she recalled later,

> was austere, but around the room lounged the ever-present disciples, male and female: the men with hair cropped, wearing turtle-neck sweaters and slacks; the women without makeup, their hair skinned back, and wearing sweaters and skirts—this highly stylized proletarian style set by the master. . . . [We] always found Elisabeth Hauptmann there, at that time literally his devoted shadow. . . . When it was time for work, the disciples left except for Hauptmann, and the two men would work steadily.

Their adaptation transferred the story to the Victorian era, but the form remained spoken dialogue interspersed with songs and musical interludes. The work was eventually called *Die Dreigroschenoper (The Threepenny Opera)*, its title suggested by Lion Feuchtwanger, who attended a rehearsal and saw the modest scenery and simple costumes, the seven-man band and the mostly nonoperatic singers.

The story of *The Threepenny Opera* follows John Gay's original closely. J. J. Peachum controls a band of beggars by giving them the outfits they need in exchange for a percentage of "charity" profits. His daughter Polly is in love with Macheath (nicknamed "Mackie Messer" or "Mack the Knife" by Brecht), a gang leader, and she has left home to wed him. Peachum enlists his old friend (and sometime accomplice) Tiger Brown, the police chief, to arrest Macheath, who flees. Mrs. Peachum then learns from Jenny (a prostitute and former lover of Macheath) that the outlaw is hiding in a brothel. Captured and imprisoned, he subsequently escapes, only to be recaught. As he is about to be hanged, the news comes that not only has Macheath been freed by the queen, but also that he is raised to a peerage.

In May, Aufricht informed Brecht and Weill that he had advanced his date for the reopening of the Schiffbauerdamm to his own birthday, August 31. Needing concentrated work without interruption, the two men retreated to the French Riviera, with Lenya accompanying Weill to the Hostellerie de la Plage, in St. Cyr-sur-Mer, and Brecht taking a leased villa near the beach at

Le Lavandou, with actress Helene Weigel (soon to be Mrs. Brecht) and their son, Stefan.

In June they were back in Berlin, and by the end of July the work was ready for rehearsal and the inevitable emendations. Weill asked Aufricht to cast Lenya in the role of Jenny, the prostitute, and, as Aufricht later wrote, ". . . she looked talented, moved well and I liked the look of her. She's rather cheeky, I thought." For Margot Aufricht, the producer's wife, Lenya was

> never beautiful, but she had a stage presence. She was very eager, very ambitious to be a success. She had an unfailing sense of what and where the possibilities were, and she knew what had to be done.

Rehearsals began in early August, but the production seemed doomed from the start, and rumors of imminent catastrophe soon spread in theatrical circles. Before the premiere, there were several unexpected crises. Carola Neher (no relation to Caspar), who had been signed to play Polly Peachum, went to her ailing husband (the poet Klabund) in Switzerland and was replaced by Roma Bahn. (Neher did, however, return to the show later.) The actor hired for Mr. Peachum withdrew. Helene Weigel, also in the cast, was stricken with appendicitis and her role was deleted. Harald Paulsen (as Macheath) and Rosa Valletti (as Mrs. Peachum) objected to the cuts in their roles and to certain risqué lyrics. Director Erich Engel walked out and eventually Brecht himself took over the direction of a show that was in complete chaos. So much for the "simple, interim work."

The final dress rehearsal, on the night of August 30, lasted until five the next morning. Everyone was upset, angry, frightened, exhausted, ready to seek new work after the certain disaster to come. At another noontime run-through, cuts were still being made—Lenya's second song, for one. Then, on that torrid August day in a cramped and airless theater, a scream was heard backstage. No one had ever heard Kurt Weill raise his voice, but there he was—enraged, after seeing the printed programs for the opening, with the inadvertent and unaccountable omission of his wife's name. Aufricht immediately arranged for a reprinting for second night.

The first public performance began unsteadily, and no one's

confidence was lifted. Lenya, as the prostitute Jenny, sang only the "Tango-Ballad," a duet with Paulsen about their former squalid life as lovers. (The famous "Pirate Jenny" song—about a vengeful maidservant—concerns a character not in the story, and was written for Polly to sing at her wedding party. Lenya, as Jenny, sang this in the film version, in the 1954 New York revival, and on later recordings. It became her signature tune.)

But as the premiere continued, the atmosphere in the Schiffbauerdamm altered dramatically. The audience, long before the final curtain, was roaring with approval, and the last several songs had to be repeated at least once each to satisfy them.

With that, a *Threepenny* fever gripped Berlin. Its tunes were whistled everywhere, and newspapers were publishing appreciative essays. The morning after opening, the eminent critic Alfred Kerr proclaimed it a magnificent evening in the theater. He also wrote about the women playing prostitutes. "Four actresses took these parts—and one of them seems to come from Munich," he wrote, mistaking Lenya's Viennese accent for Bavarian and complaining about the omission of her name. "She was very, very good . . . and her articulation was particularly good." Critic Herbert Ihering added that *The Threepenny Opera* "proclaims a new world, in which the barriers separating tragedy and comedy are eradicated." He made virtually the identical comment as Kerr about the uncredited player of Jenny. And Kurt's niece, five-year-old Hanne (daughter of his brother Hanns) saw the production:

> I have a very vivid memory of the opening scene with the man playing the hurdy-gurdy [she said in an interview years later], and then of Lenya as Jenny, sitting on a high stool, her feet crossed, wearing black stockings, her skirt raised and a hole in the stocking just at the knee.

Elisabeth Bergner, Lenya's former colleague in Zurich, attended an evening performance soon after and recalled in her memoirs:

> Weigel and Brecht introduced [me] to all the members of the cast. I had to stare at Lenya in admiration because she was so fantastic as Jenny. She must have noticed me staring, be-

cause finally she said, to me, "Yes, yes, it's me! You're not making a mistake, I'm Blamauer!" I was speechless!

Commercial success was instantaneous. "When the checks came rolling in," wrote music publisher Hans Heinsheimer,

> the commas and periods were all at the right spots, and the accountants, furiously chewing at their cigars, had to provide for extra columns in their ledgers to accommodate the thousands and ten thousands where there had only been room and need for miserable tens and for zeros.

In Munich, Leipzig, Prague and Riga there were productions mounted very soon, and by 1930 over one hundred twenty German theaters had given more than four thousand performances of *The Threepenny Opera*. Audiences took to its spirit of cynical rebellion in those days of increasing political tensions, joblessness and violence.

Elections during the summer of 1928 had given the Nazis twelve seats in the Reichstag, one of which was occupied by Hermann Göring. Economic life was becoming more and more unstable, and many unemployed were converted into ardent Nazis. *The Threepenny Opera* was not only an engagingly irreverent entertainment that shared the public cynicism about official corruption and the lack of social justice. It also capitalized on the German love of American jazz.

> We liked everything we knew about America [Weill said later in an interview]. We read Jack London, Hemingway, Dreiser, Dos Passos, we admired Hollywood pictures, and American jazz had a great influence on our music. America was a very romantic country for us.

In this he was not alone. Paul Hindemith had first heard jazz in 1921, and the 1923 recordings of "Jelly Roll" Morton had already found a wide audience in Germany. In the flapper era, this new music was even more influential than twelve-tone experimentation. And like Paul Hindemith, Kurt Weill found American jazz economical, dynamic and affirmative.

George Gershwin's "Rhapsody in Blue," scored originally for jazz band and piano, was reorchestrated by Ferde Grofé, musical arranger for Paul Whiteman, who had commissioned it in 1924 and conducted it throughout the 1920s. The American musical *No, No, Nanette* was an enormous success at Berlin's Metropole Theater, and Ernst Krenek's *Jonny spielt auf*, which had some American jazz configurations, was first staged in Berlin in 1927. American pop music (notably by Gershwin and Louis Armstrong) had been enthusiastically welcomed all over Europe by this time, and in a 1926 essay Kurt Weill himself had hailed jazz as "the expression of our time." Jazz was also taken seriously by writers and artists, who told stories and painted scenes of nightclubs and their denizens.

But the German love of American jazz coincided perfectly with another element—the new simplicity in artistic circles, the new functionalism and unembellished design. The preference for "utilitarian" music—intended, by virtue of its simplicity, for performances even by the talented amateur and not limited to the virtuoso—was openly endorsed by composers like Weill and Hindemith. In *The Threepenny Opera* Weill and Brecht, unafraid to adapt American dance and jazz idioms and English plays, saw everything as challenges to their growth as artists.

Gradually, from 1922 to 1928, Weill had become aware that much in the new music of Schönberg, Berg and Webern was inaccessible for many listeners. With *The Threepenny Opera*, Weill was now addressing everyone. According to Maurice Abravanel,

> He wanted to reach as wide an audience as possible. Theater, he knew, was not for the few but for everybody, and he knew he had to simplify his musical language.

Some of the inspiration—for both Weill and Lenya—came from the collaboration with Brecht, to be sure. "Weill with Brecht becomes more than the sum of his previous parts," as composer Ned Rorem has written.

> His notes shed dew onto Brecht's sour books . . . and for the first time since *Don Giovanni*, horror was depicted by snappy tunes.

But Brecht's characters become lively only through Weill's music, where they find their specificity and their humanity. Brecht's domain, as Rorem added,

> is bitter, yes, and objective and terse and mean and preachy. But the music, like a bridge of honey, spans the fields. . . . Song is the ultimate purgatory, lending an inner glow to even the most despondent story.

As for Lenya, the *Threepenny* fever that soon swept Germany owed much to her original participation, to her frequent return to the cast (sometimes as Jenny, sometimes as Lucy) between other acting jobs, and to the historic and hugely popular recording of selections in 1930. Still available today, this recording helps to account for her enormous fame throughout the Weimar Republic even before her exposure in the *Threepenny* film soon after. It also accounts for the direct popular association between Lenya and the work.

Under Theo Mackeben's direction, Lenya recorded Polly's "Pirate Jenny," her voice surprisingly high-pitched—in what might later be called a musical comedy or soubrette style—and swift with a sense of joyful caprice. The song tells of a poor girl who works in a London dive, dreaming of vengeance against those who have exploited her. One day, she sings, a ship with eight sails and fifty cannons will appear in the harbor and destroy the entire town except for her hotel. She will sail away, the darling of her vindicating pirates.

She also recorded Polly's "Barbara Song," her intonation slightly frantic and full of romance and regret. And in the "Tango-Ballad" (with Willy Trenk-Trebitsch as Macheath) her tonal accuracy is shimmeringly combined with a knifelike attack to both the melody and a sense of the lyrics. With Erika Helmke as Polly, Lenya also sang Lucy's part in the "Jealousy Duet" for this recording, the two women blending their voices in a lively and scrappy vivacity; Lenya's sudden slip from pitch near the end is the perfect final touch of sassy bravado. In this, as in all her cuts, Lenya's voice is that of a strong singing actress—an inimitable presence impossible to confuse with any other singing actress then or now. Her unique combination of inflection and of tone, her uncanny balance of anxiety and of insistence—and her cavalier refusal (by necessity perhaps) to attempt anything like beautiful singing—gave her the edge of character that many singing actresses have always lacked. (Over the next few years, Lenya—with various other artists—made additional recordings in Germany of selections from *The Threepenny Opera* and from the full-length opera *Mahagonny*.)

Months before the premiere, Brecht and Weill signed a contract for the division of royalties—a contract that would forever favor Brecht. Brecht insisted that he receive 62½ percent, Weill 25 percent, and Elisabeth Hauptmann 12½ (2½ percent of Brecht's share was later reassigned to the German translator of the Villon lyrics Brecht had plagiarized). More significant, however, was that Brecht always acted as if the rights to *The Threepenny Opera* were his, to transfer to agents, publishers and producers, and to negotiate and renegotiate single-handedly, without reference to Weill's interest, profit or permission. After Weill's death, when Brecht returned to Germany, his proprietary attitude and his cavalier indifference to Weill's rights continued to burden Lenya emotionally and legally—a lamentable situation that has continued to vex those responsible for her husband's rights and hers.

With his share of the proceeds from *The Threepenny Opera*, Weill bought an automobile, and he and Lenya moved to a new apartment on the Bayernallee, in Berlin's Charlottenburg district. There they held a small reception for friends and colleagues after the opening, on November 28, of Lion Feuchtwanger's play about the international oil trade, *Die Petroleuminseln (The Oil Islands)*, at the Berlin State Theater. Weill had written a bluesy fox-trot for it, and Lenya—who was available when *The Threepenny Opera* went on a revolving schedule with other works in repertory—played the role of Miss Charmian Peruchacha in Feuchtwanger's play. The reviews did not ignore her, but neither were they undiluted raves.

The Oil Islands concerns Deborah Gray, president of the Island Oil Company and owner of most of the Brown Islands. Ambitious, greedy, homely, she feeds on human folly and intends to increase her wealth through any means, moral or not. Her rival is Charmian Peruchacha, a scintillating mulatto regarded by the Brown Islanders as their guardian angel and advocate. Not only do men adore her; she is also a descendant of a former settler who had been on the island when it was still an exotic idyll. But now the idyll is being destroyed by the oil's foul smell and slick. The play ends tragically, with Deborah Gray more triumphant than ever, her enemies overcome and Charmian neatly removed as any threat to Gray's power.

"For the female characters," wrote critic Monty Jacobs in the *Vossische Zeitung*,

> Feuchtwanger has contrasted ugly and beautiful. [Director Jürgen] Fehling needed someone with first-class presence for the role of Charmian, and so it might have been more natural for him to look for a more brilliant actress than Lotte Lenya. Fehling took a risk when he chose Lotte Lenya, who had recently been discovered as a talented artist in *The Threepenny Opera*, but he converted the doubters. . . . She was exciting in an exotic way, and she was the best contrast to [the character of Deborah Gray] through her style and the high spirits of her temperament.

His colleague Max Osborn had some reservations, however: "Lotte Lenya as Miss Peruchacha is living proof of a great new talent, but she is not quite adequate for the adversary's role." Franz Köppen was more specific, criticizing Lenya as

> too immature and uncontrolled . . . [and] there was a lack of security in her reading of the dialogue. Even her movements were barely sufficient when she danced to her husband's music.

But critic Fritz Engel pointed to a quality that Lenya would improve with time:

> Then there is Lotte Lenya, striking, hot-tempered and lively. She's supposed to stand for beauty, but this she does with sensuality—for example, with her [made-up] brown skin. Some in the audience were obviously touched very deeply, and they applauded loudly.

Ludwig Sternaux, another Berlin critic, agreed:

> Lotte Lenya brings to the role her interesting profile as well as her exotic gracefulness, her hot temperament as well as the metallic sharpness of her youthful, bright voice.

And Willy Haas stated flatly that Lenya was "incomparable. She emphasizes the emotional qualities more than the flashy ones, just as the role demands."

In December of that exciting and historic year, Lenya learned of her father's death in Vienna. They had had no contact since she left Penzing for Zurich. But of immediate concern that season was her upcoming appearance as Ismene, in Leopold Jessner's production of the Oedipus cycle at the Berlin State Theater.

Rehearsals began while Lenya was still performing in *The Oil Islands*. *Oedipus* opened January 5, 1929, and many reviews concentrated on Jessner's adaptation and staging. The critic Herbert Ihering (Brecht's most enthusiastic supporter), writing in the *Berliner Börsen-Courier* reported that the performance was

> a great success, [but] . . . Lotte Lenya has to learn how to vary her intonation, inflection and modulation. She also needs to learn how to articulate each section more clearly by her use of phrasing and by breathing with the text.

At that time, a woman named Marieluise Fleisser was a twenty-eight-year-old apprentice playwright. Her mentor was Bertolt Brecht, who was also her lover. With his help and influence, her play *The Pioneers of Ingolstadt* opened on March 31 at the Schiffbauerdamm.

The pioneers of the title were a platoon of soldiers assigned to build a bridge over the Altwasser. The play, however, concentrates on the chaos the men bring to the town—and mostly to the servant girls there. A lady-killer seduces a frightened and simple-minded girl, while her saucy counterpart, played by Lenya, is mad about men and in spite of her past series of unstable love affairs delights in the arrival of the rough soldiers.

Always eager to shock his audience, Brecht (who took over the play's direction from Jacob Geis during the March rehearsals) devised a controversial sequence in which Lenya's costar Hilde Körber was ravished by a soldier. The scene, however, brought opposition from the police, who struck a bargain with Brecht. If he would remove this scene, he could retain that in which Lenya rested against cemetery headstones while she slid into an embrace with a soldier.

Critics, however, saw provocative scenes as no compensation for good dramatic construction. "The production drowned in attractive designs," wrote Arthur Eloesser. "Decorations were even projected on a linen screen, and this overwhelmed the actors, who were kept at the same dramatic level throughout." Julius Knopf agreed: "Nothing can save this production—an unwieldy and extremely boring piece—not even the excellent ensemble of actors."

Lenya's notices were better than Fleisser's, however. Herbert Ihering found Lenya's delivery of lines and her vocal nuance much improved since *Oedipus*. "Lotte Lenya as Alma," he wrote in the *Berliner Börsen-Courier*,

> exhibits striking, witty and graphic gestures. Her vocal into-
> nation, inflection and modulation are so fluid and relaxed,
> and she seems so natural. Lenya seems to be more at home
> in this role than in those she had before.

Alfred Kerr, generally regarded as the most eminent theater critic in Berlin, wrote in the *Berliner Tageblatt*,

> By the way she moved her legs, Lotte Lenya portrayed a
> particular character. A whole world is visible in the way she
> moves. She will soon emerge in the forefront of the theater.

Rolf Nürnberg agreed: "Lotte Lenya appeared fresh, clear and highly dramatic and she acted with magnificent vitality—just sometimes, maybe, a little bit too obtrusively." Critic Kurt Pinthus praised Lenya's "sensual, sweet, musical voice . . . and her gestures, which hang in the air as if undecided, are provocative."

"My husband thought the play was a great success," Margot Aufricht said years later, "and Lenya made quite a hit in her cemetery scene." And so, it seems, did Peter Lorre, who would soon become an internationally famous film star after his portrayal of a child molester in the first German talkie, Fritz Lang's *M*. (He also appeared later with Lenya in a production of Wedekind's *Frühlings Erwachen* [*Spring's Awakening*], as well as in the premier production of the Weill-Brecht *Happy End*.)

On April 10, Brecht married Helene Weigel. Elisabeth Hauptmann was so distraught she attempted suicide (in which attempt she was unsuccessful), but Marieluise Fleisser, losing no time, announced within days that she was engaged to another writer.

Lenya saw the romantic tensions swirling around Brecht, but she was not fazed by the melodramatics. Weill, on the other hand, was putting finishing touches on the score for *Rise and Fall of the City of Mahagonny*, and had little patience for anything else. And Ernst Aufricht was suggesting that on the first anniversary of *The Threepenny Opera* they all repeat its success with a new but similar theater work.

In response, Brecht suggested a one-sentence idea to Elisabeth Hauptmann, who summoned her energy and began to write a complicated play, eventually giving it the English title *Happy End*. Weill set to music Brecht's song texts for it.

Happy End presents a Chicago dance-hall as the headquarters for a gang led by a mysterious Lady in Gray. Into this setting come members of the Salvation Army, whose efforts are futile until Lillian Holiday, under the influence of the charm and the whiskey of Bill Cracker, sings a tango. For this her colleagues hold her in disgrace and she is removed from the Army. On Christmas Eve the gang manages a successful burglary and then discovers an unexpected bond with the Salvation Army: both groups resent banks, as symbols and agents of the oppression of the poor. Together the two groups plan to open new headquarters in Chicago's poshest neighborhood, claiming that there live the greatest number of souls to be saved. Lillian is invited back into the Salvation Army and marries Bill, the gang undergoes a kind of (mock) conversion, and there is a deliciously mordant "happy end."

For further work on this comedy with music in three acts, Weill and Brecht set out in May for the south of France, where they had collaborated so successfully on *The Threepenny Opera*. Here they would work on completing both *Happy End* and revisions for *Mahagonny*. But Brecht had an auto accident and returned to Germany. Weill went ahead and spent a month at the same Riviera hotel he had visited the year before.

The August rehearsals for the September 2 premiere of *Happy End* did not involve Lenya. The evening before its opening she was to appear at the Bülowplatz Theater, in Karlheinz Martin's Volksbühne production of Georg Büchner's play *Danton's Death*.

Although written in 1835, Büchner's play was not produced until 1902. It documents with powerful psychological insight and bitter humor the events leading up to the execution of the man who, once a major leader of the revolution, became a partisan of peace and was charged by Robespierre with betrayal and treason. The production was headed by Hans Rühmann as Danton and Walter Franck as Robespierre, with Lotte Lenya as Lucile, wife of Camille Desmoulins, deputy of the National Convention.

The role of Lucile is small (she appears only twice), but it is also significant: her final poetic apostrophe to Death and her loyalty to the king lead her to be the play's last victim, taken away as the curtain falls. But the strong and broad—almost operatic—reactions and emotions demanded of Lenya in the role were not apt for the more casual and naturalistic style she had been developing, with simple gestures, glances and movements suggesting rather than elaborating. Critic Franz Servaes found her portrayal "both gripping and penetrating," but others were less enthusiastic. "Lotte Lenya does not know how to give the required tenderness necessary for the role," wrote critic Wilhelm Westecker. Walter Steinthal felt that Lenya "fumbles around in a frantic manner the longer the play goes on," and even Monty Jacobs, who had championed her in *The Oil Islands*, found her miscast "because of her inner resistance to the romantic style demanded by Lucile's role."

(It is possible that Weill composed incidental music for this production, but as David Drew has pointed out, "[Lenya] is the sole authority" for this claim. "Music is not mentioned in any press notices traced so far," he has noted, although Lenya's participation adds weight to her assertion:

> It is just possible that Weill contributed to the Volksbühne production two or three anonymous arrangements of historically authentic material . . . [but] he would not have had much time to spare in August: it was only in that month that he began the orchestral score for *Happy End*.)

While Lenya was in rehearsal, Kurt's hopes were high for *Happy End*, which had the same producer as *The Threepenny Opera* (Aufricht) and the same director (Engel, again soon replaced by Brecht). There were also the same designer (Caspar Neher), the same musical director (Theo Mackeben) and the same orchestra (the Lewis Ruth band). The problem, however, turned out to be Elisabeth Hauptmann, who was still too depressed by the marriage of her mentor-lover-collaborator-idol to finish writing the book for *Happy End*. (The work was presented as based on a story by "Dorothy Lane," a suitably American pseudonym.)

By opening night the work was in such disarray and incompletion that Weigel surprised everyone except Brecht by a sudden and improvised maneuver in the third act. She drew out some papers and began to read a kind of Communist Manifesto to the audience. This was too extreme even for Aufricht's liberal, tolerant patrons. A riot broke out in the theater, the police had to be summoned, and the play—for lack of subsequent audiences—closed two days later. Not even the fervor of the cast could prevent disaster.

The failure of *Happy End*, however, was not permanent. Its "Bilbao Song" was interpolated into the famous American revival of *The Threepenny Opera* a quarter century later; several other tunes found their way into other Weill works; and "Surabaya Johnny," soon recorded by Lenya, became one of her standard songs. She offered it for years as if it had been written just for her voice and her experience, rendering a plaint of unbearable hopelessness from the song of unrequited love for a wandering sailor—a song poignant in its simplicity, its muted passion and its mood of private despair.

"Bilbao Song," "Sailor's Tango" and "Surabaya Johnny" from *Happy End* have become internationally famous, and the combination of an almost burlesque sense of satire (hardboiled comic-strip gangsters versus comic-strip Salvationists) with a comical, improbably optimistic finale continues to delight audiences six decades later.

In January 1930, Lenya wrote to Kurt from St. Moritz, Switzerland, where she was on a holiday with a friend. She was learning a new game, she reported; she was gambling at cards, which henceforth became a lifelong pastime (although rarely, later, did she play for more than pennies; no matter the amount, however, she was never a gracious loser). Kurt replied that on Sunday, January 12, Lenya's new recordings were heard on Berlin Radio—songs from *The Threepenny Opera*, as well as "Bilbao" and "Surabaya Johnny" and "Alabama Song" (from *Mahagonny*), which she had made for the Electrola and Orchestrola companies under Theo Mackeben's baton. Her fame was widening, as indeed was her talent. Weill, meantime, was busy working with Brecht on the school opera *Der Jasager (The Yes-Sayer)*, based on a Japanese play, an English adaptation of it, and Elisabeth Hauptmann's German adaptation of that.

On March 9, *Rise and Fall of the City of Mahagonny* received its premiere in Leipzig. In notes to the prompt book for the work, Weill himself provided a summary:

Two men and a woman, on the run from the constabulary, are stuck in a desolate area. They decide to found a city in which every man arriving from the gold coast can get his requirements satisfied. A "paradise city" consequently springs up, whose inhabitants lead an idyllic life of contemplation. Sooner or later however the men from the gold coast become dissatisfied with it. Discontent sets in. Prices fall. During the night of the typhoon, while it is bearing down on the city, Jim Mahoney discovers the city's new law. It is "Anything goes." The typhoon veers away. Life goes on according to the new laws. The city blooms. People's requirements multiply—prices likewise. For anything goes: yes, but only so long as you can pay for it. Even Jim Mahoney gets condemned to death when he runs out of money. His execution sparks off a vast demonstration against the cost-of-living increases that herald the city's fall. That is the story of the city of Mahagonny.

It was now evident to a much larger audience than had gathered in Baden-Baden that for Weill and Brecht Mahagonny, the "city of nets," was not specifically America. There were now alternate German names for the characters. The work had taken on a large, mythic universalism as it denounced the corruption of justice, the sadness of love bought and paid for, the ubiquity of human exploitation.

"*Mahagonny*," as Lenya said many years later, "isn't an opera about America. It's about Germany or China, about greed and emptiness everywhere, wherever there's a false utopia." And that, of course, was the core of the problem: the most diabolical element of the nascent Nazism was its lunatic commitment to a perverse utopianism. Germany must become the purest, the master race. And so it might become, Nazis thought, if the "correct" programs were pursued.

Eager to denounce both Brecht (who was a Communist) and

Weill (who was a Jew), the Nazis made sure they were present in large blocks that opening night. "Even at the beginning of the evening," wrote music critic Alfred Polgar, "storm signals were in the air. A tension, a crackling disquiet, an audible un-folding of discontent." And then, at the last scene, "war cries echoed through the auditorium. In places hand-to-hand fighting broke out. Hissing, applause like faces being slapped." Another critic wrote that there were "fist fights, wild defiances, female fainting fits, and shrieks . . . from the custodians of righteous-ness."

Brecht was not present, but Weill was, and also his parents (who lived in Leipzig) and Lenya. "Kurt's parents and I were in our seats," she remembered,

> and the performance was well under way before I was startled out of my absorption by the electric tension around us, some-thing strange and ugly. . . . Fist fights broke out, the theater was a screaming mass of people. Soon the riot had spread to the stage, panicky spectators were trying to claw their way out, and only the arrival of a large police force finally cleared the theater.

The second performance was presented with the houselights on and the walls lined with the city's police.

> It was [Hans Heinsheimer recalled] a purely political dem-onstration, carefully planned as a test of power and, as such, a great success. . . . Later performances were for specially invited audiences only. The management had got the mes-sage.

Some few rightly understood this carefully structured work as a strong reminder that people are morally responsible for the situations they create. Capitalistic greed was, for Brecht, only the clearest contemporary manifestation of a deranged social order.

Within days of the premiere, additional performances already scheduled in other cities were held without incident. But all was not serene. In Kassel, for example, Maurice Abravanel con-ducted it five days later. "It won admiration," he recalled, "but animosity too, because by that time the Nazis were very strong there and greatly feared. Petitions were circulated to get it and me thrown out of the Kassel State Theater.''

Weill and Lenya were not unduly alarmed—at least not to the point of fearing for their lives. *Their* city, after all, was Berlin, a haven of tolerance, the place where they found most enlightened and sophisticated audiences. They would await a production of *Mahagonny* there.

Three weeks after the premiere, Lenya appeared, on March 30, in another Berliner Volksbühne production, *Das Lied von Hoboken (The Song of Hoboken)*. A free adaptation of an American play, it was a kind of minstrel musical revue in which Lenya sang a few songs by the Austrian-born composer and conductor Wilhelm Grosz. Actress Dolly Haas, who appeared in it with her, remembered that Lenya was full of wily energy and humor and insisted on a costume that mixed outrageously flamboyant colors.

> We had a number in which we sang with another member of the cast, a man who tended to spit rather profusely when he spoke. Lenya made an amusing moment out of that—for his benefit and ours—by doing a pantomime about a raincoat.

Meantime, throughout the spring of 1930, Weill continued to work on the score for *The Yes-Sayer* (which had a premier via Radio Berlin on June 23 and a stage premiere the next evening). "Brecht was becoming more and more involved in politics," Lenya said later, "and all his creative ideas were now tinged with his opinionated and dictatorial political beliefs." And this, more than anything, was responsible for the unraveling of the extraordinary collaboration with Weill, who wanted to compose for the theater, not for ideologues. Because of Brecht's overarching concern for his political message, he demanded more and more control over every aspect of the creation and representation of his work.

"Brecht was a dictator, all right," Margot Aufricht confirmed.

> He wanted complete control over everything, including Kurt Weill's music. And that Kurt Weill could not tolerate. During a picture-taking session, Brecht snatched the camera from a photographer's hand, objecting that Weill should not be in-

cluded. "I don't want this phony Richard Strauss in the picture!" Brecht shouted, and he knocked the photographer to
the ground.

By summer's end, Lenya was busy preparing for another
opening—this time in October, at a Volksbühne production (at
the Schiffbauerdamm) of Paul Kornfeld's *Jud Süss (Jew Süss)*,
based on a novel by Lion Feuchtwanger. The play portrays a
Jewish ghetto dweller who improves his station in life by ruthless
means, including offering his fiancée to a duke to be seduced.

Lenya had the role of an elegant courtesan, Frau Götz—a
performance Monty Jacobs, writing in the *Vossische Zeitung*,
found full of a "humor [that] reveals the attitude of a supplicant
who obliges men of high position." Franz Köppen wrote that
Lenya and Hilde Körber gave "greater dimension to their characters [than Eleonora Mendelssohn, the leading lady]." Critic
Franz Servaes, not impressed with most leading players in the
large cast, remarked in his review that Lenya "gave color and
shape to the role of the success-oriented widow, mad about
men."

In the autumn of 1930, after legal complications over creative
control of a film version, a movie of *The Threepenny Opera* was
finally completed. It was directed by G. W. Pabst, who had
already filmed *The Joyless Street* with Asta Nielsen and Greta
Garbo, and *Pandora's Box* with Louise Brooks. The film offered
an impressive cast: Lenya (as Jenny), Rudolf Forster (as Macheath), Carola Neher (Polly), Valeska Gert (Mrs. Peachum)
and Reinhold Schuenzel (as Tiger Brown). (A French version
was filmed simultaneously, starring Albert Préjean, Florelle,
Antonin Artaud and, in the role of Jenny, the great Berlin cabaret star Margo Lion.)

Lenya's Jenny in the now-famous film is only partly the Jenny
of the stage version; it is also partly Lucy and partly Polly, for
she was given Polly's "Pirate Jenny" and portions of Lucy's
dialogue. This number, for which she was already well known
(from recordings) and for which, later, she would be even more
famous, was probably given to her in the film at Weill's insistence because her "Tango-Ballad" had been cut from it. Also,
the producers had already insisted on giving "Pirate Jenny," in
the French version, to Margo Lion; that would have supported
Weill's argument on his wife's behalf.

To this day, Lenya's performance is the memorable highlight of Pabst's film. Her Jenny is soiled and dangerous, to be sure, but she makes the girl human and credible, pathetic and tart. It was Pabst's idea to make the entire movie a chain of glances and grimaces, modulating the performers not only because of camera closeups but also to reveal complex psychological states—desires and fears and caprices only half-understood by each of them. No one knew about emotional complexity better than Lenya, and no one worked with Pabst better than she.

Her smile in the opening scene, for example, illuminates all the contradictions of characters in *The Threepenny Opera*. Carola Neher's coy gentility as Polly contrasts vividly with Lenya's swaggering confidence. When Lenya is hailed as a lady, she whines back in a voice high with mock resentment, "Me? A lady? Where? Who are you calling a lady?" Her tone (even on the primitive German soundtrack) and the flick of her wrist suggest more than boldness, however. Something tells us that yes, she was once someone's baby girl. Perhaps only Lenya, whose personal experience sometimes resembled Jenny's, could have drawn so frightening and touching yet so tender a portrait of lost innocence. "Give that guy my regards," she says of the one who accused her of being a lady—and she turns up her hip, as if offering it for a kiss. Her expression effectively italicizes the gesture. The words were provided by screenwriters, but Pabst allowed Lenya to create the movements.

When Lenya appears next, the camera moves sinuously, seeking her out in a Victorian brothel as she calmly turns over the cards in a solitaire game. Called to attend a customer, she straightens her black stockings and exits, only to find Mrs. Peachum asking her to help betray Mackie. Again her voice—high, almost that of an adolescent—is sharply at odds with her equine features and insistent plainness. All around her we see frenetic activity, or at least film actors who think acting always means action. She, however, never seems nervous, never unaware that calm confidence is often the best smokescreen against enemies. Her face is a map of confusion, tainted hopes, dim expectations.

When she finally sings "Pirate Jenny" in the bordello, she stands absolutely still, leans against a window, hands on one hip. Her eyelids are half-closed, a rueful smile occasionally appears—but the look is one of infinite weariness, of near-despair. Her victory, we feel—the victory of Pirate Jenny as of the prostitute Jenny—is a Pyrrhic one. But then she very quickly affects a look of sexual alertness, the hunger of a deprived adolescent.

Had we no other film performance by Lotte Lenya than this, she would still remain one of the most intriguing players to come from the Weimar years. Had we no other facts about her life before and after, we could infer from this coolly detached but passionately involved actress that there were reservoirs of personal history that matched all the heat and anger, the pride and resentment, the despair spiced with hope. That jumble of feelings characterized the whore Jenny, the maidservant Jenny of the song, and the once innocent Karoline Blamauer. She was playing a part of herself, turning private reminiscences into public art.

As soon as shooting was completed on the film, Lenya raced into rehearsals for another stage appearance, this time Francesco von Mendelssohn's staging of Valentin Katayev's comedy *Squaring the Circle* (translated from Russian into German as *Die Quadratur des Kreises*). First produced at the Moscow Art Theater in 1928, the play is a comedy about two mismatched married couples who, because of a housing storage, are forced to share one room. They finally change partners.

By June 1931, Kurt was busy on a new opera, *Die Bürgschaft (The Pledge)*, this time with Caspar Neher as librettist. That same month, stage director Erwin Piscator telephoned Lenya. He had seen her on stage and screen in *The Threepenny Opera*, and he had just been invited to make his first film—in Russia, as part of a cooperative venture between Germany and the Russians. Given his choice of material, Piscator had settled on a novel, Anna Seghers's *The Revolt of the Fishermen of St. Barbara*, which had won the Kleist Prize in 1928. He wanted Lenya for the role of Maria, a sailors' whore in a harbor town. She might have wondered about the similarity of the roles, but this was an opportunity to earn a handsome salary and to expand her film career internationally.

On July 28, the cast and crew left by train for Moscow, where they were registered in a grimy hotel. When Lenya placed her suitcase on a chair, she noted later in her memoir-notes, it collapsed; a faucet broke off in her hand; when she sat on the bed, its frame creaked to the floor; and one morning, she awoke to a scraping sound in the room. She had placed food on the radiator to keep it warm—it was an unusually cold Moscow summer—and rats were busy devouring it.

"We sat in Moscow," she told American television interviewer Edwin Newman in 1970,

> and we waited and waited and waited. Finally we asked Piscator when we were going to Odessa, where the filming was scheduled to begin. "Well, any day now," he said. "They ran out of typing paper for the script." So we waited until the day we were told paper arrived. "It smokes beautifully," the Russian crew members then announced. They had used it for rolling cigarettes! So we left for Odessa, and still no script.

In late October, the German cast and crew—not having shot a foot of film and now on half wages—were ordered home. The sets had taken shape slowly and haphazardly in spite of Piscator's arguments with the Russian crew, but numerous delays caused by script problems sabotaged the filming that year. (Piscator did, however, complete the project—two years later, and without Lenya.)

Lenya returned to the apartment on the Bayernallee to find Weill and Caspar Neher completing work on *Die Bürgschaft* and Neher's wife Erika hovering over them, refilling their cocoa cups. Lenya did not need explicit confirmation of what she soon learned: the Nehers' marriage had cooled. One cause of this Lenya knew—that the brilliant stage designer had at last acknowledged his homosexuality. But something else was a revelation, and Kurt freely admitted it. He and Erika were lovers.

Lenya seems to have adopted a wait-and-see attitude about this, aware that raging fires often die quickly. Whatever her reactions, she kept them to herself. In any case, by November she and Kurt were working together, preparing for the Berlin premier of the full-length *Mahagonny*.

Again it was Aufricht who brought a Weill-Brecht work to Berlin, where he planned an expensive and elaborate production at the Kurfürstendamm Theater that would have an open run. Weill rewrote completely the role of Jenny for Lenya's non-operatic voice, omitting certain sections of the music, transposing others (as, for example, her part in the "Alabama Song") and composing a new "Havana-Lied." Although Weill never intended the role of Jenny for his wife, the work had by this time been rejected by all three opera houses (and so he could allow an untrained nonopera singer to participate). In addition, Lenya had also by this time a wider popular following in Berlin, and her participation could only help the box office. The premiere was held on December 21, without fistfights or police.

Again in the role of a woman born for compromise, Lenya shone as Jenny. As the lumberjack's prostitute, she offered yet another variation on her now familiar character. "I was somehow destined for that style," she told an interviewer many years later. Critics at that time agreed: her performance was noted by several journalists who cited her energy, her confident stance, her boldness and her quite unique voice.

In *Mahagonny*, wrote the eminent philosopher, sociologist, composer and music critic Theodor W. Adorno, "the bourgeois world is presented as already moribund in its moment of twilight, and it is demolished in scandal as its past catches up with it." Further, he wrote that the music communicated

> shock from the first note to the last, functioning as the objectification of the fallen bourgeois world suddenly manifesting itself. The music restores the utterly misunderstood *Threepenny Opera* to its rightful place as a milestone between the early *Mahagonny Songspiel* and this final outcome, and shows how little this really is a matter of intelligible melodies, easy amusement, and raucous vitality; it shows how these qualities, which are unquestionably present in Weill's music, are only means for introducing the terrors of a perceived demonology into the human consciousness.

It is precisely the combination of musical-theatrical sensibility and something irrational, whimsical and slightly mad that is evident in Lenya's recordings of selections from the full-length *Mahagonny*, first registered in 1930. Her rendition of "Denn wie man sich bettet, so liegt man—For as you make your bed, so you will lie" highlighted a brassy, almost casual luxuriance in the melody; and on the words "Ein Mensch ist kein Tier!— A man is not an animal!" she has an ease of attack that is at once inappropriate to the harsh reminder and yet oddly apposite, a final moral without the preceding dilemma. Her later recordings would be starker, more pungent, but these first exercises help to demonstrate the range of interpretation possible with the Weill-Brecht songs.

While the performances continued surprisingly peacefully, Berlin life outside the theater worsened. Bankruptcy lists were published daily, factory closings were routine, banks suddenly shut their doors forever, and before the spring of 1932 there were six million people unemployed in the nation. The homeless were everywhere, according to Elfriede Fischinger, wife and assistant to filmmaker Oskar Fischinger:

> You couldn't walk ten steps without someone stopping to beg for money. Things were just awful. We lived on the Fried-richstrasse, which was the hub of the theater and film indus-tries. Beggars and prostitutes were lined up three deep on the street.

Economic collapse and social decay produced the inevitable political crises, all of which the growing Nazi party exploited for its own ends. Just before the March 10 premiere of *Die Bürgschaft* in Berlin, the official Nazi paper the *Völkischer Beo-bachter* wrote,

> Kurt Weill, this Jew, has yet to realize that *Mahagonny* led to a riot in Leipzig and that his abominable and worthless *Three-penny Opera* is everywhere rejected.

But at the same time, Kurt Weill—attempting simultaneously to invest some of his royalties and to assure equity—purchased a spacious modern home on the Wissmannstrasse, in the suburb of Klein-Machnow. Meantime, Kurt's affair with Erika contin-ued to flourish. That, and a prolonged affair of her own that Lenya was about to begin, further illuminate the altered rela-tionship between Lenya and her husband. By the spring of 1932, in fact, they were unofficially separated, and Lenya never moved to the Wissmannstrasse, as Maurice Abravanel confirmed years later. They did not then, however—nor did they ever after—rupture their relationship entirely.

Lenya had always showed a cynical attitude about love, and sexual exclusivity was not her style at this time of her life. Her attachment to Kurt Weill was based on a great admiration and a genuine affection—and a need that was professional and financial as well as psychological and emotional, for at the end of 1931 Kurt instructed his music publisher, Universal Edition in Vienna, to send Lenya's mother one hundred Austrian schillings the first of each month. Lenya was like an exotic animal—unpredictable, fascinating, in some odd way loyal to him. But Weill also saw clearly that with Lenya's independence came unreliability; he could not count on her presence, her attention or her comfort the way she at times relied on his.

In April 1932 the Weills went together to Vienna, where Hans Heinsheimer (still working for Universal Edition) was supervising a drastically shortened, one-hour studio production of *Mahagonny* at the Raimund Theater, with Lenya again as Jenny.

> Lenya fitted herself marvelously and gracefully into the excited ensemble of volunteers and rehearsed indefatigably [Heinsheimer recalled in his memoirs]. And with this motley crew we had assembled, she never hid the fact that she came from very low estate—in fact that added spice to her image. She was entirely working-class and never pretended anything else.

A week's rehearsal for the late April opening was held in a private home. The moment she and Weill arrived, Lenya noticed a slender, blond young tenor who had been engaged to sing in the opera.

> She took one look at him [Heinsheimer said in an interview many years later] and whispered to me, "That's a nice-looking boy." I knew when I saw the gleam in her eye that here was trouble. But I couldn't say anything. Her husband was there. And she had very generously agreed, like the others, to perform with us for no pay.

The young tenor was Otto von Pasetti, son of the glamorously named but minor Austrian military leader Colonel Florian von Friedensburg Pasetti. "Beyond his good looks [Heinsheimer continued], there's very little remarkable to tell about him." Maurice Abravanel agreed:

He was a light tenor, but not really a good singer—as I found out when I conducted a performance in which he sang. But to Lenya he was irresistible, a young, slender, reasonably handsome boy.

Pasetti liked her humor and aggressiveness, and he also, as it turned out, loved the fun of gambling at cards as much as she. They were soon spending nights together, and planning a holiday after the close of *Mahagonny*. Love is eternal as long as it lasts, and the infatuation between Lenya and Pasetti blazed that springtide.

Lotte Lenya, the star of the whole evening [wrote a critic in *Das interessante Blatt*], reveals a surprising talent, by which she can say more with the movement of one hand than another talented actress could convey in many hours. . . . Otto Pasetti sang the tenor part in a beautiful voice, the direction by Dr. Heinsheimer was excellent, and there was great applause.

Robert Konta, writing in the *Wiener Allgemeine Zeitung*, called Lenya's performance

the most captivating in the production. Does this artist have any equal on the operatic stage? How terribly difficult it must be to play a ravaged prostitute from nowhere in a desolate desert. Yet how genial and gripping she is as that poor creature—and yes, she also sings—sweetly, but also bitterly, and in a voice that couldn't exist on a normal opera stage—especially in the "Alabama Song."

For Paul Stefan, in *Stunde*, Lenya's performance was "a singular, special event" in Vienna; and Hedwig Kanner, in *Der Morgen*, termed Lenya "lively, with her weary grace and her finely polished 'Mahagonny elegance.' "

"The prima donna of [the Viennese *Mahagonny*] is Lotte Lenya, the wife of the composer," wrote Josef Marks in the *Neues Wiener Journal*.

She surpassed all the others in diction and acting and was almost eerie in the realism of her performance. Sometimes she seems to depart from her colleagues a bit to walk along her own path.

Her own path took her, after the half-dozen performances, to the Riviera with Pasetti. Weill returned to Germany and to work. Before the lovers departed, Lenya visited Penzing, where she found her mother still living a grim life with the brutal alcoholic Ernst Hainisch, now released from prison. There was nothing Lenya could do, and her visit lasted only a few hours.

Monte Carlo provided Lenya and Pasetti with all the gambling they wanted, cheap accommodations in the hill villages nearby and a glorious summer. "They gambled constantly," according to Margot Aufricht, who happened also to be there on holiday with her husband, "and they lost a lot of money."

Decades later, Lenya admitted to a friend that she learned nothing else of Monte Carlo except the dimensions of its gambling casino. "She told me," Harriet Pinover recalled, "that one morning a woman asked her if she'd had a swim, but Lenya was unaware that there was a beach nearby and swimming pools everywhere. She was completely absorbed in her gambling."

By autumn, however, the gamblers' cash had dwindled. Lenya wrote to Kurt for a loan, and immediately he wired the first of several large payments to her. He also reminded her that there was another way of earning money—work.

He also had a suggestion. Marie-Laure, the German-born Vicomtesse de Noailles, was a generous patroness of the arts in Paris. She had agreed to sponsor the French premieres of *The Yes-Sayer* and (as it was later unofficially called) a "Paris version" of *Mahagonny* (the *Songspiel* and four numbers from the full-length work, with a small orchestra and no dialogue). Maurice Abravanel would conduct and Weill would supervise. Kurt invited Lenya to Paris to sing at this concert in early December and promised that she would be well compensated. The opportunity delighted her, and she left Pasetti at once.

After a private audition in the de Noailles salon, the public concert was held December 11, at the Salle Gaveau. The critics were as pleased as the audience, and Lenya was singled out for her appealingly exotic presentation.

One moment she could affect the stance of a Lautrec model. Then she was a revolutionary moll, her voice full of conflict and bravado. And seconds later she could conclude with a strange quiver of anxiety. Critic Marcel Moré wrote that she possessed along with the sure taste, the perfect science and the sincere emotion of the great German singers—an indefinable tartness in her soprano voice that alone makes her the overwhelming interpreter of a music on the borders of romanticism and the art of the music hall.

The evening was even more important for Weill, who was offered a commission for a symphony from another wealthy patroness, the American-born Princesse de Polignac. Erika and Caspar Neher, who had come to Paris for the premiere, joined Lenya in toasting Kurt's success. But that month, Lenya calmly brought up the question of what might be the simplest terms for a divorce.

They remained in Paris until the new year, and Weill was socially welcomed by Pablo Picasso and composers Arthur Honegger and Igor Stravinsky, all of whom were most enthusiastic about the musical evening. Lenya, at the same time, was ushered into the homosexual circles of André Gide and Jean Cocteau. According to Abravanel,

Cocteau was really the first one to start a kind of Lenya mystique, a clique of admirers around her. He was the first in a long series of accomplished, intelligent and socially well connected homosexuals who became close friends of Lenya, and who were quite comfortable with her.

Lenya was also discovering a new element in her life, and one she could freely discuss with Cocteau and her friends. Her previous excursions into lesbian experiences—apparently only sporadic in Berlin—now led her to admit that she was willing to have an affair with the right woman. "She was always very interested in men," Abravanel said of those months, "but she was also interested in women." And Cocteau was the right one to guide her through the many lesbian circles of Paris.

But she departed the city before her social circle enclosed new lovers. Weill was returning to Germany prior to the opening of *Der Silbersee (The Silver Lake)*, a play with music on which he had begun collaboration with Georg Kaiser. Lenya traveled to the border with him, and then she went on with Pasetti.

The new year 1933 could not have been less happy, for them and for the entire world. On January 30, Hitler became chan-

cellor of Germany and demanded new elections on the pretext
that a majority assembly in the parliament had not been achieved.
The Reichstag fire then provided the excuse for Hitler to allow
Göring's Nazi militia complete control over all police actions,
and soon all civil liberties were suspended. Before the end of
March, Adolf Hitler had effectively centered all powers of state,
legal and otherwise, in himself.

On February 18, *Der Silbersee*, Kaiser's long play with Weill's
music, opened simultaneously in Leipzig, Magdeburg and Er-
furt. The Leipzig premiere was conducted by Gustav Brecher,
who had led the Weill-Kaiser one-act *opera buffa, The Czar Has
His Photograph Taken*, in Leipzig exactly five years earlier. Designs were by Caspar Neher, and the stage director was Detlef
Sierck (who when he later came to America became Douglas
Sirk and was best known as the Hollywood director of such films
as *Magnificent Obsession, All That Heaven Allows, Written on
the Wind* and *Imitation of Life*).

The Leipzig performance passed without violence, but in
Magdeburg Nazi thugs caused a riot after the "Caesar Song,"
which was a clear reference to Hitler's tyranny. On March 4, all
performances of the work were banned on the pretext that it
provoked class struggle and incited to violence. Weill's time in
Germany was obviously running out. However, by this time
every Leipzig performance of the work had sold out and Lenya
had recorded several songs from it with Ernst Busch, who had
sung in the Magdeburg production and in the film of *The Threepenny Opera*.

For years, Lenya offered a colorfully dramatic account of her
departure from Germany with Kurt Weill. They had a friend,
she said, who had infiltrated the police precisely to help those
on a list of state enemies. The friend warned them that Weill
was the next to be arrested, and so (Lenya continued) they
packed a few belongings one night and, with the Nehers, they
motored to the border and freedom. En route they were stopped
by Nazi guards; then their car broke down but they were helped
by friendly, dissenting young policemen; and finally they were
waved over the border by unsuspecting guards who thought they
were tourists. She concluded with an account of their arrival in
Paris, and the Nehers' flight southward. The details were em-
bellished, over the years, with everything except characters from
central casting and a movie score. Lenya could tell a good story.

But the circumstances of their departure were very different from her elaborate tale. For a theatrical audition, Lenya had returned to Berlin from her travels with Pasetti. There she learned that because she was married to the now-infamous Kurt Weill—who was Jewish and was professionally linked to the Communist Brecht—she was also in danger.

On March 21—"Potsdam Day," when Hindenburg and Hitler sealed an agreement—Kurt Weill and Lotte Lenya left Berlin with Caspar and Erika Neher. But just outside the city (as Margot Aufricht, Maurice Abravanel and others knew from the Weills themselves), Lenya had the car stopped. She bade farewell to Caspar Neher and good luck to Kurt and Erika (whose romance still flourished), waved them all on to Paris, and with that she headed south to Pasetti. Before they separated, however, she promised Kurt to do her best to transfer his assets out of Germany.

Lenya's next news of Kurt was brighter. He had arrived safely in Paris, where he was welcomed by the Vicomte and Vicomtesse de Noailles, and by the artists who had been receptive the previous winter. Marie-Laure would not hear of him remaining at the Hotel Splendide, and he was forthwith installed in several rooms of their home on the Place des États-Unis. Within days, Weill had another commission, to compose the score for a ballet. Boris Kochno (formerly the aide to impresario Sergei Diaghilev) and dancer-choreographer George Balanchine had formed Les Ballets 1933 in Paris, and the British patron Edward James had agreed to finance a new work most generously if it would feature his wife, the Viennese actress Tilly Losch.

At that time Losch was twenty-six and strikingly handsome. She had acted with Reinhardt's troupe in the famous production of *A Midsummer Night's Dream*; on Broadway she was a dancing partner when Cole Porter's "What Is This Thing Called Love?" was heard for the first time (in *Wake Up and Dream!*, 1929); and in 1931 she was seen with Fred and Adele Astaire in *The Band Wagon*.

Her husband, the very wealthy Edward James, was one of the most colorfully eccentric characters in modern theatrical lore. A somewhat zany modern Maecenas, he offered extraordinarily eclectic patronage, from subsidizing John Betjeman's first collection of verse in 1933 to saving the Watts Tower in Los Angeles three decades later. James (rumored to have been the illegitimate son of King Edward VII) gave generously to other artists, as well—among them the French composer Francis Poulenc and the Belgian painter René Magritte. He was also flamboyantly controversial: he had Salvador Dalí design for him a pair of sofas in the shape of Mae West's lips; Napoleon's hearse was the model for his bed (rarely shared by his wife, who—like James— preferred sex with her own gender); and his bath, lined in ala- baster, shimmered with electric images of the night sky. James's fabulously vast art and antique collection outlasted his marriage to Tilly Losch, which was dissolved after a few years of amiable social pretense.

James had admired the Weill-Brecht evening of the previous December, and he was intrigued with Lenya. A new Weill work, then, must have roles for both Tilly and her. While Balanchine was preparing ballets for music by Darius Milhaud, Henri Sau- guet and Poulenc, Weill and James sketched the scenario for a ballet to be danced and sung by two women who, in the roles of twins (named Anna I and II), represented dual aspects of a single personality. After Jean Cocteau declined Weill's invita- tion to write the text, Weill wisely and compassionately offered Brecht the chance to come to Paris. The invitation was accepted, Brecht arrived and wrote the libretto, and *The Seven Deadly Sins* was prepared for a June premiere.

Lenya, not surprisingly, responded at once when Weill and James wired an invitation for her to appear in the work as Anna I, and for Pasetti to sing in it as well. Rehearsals pro- ceeded smoothly, and the premiere was held June 7 at the Thé- âtre des Champs-Élysées. Its reception, however, was considerably cooler than anyone anticipated. Although Stravin- sky and Picasso were impressed, only a few journalists joined them—and each mentioned Lenya.

"It's not so much a ballet as a mime," commented critic Edouard Bourlet,

a sort of spoken song cycle accompanied by a series of tab- leaux that are variously acted or danced. It's all quite bold, and will probably have to be seen twice to be properly as- sessed. In fact it's not easy to discern its intentions (even if you know German), since the whole thing is somewhat ob- scure. Nevertheless, we have here something important, bold and unique. What we can say now, however, is that it offers

us two extraordinary artists, Lotte Lenya and Tilly Losch—
the first singing, the second miming and dancing this strange,
painful and touching poem.

And the American composer Virgil Thomson, who was then
living in Paris, reported to the *New York Herald-Tribune*:

> Madame Lenya sings, or rather croons, with an impeccable
> diction that reaches the farthest corner of any hall and with
> an intensity of dramatization and a sincerity of will that are
> very moving. She is, moreover, beautiful in a new way, a
> way that nobody has vulgarized so far.

(The real beneficiary of the opening was Balanchine, however. *The Seven Deadly Sins* was attended and reviewed by Lincoln Kirstein, who offered him a career in America as the creator
of a new ballet theater and school. Kirstein's detailed review of
this premiere, but without any mention of Lenya, was published
in *The New Theatre*, October 1934.)

However welcome, the good reviews were minority reports;
the work itself was coolly received by the Parisians, who found
the sets as strange as a "ballet sung in German." Two weeks
later, however, the Vicomtesse de Noailles arranged for a performance of the *Mahagonny Songspiel* (on Tuesday, June 20) at
the Salle Gaveau; its committee members included composers
Milhaud, Poulenc and Georges Auric as well as the great music
teacher Nadia Boulanger (who taught, among others, Leonard
Bernstein, Virgil Thomson and Aaron Copland) and the designer Mainbocher. The cast was headed by Lotte Lenya and
Otto von Pasetti.

Pasetti may have been pleased with the temporary employment, but by this time there was more trouble in his relationship
with Lenya than there was among the people of Mahagonny.
Whatever his gifts, and whatever his idea of a love affair, it
would perhaps have been surprising if he was not startled by the
news that she was having a passionate affair with Tilly Losch.
The two Annas of the ballet—rehearsing privately, melding their
talents and honing a unified performance—had found another
level of intimacy beyond the work's narrative. Pasetti spent several nights alone at his hotel.

"The affair with Tilly Losch went on the whole time we were

in Paris that June," according to Abravanel, "and none of us
who knew them was very surprised"—not even, Abravanel
added, Kurt Weill, who had welcomed Lenya and Pasetti to
Paris and had graciously coached them in preparation for *The
Seven Deadly Sins*.

There was a good reason for Weill's cordiality, however.
Lenya and Pasetti had, en route to Paris, stopped in Berlin,
retrieved some of Weill's possessions, sold the furniture and
were arranging a sale of the house on the Wissmannstrasse—all
of which sums and receipts they turned over to Weill. Lenya's
famous account of the escape from Berlin, and the stop-and-
search by the police, seems to have been a transposition onto
her life with Weill of what had actually happened when she and
Pasetti had motored to Paris from Berlin in May. Their safe
passage was undoubtedly abetted by the fact that neither of them
was Jewish.

In any case, the efforts of Lenya and Pasetti, and Weill's own
continuing affair with Erika Neher, put Weill in no position to
complain. Quite the contrary. In several letters to her that summer, Weill asked Lenya to relay to Pasetti his thanks for helping
with matters of German finances and official papers. On his
side, Pasetti's intentions may well have included (with Lenya's
encouragement) a boost to his own career.

Weill did not, however, remain in the midst of this increasingly complicated sexual tangle. Instead, he retreated to Italy
for rest and reading, while Lenya and Pasetti moved from his
pension to the Hotel Splendide. She wrote to Kurt frequently
that summer, reporting the amounts she was withdrawing from
his bank account for auto tax and insurance, and asking his
opinion about a name-change:

> I have left the "Lotte" from my name [on the envelope] and
> want instead to write like this—L. Marie Lenja [she wrote on
> June 8]. Isn't that better? Lotte is so like a "bosh" ["boche":
> derogatory French word for a German].

Their friendliness and continued care for each other did not,
however, prevent Lenya's intended divorce. On June 23, an application to dissolve the marriage was filed by mail; the final
decree granting divorce was handed down from Potsdam on
September 18.

This was the single act Lenya would regret for the rest of her life. "Leaving him by divorce," Lenya's friend Hilde Halpern said later, "filled her with guilt," and with good reason. She was legally severing her most important relationship. While much in her life often seems a futile attempt, by some variant of repetition-compulsion, to redress her relationship with her father, Lenya seems not to have appreciated that Kurt Weill was in fact a providing, forgiving and gentle companion—in a way exactly the indulgent paternal figure she may have unconsciously sought—and that he offered some of the very qualities she needed and longed for in a stable union. Her guilt over this action caused a permanent wound.

Edward James, meanwhile, transferred *The Seven Deadly Sins* to London for a British premiere on June 28 at the Savoy. *Anna-Anna*, as it was called there, was called "a choreographic failure" by the critic of the *New English Weekly*, "but Lotte Lenya [was] superb." The *Yorkshire Post* proclaimed her

a singer of extraordinary dramatic power. She has a strange voice with harsh notes in it, not a beautiful voice, but one with some curiously moving quality that cannot be analysed. She is a remarkable actress, too. Her miming created a feeling of attention, of unremitting watchfulness. The two Annas were perfect, but their perfection could not make the ballet other than pretentious and long.

And the Countess of Oxford and Asquith, who had once hoped to be a dancer but contented herself writing on ballet for the *Sunday Express*, commented that Lenya's

rather bitter voice reminded me of a disillusioned child singing outside a public-house, and the unexpected freshness of some of her notes was infinitely moving. The beginning and end—perfectly mimed by Tilly Losch and Lenya—were choreographically the best moments; the middle I found a little untidy and diffuse.

James had also negotiated a performance of the *Mahagonny Songspiel* for later that month, with Lenya singing once again. The composer and conductor Constant Lambert, writing a critical review for the London press in August, called her incomparable. Some may object to the rasping quality of her voice, but after all there is no such thing as intrinsically good tone in singing—there is only suitable tone.

Lambert added that Lenya "put into the word 'baloney' a wealth of knowingness which makes Mae West seem positively ingénue."

With his commissions and subsidies, Kurt was able that autumn (after a holiday in Italy and Switzerland) to lease a small house in Louveciennes, not far from Paris. It had once been the servants' quarters for the house of Madame du Barry, a notorious courtesan who became the last of Louis XV's mistresses and who was given the house and land. Her generous patronage of the arts ended only with her climb to the guillotine.

The house—bright, cheerful and modernized—consisted of three floors, with a tree growing through the middle. Weill, preferring it to the splendor of the de Noailles residence, worked well here, completing his second symphony as well as incidental music for a play (*Marie Galante*, by Jacques Deval, based on his novel), sections of the music for an operetta (*Der Kuhhandel* [*A Kingdom for a Cow*]) and portions of a music pageant. Also from this address he followed the wanderings of Lenya and Pasetti from Belgium through Munich to San Remo, described in brief notes and postcards throughout the autumn. He also offered advice about her increasing gambling debts, most of which he covered. At the end of December, they all met in Rome, where on the twenty-ninth Abravanel conducted a performance of the "Paris version" of *Mahagonny*, with Lenya and Pasetti, at the Accademia di Santa Cecilia. Also on the program was a concert performance of *The Yes-Sayer* (conducted by Robert Blum) with members of the Zurich Choir.

In Rome, Lenya learned that Kurt was beginning to talk with Abravanel about a reconciliation with her. Divorce or no, she was still the woman he loved most. He had lost his homeland, but he did not want to lose this volatile, energizing woman.

Still, Lenya spent most of the first half of 1934 in Italy, gambling and carousing with Pasetti. In January she fell ill with a tapeworm, and Kurt urged her to seek medical treatment. "It isn't serious," he wrote, "it only comes from your naughtiness." He also advised her to learn French. And then, as her debts mounted, he suggested in March that she seek a better way of solvency than the roulette wheel and the card table.

The first serious indication she gave of trouble with Pasetti was a note she sent to Kurt in March: "Should you find a nice American for me—one who would marry me quickly for the sake of an American passport—please remember him!" Within days, Kurt was insisting to Abravanel that yes, he wanted Lenya back and he would *have* her back. Weill knew all her faults but he was, then as always, obsessed with her and would do anything to keep her.

By June, Kurt was writing an urgent letter to Lenya, inviting her to abandon her gypsy life and to settle down in Paris. She could even bring Pasetti along, he added—they could live with him in Louveciennes while they sought an apartment. His strategy was inspired, for he sensed quite rightly that such a ménage would not appeal to Pasetti.

Meantime, Kurt continued to work on new projects. At the request of Max Reinhardt, he had been working since December 1933 on a Jewish musical epic then called *Der Weg der Verheissung* (*The Road of Promise*, eventually *The Eternal Road*), with text by Franz Werfel, author of *The Pure in Heart, Juarez and Maximilian,* and, later, *The Song of Bernadette* and *Jacobowsky and the Colonel*—the entire project under the aegis of Meyer Weisgal, a journalist, fund-raiser and passionate Zionist who had turned to producing theatrical spectacles. As early as February there was talk of a year-end London premiere. But while work progressed, it was soon clear that the lavish and complicated staging Reinhardt intended could not be accomplished at London's Albert Hall. Reinhardt then began talking about Paris, but Werfel felt that New York would be the better forum.

Lenya, meanwhile, had appeared for the last four years in nothing but her husband's work, and she was delighted to accept a chance for something different. For her role as "Pussy Angora" in the Kollo-Arnold-Bach comic operetta *Lieber reich, aber glücklich (I'd Rather Be Rich Than Happy)* at the Corso Theatre, Zurich, in August 1934, the management billed her as a visiting star performer.

From Zurich, she wrote to Kurt that she also hoped to prepare a recital of his songs for the Corso. She further implied that the title of the operetta did not apply to her: she was neither rich nor happy, and she and Pasetti were fighting.

In October she was back in Berlin to complete the sale of their house and to retrieve Kurt's money from bank accounts. And then, instead of using her return ticket to Pasetti in the south of France, she went to Paris. Deeply depressed, she went to a modest pension, where Maurice Abravanel rushed after her frantic telephone call.

> There she was, bandages all over her bloodied wrists [Abravanel recalled]. She had tried suicide. She wanted Kurt. If only she'd realized how much he wanted her!

There was no repetition of this uncharacteristically melodramatic scene. But neither was there any immediate reconciliation between Lenya and Kurt—probably because, on reflection, both of them wondered if it was indeed possible.

Their hesitancy, as it turned out, was well advised. That autumn Lenya met the sculptor and artist Max Ernst, founder of the Surrealists and apostle of irrationality. He was seven years older than Lenya and one of the most controversial artists living in Paris. Within days of their meeting in October, an affair was in progress. Ernst's Paris letters to her (as she traveled to and from Berlin and London from autumn 1934 to spring 1935) detail his ardent feelings, his fear of aging and his terror of impotence. She had no control over time, but sexual energy she knew something about, and apparently she allayed any fears about impotence—so successfully, in fact, that his erotic obsession for her even eclipsed his work for several weeks that winter. Their hours together were interrupted only by her confinement in a Paris clinic in early February. Ernst visited her daily after her surgery for genital warts and polyps.

This latest affair is not hard to understand, nor was it unrelated to her original attraction to Révy and Weill, among others. Ernst was one of the most original, provocative and iconoclastic artists of his time, and she was a bright, energetic, admiring, highly erotic woman with no sexual inhibitions but with complex emotional needs.

Kurt, meanwhile, was working in London the first six months of 1935. He knew from Lenya about the sudden and passionate affair, but he also knew that Max Ernst was as much a dedicated artist as himself; this, he might rightly have surmised, was a doomed passion.

That season, Lenya was an important psychological support to Weill when a mutilated version of *The Threepenny Opera* (sung on radio) had been badly reviewed. Her letter to him at that time reveals not only her understanding of him but also a reason why he still felt an attachment to her; it is also the first indication that they were by this time considering a reunion after her recovery.

Think of people like [the actress Elisabeth] Bergner, who had an equally good name as yours in Germany. It has taken her two years in order to find the right kind of a start [in England, where she had then settled]. I know that it is difficult for you right now and that you are impatient. But after all, you have that Bible thing [*The Road of Promise*] in the fall. . . . I do know you better than any other person: your impatience and your dislike of bustle. But it is a new beginning for you over there, and for that one needs time. . . . Perhaps, Weillchen, it is to be considered whether you could not move to England. We can surely arrange our life there very cheaply. As I said before, I will do anything, even housework. You can be entirely independent. I won't disturb you at all. But you know that.

In Paris, meanwhile, Lenya was pressing Maurice Abravanel to intercede with Kurt on her behalf. She wanted the security of living with him; she loathed living alone. And she seems to have known that Max Ernst would soon be a past episode. "There we were, walking in Montmartre," Abravanel recalled in an interview many years later,

and she was working on me to get Kurt to take her back. I told her what I told Kurt—that he deserved a real wife. And so she started working on others who knew them both, like Darius Milhaud and his wife Madeleine.

In spite of that, however, her sexual energy apparently continued unabated. Maria Piscator, wife of the famous director, was in Paris at the same time and she recalled that Lenya was

fiery, prodigal, freewheeling. The marriage to Kurt Weill was neither easy nor predictable, but no matter the changes in her

private life she always sang sad songs with an incredible joy-
fulness and joyful songs with great sadness.

By late spring, Weisgal's and Reinhardt's plans for a London
or European staging of the Jewish oratorio had failed, but there
was a commitment for New York. Kurt went to close the house
at Louveciennes, and a letter from there to Lenya in London,
dated July 11, leaves no doubt about the course of their revived
relationship.

> I think you are a grand person [he wrote] and that your qual-
> ities are always developing parallel to my own. After ten years,
> you are still giving me things that no one else is able to give
> me, and which are crucial. On my way here I thought at last
> we have really solved the problem of living together again—
> which is really so difficult for us—in a very beautiful and
> correct way. Don't you think so? I have a very good feeling
> about England and America as far as you and your work are
> concerned. We'll make it, won't we?

The letter concludes "With many kisses from your Weilli."

On September 4, 1935, Kurt Weill and Lotte Lenya sailed
from Cherbourg aboard the S.S. *Majestic*, which eased into New
York harbor six days later. Their shipboard mates included Max
Reinhardt, Franz Werfel and the artist and set designer Harry
Horner (who after his contribution as artistic adviser to the
Weisgal-Reinhardt spectacle would continue his career as a ma-
jor production designer for Hollywood films, winning Academy
Awards for *The Heiress* and *The Hustler*).

Weill had at first been unsure how long they might remain,
and whether there were solid prospects for him after the projected work. Lenya, however, did not care whether they remained in America, returned to London or sailed to Fiji. For
the present, she wanted only to be secure, to be with him, wherever he went. Once she had been Mrs. Kurt Weill. Now that
designation, legally abandoned, began to sound attractive for
the second time in her life.

Five

Ladies in the Dark

1935–1941

THEY WENT IMMEDIATELY TO THE SAINT MORITZ HO-
tel, overlooking Central Park, where the backers of *The Road
of Promise* had booked modest suites for them, the Werfels and
others connected with the production. Registering as Mr. and
Mrs. Kurt Weill, to accommodate the less casual attitudes toward cohabitation in New York in 1935, they sipped tea and
before unpacking left the hotel for a movie theater: Kurt insisted
this would be the best way to learn American English. The place
they chose, however, was screening a revival of *The Dark Angel*,
with Ronald Colman and Vilma Banky—a 1925 silent film. They
laughed about their mistake, tried to read the intertitles, enjoyed
the background music, and then they took supper at the Park
Lane Cafeteria, settling for waiters' slang and other diners' chat-
ter instead of Hollywood dialogue.

"Kurt had an extraordinary capacity to adapt himself," Lenya
said later. "He wanted to forget German and Germany, it had
all been so painful. . . . And he wanted nothing to do with
German refugees, because he thought they tended to live in the
past." Maurice Abravanel recalled:

> Kurt was so enthusiastically American that it would infuriate
> him if anybody would start speaking German to him. In a
> drugstore he would admire the big containers of ice cream,
> marveling at the abundance of his new homeland. I don't
> remember him ever criticizing anything American.

In March 1941, on the NBC radio program *I'm an American*, Kurt expressed his feelings about the early days in New York:

> We made a resolve to speak nothing but English when we arrived. So many foreign-born use their native language in their homes and among their friends. I used to ask my German friends: How can you ever become Americans if you still cling to the language and customs of a country that has become the most un-American country in the world?

For Lenya, however, this total immersion into English had its difficulties. Buying a sweater at Saks Fifth Avenue that autumn, Kurt insisted that Lenya negotiate the transaction in English. She asked the salesman to "Rape it, please, in a gift box." The reaction of the salesman has not been documented.

Since *The Eternal Road* (as *The Road of Promise* was eventually retitled) had been the catalyst for Kurt's invitation to America, they did not have the immediate problem of work and support—and artistic acceptance. Other artists, forced to apply for refugee status in the 1930s, or sponsored by relatives or friends, often had to accept menial jobs for livelihood. Composer Paul Dessau worked as a chicken farmer. Writer Walter Mehring was a warehouse foreman. Many artists were domestics.

But Jewish refugees to America—132,000 of them during the 1930s—had been mostly urban sophisticates in their native country and were generally well educated. American immigration authorities required a proof of solvency from those entering, so they would not become wards of the state. Although like others Jews had to produce such affidavits, they were often able to enter the mainstream of American cultural life more easily, since they were suitable candidates for professional, academic, publishing or artistic positions.

Weill and Lenya were among an impressive list of creative men and women coming to America, a list that eventually included architect Walter Gropius and designer Marcel Breuer; philosophers Hannah Arendt, Paul Tillich, Herbert Marcuse, Erik Erikson and Claude Lévi-Strauss; filmmakers Max Ophüls, Otto Preminger, Fritz Lang, Douglas Sirk, Kurt (later Curtis) Bernhardt, Billy Wilder, Fred Zinnemann and William Wyler;

musicians Otto Klemperer, Fritz Reiner, George Szell, Erich Leinsdorf, William Steinberg and Bruno Walter; composers Arnold Schönberg, Hans Eissler, Erich Wolfgang Korngold, Alfred Newman, Béla Bartók and Paul Hindemith.

At the same time, the interest of American producers and the public in European theater was already well established. The Abbey Theatre of Dublin had first visited New York in 1911, and the same warm welcome was accorded to Reinhardt's theater troupe, from Germany, the following year; to Granville-Barker's, from London, in 1915; and to the company of the Vieux-Colombier, from Paris, in 1917 and the Moscow Art Theater, in 1922. Reinhardt's return to New York now, with the Werfels and Kurt Weill, was seen as his latest contribution to the arts in America. The previous year, his spectacular production of *A Midsummer Night's Dream* opened at the Los Angeles Greek Theatre. Four thousand arc lights, flaming torches, a three-hundred-fifty-foot bridge and the entire Los Angeles Philharmonic were only some of the grander elements of the show which 150,000 people saw over the course of a week. The film version was just in release in 1935.

"His English is good," wrote a reporter from the *New York World-Telegram and Sun* who visited Kurt and Lenya a month after their arrival. The reporter also oddly noted, with perhaps some latent anti-intellectualism, that what Weill had to say was "not phony." The occasion of the interview was not only to detail the progress of *The Eternal Road* but also to discover the composer's reaction to American music.

The Weills (so they presented themselves to the press) had attended a dress rehearsal of George Gershwin's *Porgy and Bess*, America's first successful folk opera, which had opened October 10.

Porgy and Bess is a remarkable work [he told the reporter] and very close to me, too, for in my own music I try always to create a new idiom to bring opera out of its splendid isolation. Great as some of the old opera scores are, still they are what I heard someone delightfully call "museum pieces." In [*The Eternal Road*] we are definitely trying for a musico-dramatic form that will weld the lines, the action, the setting and the music into a whole.

Porgy and Bess proved to Kurt Weill that he could be, in America, the serious and respectable theater composer who would close the gap between great music and great entertainment—the way, he felt, Mozart had done.

Meantime, Lenya's role in the Werfel-Reinhardt pageant was being gradually (but, she felt, systematically) reduced, and she feared she would never be found among the forty-foot columns, the 1,772 costumes, the 245 actors, the twenty-six miles of electrical wiring and the massive, swooping constructions planned for the renovated Manhattan Opera House. Not to worry, Kurt told her. He would soon create an entire work just for her.

They had arrived in New York at a crucial time in theater history: so they were told, and so they quickly learned. Up to World War I, a kind of excessive theatricalism had prevailed on the New York stage, in the plays of Clyde Fitch, William Vaughn Moody and Edward Sheldon, in the acting of Minnie Maddern Fiske and Richard Mansfield, and in the productions of David Belasco, the operettas of Victor Herbert and the musical comedies of George M. Cohan. Then, after the war, theater in the Roaring Twenties reflected the often rash optimism and sudden wildness of the era, as spectacularly fancy comedies and thrillers filled the stage, along with a proliferation of musicals like the perennial *Ziegfeld Follies, The Vagabond King*, and apparently endless annual extravaganzas like George White's *Scandals*.

Porgy and Bess, however, was one of the great stage works of the 1930s. It was a production of the courageous Theatre Guild, the first commercially successful American art theater company. Lawrence Langner had founded it in 1918 for the purpose of producing high-quality noncommercial plays and important foreign works. (The Guild was George Bernard Shaw's American agent, offering fifteen of his plays in New York, including two world premieres—*Back to Methuselah* and *Saint Joan*.) Eugene O'Neill's historic association with the Guild had begun with *Marco Millions*, in 1928. Playwrights whose work the Guild sponsored included Sidney Howard, William Saroyan, Maxwell Anderson, Robert E. Sherwood, S. N. Behrman and Philip Barry. Kurt Weill made no secret of his desire to be associated with the Theatre Guild.

While he waited to begin rehearsals with Werfel, Reinhardt and designer Norman Bel Geddes, Kurt and Lenya attended plays almost nightly. The season's fare was rich indeed: Lillian Hellman's *The Children's Hour*, Maxwell Anderson's *Winterset*, Sidney Howard's *Paths of Glory*, Sidney Kingsley's *Dead End*, Clifford Odets's *Awake and Sing!* and *Paradise Lost*, Laurence Houseman's *Victoria Regina*—and more than twenty-five musicals and ninety dramas to choose from that season. Production costs and wages had been sharply modified after 1929, but there were still willing investors, canny producers and great talent.

Meantime, "Madame Lotte Lenja, Chanteuse"—thus she was presented on the program—appeared in a recital under the auspices of the League of Composers and the Cosmopolitan Club. Held on December 17, 1935, at that club, on East 66th Street, Lenya's recital was the first American "Evening in Honor of Kurt Weill." With ten additional singers and two pianists, the program was fully representative of the range of Weill's European theater work: there were four numbers from *Die Bürgschaft*, four from *Mahagonny*, two from *The Threepenny Opera*, one from *Marie Galante* and two from *A Kingdom for a Cow* (his score for the English musical play version of *Der Kuhhandel*). Marc Blitzstein wrote about the evening in *Modern Music*.

> The hand-picked public at the Cosmopolitan Club . . . applauded all the numbers with equal fervor. . . . Lenja is too special a talent, I am afraid, for a wide American appeal; but she has magnetism and a raw lovely voice like a boy-soprano. Her stylized gestures seem strange because of her natural warmth; but in the strangeness lies the slight enigma which is her charm.

At least ten openings of *The Eternal Road* were scheduled during 1935 and 1936, only to be set aside because the dimensions of the production, of the sets and technical inventions grew more and more monumental. At one point, a geyser of water shot up from ruptured pipes when Reinhardt and his designer ordered their workers to dig, dig, dig farther below the orchestra pit to build the lowest tier for the four-leveled set.

The first three months of 1936, Kurt and Lenya lived at the Park Crescent, 150 Riverside Drive, a residential hotel. The space was larger and brighter and the atmosphere not so commercial as at the Saint Moritz.

At the same time, they were introduced to more theater folk through George Gershwin. He had very much liked the German recording of songs from *The Threepenny Opera*, although he had not seen the first New York production, in 1933. (Few did, for the ill-conceived and badly adapted production, which opened at the Empire Theatre on April 13, had only twelve performances. The English translators were Gifford Cochran and Jerrold Krimsky, the director Francesco von Mendelssohn, and in the cast were Robert Chisholm, Steffi Duna, Evelyn Beresford and, in the very small role of Crooked Finger Jake, Burgess Meredith. The *Daily News* called the show "sugar-coated communism"; the *Evening Post* dismissed it as "appallingly stupid.")

Lenya and Weill also met artists from the Group Theatre. Founded in 1931, the Group owed its guiding inspiration to Harold Clurman, Cheryl Crawford and Lee Strasberg. Championing the works of new playwrights, the Group's first production was Paul Green's *The House of Connelly*, a play about the Old and New South's racism and class struggles. Other notable plays they offered were John Howard Lawson's *Success Story* (about a man's loss of identity as he climbs to the top of an advertising agency); the 1937 Pulitzer Prize–winner, Sidney Kingsley's *Men in White* (about the idealism of a young surgeon); and the plays of Clifford Odets—*Waiting for Lefty, Awake and Sing!, Till the Day I Die, Paradise Lost* and *Golden Boy*—works of strong social comment that prepared the way for much in the later work of Arthur Miller and Tennessee Williams. The Group Theatre also counted among its actors and directors Stella Adler, Elia Kazan, Lee J. Cobb, Ruth Nelson, Luther Adler, Sylvia Sidney, Karl Malden and John Garfield. They all evolved a unique style of unified acting and production that continued to influence Broadway and Hollywood long after the Group dissolved, in 1941.

Clurman and Crawford knew *The Threepenny Opera* and they were ready to work with Weill on his first American musical. Crawford, who had codirected Paul Green's *House of Connelly* with Lee Strasberg in 1931, took an instant liking to Kurt and Lenya. Weill insisted that he wanted a distinctly American subject, and Crawford suggested that Green would make the ideal librettist and lyricist. In May 1936, Weill and Crawford left New York to visit Green at his home in North Carolina.

Born in 1894 in the small town of Lillington, Paul Green was a farmer's son. He had left college to serve in World War I, and later he taught drama at the University of North Carolina. Incorporating local folklore into his work, he had written perceptive dramas about war and racism, and his play *In Abraham's Bosom* had won the Pulitzer Prize for 1927. During the depression he continued to write plays of social protest. (He later collaborated with Richard Wright on the dramatization of Wright's novel *Native Son*.)

Lenya finally met Green when he came north to work for the summer. Crawford arranged to lease cabins at a camp near Trumbull, Connecticut, where they could escape the oppressive New York heat and work in comfortable intensity. Green arrived without his wife, and joined Crawford, her friend Dorothy Patten, Kurt and Lenya.

"The material that seemed most promising," Crawford recalled in an interview many years later, "was the subject of World War I, in which Paul had served." In that war there were more Americans with the name Johnny Johnson than any other, and so Crawford suggested that name as title for the musical fable of an ordinary, simple American who tries to stop war even as he is drawn into it.

Green, new to the musical form, had difficulty with lyrics, and their work progressed slowly. Lenya knew there would be no role for her in a show with an all-American cast of characters, but she found Paul irresistible—tall, blue-eyed and gentle, with full curls of chestnut hair, strong hands and a soft Southern accent she had never heard before. Not long after they met, Lenya and Paul were sustaining a discreet love affair. Years later, she told her friend Lys Symonette that she had regarded the affair merely as a *"Spielerei"*—the German word for a childish amusement, a dalliance, a frivolous trifle of a pastime.

"Lenya appeared to enjoy our time in Connecticut," Crawford recalled,

> but it was hard for her because her English wasn't very good. I do recall that she and Kurt were fascinated by my collection of jazz records. Lenya sang German songs for everyone on several summer evenings, and when pressed she would sing "Pirate Jenny." But apart from two or three of us, most visitors didn't really appreciate her because of the German lyr-

ics. Now this is very interesting. Whereas he was very, very
ambitious to make a success in America, she seemed content
without being a big star.

Crawford's remark points to a fascinating contradiction in
Lenya's personality. Although she enjoyed preparing a recital or
a dramatic role (and of course relished favorable audience response and a good review), she was also "content without being
a big star." She never pushed herself to seek or to land a role,
she never sought the advice or service of an agent, and she never
felt the kind of compulsion to work—either for artistic or financial reasons—that incites so many performers. But although she
herself lacked any professional ambition, her attitude to Kurt in
this regard was ambivalent: she unhesitatingly supported his
ambition to succeed, but she was also jealous of that ambition.
And her diffidence about herself is not hard to understand in
light of her basic lack of self-confidence, which always emerged
professionally as stage fright—until the moment of actual performance. There would always be a residue of the battered child
in Lenya, who was never convinced of her own talent or personal worth.

By the end of summer 1936—thanks to Crawford's daily work
with Green on the text, and her sensitive understanding of the
unique symbiosis that prevailed between composer and writer—
Johnny Johnson was taking final shape. The story tells of the
title character, a young man of ideals, dedicated to peace. On
the Western Front during World War I, he risks his life promot-
ing peace on both sides and in both trenches. Committed to an
asylum because of his insane rejection of war, he founds there
a League of World Republics to promote arguments for peace.
At last he is freed, after ten years, to return home.

Back in New York that September, Crawford and Dorothy
Patten invited Kurt and Lenya to quit the Park Crescent and
move into a room of their large apartment (once the residence
of the Gish sisters) at 455 East 51st Street. Preparations were
now being made for a November 19 premiere of *Johnny Johnson*
and a January 4 premiere of *The Eternal Road*.

"*Johnny Johnson* was a prestige work for Kurt," Lenya commented years later, "since it was a Group Theatre production
and had fine intentions." Its director (Lee Strasberg) and its

cast (Lee J. Cobb, Elia Kazan, Luther Adler, Ruth Nelson, Morris Carnovsky, Robert Lewis and Sanford Meisner) are virtually a roll call of major artists and teachers in the American theater, but even they could not persuade the critics, who admired *Johnny Johnson* without praising it. Weill's score, however, was recognized as superb, and the spirit of the production was noble.

All that season, Lenya's affair with Paul Green (who checked into the Hotel Bristol) proceeded quietly. The romance (unlikely for Green and known to Kurt but not, it seems, to Green's wife) seems to have begun and ended with Lenya's decision for it to begin and end. That same summer, Kurt wrote for Lenya "The Fräulein and the Little Son of the Rich," a quarter-hour dramatic song to a text by Irvin Graham. This he did for Lenya's projected participation in Leonard Sillman's *New Faces of 1936*, a participation that never occurred. The song remains unpublished and unperformed. (The hypothesis that the title is a veiled reference to Green and Lenya is tempting but unsupported by evidence.)

The first night of *The Eternal Road* seemed to many to justify its title: the final curtain was rung down well after midnight. But the weary critics lavished praise. Written in the *New York Times* the morning after the premiere, Brooks Atkinson called *The Eternal Road* "a deeply moving experience in the theatre, the story of the ages, told the great dignity, power and beauty." In a lengthier appreciative essay later the same month, Atkinson singled out Weill's "triumphant score that gives [the show] enormous emotional vitality." *The Eternal Road* was most remarkable, however, as a stage spectacle, and so the critics treated it: "staggering," proclaimed Burns Mantle in the *New York Daily News*, "the most expansive of [Weill's] musical creations to date . . . a spectacle to end spectacles." The uncredited reviewer for *Time* wrote that it was "perhaps the first indoor theatrical event ever to justify the cinematic adjectives Stupendous and Colossal," and John Mason Brown, in the *New York Post*, summed up the consensus when he called the work "the stage spectacle of all stage spectacles." Although the show consistently played to full houses, the half-million-dollar budget forced its closing, after one hundred fifty-three performances, on May 17, due to increasing deficits.

And so Reinhardt's grand staging itself was reviewed, and

individual performances were hardly mentioned at all. The composer's wife was singled out only by the visiting reviewer from the *Hollywood Reporter*, who offered "a bow to the singing of Lotte Lenya." But such an omission by the New York press is not, even in retrospect, remarkable: as Moses's sister Miriam, Lenya sang briefly about the discovery of the infant Moses by the pharaoh's daughter and his leadership of Israel in Egypt. She also appeared in another short scene, as the witch of Endor.

But she was not, on opening night, the wife of Kurt Weill—a situation that might have justified some press had that been known, and a situation they quickly remedied. Two weeks later, in the Westchester County village of North Castle, Justice of the Peace Julius A. Raven presided at the vows of Kurt Julian Weill and Karoline Blamauer. On the way to the ceremony, they stopped at a Woolworth's variety store. "We spent fifty cents and we got two cheap rings," Lenya told film editor Hans Dudelheim years later.

The reason for the remarriage was not to avoid an unsavory bit of gossip; much less was it for material benefit. By early 1937 both Lenya and Weill seem to have realized, without ever articulating it for anyone's benefit, the particularly strong psychological interdependence that bound them. In spite of her occasional sexual infidelities precipitated by deep insecurities, she was emotionally and professionally loyal to Kurt, and she was unwaveringly attentive to his art and his success. She might want to follow her own path from time to time, but the road home was always to Kurt. For his part, he took advantage of later sojourns in California for occasional transient affairs with young women.

By this time, their unconventional relationship had been seasoned by a mature acceptance of their differences. The marriage was based on a deep friendship with its own categories and its own truth, and it was honesty and frankness—the absence of artifice and deceit—that drew them together and enabled them to sustain one another's differences.

"I think there was a really deep affection between Lenya and Kurt that had once been sexual," recalled Gigi Gilpin, who became a close friend that year.

But she had a very strong sex drive that needed a lot of expression. Her affairs didn't lessen her devotion to him, and his love affairs didn't lessen his for her. If any problem came up, they were together.

The morning after the wedding, Kurt departed for Los Angeles, where a schedule of appointments and movie contacts had been set for him by Cheryl Crawford. He remained in Hollywood the first half of 1937, writing music for a film that was never completed. Later, he composed scores for Fritz Lang's *You and Me* (released in 1938) and for Gregory Ratoff's *Where Do We Go from Here?* (1945). Weill was not, of course, the only serious composer to accept such an invitation. Hollywood film scores (used or unused) were also commissioned from Virgil Thomson, Aaron Copland, Igor Stravinsky, Arnold Schönberg, Darius Milhaud and Erich Wolfgang Korngold, among others.

While Kurt rented quarters in hotels and rooming houses (and sometimes stayed in colleagues' homes), Lenya—still in *The Eternal Road*'s brief run—remained with Cheryl Crawford and Dorothy Patten. It was at Crawford's suggestion that Lenya soon enrolled in an acting class.

"I met Lenya just after *The Eternal Road* closed," according to Gigi Gilpin.

Benno Schneider had directed the Group Theatre's production of Leopold Atlas's play *But for the Grace of God* the previous January, and I was [in June] in his acting class with Lenya. He [Schneider] ran a studio group composed of professionals who prepared scenes, performed them and then were given criticism. My friends Samson Raphaelson [the playwright and screenwriter] and his wife Dorshka introduced me to her. . . . Lenya was very serious about her acting class, but it was difficult for her to work in a strange language. But in the scenes she prepared I recalled her being very truthful, very emotional and very intelligent. She caught on quickly and she was wonderful in a short scene in which she played a girl from Brooklyn. She was the type of person who took something from every situation, gleaned something from everyone she met, and saw through a lot. And she used everything in a scene. She loved talent in others, and intellect.

When she joined the class, Lenya tried to improve her appearance. "She was always trying to make herself beautiful," Gilpin recalled.

She was always trying to lose her hips, improve her makeup, build her bust. That's common enough for actresses, of course, but in Lenya's case it had to do with her relationships with men. Men of all ages were crazy about her.

Kurt returned to New York in August and announced to Lenya that he was taking his first steps toward formal citizenship. In order to change from a working visa to citizen application, however, it was necessary for him to leave the country and return. And so, on August 27, he went to Canada and reentered on an immigrant visa. Very likely Lenya accompanied him, since their applications for citizenship status then progressed similarly.

With the money from Hollywood, the Weills could now afford to rent an apartment, and in September Kurt took a duplex with terraces and a roof garden, at 231 East 62nd Street.

In October, Lenya made her American radio debut, singing a small role in Marc Blitzstein's music drama *I've Got the Tune*, commissioned as part of a series by CBS radio. In this strange tale of a composer's odyssey, Lenya as a lovesick but demented New Yorker sang a "Suicide Song" before leaping to her death from a tenement rooftop. The extant broadcast tape features a nervous, somewhat thin voice in the upper reaches, but a sure sense of drama in the final moments. As always, character and mood dominated with Lenya, and the small part was perfect for one whose major asset was never as a traditional singer with a beautifully trained voice.

On October 13, Kurt wrote his first letter to playwright Maxwell Anderson. In the short time the Weills had been in New York, Anderson had had three Broadway plays produced— *Winterset, High Tor* and *The Star Wagon*. Each was directed by Guthrie McClintic, each starred Burgess Meredith. After seeing the last, Weill had to write Anderson that he was "deeply moved [and] impressed by your mastery in binding together reality and fantasy. . . . You have found a new kind of poetry which has the simplicity of a folk song."

By sheer coincidence, at the very same time Burgess Meredith and Maxwell Anderson were discussing future plans. "I had had a small part in the brief 1933 run of *Threepenny Opera*," Meredith recalled,

> and I had very much admired Weill's music. When Max asked me what I wanted him to write next, after *The Star Wagon*, I said a musical, with Kurt Weill. Anderson wasn't opposed to the idea, and I brought Kurt—whom I'd met through Lee Strasberg—up to Rockland County to introduce him to Max at his home in New City.

Weill and Anderson became friends, and by early March 1938 they had, at Anderson's suggestion, found the source for a musical they would create. "Max," according to Meredith, "came up with the idea of adapting something from Washington Irving's tale of early New York." As the work took shape, however, the part planned for Meredith was weakened, and the part of old Peter Stuyvesant—which finally went to Walter Huston—became the lead. The show was *Knickerbocker Holiday*, and its most famous song, written especially for Huston, was "September Song." Meredith withdrew (to work with Orson Welles and John Houseman), and the Weill-Anderson collaboration and friendship deepened.

Maxwell Anderson, born in Pennsylvania in 1888, was the son of a small-town minister. Educated at the University of North Dakota and at Stanford, he had notable Broadway successes beginning with *What Price Glory?* in 1924, continuing with historical dramas *Elizabeth the Queen* (1930) and *Mary of Scotland* (1933) and his Pulitzer Prize–winning satire on political hypocrisy, *Both Your Houses* (also 1933). The highlight of his career before the collaboration with Weill was achieved in the trio of verse plays for Burgess Meredith—especially the first, *Winterset*, a tragedy inspired by the case of anarchists Sacco and Vanzetti.

"He looked like a lovable tame bear." So was Anderson described by the attorney John Wharton, one of Anderson's partners in the Playwrights Company. That production company was formed by a consortium of writers for the stage—Elmer Rice, Robert E. Sherwood, Maxwell Anderson—as well as Wharton and producer Roger Stevens. Victor Samrock later joined them as general business manager, and the Company

eventually also included producer Dwight Deere Wiman, Kurt
Weill and playwrights S. N. Behrman and Robert Anderson.

But [Wharton added about Maxwell Anderson] he could be
as violent as the wildest of wild bears. . . . He was attractive
to women, but two of his three marriages were unsuccessful.
He was mercurial, a bit paranoid; I never knew just where I
stood with him.

Kurt Weill, however, was the perfect collaborator for Anderson. Whereas Weill respected Brecht, he had great personal
affection for Anderson, and found him quick to understand the
demands of lyric-writing, willing to modify words, instantly
sympathetic with the workings of a musical sensibility. As their
friendship progressed, so did that of their wives. And Max's
children also drew close to Lenya—sons Quentin, Alan and Terry
(by his first wife Margaret) and daughter Hesper (by his then
current wife, former actress Margaret Maynard, whom everyone called Mab).

The collaboration on *Knickerbocker Holiday*, which began in
March 1938, was interrupted when Kurt returned to Hollywood
to work on Fritz Lang's *You and Me*. During his three-month
absence, he missed the opportunity to see and hear Lenya's club
debut at Le Ruban Bleu. For four weeks, beginning April 7, she
sang selections from *The Threepenny Opera*, from *Mahagonny*
and from *I've Got the Tune* and she premiered Weill's new song
"The Right Guy for Me" (which he composed for the Lang film
shortly after his arrival in California and sent to her). "Club
dates," as they were called, were not ordinarily reviewed at that
time, although the *New York Times* departed from that custom
and on April 17 a short notice praised Lenya as "an engaging
young lady" ("I don't put much value on 'lady,' " she wrote
to Kurt), and the *Hollywood Reporter*, on April 25, termed her
"a swell singing comedienne." But for the most part her success
was due to word of mouth, and her support came from regular
patrons of the café and from friends. Those who attended recalled Lenya almost faint with stage fright before she went on
but the complete, relaxed professional when she faced the audience.

"When Lenya arrived in America she wasn't as well known
as she'd been in Germany," as Burgess Meredith said.

From Americans' viewpoint, she wasn't easy to cast, and of course there was her accent. The first time she was really known was at Le Ruban Bleu, where European stars were often popularized. There she began to take hold. Having never heard her sing except on record, I remember being impressed with her appearance and her performance there.

Her engagement was financially as well as psychologically beneficial for her. "The late 1930s were a struggle for both of them financially," Meredith continued.

It was also a struggle to achieve their identity, to re-establish themselves in America. And it was a struggle for them to stay together, too. There was some very modern arrangement between the two of them, because although she was never a great beauty, she had an attractive personality—a powerful personality. Kurt was not promiscuous, but Lenya was.

Three thousand miles away, Kurt dealt with loneliness his own way. "In Hollywood, any number of starlets rationalized that by going to bed with important people their careers would be helped," Maurice Abravanel said in an interview after Weill's death. "So Kurt took his pick and had a marvelous time for three or four days. Then it was back to work." ("My husband had many affairs," Lenya told Maxwell Anderson's biographer Alfred Shivers many years later [without admitting her equivalents]. "But that didn't interfere with our fundamental commitment to one another.")

The Weills sustained an avid correspondence that spring. From the apartment at 231 East 62nd Street, Lenya wrote (almost always in German) to Kurt at the Villa Carlotta, 5959 Franklin Avenue, Hollywood. On March 29, during her rehearsal period, she balanced news of her preparations ("It was very good I tried this—I have learned a lot") with observations on local events: "Four Nazis here attacked a Jewish newspaper editor in his office in the middle of the day and made a mess out of him. One really feels sick to think all that might start here too some day."

"Yesterday it was so crowded," she wrote in high spirits on April 20. "I am really good now . . . I sing 'The Right Guy' very softly now and it is a big success every time. Last night they were really crazy about me." A week later she elaborated: "I am now enjoying myself and I'm glad I accepted this. I'm learning very much. I now know how to take an audience."

Lenya's letters to Kurt reveal her enjoyment of New York nightlife and of the celebrities who came to hear her at Le Ruban Bleu. "Tilly [Losch] war besonders sweet," she wrote Kurt on May 4 after a visit from her old friend—"Tilly was especially sweet." German was easier, but she was trying—if somewhat halfheartedly—to write in her new language. And on April 28 Lenya (still writing in German) was most enthusiastic:

> Last night suddenly there was Marlene [Dietrich]! She looked marvelous and behaved incredibly nicely toward me. . . . When [I was brought back for a bow] she said quite loudly, "How wonderful!" and applauded like crazy, which of course made a great impression on everyone. I sang "Surabaya Johnny" for her, and she brought me over to her table. Well, you should have seen all the others. . . . And tonight Cole Porter was there. He sat with Horst, the photographer from *Vogue*.

Also at Le Ruban Bleu she met Otto Halpern, a professor of theoretical physics, and his wife, Hilde, whom they had met aboard the *Majestic* and who became instant friends. "Lenya was very happy to have this nightclub engagement," according to Hilde Halpern. "Weill was so busy composing, this was just what she needed."

The most important social contact of the nightclub engagement, however, turned out to be not with a movie star or film director. At the club one evening was George Davis, a novelist and magazine editor. Eight years younger than Lenya, Davis had lived and written in Paris and was now at the center of a small but intense literary-social circle in New York. He stood five feet nine inches and was rather pudgy, and his brown hair was thinning. But he spoke and moved with an urban polish that Lenya found attractive. He had an intelligent, open face and enormous poise, but it was his mind, his articulation, his wit that most appealed to her. On April 20 she wrote to Kurt that she had invited him to a dinner party she gave, and that he had taken her to see Ruth Gordon in *A Doll's House*—a production, she wrote, that was "like a slow motion movie, everything so full of deep significance. And this Ruth Gordon can drive you to distraction.'' This letter was among the first written entirely in English, and it reveals Lenya's quick development of a witty, laconic style. By 1939, she was admirably fluent and in fact told Kurt that she was by then dreaming in English—a shift, he said, that meant she had found her new home at last.

Soon Lenya's constant companion was George Davis—with whom there was only simple companionship and no romantic entanglement, for George was homosexual and had no inclination otherwise. They continued to attend theater together, to dine several times each week after her club engagement, and to join friends for card games. More fascinating than any pastime for Lenya, however, were George's unretouched accounts of his earlier life in Paris.

In 1929, at the age of twenty-three, George Davis had joined the American literary expatriates in Paris, where he was accepted by a small but select cultural circle as he embarked on a writing career. His French was fluent, and soon he was commissioned as translator of works by Colette and Jean Cocteau. The latter introduced him to artistic homosexual groups that also included European and American composers, artists and writers. ''He was a sulky, ultra-sensitive, brilliant character and a deadly wit,'' according to Janet Flanner, who chronicled the Paris scene for *The New Yorker* for many years and was also a member of Paris's gay community.

George took a tiny room near Saint Germain-des-Près, where he worked on his first novel. Harper's published it with the title *The Opening of a Door* in 1931, and the author was soon reading the kind of reviews others merely fantasize: ''This novel is a high achievement in creative literature,'' wrote the critic of the *New York Times Book Review* on August 30, 1931.

> It is a work of beauty . . . a novel worthy to rank with the best of its time. . . . With its appearance a new American novelist of importance swims into our ken.

And Rebecca West, writing in London's *Daily Telegraph* on September 11, agreed: ''Mr. Davis writes exquisitely.''

But that success was not to be followed by another; a second novel for which he had been paid an advance never went beyond chapter two. George was, however, the social rage of the American contingent in Paris, and because he quickly spent whatever cash he received, he had soon dispensed both the royalties on *The Opening of a Door* and the advance for the second novel. Any drama that book might have had, however, was transposed onto his life, which soon became a whirlpool of intrigue, whimsy and footloose extravagance.

George's expenses did not include elegant restaurants or clothiers; instead, he doled out money for casual evenings at cafés and bars with friends and acquaintances. And a large portion of his cash went for ruder and more dangerous entertainments. George Davis—always "incurably self-destructive," as writer Irving Drutman recalled—frequented the darker alleys of Pigalle, Montmartre and (on weekend jaunts south) of Marseilles and Nice, where he paid hustlers and sailors for sexual activity he preferred violent.

George's preference for what can only be called acts of pathological sadomasochism often led him to the brink of disaster. On one such evening he brought to a provincial hotel room not one but two apparently compliant sailors. Once the door was closed, however, the sailors repeatedly raped and beat George, then robbed him and left him tied to the bedposts. "And the worst of it," he told writer Paul Moor years later, "is that ten years from now I'll probably look back on this as one of the happiest times of my life!" (To spare Lenya embarrassment, Drutman—in writing about the event—connected it to an anonymous third party instead of to Davis. But both Moor and Victor Carl Guarneri—a close friend to both George and Lenya for many years—knew from George himself that it actually happened to him.)

Moor (also a friend to Davis and Lenya later) knew about this time, too:

> George told me all about his experiences in France, where he got to know the street whores. "And the best they saved for me," he told me with audible pride. He had, you see, become a fixture at a whorehouse, and the whores would save the best customer for George, who had an insatiable appetite for sailors in most situations. The muggings unfortunately became a pattern.

In George Davis's life, then, there was a sad and disarming paradox of character that defies comprehension. Gifted, articulate, warm and loyal, he had a deep respect for art, for friend-ship, for confidences, and he had as well a keen appreciation of his own and others' talents. Perhaps he was consumed by a rage of psychoneurotic guilt; whatever the reason, the man who at-tracted so many admirers, and who several times was on the brink of an extraordinarily fertile and successful career, seems to have harbored an astonishing self-hatred.

Poverty eventually drove George back to America, where he arrived without money or clothes and began a habit of asking for castoffs from friends. He had descended the gang-plank in torn trousers and carpet slippers, rather like a pa-thetic mimic of his friend W. H. Auden, who was notorious for unkemptness.

His talent, however, was not so threadbare, and after a stint as an articles editor at *Vanity Fair*, he was (from 1936 to 1940) fiction editor at *Harper's Bazaar*. During this time he managed to arrange for the magazine to send him to London, where with a combination of consummate charm and genuine literary sen-sitivity he coaxed articles from Virginia Woolf, two of the three famous Sitwells, Auden and Christopher Isherwood. His tenure at *Harper's Bazaar* ended abruptly, however, when editor Car-mel Snow fired him for not keeping regular office hours.

Lenya's busy social and professional life did not deter her from concern for Kurt. When he wrote of his discontent with the methods of Hollywood production, she replied on May 8:

I am firmly convinced that your present attitude of telling these idiots off right to their faces—regardless of any future job (which you would undoubtedly get as soon as you have a show running on Broadway)—is the right one. It's better to speak up and show them that you are far more capable than all the others, and that it's their own fault if they don't under-stand this. It's such a shame (but one experiences it time and again) that one doesn't achieve anything merely by decent behavior.

But for most of this letter (and for most of all her letters) the focus was securely on herself, and she reported that her club engagement was about to conclude in early May:

Many people have liked me very much, and if I were to be
in a show next fall, I would be able to tell what good it has
done me to have sung here. My program was somewhat limited . . . but I have retained a good feeling and learned that
I can get a bunch of drunks to shut up for a few minutes. . . .
If nightclubs were my only ambition I would be totally content. But thank God I still have something more in my knap-
sack. So you won't hear anything further about the nightlife
in New York in the near future, and I will sleep once more
like a normal human being. . . . I bought little trees for our
roof, and a reclining chair for my Hollywood plant when he
comes home to take sunbaths.

"I am feeling fine since I finished this nightclub job," Lenya
wrote to Paul Green in May. "I had a hell of a time trying to
cheer up those drunkards every night, me included." That brief
note to her (by then) ex-lover was apparently the last he received.
About him, Lenya wrote a curiously ambivalent letter to Kurt
on May 12:

[Green] is so block-headed that I get nervous. . . . He reacted
somewhat sour when, half-jokingly, I said I could come to
Chapel Hill [where Green lived and taught]. Well, okay, then
not. I can get along without that, too. He will be staying here
for a few days, had come from Washington. He really is a
hopeless case.

By summer, Kurt had returned, and with the money from
Paramount Pictures for his work on *You and Me*, he and Lenya
rented a small country house on Route 202 near Suffern, in
Rockland County, New York. Near Maxwell Anderson (with
whom Weill resumed work on *Knickerbocker Holiday*), this section of the Hudson Valley was sparsely settled in 1938. The
towns of the county have traditionally been home to a number
of theater folk, writers and artists who cherish quiet and privacy
but also require proximity to Manhattan. Planted thick with
centuries-old trees, the properties—with their sturdy eighteenth-
and nineteenth-century houses—are generally large parcels of
land separated by meadows and laced with streams that run to
the Hudson River. The villages, too, are rustic and pictur-
esque—a few stores, a post office and a filling station—and until

the 1960s residents had to travel more than fifteen miles to find a movie theater, a restaurant or an apartment building.

Not long before the premiere of *Knickerbocker Holiday*, the Andersons invited the Weills for a dinner party that was also attended by the show's star, Walter Huston, and his wife, Nan Sunderland. The Hustons brought a close friend from West Virginia who complemented her life as a school librarian with frequent trips to New York for theater and social life. Her name was Mary Daniel, and she and Lenya became friends immediately.

For the next four decades, Mary Daniel would play an increasingly important role in Lenya's life. Devoted, energetic and self-sacrificing, Mary became a confidante and sometime companion to Lenya—indeed, she became a kind of willing slave. When there was illness or unhappiness in the Weill home or the Hustons' or the Andersons', Mary Daniel would soon arrive.

For Lenya, however, this sophisticated woman reserved a single-minded attachment, and nothing was an inconvenience to her. As a visitor Mary Daniel scrubbed floors, shopped for food, cooked, cleaned, sewed—essentially she performed all the duties of housekeeper and cook whether or not she was asked, and whether anyone was ill or otherwise engaged. She held her own needs, her own freedom, her own relaxation as entirely incidental to that of her beloved Lenya. She was, to put the matter simply, henceforth entirely obsessed with Lenya, Lenya's comfort and Lenya's contentment.

How she may have felt emotionally compensated for her allegiance may never be clear, for Mary Daniel's own needs seem not to have been expressed, and of the correspondence only Lenya's letters to her have survived. There is no evidence of any sexual intimacy between the two women, but it is obvious that the relationship was deeply tender and and extraordinarily intense. Lenya was grateful to be the recipient of Mary's devotion and attention, and she was especially pleased that Mary relieved her of many practical daily tasks and decisions at home. For almost forty years Mary Daniel traveled to visit and to help Lenya, she worked to make Lenya's life smoother, she subjugated herself entirely to Lenya.

Knickerbocker Holiday, which opened on October 19, takes place in seventeeth-century Manhattan, where Governor Peter

Stuyvesant takes over the reins of a corrupt city government. At the same time, he woos Tina, the daughter of a councillor, who is really in love with the fiery workman Brom Broek. Full of scorn for the council, Broek is thrown into jail. He escapes and rouses public support against Stuyvesant's tyrannical ways. Just as Brom is threatened with execution, Washington Irving steps into his own story, and converts Stuyvesant to democracy. The governor introduces necessary reforms and gracefully consents to the marriage of Tina and Brom.

After *Knickerbocker Holiday* (which ran for one hundred sixty-eight performances, into 1939), Weill worked on a new (and eventually unfinished) project with Maxwell Anderson, a drama of the American South called *Ulysses Africanus*, originally intended for Paul Robeson. He also wrote incidental music for two plays (Sidney Howard's *Madam, Will You Walk?* and Elmer Rice's *Two on an Island*); the music for the pageant *Railroads on Parade* at the New York World's Fair; a song based on a poem by Robert Frost ("Stopping by Woods on a Snowy Evening"); and *The Ballad of Magna Carta*, a fifteen-minute cantata for radio to text by Maxwell Anderson. He also composed a Christmas present for Lenya—"Nannas Lied" ("Nanna's Song"). The text (from a Brecht play for which he once suggested Lenya) describes the feelings of Nanna, who has been "on the love market" for years and regrets that with age her feelings have become cool and blunted. (Although Lenya never offered "Nannas Lied" in concert, she did, however, sing it privately for Brecht, when he visited the Weills a few years later; he described her delivery of it as "absolutely unforgettable.")

From this time, there would never be financial trouble for the Weills again, since the Hollywood income (from film compositions and, eventually, sales of film rights to his stage works) always supplemented his theater work, and the savings account records a sustained balance of at least $3,000 throughout 1939. (After his death, Lenya rarely touched this account, and when she closed it in 1957 she was able to withdraw a total of $10,153.43 due to interest accrued.)

Lenya settled happily into Rockland County domestic life. With nothing to engage her professionally in 1939, she also refined her English and expanded her library as she read contemporary plays (by Thornton Wilder, Eugene O'Neill and William Saroyan) as well as British and American poetry.

Kurt, meantime, had found a new collaborator (Maxwell Anderson now having other commitments). He had met playwright Moss Hart at a party, and they renewed acquaintance through the Andersons. Hart was in psychoanalysis and eager to work on something that would concern psychotherapy's effect on romantic life. Very quickly, he and Weill agreed to collaborate and persuaded Ira Gershwin to join them as lyricist. The result, a year later, was *Lady in the Dark*.

With Kurt busy, Lenya resumed her social contact with George Davis throughout 1940. That summer Lenya entertained him and the gifted but emotionally unstable writer Carson McCullers.

George, then still literary editor at *Harper's Bazaar*, had been impressed by McCullers's first novel, *The Heart Is a Lonely Hunter*, which he had read in manuscript and which was published that June. He had asked McCullers for more completed works, and with her approval he rummaged through her files and found a second novel called *Army Post*, which he then guided to its final form as *Reflections in a Golden Eye*. George scheduled it for publication in *Harper's Bazaar* in two installments (October and November 1940), and Houghton Mifflin then contracted to publish it as a book the following February.

When George and Carson visited Lenya, there was, however, not much serious literary conversation, for Carson had few interests outside herself, and when this subject was circumvented she usually retreated into heavy, sullen drinking. In that refuge George could match her, and on more than one afternoon the writer and her editor sipped their way to either a giggling incoherence or a taciturn withdrawal that was practically a summer snooze. Lenya, who enjoyed a drink but was rarely even tipsy, boiled frankfurters and fed her guests an early supper. George's charm was worth whatever eccentricities his friends paraded.

Lenya always admired George's talent as editor, career guide and general manager for the gifted and insecure McCullers, who told Lenya how George had often come to her Greenwich Village apartment and soothed her when she was depressed. George shared not only McCullers's passion for fiction; they each also had a sad history of unfulfilled homosexual attachments. Lenya was intrigued with their tales of inchoate and unhappy love affairs. She kept their glasses half full of iced tea late that summer, always leaving space for the sherry or gin Carson liberally added.

In September, George had news for Lenya. He had found a three-story brownstone available for lease at 7 Middagh Street, Brooklyn Heights, very near the Navy Yard. He, McCullers and Auden were to be three founding members of a creative community that was rather like a live-in salon. Lenya kept in touch with George throughout that fall as he and his friends settled in, and she thought the addition of the next resident, Gypsy Rose Lee, was a fascinating development.

Gypsy Rose Lee had long been a friend to George, whose circle was always an unpredictable potpourri. At his encouragement, the striptease and burlesque entertainer tried her hand at a novel aptly titled *The G-String Murders*, which Davis virtually wrote for her.

By 1941, the house at Middagh Street had become a kind of academy for some of the best work then being created in America. Virginia Spencer Carr, Carson McCullers's biographer, has quoted the Swiss critic Denis de Rougemont, who claimed that "all that was new in America in music, painting or choreography emanated from that house."

From late summer 1940 to early 1945 Davis (as titular landlord) and his cofounders welcomed for short- or long-term residence the poet Louis MacNeice; composers Marc Blitzstein and Benjamin Britten; the stage designer Oliver Smith; and the writers Chester Kallman, Paul and Jane Bowles, Christopher Isherwood, Richard Wright and Colin McPhee. Transients included Virgil Thomson, Aaron Copland, Leonard Bernstein, Lincoln Kirstein, David Diamond and Salvador Dalí. Tenants had to be working in the fine arts or writing or musical composition. Even Gypsy Rose Lee had to be at work on a novel in order to check in. And while to his brood George was mentor, sometime Father Confessor and guiding housemaster, he was also a savagely witty raconteur, and Lenya was an appreciative listener to his accounts of life there. Middagh Street was not only an artistic haven but also the place for a complex game of musical beds. Nothing was ever conventional about its residents' habits, and Lenya loved George's tales of the late-night whispers, the shutting doors, creaking beds and endless intrigues.

* * *

When *Lady in the Dark* opened on January 21, 1941, Kurt had the enormous success he had hoped for. It ran almost five hundred performances and the film rights were sold for the highest price paid for a Broadway musical to that time. Gertrude Lawrence earned wild applause in the role of Liza Elliot for her song "The Saga of Jenny" and for "My Ship." And the previously unknown Danny Kaye, whom Moss Hart had discovered singing in a nightclub, made a smashing debut. The story described the fantasies and psychological problems of Liza, editor of a fashion magazine, whose romantic dreams and attempts to recapture and remember a childhood melody lead her into psychoanalysis. She finally comes to terms with her past and realizes who is the right man—none of those on whom she had attached unrealistic dreams (her lover and a film star), but a colleague with whom she has been at odds.

A month after the opening, Kurt was able to write to his lyricist Ira Gershwin (who had returned to his California home): "It looks very much that we are going to buy [the actor] Rollo Peters' house in New City, just next to the Andersons." And so they did. With the proceeds from the film sale of *Lady in the Dark*, he paid $16,000 for a nine-room house and fourteen acres of land at 116 South Mountain Road, which Lenya herself had found. On May 28, Kurt wrote again to Gershwin,

> Today I signed the deed for the new house. We have been busy with carpenters, plumbers, painters, etc. Lenya is dashing around all day and we are having lots of fun buying furniture, etc. and I think it will be very nice.

Lenya adored Brook House, as it was called, because of the trout stream that flowed through the property, right behind the house. Half-hidden by a stone wall covered with roses and honeysuckle, it reminded them of a European country house. Peters had converted the fieldstone cellar into a lower-level kitchen and dining room, and the house, charmingly filled with antique American furniture by the Weills, took in good light all day. The property also had good running space for their two English sheepdogs, a gift from Moss Hart.

New City welcomed the latest members of its small artistic community. In addition to the Andersons there were Milton Caniff, the artist and illustrator of "Terry and the Pirates" (and later of "Steve Canyon"); Burgess Meredith and soon his wife Paulette Goddard; painter Henry Varnum Poor and his wife, the novelist Bessie Breuer; and writer William Sloane and his wife Julie. Not far were a number of actors—Helen Hayes among them—who found the hour's drive convenient to New York but who could still enjoy the quiet of country living.

Maxwell Anderson's daughter Hesper was in grade school at this time, and Lenya befriended her, beginning a lifelong devotion that was mutual and uninterrupted.

"I adored her," recalled the screenwriter and poet Hesper Anderson years later.

> Although she wouldn't sing on command for the adults in social gatherings, she would for me, when it was just the two of us in her kitchen. Her unmoored washing machine had a startling way of bumping and jumping across the kitchen floor, and when I was with her she started to do a song and dance to the rhythm of the washing machine. What a spontaneous performance! And I remember that she always had an approach to the details of life that then seemed to me wonderfully European and sophisticated, which is of course just what she was. Once I took a phone message for her, and next day inquired whether she had received it. "Oh, yesterday!" she said airily, "that is the past already!"

The oldest of Maxwell Anderson's sons, Quentin (who became a noted university professor and American literature scholar), retained equally acute memories.

> Long before I ever met them, I had heard a German recording of selections from *The Threepenny Opera*, which I played almost to the point of my mother's madness. There was, then, an implanted readiness to attend to that extraordinary mixture of cacophony and melodic sweetness and seductiveness that characterized so much of Kurt Weill's music. . . . I was enchanted by Kurt and Lenya. One of my most vivid recollections is of Kurt singing songs from a show he and my father were working on. In a somewhat inadequate but altogether charming voice he sang something called "The Last Time I Saw Ho-Ho-Kus." Kurt was, during the entire decade of the 1940s, my father's only really close friend. My father was not

a terribly social man—indeed, he was rather reclusive most of the time. Kurt was a small, beautifully composed man, and he took obvious delight in the company of this large, graceful man who looked (as indeed he had been) every inch a farmer. My father had a capacity for friendship, but no one ever drew as close to him as this man from abroad who marched a good way into the territory of this country. He had an extraordinary ability to compose for the lyrics given to him by the writer—and this he did with a willingness other composers often lack.

When they were settled into Brook House, the Weills invited neighbors for evening card games.

"Lenya was the best card player I ever met," according to Milton Caniff.

She was good enough at all the other games so that we taught her to play poker, and she got to be the best in the group and usually took us to the cleaners. I was very often the number one victim of her talent.

On this point, Quentin Anderson recalled "a dominant image of Lenya playing cards with [Maxwell Anderson's second wife, Quentin's stepmother] Mab. They played endlessly. They were both women who demanded occupation. They could not sit back, relax, talk, remain quiet." And Hesper Anderson could never forget "the image of the three heads I saw from the upstairs landing as a child—the blonde, Bunny Caniff; the brunette, my mother; and the redhead, Lenya," who by this time was regularly dyeing her hair a brighter color than her natural brown.

Kurt, Caniff also remembered, was always kind and proper, but also very direct:

If I relayed to him something from the newspaper about the arts, he might say with some sarcasm, "*Ach*—new knowledge!" Now it may well have been new knowledge, at least for him, at that moment. But his terse reaction was discomfort with the source, and his way of learning it. When he wanted to leave a gathering, he could be just as direct. "Lenya, ve go," he said, and dey vent.

Lenya, Caniff felt, was no less interesting than her husband, and she seemed more accessible. Caniff found that Lenya could discuss any topic; if she had no knowledge of a certain subject she asked questions, asked what to read and where to seek,

> and always she told wonderful stories, whereas Kurt was not so inclined to tell stories and just chat. She was never bored with learning more about American culture and life. She felt she had an enormous gap to fill in. She had a terrific curiosity about newspaper comic strips, for example.

According to Burgess Meredith, the Weills were soon more settled in than any other members of the community. "They were surrounded by American antiques, a brook flowing by, and little by little they assumed a kind of conservative lifestyle. At least it seemed that way on the surface."

But after a year the quiet domesticity had begun to bore Lenya; her natural creative gifts needed a professional expression, but she did not actively seek that expression. "She was pacing like a caged animal after a while," according to Quentin Anderson,

> because her talents were not being used. It was the first time I thought about their marriage. I wasn't conscious either of a division between them, nor of affection between them. It was as if they were by now partners who knew each other so well and relied on each other. But as a marriage I could never quite take it in.

Perhaps because Lenya did not actively pursue her career, Kurt (always sensitive to his wife's needs and her changes in mood) spoke to his friend Maxwell Anderson. Soon Max paid Lenya a visit. He had just added a role for her in his new play, he said, and it was about to begin rehearsals. She accepted on the spot.

Six

The Maid
and the Duchess

1941–1950

"MAX WENT OUT OF HIS WAY TO WRITE THE PART OF Cissie, the maid, for Lenya," according to Burgess Meredith. "Unlike other playwrights, he did something like that quite easily, almost at will, for several friends."

Maxwell Anderson's play *Candle in the Wind* concerned the efforts of an American actress (Helen Hayes) to rescue her French lover, a resistance fighter (Tonio Selwart) from a Nazi concentration camp. After several weeks of rehearsal under Alfred Lunt's direction, the play opened at Boston's Colonial Theatre on September 15, 1941, and at New York's Shubert on October 22. As the occasional maid who needs help to obtain a passport, Lenya had a very small part indeed—only a few hundred words in a lengthy, three-act, seven-scene play. But in it, the playwright drew from Lenya's memories to create her role. "I have had experience with German soldiers," Cissie/Lenya says in her first scene, "first in Vienna, because I am Viennese." Later in the action, Anderson returned to Lenya her own comment about assimilation: "They say when you dream in English, then you are no longer German, then you can be an American."

Her performance was noticed by the press out of all proportion to the size and importance of the role. "Miss Lenya is dynamic enough to play the lead," wrote one critic in words that may not have been so welcome to the star. "She comes

close to stealing Miss Hayes' thunder,'' wrote another critic;
and *Variety* called Lenya's ''an excellent performance.''

And so it continued:

> A rather remarkable girl named Lotte Lenya gives a gem-like
> performance.

> Lotte Lenya's conversational description of the behavior of
> the Gestapo in three successive cities where she had been
> trapped is written in natural terms worthy of the talent of so
> good an actress.

> There is a Lotte Lenya, whose performance of the eternal
> refugee maid is a shining thing. To come upon such an actress
> is like an unexpected bonus.

The play was not so enthusiastically received as Lenya, however. A typical reaction appeared in the *New York Herald-
Tribune*, which called *Candle in the Wind* ''pedestrian in its
writing, its thinking and its emotions.'' In fact only the star
attraction of Helen Hayes was responsible for its endurance beyond opening week.

Once the play had settled in for a modest run of ninety-five
New York performances (until late January 1942), Lenya lived
in a room of Gigi Gilpin's large apartment at 200 West 54th
Street. This was a convenient location in a famous theatrical
building whose other tenants included Harold Clurman, Stella
Adler, Sylvia Sidney and Luther Adler. Kurt ordinarily worked
and resided at Brook House, maintaining constant correspondence with Lenya at a time when telephone calls between New
York and a town fifty miles away were neither inexpensive nor
invariably possible.

Lenya's relationship with other cast members was friendly,
with one exception. ''She admitted to me that she didn't like
Helen Hayes,'' recalled Lenya's neighbor Ken Andorn years
later. ''Miss Hayes had timed a speech so that after a certain
number of steps she sat in a chair without looking. But one
night, after they had disagreed about something in offstage conversation, Lenya moved the chair and Miss Hayes did a graceful
fall. There was a naughty schoolgirl in Lenya, and she was
proud of it.''

Lenya enjoyed working and living independently in New York and on tour with the play, which took her out of town from January through May (to Pittsburgh, Philadelphia, Evansville, Chicago, Detroit, Montgomery, Birmingham, Nashville, Memphis, New Orleans, Austin, Houston, San Antonio, Fort Worth, Dallas, Little Rock, Wichita, Des Moines, Cleveland, Flint, Ann Arbor, Tulsa, South Bend, Lansing, Erie—a total of more than forty cities).

What Lenya could not know, as she went from city to city, was that Kurt was suffering the first signs of an illness that would kill him. Now, at forty-two, he was to all appearances a calm, reserved, polite gentleman. But his doctor found that already his blood pressure was alarmingly high, and his heart rhythm erratic. There was a family tendency to hypertension that did not yet worry Kurt, however, and he told the physician that he needed only a few quiet days, or a new Broadway project. Antihypertensive medication without serious debilitating side effects was not so readily available in the 1940s, and Kurt did not want to be lethargic or impotent, common side effects of the medication.

Instead of relaxing, however, he completed three songs to texts by Walt Whitman, worked on a musical contribution to the Ben Hecht–Charles MacArthur "Fight for Freedom" pageant at Madison Square Garden, and composed a number of songs for the Lunch Hour Follies, on whose production committee he served.

"Kurt had deep gratitude about America," according to Gigi Gilpin, "and he loved it like no one I ever met. Very few refugees could match him for that. During the war, I think most people forgot how lucky they were to be here. Kurt wanted to go enlist, but he had to content himself with the Lunch Hour Follies."

The Follies was a program funded by the American Theatre Wing to provide entertainment for factory workers in war-related industries. Modeled on England's ENSA program, the Follies was a touring show with rotating singers, musicians and performers to entertain workers and to encourage productivity. Moss Hart also contributed time and talent, as did Frank Loesser, Cheryl Crawford, Maxwell Anderson, Marc Blitzstein and others.

"They were held in various places, all around the clock," as Gilpin remembered,

> since munitions and factory workers were always at work and there was always a lunch hour somewhere. A platform was erected in the middle of a factory, and the workers came with their sandwiches and ate while a little show was staged for them. These were offered everywhere—Brooklyn, Hoboken, Bridgeport, wherever there was a war-related industry.

Kurt visited Lenya only once while she was on tour, in Detroit. On his return home, he found a letter from her—the first of many she wrote between 1942 and 1944 in which she makes amusing, affectionate and risqué comments about his genitals, often accompanying them with little graffiti: "a monkey's tail," she labeled one surprisingly detailed sketch; later she caricatured his "little asparagus." Most elaborate of all was a cartoon of Kurt ejaculating on blossoming shrubbery and surrounded by the words "Spring is here!" and a few musical notes. These are typical of Lenya's robust, peasant humor, which Weill (like others) always found refreshing and unself-conscious, without meanness or tawdriness. The drawings and comments also evidence the easy intimacy that still prevailed between the Weills.

Not long before Lenya accepted Anderson's offer of the role, she had met a twenty-year-old air force pilot named Howard Schwartz. "Lenya was mad for him," according to Gigi Gilpin, who was first to learn of the affair. "She adored him, and Kurt liked him too. She went South to visit him and his family in Texas just before the war, and he often came to New City if Kurt wasn't there." Because he was not sent overseas to combat, Howard Schwartz visited Lenya on tour when he had leave.

Her letters to Kurt during these months are remarkable for their observations of American life in wartime and her succinct comments on human nature; and they reveal, too, her unique style in a now polished English, and her keen eye for the telling detail about the life of a touring actor. On January 27, 1942, she wrote from the Pittsburgher Hotel:

> Well, darling, this is Pittsburgh. A gray, smoky, unfriendly town, which would be ideal for a minstrel show. You don't

have to blacken your face, the city does it automatically. . . . The bank is the friendliest thing I have seen. My stomach is terribly upset from the water, it's full of chlorine and tastes awful. . . . The food is medium, wherever you go. Last night's opening was pretty awful. A very cold, coughing audience. Charming old theater with nice big dressing rooms, tremendous stage. . . . One nice thing here, you hear the boats from the river, like Louveciennes.

Next day, from the same hotel, she wrote:

Darling, thanks so much for your letter. I was waiting anxiously for it. I would have forgotten our wedding anniversary [she refers to their first marriage, on January 26, 1926]. But darling, this town almost makes you forget you are alive. What a town for [the great Italian actress Eleonora] Duse to die in [which she did, on tour, April 21, 1924]! . . . You can feel all the way through that the audiences don't like this play, and it is only pushed through by Helen [Hayes]. It is an unhealthy child. I am very happy to hear that our Lady [*in the Dark*] is still doing good business. . . . I bought you three pairs of pyjamas and a dressing gown from the money I saved.

From Syracuse, on February 3, she wrote to Kurt for the first time about the war; she also alludes to her family's hardship in Vienna:

That book *Darkness at Noon* [by Arthur Koestler] is very interesting. The only discouraging thing is that the methods of the Russians are so similar to the ones of the Germans. I hope democracy will survive! I am worried about my people in Vienna. If you talk to [Kurt's sister-in-law] Rita again, ask her if she could find out whether it is possible to send through the Red Cross food packages to civilians. That would be of some help.

En route to Columbus, Ohio, for a performance on February 9, Lenya won five dollars playing stud poker with the stage crew, and she was in good humor. Asking about their New City neighbors, playwright Elmer Rice and his wife, actress Betty Field, she inquired, "How are Mr. and Mrs. Rice-Field?"

But soon the pleasure of the tour faded for Lenya, and she began to negotiate (unsuccessfully, as it turned out) to be released from her contract. "I am horrified," she wrote from Milwaukee on February 11. "We have to work out something so I can get out. It would be too awful if I had to stay until June 1." From this point, her comments on the cities and towns of her tour became increasingly negative. Indianapolis, she wrote on February 13, is "about the ugliest town so far." But the people were a good audience, she added, and they gave her pause for thought:

> I discovered my love for acting again. I had forgotten how much of an actress I am after all those years of sitting still.

Two days later, she announced that she had won fifteen dollars playing gin rummy against another cast member who was leaving for Hollywood: "There goes my income!" she wrote to Kurt, regretting the actor's departure.

Then, in St. Louis on February 16, the horror of the war brought on a nightmare. She telephoned Kurt at three in the morning and then at once wrote him a letter:

> I woke up trembling after that horrible dream. I finished that book last night, *Darkness at Noon*, and I guess that was the cause of that nightmare. What a depressing book. Who is right? Getkin or Rubashow? They both believed in the same thing and still the one who knew so much more and had the much better brain had to die in the end. Is there any answer to such a story? I shouldn't read books like that without having you around me. I can't digest them alone. But I suppose I am not the only one who doesn't know the answer in what to believe. . . . What in the world is going to happen? . . . As a whole, this tour is very boring. But I don't see how I'll ever get out of it and whether I should. It's still the easiest way for me to make money; and for later, if I want to go on acting (which I want more than anything else) it's better to have a clean record and be known as a good trooper.

And a good trouper she was. Next afternoon she went with a few crew members to see the Disney animated feature *Dumbo*:

That's the most beautiful thing I've ever seen [she wrote to Kurt on February 18]. I cried my eyes out. When that mother elephant takes Dumbo in her arms, that's like a Botticelli Madonna. Just beyond words. And that beautiful pink ballet. Oh, I could go on forever!

The following month, Kurt wrote Lenya about contact with Brecht, who had planned an all-black production of *The Three-penny Opera* in California. The idea precipitated considerable correspondence between Weill and Brecht. Kurt insisted that *The Threepenny Opera* would only be successful in America with a completely new adaptation. But he also insisted that his music and orchestration not be violated.

I believe to a certain extent [Lenya wrote Kurt in March] what he writes about the procedure of that *Threepenny Opera* project, but I don't trust him at all [regarding the artistic intent, the financial arrangements and the division of royalties from an American production]. I never believe that he can change his character, which is a selfish one and always will be. I am sure he went through a lot of unpleasant things, but not so unpleasant that it would change him. I know, darling, how easily you forget things, but I do remember everything he did to you. And that was plenty. Of course he wants to collaborate with you again. Nothing better could happen to him. But I am convinced that after a few days you would be so disgusted with him that I could write down for you what would happen. Think of people like Moss [Hart] and John Steinbeck and Max [Anderson] and all the rest we know, and compare them—then you; you'll know it's impossible for you to take up that relationship again. It's not surprising that somebody gets nice and soft when they are down and out. That's the natural way. But just let him be a little successful again and he'll be the old Brecht again. No, darling, I don't believe in changes like that. . . . I always believed in decency and a certain fairness. And Brecht hasn't got much of it. So please, darling, don't waste much time thinking about what they will say about you. . . . Write him and tell him you are working on a new show now, but if he has any ideas he should tell you about [them] and you'll see what you can do. . . . If it makes you feel better, send Brecht $100, but don't send him anything monthly. It's very hard to stop it and one can't go on doing it. It would be just up his alley to spoil your carefully built-up good name. I have no pity or sympathy. They are too mean, that German bunch. They just use you, whenever they need you.

Soon after that, Howard Schwartz, en route to a New York assignment from his home in Texas, stopped to visit Lenya in Memphis. Kurt knew of their affair while Lenya was on tour. He knew, too, that although she was more than twice Howard's age Lenya matched the young man for passionate intensity.

Darling [she wrote to Kurt on April 17], I just came back from the station. Howard has left. He came yesterday evening and stayed overnight. That was a tough job, to cheer him up. He was terribly depressed and unhappy and I am just the wrongest person in the world for cases like that. As you know, I am so flexible and adaptable to everything, that it was a great effort for me to understand somebody who is on the verge of committing suicide just because he has to peel potatoes three times a week. But when he left he felt quite happy. It was a beautiful day and we walked along the Mississippi, which is the most beautiful river I have ever seen in my whole life.

Lenya's rendezvous with Howard Schwartz continued. Very little else is known of this young man; his place in history may have found its moment of glory in his relationship with Lenya.

Back in New City after the tour, Lenya joined Kurt and her neighbors in sharing watchtower duty for Civilian Defense. "We did our little contribution to the war," Lenya recalled years later in a letter to Milton Caniff,

by playing canasta at the airtower. Well, I tried to figure out from where the planes were coming. By the time I straightened out where south, north, west, southwest, etc., was, we could have easily lost the war.

An Allied victory was far from certain in 1942, and for German immigrants with families in Europe there was an inevitable conflict, always an inner collision of hopes and fears.

Lenya and I shared long hours on the tower in Pomona that winter [Milton Caniff recalled]. We all expected Hitler to invade New York any minute. Christmas Eve Lenya and I were alone keeping watch, and for once all her memories, her nostalgia came out. She described the makeshift gifts her mother had tried to put together for the children, and the paltry treats at holiday time. She was very concerned about her family in Vienna, whereas Kurt's family had gone to Palestine. She tried to go along with all the American ways and ideas, as Kurt did, but sometimes it was hard for her, especially during the war.

As another way of contributing to the war effort, and in addition to the music for the Lunch Hour Follies and the "Fight for Freedom" pageant ("Fun to be Free"), Weill composed incidental music for a radio broadcast about the American navy; a number of propaganda songs; a quartet of short musical melodramas for speaker, chorus and orchestra (called "Mine Eyes Have Seen the Glory," and commissioned by Helen Hayes and Victor Records); and the memorial "We Will Never Die," dedicated to the Jewish war dead in Europe.

Hesper Anderson recalled the same time:

My mother [Mab Anderson] was head of Civil Defense for Rockland County, and every night she and Lenya were part of the watchtower vigil that summer, looking for enemy aircraft. That was natural for Lenya. She loved being in America as much as Kurt. Of course the watchtower vigil didn't mean there weren't wild poker games when they weren't on duty. I can remember them at home—Lenya, my mother and Bunny Caniff, playing cards. I remember sitting on the staircase of our house, looking down at the three women while they played cards, smoked, laughed—sometimes until two or three in the morning. I think all three women felt unfulfilled at this time in their lives, while their husbands were so successful or at least working hard and getting paid for it. They were the wives of the great ones.

"Unfulfilled" is a description that seems to apply most to Mab Anderson at that time. Strikingly beautiful and often winsome and cheerful, she was also deeply insecure and given to periods of manic instability.

"She was a very troubled woman," according to Milton Caniff, "and this we all sensed right from the first meeting." Her emotional anxiety took the form of an acute nervous distraction, and her fingernails were always badly bitten. Quentin Anderson said of his stepmother:

> Mab's was a life that required a lot of external stimulus because there may not have been sufficient resources within. There was an emptiness that had to be filled with incessant occupation.

Mab had never realized her ambition to become a major star. Now, seeing her famous husband always occupied, Mab was even more depressed.

According to her daughter Hesper:

> The friendship between my mother and Lenya was very devoted, but complicated. I think my mother resented Lenya's talent, and also her virtual indifference to whether she worked or not—whereas my mother wanted passionately to be performing something, all the time. I also think my mother was in love with Lenya, but that this love was neither acknowledged nor ever expressed. Lenya represented something exotic, gifted and monumentally casual—all of which Lenya indeed was, and all of which were qualities my mother coveted.

Lenya also claimed she enjoyed acting and wanted it, as she had written to Kurt from the tour, "more than anything else." But as before she exerted no effort to win roles, to meet agents and producers, to advance her career. If a role were offered to her (as Maxwell Anderson had, and would again), she might accept it. But apart from one Kurt Weill musical soon to come, she was never ambitious about her career.

The result of this friendship was a mercurial bonding, with Mab often dependent and Lenya resentful of that dependence, yet with Lenya often touched by Mab's sadness and despondency and eager to alleviate her neighbor's poignant alienation.

As for the Weills' marriage, "On the surface, Kurt and Lenya kept it going," Burgess Meredith said, "and there was a kind of understanding between them." The understanding enabled Kurt to pursue occasional romantic affairs—for solace and comfort more than any rush of sexual passion—when he was working in Los Angeles. Lenya knew about these liaisons, and realized that Kurt's tolerance of her affairs with Pasetti and Schwartz made it impossible for her to complain now. According to Hesper Anderson,

> She told me that her affair with [Pasetti] had been a stupid mistake and that all during it Kurt had been patient and understanding with her. She admitted that she had been foolish, and she reminded herself of this during Kurt's affairs with women.

By June 1943, however, Kurt at last found a new project for Broadway, and new collaborators. With S. J. Perelman and Ogden Nash writing the book and Nash the lyrics for his songs, Weill would work on a musical version of the novel *The Tinted Venus*, by F. J. Anstey (pseudonym of the English writer Thomas Anstey Guthrie). A variation on the Pygmalion-Galatea myth, the show (produced by Cheryl Crawford and directed by Elia Kazan) finally opened on October 7 and was presented five hundred sixty-seven times as *One Touch Of Venus*—among the most literate and witty of American musicals, and that which established Mary Martin as a popular musical comedy star. Weill's brilliant score includes the songs "Speak Low," "That's Him," and "The Trouble with Women."

One Touch of Venus tells the story of a barber who places an engagement ring on a statue of the goddess of love. She promptly comes to life and pursues the barber, but when she discovers what sort of life the typical housewife leads, she returns to Mount Olympus.

Before Kurt began working on *Venus*, Lenya had an opportunity to sing Kurt's earlier songs in public. The occasion was "We Fight Back," a program produced by Ernest Aufricht (then living with his wife in New York) and Manfred George (editor of the German-language New York weekly newspaper *Aufbau*) featuring refugee talent, and designed to recruit the émigré community for the war bond drive. With Kurt at the piano on the stage of Hunter College in Manhattan in April, Lenya sang "Surabaya Johnny," "Pirate Jenny," and the "Moritat" from *The Threepenny Opera* (all in the original language). She then presented the premiere of Weill's setting of Brecht's bitter poem "Und was bekam des Soldaten Weib?" ("What Did the Soldier's Wife Receive?"). The song is a cool description of items—shoes, a fur piece, a hat, lace, a silk gown—sent home as gifts by husbands at war in Prague, Oslo, Amsterdam, Brussels, Paris and Bucharest. The lyrics conclude, "And what did the soldier's wife receive from vast Russia [the place of the most massive suffering and death that year]? The widow's veil for the funeral."

Weill had received the lyrics from Brecht during their increasingly tense correspondence over a possible all-black production of *The Threepenny Opera*. Brecht, perhaps making a kind of peace-offering, wrote that the recently written poem might make a suitable song for Lenya.

Gigi Gilpin was present that evening.

> She came out and sang in German, and her voice—very strange to American ears and even to the immigrants present—entranced the audience in moments. That quivering, funny little tone we're not accustomed to—it made people cry. It was her intonation, her inflection. Even if you didn't know German, you had to be touched by it. She wasn't a beautiful woman in any typical sense, but when she sang that night she became beautiful.

On the same program, Elisabeth Bergner recited Brecht's "The Children's Crusade, 1939," and Herbert Berghof read antiwar epigrams from Brecht's *Primer of War* (with accompanying slide projections prepared by Erwin Piscator, then director of the famous Drama Workshop at the New School for Social Research in Greenwich Village).

The evening's event was broadcast by the Voice of America, and the following year Weill and Lenya recorded the new Weill-Brecht song for broadcast behind enemy lines by the Office of War Information, as well as Weill's setting of Walter Mehring's text "Wie lange noch?"—a woman's song of despair over her faithless lover that takes on an anti-Fascist gloss in the second verse.

About the second time, Weill arranged six songs for Lenya and piano, which they recorded for Bost records on three discs: two songs from *The Threepenny Opera*, one each from *Mahagonny*, *Happy End* and *Marie Galante*, and "Au fond de la Seine," originally written in 1934 for the French cabaret singer Lys Gauty. Lenya's voice on these recordings is a voice that was changing. No longer the highly pitched, thin soprano of the 1920s, hers was now less energetic, slightly husky (she was forty-five, and a heavy smoker) and occasionally—as in the shifting tones of the second and third lines of "J'attends un navire" from *Marie Galante*—not always quite on pitch. On the other hand, her delivery has been sharpened, her intention clarified. "Surabaya Johnny" has an angry bite, and a tincture of despair in the final notes informing the listener that here is a woman who has brought her past to the present task. She does not sing the songs, she offers them as stencils of experience that are hers, to be sure, but in some ways might be her listener's too. It was Lenya's peculiar ability not to "disappear" behind the songs (as if that were in some mystic way possible); on the contrary, she capitalized on her unique pitch and style, and gave us her feelings so directly, so simply that they stand as markers of life experiences beyond her own.

For several days that spring, Bertolt Brecht visited the Weills at Brook House, and plans were discussed for a revived collaboration on at least two projects—musical versions of *The Good Woman of Setzuan* and *The Good Soldier Schweyk* (which was to have had a major role for Lenya). Neither was realized.

On August 27, Kurt swore his oath of American citizenship—a favor granted earlier than scheduled by law because of his patriotic work, which had been pointed out to naturalization authorities by friends in the theater. Lenya's became effective the following May.

(The judge at Lenya's citizen inquiry asked only one question, the name of America's first president. "Abraham Lincoln," was her reply. The judge smiled and said that was good enough. "I'm lucky he asked me that one," Lenya told a neighbor, the actress Dolores Sutton, years later. "If he'd asked me anything else about the presidents, I'd have answered wrong.")

* * *

During preparations for the October premiere of *One Touch of Venus*, Lenya became increasingly anxious about Kurt's persistently high blood pressure. When rehearsals ran late and Kurt was delayed with players and musicians, Lenya's concern became outright anger. Maurice Abravanel, who was conducting the show, remembered Lenya's arrival at rehearsals.

If we were late, Lenya was furious. She marched up to us and cried, "For heaven's sake! Kurt has been here for eight hours! Isn't it time to go home? This is ridiculous!"

The strain of preparing for a Broadway opening is enormous even for those in the best health; in Kurt's case it was increasingly dangerous. "Most people," he wrote to his parents in Palestine in January 1944,

forget, or most of them don't even know it at all, what a tremendous amount of work and what nervous strain it takes to get such a Broadway show together, especially for someone who is comparatively new in this country. It has taken a year and a half of incessant labor to get *One Touch of Venus* on its feet. A year and a half of aggravations, disappointments, intrigues and hard work. [He was referring to the time-lapse since *Lady in the Dark,* not the actual period of composing *Venus.*]

By the summer of 1944, Dr. Francis A. Glass of Haverstraw (a village near New City) reported to the New England Life Insurance Company on Kurt's behalf that his patient's marked emotional stress contributed to increasing high blood pressure that season.

One of the causes of the emotional strain that aggravated Kurt's hypertension was the disparity between his success and Lenya's. Although she was not pursuing her career more avidly at this than at any other time, she still hoped that the right role—which usually meant something in a work by Kurt Weill—would come to her.

But her good notices in *Candle in the Wind* were just happy memories now, and there were not many roles for forty-five-year-old women with thick Viennese accents. She was hard to cast, and they both knew that. Still, her inactivity except for an occasional recital rankled both of them by 1944. When Maurice Abravanel urged Kurt that year to write an opera, he replied, "Yes, Maurice, yes—but first I must write something for Lenya."

As early as the *Candle in the Wind* tour, Kurt had written to Lenya that he wanted to write something for her:

> There is no doubt in my mind that you can be a terrific success in this country if we only can get the right play. I thought of sitting down and writing one. The only thing I couldn't do is write good dialogue.

From that time, Lenya had frequently reminded Kurt of his promise. Now, in early 1944, he found a source for a show that would enable him to honor his pledge.

His choice was a 1924 play by Edwin Justus Mayer, *The Firebrand*, which concerned the Renaissance sculptor and rogue Benvenuto Cellini. The plot is a series of interconnected escapades involving the love of the Duke of Florence for Cellini's model and Cellini's love for the Duchess.

Lenya, Kurt had decided, would have the supporting but crucial role of the Duchess in a work conceived as an *opéra comique*, rather like Offenbach's *Grand Duchess of Gerolstein*.

"You are ideal for the part," Kurt wrote Lenya from Los Angeles on July 17, 1944, where he was busy with Mayer (who was working on an adaptation to musical drama) and, again, with Ira Gershwin as lyricist. "I had been waiting to find a part for you for years. . . . I am determined to have you play it."

This immediately aroused her interest, for as Gigi Gilpin said of that time, "Things were fairly routine and boring for her at home. Mostly it was evenings of cards with her women friends."

But there were other diversions. "I had a brief affair with Lenya," Quentin Anderson said in an interview years later.

> I had just been separated from my first wife, and my relationship with Lenya was quite intense while it lasted. Into everything she did, she put every bit of emotional energy she had—her work, her attentiveness to friends, her love life, her commitment to Kurt Weill's music. What Lenya wanted in the world, she took and enjoyed.

That same season, she once again enjoyed the company of George Davis, who spent several weekends at Brook House. "I always was kind of fond of that old poop," Lenya wrote of him to Kurt on August 4. As before, the friendship was platonic; George was her witty houseguest and entertainer, and she was an appreciative audience to his literary news and society gossip.

Kurt, meantime, was having trouble with the new work. "I am very anxious to know what kind of music you will write for the show," Lenya wrote on July 21. "It must be wonderful for you to do something so different after *Lady* and *Venus*." She then tackled the central problem of that summer: Ira Gershwin's insistence that Kitty Carlisle, the wife of their fomer collaborator Moss Hart, would be a better choice for the role of the Duchess than Lenya.

> Darling [she wrote in the same letter], to push me through will need a lot of fighting and arguing, but you have to do it without any emotion. If you have a sleepless night every time that question comes up, you won't get any sleep at all. I am fully prepared for fights. . . . [Ira] will probably be the first one, if I turn out all right, to say he always wanted me. . . . Don't get excited, take things as they come—be firm, though. You just have to hammer it into their brains. What does a guy like Ira know about acting? It's not my fault that he never heard about me. But he is nice. Just weak. So let's use his weakness.

In a letter to Kurt dated August 10, however, she never mentioned the role, and instead turned reflective:

> I got a very nice letter from [Nan] Huston [wife of Walter], with a long paragraph about how unimportant life is and how wonderful death is. I don't know why, but I get terribly hungry when I read things like that. So I went to the kitchen and made myself coffee and felt that there is nothing more beautiful than life. God has to agree with me on that. You think he will?

Kurt's reply came at once, dated August 12:

That is just like you, to go to the kitchen and have a cup of coffee after that letter about death from Nan. I love your vitality, and your lust for life, and I am sure God likes it too.

The seriousness continued into his next letter.

Darling, the world news has been so exciting these last days that everything else seemed awfully silly and small compared with the events in Germany and Japan. For more than ten years now we have been waiting for what is going on in Germany now. There is no doubt that this is the real thing . . . I saw a picture by the Army Signal Corps, photographed entirely in battle. It is about the war in the Pacific, the invasion of New Britain. It is incredible what these boys are going through, carrying with their hands their battle equipment through jungle, through knee-deep mud, always under enemy fire—quiet, modest, without fear or emotion. In seeing that, one feels that one should stop complaining and worrying about the little difficulties as long as one has the privilege of continuing his normal life and work. . . . Gosh, wouldn't it be wonderful if Hitler were dead and the war over before I get back. What a party we will give!

The party, like the show he was composing, was delayed, and in fact the new work was not in rehearsal until the end of 1944. By that time, it seemed to some that Edwin Justus Mayer's trifle of a libretto had not nearly enough strength to sustain Weill's ambitious score and not enough real wit to justify Gershwin's complex, highly inflected lyrics.

With rehearsals there began what conductor Maurice Abravanel afterward called "a catastrophe." First, it was quickly evident that the major players were badly cast. Earl Wrightson, the leading man, was simply not strong enough to be convincing; Beverly Tyler, the ingenue, looked lovely but could not sing; Melville Cooper (a replacement for the more desirable Walter Slezak as the Duke) substituted British buffoonery for subtler comedy. As for Lenya: "It could have been a tremendous part for her if it had been better written and well directed," according to Lys Symonette.

On February 23, 1945, the show—originally titled *It Hap-*

pened in Florence and then *Make Way for Love* and now temporarily called *Much Ado About Love*—opened for a pre-Broadway tryout in Boston.

"Unfortunately," complained the *Boston Post* on March 4, "one of the principals is not suited to her role.

> Lotte Lenya, as the Duchess, is hardly up to the comedy and the songs which have been given her. Her ability is not in question, nor her personal charm. But someone else should be playing the Duchess, for the sake of all concerned.

Detached as she tried to appear, Lenya was unutterably depressed. She knew not whether to be angry with herself, for failing Kurt, or with Kurt, for failing her. She openly admitted her problems with the staging and with the director John Murray Anderson, a genial man who had been engaged because of his experience with epics and spectacles but who was unsympathetic to the tradition of operetta and to the Gershwin-Weill aim of a seriocomic musical. Her delivery of songs in English had also been a problem; this she knew, too.

George S. Kaufman rushed to Boston to apply his famous doctoring skills, cutting a scene here, rearranging there, altering actors' entrances and blocking in this scene, hastening the pace in that one. By the time the musical was scheduled for New York—with a last-minute name-change to *The Firebrand of Florence*—Lenya was sick with anxiety, for she knew they were not in a remediable production. Not even her old friend Maurice Abravanel, again the conductor, could allay her fears; in fact he shared them. The production was altogether too gravid, overweighted with all the elements of costume drama but with no smoothness of staging, acting or integrating direction that would have given the show unity.

After the Broadway opening at the Alvin Theatre on March 22, 1945, the *New York Times* reported that the work "lacks sparkle, drive or just plain nervous energy. Lotte Lenya is miscast as the Duchess." As she admitted, she had the best number in the show, "Sing Me Not a Ballad," neatly tailored for her voice and for her personality such as Weill and Gershwin knew it. In this song, the Duchess asks not for the words of love but for the gestures of lovemaking: a bit of bawdiness is what she wants, but no songs. (There was a bit of bawdiness backstage, as it turned out, for Lenya carried on a passionate, brief affair with a younger, minor player in the show.)

Weill's stated reaction to the closing of the show after forty-three performances was not one of great sorrow or disappointment. In a letter to his parents from Los Angeles, he admitted:

> the last few months were full of agitation . . . because the dramatist [Edwin Justus Mayer] who had written the libretto was a total failure, and I felt especially responsible because it was a very expensive show, and of course also because Lenya had appeared in it. . . . Apart from the momentary unpleasantness and aggravation which is always tied up with things of this kind, the minimal success of [the show] has not touched me very much. . . . I had got used to the up and down curves of success for a long time, and I have been very aware that after two giant successes [*Lady in the Dark* and *One Touch of Venus*], a set-back was definitely due once again. Somehow I am even content that I do not fall into the routine of a regulated successful career. As long as I am trying with each new work to do something fresh, which in many cases is ahead of my own time, I have to make allowances for such set-backs—which of course is that much easier, because financially I can hold out; therefore—on to new tasks!

More important, he was in the same letter able to place his own life and career in a larger perspective:

> Everything one experiences personally is by now being over-shadowed by the tremendous happenings taking place in the theater of the world. . . . One is full of hope and confidence, when one is permitted to experience the victory of justice, when one sees how after a short while the bad is punished and the good is victorious. I don't believe that in the history of humanity a nation ever has suffered as terrible a defeat as Germany, and that never before a people has deserved humiliation as much as these barbarians who have presumed the right to destroy everything good and decent human beings have been building up for thousands of years. If one considers with what courage and pride the English, Dutch, French, Russians, Yugoslavs and most of all the Jews have borne their

pain one is filled with deep disgust when one sees the cowardice, the degradation, the sickening rage of self-destruction which the so-called master race is demonstrating at the time of their defeat. It borders on the miraculous what the allied armies have accomplished in four short years, because it was so totally a war of good against evil.

And with that Weill returned to his work, which included plans for a one-act radio opera based on Kentucky mountain folk songs. *Down in the Valley*, as it was eventually called, with text by Arnold Sundgaard, was reworked in 1948 as an educational opera. Weill used robust American musical motifs and rhythms in the tale of a condemned man's escape from prison and his last hours of reunion with his girl.

Only one nagging anxiety remained with him that peaceful, creative summer: his blood pressure was not under control. He continued to hope, however, that rest and a careful diet would alleviate the problem.

There was, in addition, Kurt's anxiety over the rights to his best-known work—a matter that would increasingly tax his patience, then Lenya's, and finally even her estate's. In a letter Kurt wrote to the Department of Commerce on August 31, 1945, he clearly set forth the basic dilemma:

. . . In 1928, before [*The Threepenny Opera*] opened, Mr. Brecht and I signed a contract with a large German theatrical publishing and agency firm, Felix Bloch Erben, Berlin, to handle all the theatrical rights for "Dreigroschenoper," to prepare contracts, to collect money, etc. They received a commission of 20%. . . . When Hitler came into power, the "Dreigroschenoper," together with all my compositions, was banned in Germany. Shortly after this, Mr. Fritz Wreede, president of Felix Bloch Erben, committed suicide. Since then, neither Mr. Brecht (who lives in California) nor I have heard anything from Felix Bloch Erben, nor did we receive any of the quarterly statements which, according to the contract, they were supposed to send us. Both Mr. Brecht and I consider our agreement with Felix Bloch Erben null and void since this firm, under the Nazi rules, was unable to handle our business and to fulfill the obligations of our contract. . . . The question is now, what has become of the rights for "Dreigroschenoper''? Who, for instance, gave the right to perform this play, to the theatre in Budapest? What royalty arrangements did they make and to whom did they pay? I also learn from an English newspaper that it is being produced in Berlin now. I wonder who made contracts with the Berlin producer, and who gets the royalties? . . .

The American government could not help Weill sort out the matter, which became increasingly complicated and, as the Weills would soon learn, tainted by the arbitrary and despotic actions of Brecht himself.

Lenya, meantime, was pitched into grief by news of the death of the young and ardent Howard Schwartz, killed in an airplane crash. Gigi Gilpin and others recalled her as utterly broken by the news, unable to sleep or to eat for days. For weeks she was inconsolable. The summer in Rockland County was blazingly humid, but for Lenya the world had turned to winter. With the collapse of *Firebrand* still fresh, she now had to accept more poignant condolences—about Howard—and the attitude of grief did not suit her.

"When Kurt returned from Los Angeles," as Hilde Halpern remembered,

> she had nothing to do but be a housewife, entertain their friends and make a good home for him. But that was not sufficient to engage her interest nor utilize her energies.

By contrast, the years form 1946 to 1949 were the busiest of Kurt's life. He composed numerous works, including a folk-opera and three major Broadway musicals.

Street Scene, the first musical, was based on Elmer Rice's 1929 Pulitzer Prize play. A story of adultery and murder in a New York tenement, it was remarkable for describing the routine life of a building's tenants and offering a musically naturalistic portrait of urban compression and decay. Rice wrote the libretto, poet Langston Hughes the lyrics. The eminent music critic Olin Downes called *Street Scene* "the most important step towards significantly American opera yet encountered in musical theatre," precisely the reason that (along with its lack of a name star) limited its Broadway run to one hundred forty-eight performances.

In 1947, Kurt received word of the death of his much loved

brother Hanns, at forty-eight, from complications of postsurgical hypertension. This news saddened and upset him greatly and renewed his concern about his own high blood pressure. His frequently recurring psoriasis, exacerbated by anxiety, then afflicted his skin more painfully than ever, and in a state of extreme depression he decided to travel to England, France and Switzerland; he then spent time with his parents in Palestine. On his return to America, he was honored with an Antoinette Perry Award, a special "Tony" for his achievements in the theater. The most dramatic event in Lenya's year was an emergency appendectomy.

Refreshed by the time with his family, Kurt returned to New City and offered to pay for Lenya's mother and sister to visit them from Vienna. At first, Lenya objected because of the expense. But as Hilde Halpern recalled, Kurt prevailed, insisting that their money not only be spent as they wished, but in a way that would make others happy, too.

And so, on September 29, 1948, Johanna and Maria arrived; their husbands, Ernst Hainisch and "Peperl" Hubeck had remained in Vienna. Kurt and Lenya drove to LaGuardia Field to meet their flight from Vienna.

"Mother had hardly changed at all," Lenya wrote in notes for her memoir a few years later. "Still looked like a woman of sixty [she was eighty]." Those notes, alternately funny and poignant, bear the stamp of her own shrewd observation and offer a lively account of her family's visit.

Mother at once began talking about the chewing gum on the plane. We drove through Manhattan and stopped off at St. Patrick's Cathedral because both wanted to offer thanks for the safe flight. . . . Before we turned north on the West Side Highway, Mother had her first and most significant comment on America: "American men all walk with their hands in their pockets!" A moment later, as we were driving along the Hudson River, Mother exclaimed, "Look, the Danube, the Danube!" I told her they had left the Danube on the other side of the ocean, but Mother kept staring out the window, repeating with calm obstinacy, "The Danube, it's the Danube!" Maria leaned over and whispered, "See how mean she can be?" It may have been meanness; it may have been hard Austrian logic—such a big and beautiful river, wherever it was, could only be the Danube. . . . During their six weeks with us, we often took them to the city, to Radio City and to the Ice Show, but Mother was quickly bored. . . . She asked for nothing, and let me buy her only one dress; she chose it herself, with a quick nod and unerring taste, a royal-blue knitted dress, expensive, simple. . . . They locked themselves in their room [at Brook House] at night, it took them quite a while to realize they were safe. Early in the visit, as she put on her silver-rimmed glasses to knit, I noticed that the right lens was gone, but she refused to have it replaced: "Leave it as it is, I've already seen enough of the world," she said. She's a wonderfully adjusted woman, not a trace of sentimentality, never envied anyone. . . . She still lives in the same apartment where Maria was born, where we moved when I was eight, a huge tenement now surrounded by factories. . . . Ernst Hainisch had changed for the better now. He had been a sailor, was the kind of big man she liked, was very decent to her now, was fifteen years younger than she. Mother knew all about the servant girls he used to pick up at the movies, but he didn't pursue them any more, and she was extremely happy with him and delighted to have all her children gone. . . . Maria still has her job in the candy factory. . . . A few nights before they left, Mab Anderson gave a little farewell party for them, but mother sat silently most of the evening, smiling down at three red roses that Mab had cut for her from the garden, holding them stiffly but with a strong noble grace. . . . Then a few days later Mother suddenly said, "Now I have seen it, I could leave now."

The two women departed on November 20. "We embraced [Lenya concluded in her memoir], in the good-bye of a mother and daughter who would never see each other again, and then they were gone."

The visit had coincided with the premiere of Kurt's next musical, *Love Life*, with was premiered on October 7. With a book and lyrics by Alan Jay Lerner and direction by Elia Kazan, *Love Life* was a cool and cynical portrait of American marriage. The structurally complex play presents seven stages in the marriage of a single couple who transcend time, from the eighteenth to the mid-twentieth century. Although it ran for 252 performances, *Love Life* was not a critical success. The day after the premiere, Brooks Atkinson (in the *Times*) termed it "joyless."

Cheryl Crawford felt "it had no heart, no passion," and that Kurt's score lacked "the warmth of his best ballads." In his eight-hundred-page autobiography, Elia Kazan made no mention of *Love Life*.

By this time Lenya had virtually retired from the stage; the wounds from *The Firebrand of Florence* had never entirely healed. But Kurt's professional life was in perpetual motion. Throughout 1949 he and Maxwell Anderson worked on an adaptation of Alan Paton's book *Cry, the Beloved Country*. The libretto for what they finally called *Lost in the Stars* concerns a black preacher in South Africa whose son is accused of murdering a white man.

As the production neared its autumn opening, the usual stress took a dramatic toll on Weill's health. "He was thoroughly involved in the plans for the production," recalled George Jenkins, who designed *Lost in the Stars*, "and when I visited him and Lenya at Brook House there was no indication of any illness or concern. He was quiet and attentive, and Lenya, as always, was his greatest supporter."

But in fact by that time there had been an alarming incident. In July, Kurt and Alan Jay Lerner were playing tennis in New City when Kurt suddenly dropped his racquet, complaining of the heat. He staggered to a chair as the right side of his face twisted in a grimace and the color drained. Lerner thought his friend had suffered heat prostration. But Kurt did not respond to questions and he had to be carried inside. After a few moments the stroke—for so it was—seemed to pass its crisis, and when Lerner went to order an ambulance Kurt forbade him, saying it was only a bad stomach, that he would see his doctor, that Lenya must not be told.

By the time *Lost in the Stars* began September rehearsals, Kurt was clearly in a state of nervous anxiety. More than ever, he depended on Lenya to be with him in New York. In a letter to his parents, he said Lenya was taking good care of him, seeing that he was not overworked and was eating sensibly. *Lost in the Stars*, a commercial and critical success, opened on October 30, 1949 and had a run of two hundred seventy-three performances.

During the winter of 1949–1950, Weill and Anderson continued to outline plans for a musical based on Mark Twain's *Huckleberry Finn*. But everyone around Kurt sensed that his irritation, even at trifling matters, betokened some deeper problem. When questioned about his health, he waved away the questioner; if concern was expressed about his spirits, he rebuffed the inquirer. Lenya, who had always been expert at sensing when he needed solitude and when he wanted company, was locked out of his confidence for a time too. And Max could not understand Kurt's excitability and surprising shifts of mood.

On March 2, the day before his fiftieth birthday, Kurt took to bed, complaining of his psoriasis and flulike symptoms. A week later Lenya was so alarmed by his continuing lassitude that she called her neighbors, Mab Anderson and Bunny Caniff, to see if she were misreading some danger signal—either of physical or emotional breakdown. The women were sympathetic, as were their husbands, but Kurt insisted a week's rest was all he needed. Lenya, by March 12, was terrified. Kurt ate little, his sleep was erratic and restless. Then, on the night of March 17, he awoke and called for Lenya. She found him gasping for air and clutching his chest. A doctor was summoned and, at the Anderson's insistence, a cardiac specialist who administered an injection for pain and sedation.

Lenya burst into tears, and the Andersons and Caniffs remained with her. They all stayed nearby the whole night, for Kurt's pain was intractable and his breathing severely compromised. On Sunday morning, the doctor ordered an ambulance, and Kurt was transferred to Flower–Fifth Avenue Hospital in Manhattan.

Once there, he fell into a coma, and through the oxygen tent Lenya watched his colorless face. She and Mab checked into the midtown Dorset Hotel, where Lenya alternated telephone calls—to the hospital nurses' station, to the doctor's office, to her New City neighbors, and to George Davis, who had just the previous month been up for lunch after a year's absence.

On Wednesday, Lenya was sitting on a footstool in Kurt's hospital room when he opened his eyes. She leaped to his side, and heard him say, "Zurück von der Unterwelt—Back from the underworld!" He then asked for his notebooks, the sketches for *Huckleberry Finn*, and the page proofs for the imminent publication of *Lost in the Stars*.

An electrocardiogram next day revealed a massive heart attack, and Dr. Leo G. Weishaar, Jr., told Lenya that although her husband felt better he must remain in the hospital. Over the next week, Kurt indeed seemed to rally. "Two more things I want to do, Lenya," he told her from behind a newspaper one morning.

"*Huckleberry Finn* and *Moby Dick*, my contributions to America. Then I relax a little." By April 1, Lenya had moved back to Brook House and was making the hour-long daily trip. Even she was encouraged at Kurt's apparent beginning of recovery.

On the afternoon of April 3, however, she arrived at his room to find a parade of attendants and technicians around his bed. She was asked to remain outside, and presently an intern suggested she call other family members or friends. The Andersons sped from Rockland County and Margot Aufricht from her New York apartment. They found a dazed Lenya, encircled in the smoky confusion of the visitors' lounge. She had been permitted only a few minutes with Kurt, and he had asked her, "Lenya, do you really love me?" His hand was resistless and dry at her touch, as she replied, "Only you."

And as she recounted this to her friends, a staff physician came to the waiting room. His manner told them Kurt was gone.

Next evening, the body was returned to Brook House, where friends and neighbors gathered. "The Andersons and my wife and I were with her," Milton Caniff recalled,

> and a young friend of ours, a psychiatric intern, came with us to comfort her. Lenya was just numb, but she looked around, saw the intern and asked, "What's he doing here? This is no place for a young person—he shouldn't have to witness this grief." Her tone was not resentful or harsh, in fact she was quite compassionate, as if youth were out of place in an atmosphere of death.

"I didn't know what to say," Hesper Anderson recalled of her first teenage experience of death, "and so as Lenya and I stood by the open casket I told her I thought the flowers were beautiful. '*He's* beautiful, Hep,' she said, and she put her arm around me." Quentin Anderson was there, too. " 'It really doesn't matter what you and I did, does it?' she asked me as we stood by his coffin. 'That was no separation from Kurt.' I felt I understood what she was saying—that she had an unbroken devotion to him, and that in a mysterious way it had been a profounder bond than she had had with anyone else."

In spite of that bond, however—a bond which she would often have to reclaim for herself—Lenya was no romantic, and in later years she was capable of a dispassionate clarity about Kurt Weill. "There was always a wall around him," she told an interviewer in 1980. "People never really knew him. And I'm not sure *I* ever really knew him, even after twenty-four years of marriage and the two years we had lived together before that. And when he died I looked at him and asked myself, did *I* ever really know him?"

More to the point perhaps was the question whether Lotte Lenya was ever in love with Kurt Weill. Did she ever feel for him anything like the passion he clearly demonstrated (and documented in letters) for her? The answer seems to be that she loved and admired him as a friend and as a genius, and she very much depended on him—psychologically as well as professionally and financially. Even when dallying with lovers (Pasetti, Ernst, Schwartz and others) she looked to Kurt as the person who was—like a father—responsible for her. In addition, as Lys Symonette recalled,

> Lenya's emotions were mercurial, constantly torn. One moment she could be a darling, and the next terribly mean—almost brutal. And she couldn't give Weill any security, he couldn't find any solace with her, her moods shifted so from one day to the next. No, basically this was not a great mutual physical love. She was drawn to his music, and he was enormously kind and had a great sense of humor, and this was attractive to her, too.

Albert and Emma Weill, at their home in Israel, received word of the death of another son, the second of their four children. They were themselves too old and frail to make the journey for the funeral.

At a graveside service on April 5, in Haverstraw's Mount Repose Cemetery, Maxwell Anderson spoke briefly in honor of his best friend and collaborator. Rouben Mamoulian, who had directed *Lost in the Stars*, was there, and Robert E. Sherwood, Elmer Rice, Marc Blitzstein, Charles MacArthur, Marc Connelly and Arthur Schwartz, among others. Then, as a cool spring rain fell over the valley, Kurt Weill, dead at fifty, was buried, very near the old Civilian Defense watchtower.

Seven

Revival

1950–1955

A WEEK AFTER WEILL'S DEATH, COMPOSER VIRGIL Thomson paid tribute to his art in a Sunday *Herald-Tribune* memorial. "Your article was kind and good," Lenya wrote Thomson, "and I thank you for it. . . . I would love to see you—just how soon I can't tell right now, but I will call you and maybe we have an evening of old memories, if you can take it."

But it was not a question of whether old friends could take being with her; rather, it was doubtful whether Lenya herself could endure the grief. Immersed in a paralyzing pain, she was overcome (as she readily admitted to friends like Milton and Bunny Caniff, and to Maxwell and Mab Anderson) with an abiding sense of guilt. Kurt had married her and had included her in his *Threepenny Opera*. He had lived with her continuing infidelities, he had given her and her lover Pasetti work in Paris. He had remarried her in America, he had finally written a musical for her, and no matter the result he was always proud of her performance in it. But she felt she had let him down, from their separation in Germany to her affairs there and in America, and to the failure of *The Firebrand of Florence*. And she also knew the guilt of the survivor, common to very many who lose a spouse or companion. "She knew she hadn't given Kurt solace," according to Lys Symonette,

and that she hadn't been that kind of provider for him—but if someone *else* wanted to offer that to him, she'd raise hell. There were enormous conflicts within her like this throughout

162

her life, and they sometimes caused her—and those she knew—great suffering.

Hesper Anderson remembered Lenya's mourning the month after Kurt's death. "How she grieved! She just couldn't be left alone. Either my mother or Bunny Caniff stayed with her every night, or she with one of them. And she cried, night after night after night. She just did not want to live." For weeks, the solace of friends could not diminish her guilt, nor did their company alleviate her sorrow.

By early May, she seemed to have found a way of coping with her loss, her grief and her guilt. A letter written on May 11 to Manfred George, who had coproduced the 1943 Hunter College recital, focused her emotions and expressed her new commitment—a commitment that was itself the mechanism triggering her survival. Her life would henceforth be dedicated to the legacy of Kurt's music.

The only thing that keeps me going is his music and the only desire I still retain—everything I learned through him in these twenty-five years—is to fight for this music, to keep it alive, to do everything for it in my power. There are only a few who know about his importance, especially here, where only a part of his work is known. And I believe that it will have to be the task of my life to make this music known. Everything is still very hazy and I don't know as yet where to begin. But the only thought that again and again emerges out of my confused inner self is his music. . . . This is the only thing that still keeps me alive. . . . I hope I am choosing the right path by going on living just for him, so he won't be forgotten too quickly in a time that has no time to remember what happened yesterday.

There were now also practical matters relative to Kurt and his music that demanded Lenya's attention, and as they can, such tasks helped the healing process, too. Kurt's estate was now in her care, as executrix, and that meant a tangle of responsibilities. Copyrights, performance rights, royalty statements and divisions, contractual obligations, legal disputes, negotiations with music publishers and collaborators (and the estates of collaborators), deals for recordings and for both professional and amateur productions, the representations of foreign and domestic performances, the supervision of adaptations and translations, and the survival of Weill's manuscripts—these and an endless skein of business affairs exercised her for the rest of her life.

"Weill always kept such matters from her," Lys Symonette recalled, "and he also kept her from participating in his professional financial decisions—maybe because he felt she wasn't capable, maybe to save her the trouble, maybe because he wanted complete control himself." Whatever the reasons, Lenya in 1950 suddenly undertook a serious and difficult education.

She was, at the outset, introduced to the fine points of international legal maneuverings, obstacles and the almost infinite problems accompanying both the broadcast and performance rights of works by a deceased artist. There was the task of persuading Universal Edition, Weill's Viennese publisher, to republish or reprint his scores, most of which Weill himself—up to the time of his death—had thought lost forever. Lenya also realized that Weill's American works were unknown in Germany, and his German works were unknown in America—that the two countries essentially knew two different Weills—and her intention was to unite the complementary perceptions into the accurate sense of one developed genius. It is no exaggeration to state that for the last three decades of Lenya's life, a great deal of her time and energy each month was devoted to the business and legal complexities attendant on fighting for Kurt Weill's public stature as a composer and—quite literally—for the survival of his music.

In May 1951, for example, Lenya hoped to arrange a performance of the Weill-Brecht one-act opera *The Yes-Sayer*, and she wrote to Universal Edition for the score and orchestra parts.

Gradually [she wrote to Alfred Schlee at Universal, on May 14], I hope to have all Kurt Weill's works staged, one by one, and I hope you will be helpful in this matter. Also, I have received a number of questions regarding his chamber music, and so I also need the orchestra material for that—about which I will write to you, and about photostatic copies of all his other works, in my next letter. When you send the material for *The Yes-Sayer*, please also send the partitur for *Quodlibet, Zaubernacht* and *The New Orpheus*.

Karoline Blamauer, age three (third from left, front row), and her brother Franz, age four (sixth from left, front row), in Vienna, 1901.

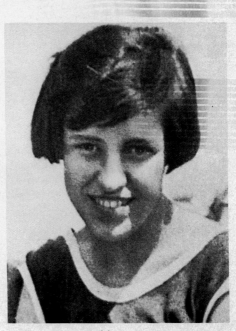

Age fifteen (1913).

In Zurich (1915).

As a dancer in repertory, Zurich (1916).

Kurt Julian Weill, in Leipzig, age seventeen (1917).

Georg Kaiser.

Lenya and Weill on their wedding day, January 28, 1926.

Front row: Kurt's parents, Emma (Ackermann) and Albert Weill. *Back row:* Kurt and Lotte Lenya Weill, Rita Weill, Leni and Nathan Weill.

Lenya (front left), with Bertolt Brecht (behind her) and Weill (top left), at Baden-Baden, summer 1927.

Lenya (center, hand raised) and Irene Eden, in the original production of *Mahagonny Songspiel*, Baden-Baden July 1927. Weill is at the rear, behind ropes (third from right).

Photo by Lotte Jacobi. Reprinted courtesy of Lotte Jacobi Archive, Media Services, Dimond Library, University of New Hampshire.

In Berlin, 1929, in a famous photo by Lotte Jacobi.

Hilde Körber and Lotte Lenya in Marieluise Fleisser's play *The Pioneers of Ingolstadt*, Berlin, 1929.

Lenya and Weill, Berlin, 1929.

Lenya, at the Reichstag, 1930.

Bertolt Brecht.

In Frank Wedekind's play
Spring's Awakening,
Berlin, 1930.

Peter Lorre and Lotte Lenya in *Spring's Awakening*,
Berlin, 1930.

Lenya and Harald Paulsen in *Mahagonny*, Berlin, 1930.

Lenya in G. W. Pabst's film of *The Three-penny Opera*, 1930.

Tilly Losch and Lotte Lenya in the original French production of *The Seven Deadly Sins*, Paris, 1933.

Photo by George Hoyningen-Huene.

Lenya in Odessa, 1931.

Louise Dahl-Wolfe

Kurt Weill and Lotte Lenya, New York, 1935.

George Platt Lynes

Lenya, publicity photo, New York, about 1938.

Lenya with Evelyn Varden in Maxwell Anderson's *Candle in the Wind*, 1941.

Maxwell Anderson (with hat), Kurt Weill and neighbors, on air-raid tower, Rockland County, New York, 1942.

Weill at New City, about 1943.

Weill and Lenya at Brook House.

At New City, about 1944.

In California, 1944.

Lenya with Melville Copper in *The Firebrand of Florence*, New York, 1945.

Maxwell Anderson.

Rehearsing at Lewisohn Stadium, New York, 1950.

George Davis with Lenya, at Brook House, 1951.

George Davis, 1953.

S. Neil Fujita

Scott Merrill and Lenya in the Theatre de Lys production of *The Threepenny Opera*, New York, 1954.

Singing "Pirate Jenny" in the Theatre de Lys *Threepenny Opera,*
1954.

S. Neil Fujita

During her first postwar visit to Berlin, 1955.

At the recording session for *Mahagonny*, Hamburg, 1956.

Recording for Columbia
Records, New York.

With Louis Armstrong during his recording session of "Mack the Knife," 1956.

Lenya (right), Allegra Kent and partner in the New York City Ballet production of *The Seven Deadly Sins* (1958).

In Munich, 1960.

With Warren Beatty in José Quintero's film of Tennessee Williams's *The Roman Spring of Mrs. Stone*, 1961.

As the Contessa Magda Terribili-Gonzalez in *The Roman Spring of Mrs. Stone*.

Hulton Picture Library/Bettmann Archive

With Russell Detwiler in London, 1962.

The Detwilers in Berlin.

As Rosa Klebb, with Daniela Bianchi in *From Russia with Love*, 1963

As Mother Courage, Recklinghausen, 1965.

Rosmarie Pierer

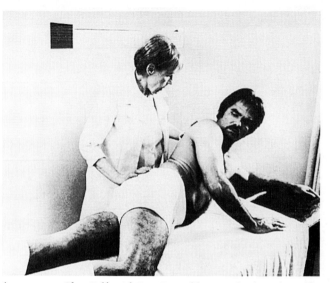

As masseuse Clara Pelf, with Burt Reynolds in Michael Ritchie's film *Semi-Tough*, 1976.

In Munich.

Felicitas

At Brook House, 1977.

© by Gerard Malanga

On her eightieth birthday, October 1978.

At home, 1979.

John Ardoin

At a Kurt Weill symposium at Goethe House, New York, March 1980.

Erika Stone

On August 18, 1952, Lenya wrote to Ernst Hartman at Universal Edition that negotiations were in progress for a production of *The Threepenny Opera* in America. "It is very important that you send me, for the negotiations here, a copy of the original contract [with Bloch Erben, the dramatic licensing agency, and with Universal]—and please, as soon as possible." She then asked him, for reasons of sentiment, also to send the original score in Weill's own hand, "since it was Kurt's and my first great success"; she further offered to have a facsimile made at her own expense and returned to him. And in the hope that a theater group would soon stage the *Mahagonny Songspiel*, she also asked for the songs for that (and for *Happy End*)—"by air mail, at my cost, and the same goes for the contract." It was a great joy, she concluded,

> to see how an interest in Kurt Weill's music is growing. What I would really prefer is to have all his works on microfilm here, so that no time would be lost in getting things from Vienna. I would also like to know what of his music was lost or destroyed. Are all orchestrations for his works available? I am very sorry to bother you with so many things all at once, but of course this is also in the interest of the publishing house. . . .

And so Lotte Lenya became the ardent guardian of the Kurt Weill legacy. There was certainly a strong component of what might be called repentance in this mission—a sense of making restitution, of expressing her gratitude and compensating for her former infidelities. But her strong sense of duty, repeatedly activated, should not be simply conceived as a prolonged manifestation of guilt. She always sustained a deep belief in and an authentic commitment to the art of Kurt Weill. He would never have a more ardent devotee than she, and to him and his art she always submitted herself and her own place in history.

There was a supreme irony in this commitment. She knew—Kurt had told her, after all—that she came "right after" his music in his devotion and valuation. Now, after his death, that music became her priority. In life he had loved it more than her, and now in a way she loved it more than she had loved him.

"Don't write about me as a performer," she told writer and teacher Guy Stern after almost a decade of supervising Weill's estate. "That, I think, has been done more often than I really deserve—but I'd like it if you would tell what I have done to keep Kurt's music alive."

But a personal comforting and encouragement and a return to some kind of social life were still lacking—until by chance she met George Davis again one afternoon, at the Second Avenue apartment of a mutual friend, art dealer Victor Carl Guarneri. George invited Lenya to lunch soon after, and then to a party given by other friends.

"I scarcely recognized her," George said later of that first meeting after Kurt's death. "It wasn't merely her appearance, either. Her face was veiled by apathy. Here was a person who had lost interest in everything. She had abdicated from life." George's sympathy for her and his own enthusiastic appreciation of Weill's music emboldened him to reach out to Lenya in her loneliness.

"Thank you for a lovely evening," she wrote to him on June 6 from Brook House,

> and I wanted to ask you not to let too much time pass until we see each other again. Please do let me know where you are hiding. If you really feel like disappearing for a weekend, you know that you can come out here [to New City] any time. Nobody will bother you. Drop me a note or call me.

Soon they were visiting frequently, either in New York or at Brook House.

When Kurt died, George was regarded in New York publishing and social circles as a bright, undependable entrepreneur. He was still known as the discoverer of the talents of Carson McCullers and Truman Capote, and he was appreciated as the man who had given them first publication in magazines before any book editor knew of them. But by 1950 publishers also knew of his untidy private life and his refusal to conform to ordinary procedures and formal deadlines.

During the academic year 1947–1948, George had taught writing in the School of General Studies at Columbia University—a position he accepted for the twelve-hundred-dollar salary. Then, in the fall of 1948, Cowles Magazines (publishers of *Look*) announced a new literary and fashion periodical, to be called *Flair*. Fleur Cowles, its editor-in-chief, invited George to leave *Mademoiselle* and join her new staff. *Flair* began with great promise: its premiere issue, dated February 1950, included a new Tennessee Williams short story, "The Resemblance Between a Violin Case and a Coffin." But the magazine soon ceased publication, a casualty of competition and of fierce intramural battles.

George's wit, nevertheless, survived lack of permanent employment. When a malevolent acquaintance crashed a dinner party and announced, "My, it looks like the Last Supper," George countered in a stage whisper, "Yes, now that Judas has arrived." And when Ernest Hemingway, after disappearing in the African jungle, was found hurt but alive—thus oddly disappointing those who had already composed extravagant obituaries about his flamboyantly apposite death—George commented, "Somehow it makes one think less of him as a writer."

With the collapse of *Flair*, George moved into a room at the Hotel Columbia, on West 46th Street. (He had been living with writer Colin McPhee in pleasanter quarters on East 86th Street.) "He could help others more than himself," Victor Carl Guarneri recalled.

He was flat broke, and no one was exactly throwing checks at him. For a time he stayed with me, and his only income was an occasional small residual for old work at *Mademoiselle*. He could never hold a penny in his pocket. Within a day of getting a check, he asked for a twenty-five-dollar loan.

George readily accepted Lenya's invitations to Brook House that summer of 1950, and there he regaled Lenya with updated accounts of his past and present life, neither glorifying his promiscuity nor glamorizing his poverty. She found his vitality and candor refreshing, and he appreciated that she made no judgments nor expressed disapproval about any part of his life. Soon they were together several times weekly.

The relationship certainly was not romantic. But Lenya did not want to be alone, she liked someone to escort her to social gatherings, and George was a genial and undemanding companion who shared her passion for Kurt's music. Precisely because George was devoted to Weill, she was soon devoted to George.

And because he was homosexual, she could keep a kind of fidelity to Weill, to whom her former infidelity now caused her such retrospective guilt.

Soon she was depending on George for advice as well as for companionship, and he was depending on her not only for life's luxuries, but even for its basic necessities. When they dined in New York, she paid; when they drove to and from New City, it was in her car; when they invited friends to dinner at Brook House, Lenya paid the grocer. She also supplemented his modest wardrobe with new suits and accessories.

With George, Lenya loosened the strings of her purse for perhaps the first time in her life. Thrifty since childhood, she had grown up with the habit of clothing herself simply and inexpensively, of avoiding even a small luxury and of never spending money she could bank. "But I'm not stingy!" she liked to insist when she rejected an invitation to a Dutch treat luncheon or a theater party. "I just don't like to spend money!"

Victor Carl Guarneri knew the reason for her parsimony:

> Lenya's exaggerated thriftiness came from her childhood days, and she never got over that insecurity. Often she said, "I saw the prettiest blouse today," or a skirt, or a handbag. When I asked why she didn't buy it, she always replied, "Oh, but it was thirty dollars!" That price was not beyond her means, but she thought that if she spent money she wouldn't have a dime by the end of the year, that soon she'd be poorer than she was as a child. George had to complain about it sometimes—"She never believes she has a nickel!" She just wouldn't go out and spend the money. But if a close friend were in *real* need she could be spontaneously openhanded.

Gigi Gilpin had a similar impression.

> She could be so chintzy! I remember her screaming at me when I visited Brook House. She thought I was using too much hot water in my bath! But then, like all of us, she could be so inconsistent. She bought a large and expensive gold locket for my baby girl, saying she hated the tiny, cheap kind, and that was that.

Lys Symonette also remembered the contradictions. Once Lenya gave her and her husband several hundred dollars to help defray the cost of a professional trip to Europe. But Symonette also remembered that friends visiting Brook House had to keep records of timed telephone calls to reimburse their hostess before departing—a custom begun when Kurt complained about her own long calls to friends in earlier years. And even years later Lenya complained if someone wanted two eggs for breakfast.

"She was always afraid of running out of money," recalled her friend and accountant Milton Coleman, who managed Lenya's financial affairs from 1948, and who for more than thirty years thereafter had Lenya's confidence and trust.

> She never realized, dollar-wise, what she really had. She could not think in those terms. I continually had to reassure her, even to the point of redundancy, that yes, she could afford to buy a new dress or a new car. She always took a hard look at money and money matters, and this had something to do with her early years. She made you feel she had had a very rough childhood. And that helps to understand why she could cry out, "My God, what are all these phone charges?" even if the phone calls were made by her husband!

As for her frequent protestation that she was not "stingy," she was right to suspect herself. "She was not," Coleman added,

> one who gave to charity. I always told her in later years that in her bracket it would at least be a tax advantage to give some money away. But she said, "Those people [the needy] just dissipate the money," and that was the end of it.

But for a time in 1950—because George's companionship was so necessary for her—Lenya indulged his requests and spent money for a bottle of fine old Scotch whiskey and frequent maid service, a handyman and a much needed new car.

On July 10, 1950, Maurice Levine led the New York Philharmonic at a Lewisohn Stadium concert in memory of Kurt Weill. There were excerpts from *Lost in the Stars* (which Levine had conducted on Broadway) as well as a tribute by Maxwell Anderson, a presentation of *Down in the Valley*, and songs from

Love Life, *One Touch of Venus* and *Knickerbocker Holiday*. Lenya, however, did not appear onstage. On August 7, she and Mab Anderson attended the San Francisco premiere of *Lost in the Stars*. Still, there had been only vague conversations about Lenya singing the music of Kurt Weill in public.

Her first appearance before an audience, almost a year after Kurt's death, was arranged by her old friend Ernst Aufricht, who asked her to sing in a concert version of *The Threepenny Opera* during a Kurt Weill tribute at Manhattan's Town Hall on February 3, 1951. Lenya agreed to participate only because George insisted, arguing that her commitment to Weill's music required a tangible proof that only her voice could provide.

The program was divided into two parts. The first, with soloists and a quartet, included selections from *Knickerbocker Holiday*, *Street Scene*, *Mahagonny*, *Happy End*, *One Touch of Venus* and *Lost in the Stars*. The second part was the *Threepenny Opera* concert version, in the original language.

"I don't remember even being alive at that time," Lenya said later. "I did it because I had to do it, and this was the beginning."

Just before she was to sing, Lenya burst into tears backstage. "I can't do it! I can't do it!" she cried to Margot Aufricht. "I can't sing the music! It's impossible!" And then George came to her, led her away and spoke quietly to her. Moments later she stepped onstage.

Hesper Anderson was in the audience that night.

> When she first came out, it was clear that she was shaking with fright. When she started to sing, her voice trembled a bit, but then on she went, gathering strength from the music, and she was magnetic.

The stage fright is easy to understand, and not only because she was about to perform onstage for the first time in six years. She had also committed herself to Weill's music, she was duty-bound to him and his art, and she was terrified of failing Kurt again, and of failing George's confidence in her now.

What was magnetic for audiences that night and at her concerts ever after was Lenya's blend of passion and stillness. Arms at her side, she seemed lost in a bittersweet reverie, her apparent emotional distance from her audience actually drawing them nearer the complex adult emotions the songs described. Her attitude was one of cynical inexpectancy, and even the slightest gesture or lift of her arms was full of meaning, like every note in the strident restraint, or the sudden hush in her voice—now no longer high-pitched but faintly boozy, grown husky and smoky.

The concert—so successful that it was repeated two weeks later and a third time in March—was a triumph for the reputation of Kurt Weill and for the strength George Davis was infusing into Lenya. Virgil Thomson referred in the *New York Herald-Tribune* a few days later to "the impeccable singing actress Lotte Lenya-Weill."

"Now she began to live," as Hans Heinsheimer said. "Without the presence of Kurt she could become a real star. But she could not have emerged without George Davis."

Maurice Abravanel agreed: "The Lenya legend did not begin until after Kurt's death, when she emerged from his shadow under the gentle guidance of George Davis." And Paul Moor, who had known George at Columbia University and would be a close friend to him and Lenya, remembered that

> when Lenya said she never wanted to work again, he forced her—and of course he was right. He began to shape and re-fashion her entire image. She had totally lost her nerve and effectively gone into retirement. He saw to it that she re-emerged into the limelight.

George's encouragement was appreciated in another context when, three days after the concert, Lenya learned of her mother's death. In her eighty-third year, Johanna had quietly expired at a Vienna clinic after two heart attacks. Lenya had the flush of success and George's pride in her, and his comfort, to soften the news.

The evening at Town Hall thus further cemented the intimacy between George and Lenya. "His influence as an editor was a thing of the past," as Milton Caniff said,

> and now he saw that he could devote himself to the career of Lenya—not just for a year, but as a permanent occupation. He determined that she would be known as Lenya, not just as the widow Weill.

By summer 1951 Lenya and George were constant companions, and at the beginning of July they invited a few friends to lunch at Brook House and announced that they were to be married.

"When she told me the news," Lys Symonette recalled, "she looked like a small schoolgirl, she was so happy, so completely changed."

But about this union Lenya never had any illusions. "George married me out of friendship," Lenya admitted years later, "so I wouldn't be alone—it was a gesture of kindness, because I was so lost." The kindness, she might have added, benefited him as well. She was giving George gainful employment, enabling him to earn the support she was providing even as he was providing her with an outlet for her dedication, a new professional status and a man to escort her. And by giving to George—who was helping her to celebrate Kurt's art—she was giving simultaneously to Kurt.

Before Weill's death, she needed other men's admiration to support her self-esteem; now she longed for simple companionship. But her insecurities remained, although they took a different manifestation. Lenya's second, third and fourth husbands were homosexuals with tragic self-destructive tendencies—men who were simultaneously unthreatening to her but also dependent on her. Even while she was aging, therefore, she could offer—as alternatives to sex—the material security these men were incapable of realizing on their own. And like many women in earlier generations, she felt and said that her life had significance only when attached to a man's.

Much in the Lenya-Davis marriage was, therefore, an amiably mutual interdependence. But given their own uneasy histories—George's dangerous, destructive passions and Lenya's overarching insecurities—it was perhaps inevitable that there would be heartache accompanying the happiness of achievement. In addition, neither of them foresaw the risk of combining his material dependence and his impulses toward danger and pain with her fear of loneliness and her need to be somehow attached to an unthreatening, dependent man. Their needs, in other words, were doomed to clash, for in a conscious and finally tragic way George did not want the security Lenya longed to provide.

"I think she felt a maternal feeling toward George," Milton Caniff reflected.

It was certainly not a love-match. We were actually quite startled when they announced their marriage. But at that time George was absolutely broke and had no job potential. Lenya understood him, liked his company and decided to do something about his situation. So she married him.

The arrangement, however, was no more exploitive than it was sexual.

I would love to see you [she wrote to him after a Christmas hiatus in early 1951]. That you know. So I'll just wait, darling, until you feel like seeing me. . . . But don't wait too long.

The plaintive note, which suggests her growing emotional dependence on him, concludes, "All my love as always, yours, Lenya."

And so George Davis helped Lenya back from grief to social life. That he counted on her materially was no embarrassment for them. She was grateful that witty man wanted to be with her, no matter the mixed motives. She knew that her relationship with him was a pragmatic symbiosis, and she accepted its limitations as she accepted its advantages. She saw herself (and she was) more practical than George, and her money gave her a benevolent upper hand. But he shared her commitment to Kurt and his legacy, and that placed a great value on his presence in her life.

On July 7, in Maxwell Anderson's living room, George Garfield Davis and Karoline Blamauer Weill exchanged vows before a justice of the peace and a few friends. Their wedding license listed their residences as South Mountain Road, New City, and 1031 Second Avenue—actually Victor Carl Guarneri's Manhattan apartment, where they took over a room for city visits, and which had virtually become George's New York address. As if for a wedding present, Maxwell Anderson then announced that he was nearing completion of a new play, and he wanted Lenya in the cast—not a minor role this time, but the female lead.

After the ceremony, George took Lenya to visit his family in

Ludington, Michigan, and then to his friends, the writers Allen Tate and his wife Caroline Gordon, in Princeton, New Jersey. "I was one of the writers George had discovered and encouraged," recalled Marguerite Young, later best known for her novel *Miss MacIntosh My Darling*.

> I was there in Princeton to meet them with the Tates, and I recall Lenya asking us not to tell Caroline that she was an ex-Catholic. She was afraid that Caroline, who was very devout, might try to reconvert her—which was very silly, since Caroline was a discreet and respectful person. . . . From there George invited me to return with them to Brook House for a few days, which I did. She was quite content to let him do the cooking, which he loved and she didn't.

Anderson's play *Barefoot in Athens* concerned the last days of Socrates, when he faced charges of treason against the state. "The play wasn't exactly written for Lenya," according to Max's son Alan, who directed it, "but my father realized that year that he could put her in it." Lenya sailed with high energy through the role of Socrates's waspish wife, Xantippe. She had no trouble memorizing lines, her English diction had improved (although she was the only cast member with a heavy accent), and she made a serious effort to enliven every scene.

Barefoot in Athens was a problem play, in two senses. Like all Maxwell Anderson's works, it had a noble theme and concept, but in this case there were serious flaws in dramatic construction and narrative development. Anderson simply tried to fit too much into his play: the fall of Athens to Sparta, the establishment of an oligarchy, Socrates's trial and conviction by the free electorate of his beloved city—all these were thematic supports to the central issue, the trial scene in the second act.

After the October 16 premiere, the Philadelphia critics chose to emphasize the performances in their notices. "The playing is of superior grade, particularly the performance of Lotte Lenya as Xantippe, that most quarrelsome of wives," wrote Jerry Gaghan in the *Daily News*. Henry T. Murdock wrote in the *Philadelphia Inquirer*, "The much maligned Xantippe comes to life with all her understandable exasperation in Lotte Lenya's portrayal."

But the play itself was not so enthusiastically reviewed, and in an attempt to give it new life the producers, to everyone's surprise, decided to replace Lenya with an actress who had no accent. The replacement, however, turned out to be disappointing, and so Lenya was invited to return to the role—which she cheerfully and uncomplainingly did, without any tincture of the prima donna's posing or resentment.

When the play finally opened in New York on October 31 at the Martin Beck Theatre, the kudos for Lenya continued. "Lotte Lenya is admirable," pronounced John Chapman in the *Daily News*. Walter Kerr, in the *Herald-Tribune*, felt that Lenya brought "just the right balance of style and feeling" to her performance. And Brooks Atkinson, in the *Times*, praised Lenya's "excellent performance as Socrates's harassed, acid-tongued though affectionate wife." But Atkinson then added that the play was "not only barefoot but heavy-footed and slow, high-minded and pedestrian, sincere and perfunctory."

Lenya's gratifying notices could not prevent *Barefoot in Athens* from closing after only thirty performances, and no road tour was booked. She was not at all depressed, however, for she was still enjoying her new status, which she indicated in letters as "Lotte Lenya Weill-Davis." Throughout the autumn and early winter, while she was in Philadelphia and New York, George tended Brook House. Then, with the closing of the play in late November, she returned to her husband, who announced that he had scheduled job interviews with magazine editors and promptly left to spend several weeks at Victor's New York apartment. "Darling, it's a beautiful day and I am so happy to be married to you," she cabled him from New City to Manhattan on December 7.

But there were no professional appointments on George's calendar. His days were spent gossiping with old friends, and his nights were spent picking up strangers for casual sex. When her friends thought Lenya was unaware of this, they misjudged her sharpness. "Lenya knew all about these nighttime wanderings of George in New York," according to Paul Moor, who learned the details from Lenya herself later. Milton Caniff agreed:

Lenya didn't seem to mind that he preferred the company of gentlemen—if anything, she mentioned it to us. Everybody knew about George, there was nothing secret about it. Lenya simply chose to stress their common interests. In most ways the marriage, which was one of mutual practical convenience, worked quite well. And she was endlessly patient and indulgent with him.

And so her marriage to George was carrying her at once more deeply into both hope and hopelessness, into creation and diminishment. She sustained the unpleasantness and danger in his life because he shared her devotion to Kurt Weill, and because he had unshakable belief in her talent and her future.

But during 1952 the problems accumulated. Lenya began to insist that George spend more time at home. Just when domesticity was so appealing to her, however, it was appalling to him. And with his inevitable boredom came depression, which often alternated with his high spirits and good humor.

As early as May 10, 1951, a lengthy journal entry had testified to George's fears about a creative life grown arid. His depression was apparently linked with both the desire and the fear of death— and even, perhaps, to that deep-rooted self-destructiveness responsible for his trysts with catastrophe.

A day and night to remember: the saddest, the loneliest, the most appallingly empty in a lifetime. Beyond tomorrow, if I cannot force myself to work, to wrest victory from defeat, I must give way to the most abject self-pity. I write these words now, in the middle of the night, because it is important for me to remember why I began this, my second book: to escape that person I most dread becoming. Now at last my fear of writing seems conquered by a greater fear, the fear of not writing, of not being, or worse of being without wanting to be. This is the night when evil seems to wait outside, just by the window, my murderer on the fire escape. It is as though I had called him there, paid him in advance for his nasty job, warned him that he must not let [me] beg my way out at the last moment. My ears strain, I hear a faint rustle . . . and suddenly I remember that only a few days ago I saw lilacs on Lexington Avenue, lilacs crammed into a square glass jar, with a sign 50 cents a bunch. And suddenly I hear [a] voice, "Little boy . . . little boy . . ."

But George had not only himself to be responsible for now. He had a genuine concern for Lenya and her career, and this was intimately bound up with his own. And he began to see the way out of his own depression as connected with helping Lenya out of hers. The legacy of Kurt Weill was Lenya's self-proclaimed mission; and Lenya as the propagator of that legacy would be *his* mission. Soon there was a clear path to realize that twofold goal.

In late 1951, Lenya and George met with composer Marc Blitzstein, who had first heard *The Threepenny Opera* in Berlin, and who had known Lenya since her radio debut, in one of his works, in 1937. By 1951, Blitzstein believed that the work could attract new admirers if it were performed in a new English version, and at the encouragement of no less an expert than Maurice Abravanel (who had conducted Blitzstein's opera *Regina* in New York in 1949), Blitzstein prepared an entirely fresh English adaptation. On June 14, 1952, with Leonard Bernstein conducting, a concert version of *The Threepenny Opera* was presented at Brandeis University, with Lenya as Jenny. The event was a major moment in the growing revival of interest in Kurt Weill and in *The Threepenny Opera*.

The extant recording, preserved in the archives at Brandeis, reveals Lenya's voice in "Pirate Jenny" as initially tentative, but after the first touch of stage fright there is a gathering force. When she reaches "But the ship, a black freighter . . . ," there is the indication of a major shift in Lenya's voice from the 1930s, and of her ability to turn the almost baritonic stridency of her mature years to her advantage in the role of Jenny the prostitute. Vocal straining for high notes conveys a barely suppressed frenzy of anger and vengeance. On the words "Kill them now or later?" there is a ferocity that is almost manic, and of whose deadly outcome she sounds entirely confident.

In the "Tango-Ballad," her hoarse, dry voice—again weaker at the beginning—is turned to her benefit. Lenya is almost a *diseuse*, often speaking, rasping the words, acting the story of a woman in a doomed and squalid love affair. And in the "Solomon Song," with an electric organ accompaniment, she receives her strongest audience response: where other performers received polite applause, the recording preserves the wild reaction of her hearers at Brandeis that night, laughing at her cynicism, clapping loud and long at her conclusion.

For the moment, however, there were no further plans for Lenya or for *The Threepenny Opera* after the Brandeis concert

version. George and Lenya had, however, a related enterprise
that united them in a common effort and exercised their devotion
to Weill, and it was George's idea: a critical biography of Kurt.
That, after all, would be something in which George could be
actively and directly involved; it was also a way of earning his
keep, since there was no doubt the text would have to be written
by him. From the summer of 1952, at George's encouragement,
Lenya signed letters he typed, requesting information or interviews from former friends and from Kurt's associates, ranging
from Fritz Stiedry to Alan Jay Lerner.

"I am a different person since I have [the book] in mind,"
Lenya wrote from New City to Lys Symonette on September 3,
1953, after a year of preliminary research among letters, papers,
scores and documents at home. "All of a sudden, my life takes
on meaning again. It's been buried so long under just trying to
kill time." And on October 16 she added: "George is of invaluable help. Without him, I wouldn't have dared attempt it. But
so far, so good. . . . I am sitting at the library many hours a
day to collect material."

In spite of several years of hard work, however, the project
never reached a first draft of manuscript. George found the details of Lenya's life far more interesting (and accessible) than
Kurt's, but she wanted the emphasis squarely on him.

But as their work progressed, it became clear to George that
a serious critical biography of Kurt Weill's life would demand
considerable time working with Lenya in German libraries and
music publishers' files. George had no fluency in German, and
a life of Weill was a task for someone with musical training;
Lenya was, therefore, delighted years later when the British
scholar David Drew, already a Weill enthusiast, offered his considerable talents for the task. To him Lenya gave time, attention
and access to an enormous array of materials, and for years
David Drew and Lotte Lenya worked closely on a biography of
Weill which Drew eventually undertook on his own.

The initial efforts the Davises put to the task reestablished
their common commitment, however, and soon, as they freely
admitted to friends, their marriage had taken yet another un-
foreseen turn—for a time at least, they shared the same bed.
This seems to have satisfied Lenya's ego more than George's
desires, however, for in October 1952 and early 1953 he was
back in his dark New York haunts. Hesper Anderson recalled

that one of his forays into the city led to a dreadful assault, after which George was taken to a city hospital ward.

It was a terrible sight, crowded cots lined against walls, elderly indigents in a foul-smelling ward. No one was available to help us find George amid all this. She and I went along rows and rows of patients until finally she saw him in an alcove, his face bandaged. We went to his bedside, and Lenya said, "George, George, I have to get you out of here!" But he turned one swollen eye toward her and said, "No, Lenya, just leave me here with these old guys. This is where I belong."

Next day, Lenya had him transferred to a private hospital room. The situation was summed up by Virgil Thomson: "Lenya took care of everything. She was accustomed to emergencies—and to low-class life."

On another occasion, the Caniffs were summoned to accompany Lenya on a similar hospital duty. "He was so badly beaten," Caniff recalled. "No one ever forgot it, but no one ever spoke about it, either. Life just went on. That kind of thing occurred more and more often in the 1950s as the stress between them deepened."

But this was not, as Lenya knew, a fresh development in George's life. All during his earlier time at Middagh Street, it was the low life of the Bowery that attracted George, and the far west end of Greenwich Village and its grimy piers, and the Brooklyn docks. He was bruised in fights in Sammy's Saloon, tossed out for lewd conduct at the notorious Silver Dollar Bar, and caught in the whoosh of knife-fights at the Bucket of Blood. He once defended his bedtime choice of a particularly untamed and nasty character by shrugging off the objection. "Well, if that's the sort of thing one likes," he said airily, "you must admit it's the best example of its kind."

One of Lenya's methods of dealing with George's wanderlust, however, was not entirely understanding, as Caniff further recalled.

She put him on a very strict budget, a short leash. He was given return train fare and money for lunch at the Automat each day. And he had to take it because he had absolutely no

source of income, and there was no way he could get out of
her clutches in this regard. Just as she resented the violence
in his life, so he began to resent his dependence on her. But
he never turned against her, never rebelled.

The unpleasant intervals were not limited to Brook House,
however. That year Maxwell Anderson had planned to divorce
Mab, whose emotional illness had become appallingly burden-
some to him at the same time as he had fallen in love with
another woman. Neurasthenic, anxious and deeply troubled for
many years, Mab had already attempted suicide several times.
She and Max had each sought solace with lovers—he with a
woman he eventually married, she with a younger man.

The friendship of Lenya and Mab had been an accident of
their husbands' collaboration and affection. Joined by their marriages to famous, successful men and attracted to show business,
both Mab and Lenya drew a large part of their identities from
Max and Kurt. Although she found Mab exasperatingly self-
centered and demanding, Lenya was nevertheless sympathetic,
and she would often listen for hours to Mab's troubled laments.
In any case, her enduring affection for Mab's daughter Hesper
made Lenya a patient neighbor.

Mab's desperate attempt to stitch together the torn pieces of
her life had finally worn her down. On March 21, 1953, when
Mab had not appeared in public for several days—which was
unusual because Max was working in Los Angeles and she
ordinarily required even more companionship during his absence—Lenya and Bunny Caniff went to her house.

"Without stopping," Lenya told Maxwell Anderson's biographer later, "I went straight to the garage, and there she was
in the front seat. She had on a mink coat, and a nightgown."
The gasoline tank had been depleted during the night, but not
until the engine had done its task. Mab Maynard Anderson was
dead at forty-eight.

Lenya at once reached out to comfort Hesper, who always
remembered her strength and her astonishment at Mab's suicide.

I remember her standing at my mother's casket, shaking her
head and saying quietly—it was a reference to my mother's
anger at my father's affair—"You are such a poor sport, Mab,
such a bad sport." Then I learned that my father reburied his

first wife's ashes with my mother's ashes when *she* was buried—thus ending the odyssey of what I always knew as "Margaret's [Max's first wife's] floating ashes." I was shocked at this and said so to Lenya. "Oh well, Hep," she said calmly, "one woman, another woman—what's the difference?"

By late 1953, Bertolt Brecht had finally approved Marc Blitzstein's adaptation of *The Threepenny Opera* (and the terms of Brecht's share in any American production), and the way was now clear for what would be Lenya's greatest theatrical success.

Coincidentally, two young men named Carmen Capalbo and Stanley Chase, who had been story editors and production assistants, had decided to try theatrical producing. They learned that an old Greenwich Village movie theater on Christopher Street was available for rent. Capalbo and Chase leased the Theatre de Lys (as the owner, Bill de Lys, had called it) and first intended to stage Albert Camus's play *State of Siege* with Marlon Brando. When that could not be realized, they heard about Blitzstein's adaptation. A longtime admirer of the music, Capalbo (who would eventually direct it) took Chase to Blitzstein's studio on East 12th Street to meet him, George and Lenya, on an October day in 1953.

"On first meeting, she seemed reticent," Stanley Chase recalled in an interview years later. "She didn't talk very much, but George did. He became a rock, not only for her, but also for the show. He sensed our eagerness and our innocence and our willingness to respond to the material."

Capalbo and Chase told Lenya they wanted to stage *The Threepenny Opera* at the 299-seat Theatre de Lys, using only the eight musicians of Blitzstein's arrangements (Weill's score had been for seven musicians playing twenty-one different instruments). They wanted the intimacy of a European production, like the Schiffbauerdamm original. George responded enthusiastically: having lived in Paris, he heard about the Vieux-Colombier and mentioned it when the Theatre de Lys was suggested. The Vieux-Colombier was a theater opened in 1913 by Jacques Copeau. Objecting to the exaggerated and lavish realism of the plays of his time, he aimed in his productions at extremely simplified stage designs that would still communicate the strength of the classics.

Lenya listened patiently, her appearance making a sharp impression on the young producers. By this time she had, at George's encouragement, dyed her hair redder than ever—a kind of Technicolor red, which contrasted with her pale face and highlighted her slash of red lipstick. The image was almost violent.

Capalbo further told Lenya that only she could play Jenny: she *was* this show, he insisted, and she would give the production its authenticating spirit. "She did not want to play the role of Jenny, however," Chase recalled. "I think she was very insecure about herself at this time."

His partner agreed that she seemed not at all sure about her own place in the Weill work. In addition, she was now fifty-five; in the original, she was not yet thirty when she had played Jenny the whore. "She was also concerned," Capalbo added,

> that no one would want to come all the way down to Greenwich Village to see this little show. And she was worried about being rejected by an audience again [as she had been in *The Firebrand of Florence*]. I knew it was up to George to convince Lenya to approve the production and to star in it. Eventually she said yes—but very reluctantly. "If you want to replace me after rehearsals begin," she said, "that will be fine." She thought she was too old, and she had, so far as I could see, not a drop of confidence in her ability.

To George Davis fell the responsibility of encouraging Lenya, and he became, as David Drew has written,

> the strategist of the so-called "Weill renaissance" of the 1950s. It was he who convinced the ever-sceptical Lenya that her own contribution as singing actress was indispensable; he who coaxed her back to Europe and into recording studios; and he above all who sensed that an international career would enable her to fulfil, in a manner Weill himself had not foreseen and with an efficacy he could hardly have dared hope for, the responsibilities vested in her as sole executrix of the Weill Estate.

As for her hesitation about audiences coming "all the way down to Greenwich Village," that was understandable at the time. The larger legitimate houses of uptown, near Broadway, still offered producers and performers the best chance of success in 1953. But there was the recent example of Tennessee Williams's play *Summer and Smoke*, a failure in its 1948 Broadway staging, but a great success when it was revived in 1952 by producer Theodore Mann and director José Quintero at the Circle in the Square Theatre, at Sheridan Square (about a two-minute walk from the Theatre de Lys). That remarkable production, with Geraldine Page's luminous performance, was effectively responsible for the birth of what became known as "off-Broadway theater" in New York.

"Eighteen hours a day," according to Carmen Capalbo, "we did everything ourselves preparing for the production—bought props, sewed costumes, did publicity." Stanley Chase recalled that they had no office: "We couldn't afford one, [and we had] no phone. Most of the money was raised from a phone booth in Cromwell's drugstore [on Sixth Avenue near Christopher Street]." The producers raised the budget of $8,789, which was, as Capalbo said, "exorbitant for off-Broadway in 1954, where most shows cost a thousand or less. There were twenty-three backers for our show, the highest offering seven hundred fifty dollars, the least one hundred. Mostly they were our friends."

George Davis, meanwhile, continued as the psychological power behind the production. "George and I scoured thrift shops," recalled Victor Carl Guarneri, "and we found props and outfits on the cheap. No one was really confident except George that this was going to be a hit, and because there wasn't much budget we had to count every nickel." There was also another show booked into the Theatre de Lys following the contracted short run of *The Threepenny Opera*. But George ignored that. He carefully orchestrated a massive publicity campaign, Guarneri remembered, placing in the magazines photos and news items about the world of Brecht, Weill and Lenya.

On Tuesday, February 9, 1954, rehearsals began. Two days earlier, Lenya had signed a standard Actors Equity Association contract. According to its terms she was to be paid the usual minimum fee: five dollars a week for the four weeks of rehearsal and twenty-five dollars a week for performances. (This sum was later raised to an unprecedented sixty-five dollars a week, but only if the box office took in more than $6,500.) After the cast paid for meals and transportation to and from the theater, and for photographs and agents' fees, they were practically working for nothing.

But another contract she could not sign. On March 1, Lenya was asked by Blitzstein's agents to agree that his adaptation of *The Threepenny Opera* would be used exclusively for a five-year period in the United States and Canada. Six months later, writing to Leon Kellman at the William Morris Agency (Blitzstein's representative), Lenya explained, "My own instinctive feeling was that I had no right to sign such an agreement, and I have been advised now that I do not have that right." But in the first draft of her reply she had written a sentence she soon deleted: "I had to think carefully what would have been Kurt's own feeling in the matter."

As she approached opening night, Lenya seemed both joyful and nervous. Her energies were acute, and she exhausted her colleagues by insisting on just one more rehearsal of the finale, or one more run-through of a chorus.

At the same time, she never shirked the eternal responsibilities of the Weill estate. Informed about a Paris production scheduled for April 1954, she asked Kellmann to instruct Alfred Schlee at Universal Edition: "Any enlarged orchestration [which the Paris producers had requested] must not constitute a change or distortion of Weill's music." And another battle had just begun with Universal Edition, about the apportionment of royalties from this new production. She also had to cope with legal problems abroad and at home regarding past and projected versions of other Weill works.

The Threepenny Opera opened on March 10, 1954. "Lenya arrived at the theater," Capalbo recalled,

> put on makeup and then left the company of the others who were crowded into that small dressing room upstairs. She paced back and forth in the alley outside. She was terrified to go onstage. She also seemed to me to be in some mysterious way communing with Kurt Weill.

Only George's soothing encouragement, once again, enabled her to take her place on cue.

"I remember seeing her in that production," conductor Julius

Rudel recalled. "There are some few people who have an incredible magnetism. If they stand in a particular place your eye invariably moves toward them even if they're doing nothing while everybody else is going crazy. That was Lenya."

The critics hailed the show, of whose success no one, by opening night, had been confident—except George Davis.

"One of the authentic contemporary masterpieces," wrote Lewis Funke in the *Times*. "A show full of beauty, humor, compassion. . . . Miss Lenya delivers her role with the necessary strength and authority." Brooks Atkinson, writing an extended review ten days later, concurred: "Lotte Lenya helps to tell the story without making a personal incident out of her presence in it—again, the renunciation of showmanship in the interest of the theme and tone of the play." And Jay Harrison, in the *Herald-Tribune*, pointed out a moment in the second act, when

> Lotte Lenya stepped to the front of the stage to sing her air about Pirate Jenny. At that moment the miniature confines of the theater stretched and were replaced by a broad and sweeping arena of genuine sentiment. For that's what art can do, and that's what an artist does.

Virgil Thomson felt that she had made it

> hard to believe that she ever sang those extraordinary songs in anything but English. It is my impression that the authenticity of Blitzstein's translation and of Lenya's singing are the tonic elements in the production.

And of this revival, music critic Alan Rich said years later:

> She was really a personality rather than a singer. We all know that she sang the songs transposed. . . . Very little was known about Kurt Weill in 1954—his musicals had vanished without revival, and to have her presence meant not only the rediscovery of his music but the rediscovery of it through her, an original and historic presence.

Commercially, the show was an instant success. Although it had to close after less than one hundred performances on

May 30 (to allow another scheduled play into the theater), plans were already being formed to revive it the following year. Offers were made to move to Broadway, but the "enlargement" of the show, the upscaling of design and production and the new musical arrangements for a larger orchestra all encouraged Lenya to turn down such offers. When it returned, *The Threepenny Opera* was presented at the Theatre de Lys uninterruptedly for an additional 2,611 performances, until December 7, 1961—by which time its investment of less than $9,000 had realized a gross income of almost three million dollars.

Three songs were given to Lenya for the New York production: "Pirate Jenny" was (as in the Pabst film) taken from Polly and given to her, and she also sang her original number, the "Tango-Ballad," and the restored "Solomon Song."

Before the year was over, MGM Records produced the original cast album, the first off-Broadway show to be so memorialized; twenty thousand copies were sold before year's end. Rereleased years later on compact disc, the studio recording reveals the brash, unsentimental attack to Lenya's songs that must have sounded like a slap in the face of audiences used to polite, musically traditional renditions.

In "Pirate Jenny," for example, it is clear that by 1954 Lenya's voice was frankly harsh—but with more character than ever. When Jenny swears vengeance on all who have abused her, fantasizing the day a pirate ship will come to take her away and destroy the town, she predicts the arrival of "a ship, a black freighter," and suddenly there's a swooping glissando effect on the last word (as later, on "harbor") that italicizes both loneliness and menace. When she draws a verbal picture of a ship "with a skull on its mast," the "skull" is given a deadly hollowness of tone. "Nobody gonna sleep here—tonight," she promises, and the half-singing, half-speaking is so perfect for a character shorn of pity that the merest crack in her voice suggests not so much the age of the singer as the effects on the character of too many brutal years. By the end of "Pirate Jenny," when she sings of the ship that "sails out to sea, and on it is me," the last word is spun out with a thin vibrato, full of a pathetic triumph.

In the "Tango-Ballad," Lenya's tone is quite different. First alternating and then joining stanzas with Scott Merrill (as Mack), she begins brilliantly, straining for the high note: "That was a time, and now it's all gone by," she sings, and the very impossibility of reaching the right tones underscores the bittersweet memories of Jenny's former life with Mack. "But when the day would bring no job to me/He'd curse and say, 'How lazy can you *be*?' "—and Lenya speaks the last three words, as tough and demanding as Mack would have been. At this point one senses that for this singing actress at least there is to be no pretty elaboration, no slick conformity to operetta, nor to a musical idiom inappropriate for the tired plaint of a withering prostitute. Her memories provide no comfort, and her voice cracks with a regret that is half anger, half shame. Remembering "that foul two-by-four where we played house," she introduces a shimmering vibrato (it certainly does not sound like the voice of a woman almost fifty-six years old); on "played house" she applies the right tincture to her voice, a melancholy behind the words. "You stayed in bed," she then chirps to Mack, and points the double meaning with a shift to spoken words, "and don't you smirk!"

Lenya's third song in the revival, the "Solomon Song," is a parody of the conventional terms of wisdom and courage, ideals now lost in the unglamorous Victorian backwaters of *The Threepenny Opera*. She almost spits out the lyrics: "I thought that brains were good—guess not! . . . Is it worth it to be top dog? Guess not!" In Lenya's unself-conscious style—which was of course a carefully calculated, intensely prepared performance— the music of Weill, the narrative of Brecht and the new text by Blitzstein are not simply the terms of an angry invective against hypocrisy and betrayal. In her performances (and the recordings and films that preserve them) we have access to a singular type of artistic movement, in which the interpretation of character disappears, the overt sense of technique vanishes, and we hear and see a woman who has heard and seen everything she describes. Lenya's art is an art of immediacy.

Mary Daniel had visited from West Virginia before rehearsal. "By now you probably know," Lenya wrote to her on March 22, 1954,

> that *The Threepenny Opera* is a big success. I am very happy about it, most happy about Kurt's wonderful notices for his music. I am pushed around from one tv show to the other,

all for publicity. But it is worth it. At the moment I am utterly exhausted, but nobody seems to care and so I go on. I can't write a long letter, dear Mary, this is just to let you know that I love you and think about you and wish you could come here just to see the show. It is quite an experience. . . . I am just on my way out to [Brook House], haven't been there for the last five weeks.

Although she could afford to stay at an apartment hotel, Lenya saved money and instead relied on the generosity of Victor Carl Guarneri, setting up house in a room of his Second Avenue apartment.

But with Lenya's success came an odd twist in her relationship with her husband. The stress that her friends had seen and expressed was aggravated, both by emotional and geographical distance, and by what was happening to them in and out of the public eye.

"She was one thing during the daytime and another at night, onstage," Caniff recalled.

By day she was the purse-keeper, the woman who kept him on a tight budget and preferred that he be with her as a devoted companion. But at night she became the performer that he had virtually molded in his own hands. It was a very strange situation: half the time she was a Mama who saw to it that the line was toed, and then she became at night his creation. And this annoyed her. She had put herself in this apparently irreversible position, and she had to go on with it.

The curious variation on Pygmalion and Galatea was entirely consistent with the backgrounds of each. For all her pleasure at performing, hearing applause and accepting praise, Lenya was still constantly afflicted with stage fright. Admiring audiences, autograph seekers outside the theater, requests for signed photos, public appearances, invitations to fashionable parties—all these were very pleasant indeed. But she may not have escaped the conviction that it had been too easy, that it had all been (and might always be) because she *was* the widow Weill, and because she could take advantage of the important connections that could provide. In addition, she depended on George for the emotional security that came from his attentive professional support and encouragement. She was lonely and angry when he left her for a few days.

Because of this, she continued to exert her control the only way she knew, by a virtual tyranny over George's time and money. "I am nothing but the husband of the widow Weill," George began to complain to Milton Caniff. This financial control was, of course, a self-defeating attempt by Lenya, and it had precisely the opposite effect. When she returned to Brook House in June (after the temporary closing of *The Threepenny Opera*), it was as it had been after *Barefoot in Athens*. Within days, George had left for a time in Manhattan. "He didn't want to spend all that much time at the country house with her now," Guarneri remembered.

He preferred life in New York. Everybody else thought the stream flowing near the house was so beautiful, for example— so peaceful. But George snarled, "That damned thing sounds like a rumbling subway under the house!"

The June journey to New York produced yet another and even more violent result, however. In a tragic recurrence of the pattern that had begun in France, he was again beaten savagely, as Guarneri remembered.

Lenya had a call from a hospital on Welfare Island, and we went there to find George, his jaw wired up, his eyes swollen shut. And the awful and mysterious thing was that he had known the two men who had done this to him.

Next day, Lenya again arranged for him to be transferred, this time to Roosevelt Hospital. She did everything to make him more comfortable and speed his recuperation, both there and at Brook House. "After that beating," Guarneri concluded, "he was depressed for a very long time, even though he continued to do everything for Lenya's career, in New York and in Europe."

"George was the architect of the entire Lenya enterprise in the 1950s," Milton Caniff said in an interview years later (expressing the consensus of all who knew the Davises). "He con-

tacted those who could make a deal for a recording and for
productions, and it was done.''

And in 1955 it was George who had the idea to call acquaintances at Columbia Records, to test the waters of interest for
Lenya to record Kurt Weill's songs. The deal turned out, after a
long and arduous process, to be more exciting than Lenya could
have guessed, however; it was to be a cooperative venture with
Philips Records in Europe, and Lenya was to make a ''new
historic album'' (as the Columbia people were soon calling it)
by recording in Germany.

When George told Lenya, her first reaction was not so enthusiastic, and—thus Caniff—''he had to bulldoze her into going
back to Germany to do those recordings.'' Despite the recent
success, her insecurity about her age and her own value to the
works revived with a vengeance as she imagined how she and
Kurt's music might (or might not) be received in Germany. But
George prevailed, insisting that in addition to the recordings
they would also, in Germany, interview former colleagues and
friends for the still projected biography of Weill.

After a farewell party tendered by Mary Daniel (by now a
frequent visitor to Brook House), the Davises sailed for Germany in April 1955. Margarethe Kaiser, Lenya's former friend
and employer at Grünheide, was now widowed, and she found
them an apartment on Berlin's Paulsbornerstrasse and welcomed
them warmly.

> Our second day in Berlin [George wrote to Mary Daniel], we
> toured the worst of the ruins, which literally sent Lenya to
> bed for days. It was great luck that [the poet W. H.] Auden
> came the second week, and we got out and met new people;
> from there on the progress was erratic but on the whole good.
> However, Lenya was simply unable to keep up; her color was
> gray, her energy down to an alarming point. Finally she ad-
> mitted that she needed to see a doctor, and did; [the] diag-
> nosis, exactly what I have said for years, [is] low blood
> pressure, [and a] slight but debilitating case of anemia.

Lenya described her own reactions for Mary in another letter:

> By now we are used to the rubble, which they clear up reli-
> giously and indefatigably. What a determination to get on top

again! One could admire it, if one would not be afraid that somewhere lurks another Hitler. But you can't seem to find a single Nazi in Germany! Nobody was one! It was all a dream!

In Berlin at the time was a young student of musicology and theater arts named Andreas Meyer-Hanno. One of his professors recommended him to Lenya as a research assistant, and soon Meyer-Hanno, Lenya and George were rummaging for articles on Weill and his music in newspapers and journals in the German State Library. The young man then suggested that, since Brecht lived quite near the library, she meet him. Soon they went to the Dorotheenstrasse, where Brecht and Helene Weigel then lived.

I had never been in Brecht's apartment before [Meyer-Hanno wrote in a memoir later]. It was light and airy, furnished with only a few old, heavy wooden tables and chairs. There were hardly any pictures; the walls were decorated instead with a variety of old household utensils made of zinc and iron. It was all rather impersonal and surprisingly sparse for the home of the most financially successful German author of the day. . . . Brecht's manner was extremely reserved, [but] there was much talk about theater, about *his* theater, and they never basked in memories of their shared past. All conversation centered on the here and now: and finally about tomorrow.

Lenya mentioned that she was preparing for the Philips recording in Hamburg (the ''Berlin Theater Songs'' album), and Brecht immediately offered to assist her. ''Soon after,'' Meyer-Hanno recalled, ''Lenya flew to Hamburg for rehearsals, but returned to East Berlin'' to work on the songs with Brecht.

I showed him the songs [Lenya told a British interviewer in 1980], those I was going to record for Columbia in Hamburg. At that time everything was epic-this and epic-that with him, and all about alienation. And I thought, oh, the hell with all this, I'll just sing it as I always have. Brecht sat and listened, and I stopped and said, ''Maybe this isn't epic enough for you, Brecht—maybe you don't like it?'' And very gently he came over and touched my face and said, "Lenya, darling, whatever you do is epic enough for me."

And then the tough and cynical Brecht, whose warmth and humanity had been so rarely displayed to anyone but his women and children, began to weep. He and Lenya sipped warm milk and were soon talking about the old times, about Aufricht and the Schiffbauerdamm, about the all-night rehearsal before the opening of *The Threepenny Opera*, about the riots at the Leipzig *Mahagonny*. And when Lenya asked permission to record "Surabaya Johnny" on the album of "Berlin Theater Songs" Brecht looked up and whispered, "I have completely forgotten it. Won't you sing it for me?"

There in the dimly lit study, without accompaniment, Lenya sang her favorite torch song, about a young girl and her faithless sailor-sweetheart who deserted her. Brecht nodded his head in rhythm and gently poked the air, as if conducting. "Once again," he said when she finished. "I want to tape it. No one will sing it like this again. I won't ever forget this poem now. You sang it the way I wrote it."

Several days later, George accompanied Lenya on another visit to the Brechts, detailed in a letter he wrote to his friend Irving Drutman.

I went over with her to spend the afternoon with [the Brechts], preceded by a walk around that part of East Berlin. It is a grim and bleak spectacle, not only for the physical desolation but for the terrible blankness on the faces, a blankness worse than any real display of despair (and this comes over me every time I go there). Brecht and Weigel live in a charmingly furnished house overlooking an old French Huguenot cemetery, and we had coffee with them and delicious Viennese cakes made by Weigel in Lenya's honor. Together Brecht and Weigel look like a pair of shrewd and hard-bitten peasants—with at times another atmosphere coming through, of two shady con artists, or a couple that might be running a pawn shop as a blind—and so for me, as you'd guess, overwhelming charm. He has the Stalin Prize, but make no mistake, she's the political power, the schemer, the really dangerous member of the team. Like Mother Goddam she has *survived*, and she wants you to know it. Looks rather like a battered Martha

Graham . . . with a grindingly harsh voice and the grip of a longshoreman. . . . Weigel herself is all will power and painful study, over and over . . . and I think she would be delighted to have you lined up against a wall and shot if you didn't like [her performance in Brecht's *Mother Courage*, then staged in East Berlin]. . . . Needless to say, Madame Lenya doesn't, and isn't in great pains to hide it; and somehow Weigel takes it from her, even to the bitchiest compliment of all from Lenya, "Isn't it amazing, what you've learned." It was Weigel's job to ask Lenya if she would appear with them in Paris at the Theater Festival—they offered her all the songs. But Lenya answered, "It's awfully sweet of you, but I really value my American passport too much for that." And so it goes.

From the gloom of East Berlin, Lenya and George traveled to Düsseldorf where the premiere recording of Weill's *Der Jasager* was being prepared. "And brother, is that a difference," Lenya wrote to Mary about Düsseldorf. "Rich, elegant, arrogant, expensive."

They also saw Düsseldorf's famous "Paris Week," a festival of special events and spectacles. "We thought it would be cheesy and cheap," Lenya added in the same letter to Mary, perhaps referring to the drag and strip shows she and George expected. "But it was extremely beautiful, wonderful costumes and very pretty though naked girls."

Then they went to Wiesbaden, site of an American army base. "We saw more pregnant army wives in one afternoon than we saw in Berlin in six weeks," she told Mary. They returned to Düsseldorf via the Rhine's famous boat-trip, where Lenya imagined the Lorelei singing from the old castles: "I almost started combing my hair, if I had any," she wrote to Mary, referring to her short-cropped and thinning hair. However much she enjoyed the trip through Germany, Lenya was eager to return home: "George loves it here," she wrote to Mary Daniel on May 16, 1955, "and is not as eager to get home as I am. But by [summer], we will have run out of money and that will settle all arguments."

In late May, Lenya went alone to visit her sister in Vienna, while George remained in Berlin to interview Elisabeth Hauptmann for the Weill biography. Brecht's former mistress and co-writer dictated a memoir, on May 27, in which she painstakingly recreated the minutest details of the Weill-Brecht collaboration from 1927 through 1930. This interview, equally painstakingly recorded by Davis and soon transcribed by him, became the basis for the famous autobiographical sketch "That Was a Time!" published over Lenya's name, written by George Davis, and first published in *Theatre Arts* magazine in May 1956.

Lenya, meanwhile, stayed at a hotel near her sister Maria, who was still living in the same apartment building in Penzing. She wanted to bring her sister a gift and decided on a family of small dolls. "You don't know how poor we were when I was young," she had told Tonio Selwart. "My sister and I never had anything of our own—even dolls."

The visit was a healing experience for both women—not because any family history was analyzed, but simply because they had time together to explore Vienna, to share meals, to buy silly hats. "The Gobelins are Flemish," Lenya wrote about the tapestries on a card to George after she and Maria visited the Hofburg. "One just stands there gasping. And those beautiful baroque stoves and chandeliers! After all that destruction in Berlin, this is a relief to be in a singing city."

Several days later, after attending a wine festival, Lenya wrote George her longest letter.

> This is the holiday of First Communion and boys usually get their first wallet. I don't know what the girls are supposed to get (I was never that lucky) [but] they drive in flower-covered cars to the Prater. . . . Last night we drove to [the wine festival] where one drinks the first new wine of the year. The one we went to, one brings one's own food but one buys the wine, and a very streamlined affair it is indeed. It's owned by Toni Karras, he was the one who played the zither in *The Third Man*. . . . We took my late brother's wife along. She needs about three chairs to sit on, but I have always liked her, though she smells now like all fat women do—bad. . . . This afternoon we visited my cousin and my aunt (the one who was a thief in the family [not Sophie, who had taken Lenya to Zurich]). Oh, darling, what a dreadful afternoon. She is paralyzed for six years now, and when we came, she was dying and did not recognize anybody . . . I tell you it was ghastly. She might be dead by now. We went home as soon

as we could and we could hardly eat anything thinking of that old spitting, dying woman. Then we went to the Schönbrunn, and we felt warm and comfortable in the glass house with its tropical heat for the orchids. In the coffee house they played "September Song" with nice German words. Then home to Maria's again. All of a sudden that terrible proletarian smell of the house hit me and my fear of poverty made my heart pound. My sister's little apartment is immaculately clean, but the smell of the house creeps through the door. Tomorrow I go to U.E. [Universal Edition] to see what those sleeping beauties have to say. I just phoned and they are still on vacation. That's Austrians for you.

The visit to Universal Edition only confirmed what Lenya had suspected since Kurt's death: that the details of publication rights and sharing of royalties, that the representation of his German works in America and his American works in Germany were a labyrinthine muddle, the clues to which required the skills of historians, archivists and attorneys. Lenya also devoted days then—and much of her time later—objecting to the licensing of performances that compromised the integrity of Weill's scores. As the vast correspondence grew (matched by the complex legal documentation Lenya filed and which she bequeathed to the Kurt Weill Foundation for Music), so did the problems with European agents, publishers and attorneys—problems that continue many years later.

Lenya was constantly plagued, to the end of her life, by an endless series of legal battles with Brecht's second publisher of *The Threepenny Opera*, Suhrkamp. Her tenacity resulted in an increase of royalties for the Weill estate for that work, from twenty-five to thirty-five percent. There was later, as well, a protracted dispute with Helene Weigel over *The Seven Deadly Sins*, its proper division of royalties and its licensing by dramatic or music publishers. Lenya's personal and professional life was never free of the burden of these responsibilities. For the most part she bore them courageously, although sometimes she became understandably angry. Lenya's impatience, readily comprehensible to anyone who has ever had to cope with such matters, seldom compromised her perseverance and her vigilance.

* * *

On June 22 she and George proceeded to Hamburg for Lenya's scheduled recording session, which featured three songs each from the full-length *Mahagonny* and *Happy End*, one from the *Berlin Requiem* and two from *Der Silbersee*, among others. The rehearsals and recording were held at the Friedrich-Ebert Hall, Hamburg.

It's a cold, gray, North Sea day in Hamburg [George wrote to Mary Daniel on June 23], swallows are swooping around outside our window and Madame is curled up in bed. She is spoiling herself before the big job, to be done in three recording sessions July 5, 6, 7. Tomorrow she begins work with the conductor, and from then on she will be busy, busy, busy—and, may we say it mildly, easier to get along with. . . . This wonderful thing [the recording of the songs] is something [Columbia and Philips] and I have planned for months, kept secret from Lenya until the very last moment.

On July 2 he wrote again to Mary:

Lenya is out rehearsing, and as always when she gets right on top of a job, very much in control, steady, no nonsense, the artist that she is. But boy! leading up to there, jumps, jitters, the vapors, yes, and even a rash (which may have been fish or berries or me). By now, though, she has rehearsed with the assisting singers, she likes the young conductor, and I think is wholly prepared for next week's sessions. And then longs to get the hell on that boat. . . . Our hotel is, well, I guess comfy is the word; cluttered with Victorian bric-a-brac animal vegetable and mineral, and we look out on a lively river where they sail and row and scull and throw sticks to dogs and bread to swans. Me, I lie down and read Agatha Christie. The other night, we were over in the old part of town, like Coney [Island] and Times Square and the Barbary Coast combined, deliciously squalid, and we scampered through what is called the Puffstrasse—street of the brothels—walled off at each end and filled with jostling men and sniggery boys. The ground floors of the brothels were like showcases, the girls bedizened to suit various fancies and leaning out the windows. One yelled to Lenya, "What are you here for—to *criticize*?"

The album of "Berlin Theater Songs" was yet a new triumph for Lenya; heard years later it yields at every cut fresh aspects of her art. The urgency of the "Alabama Song" from *Mahagonny* sounds comic enough—until she overlays "I tell you we must die" with her breathy vibrato, and from there sweeps into the first repetition of "Oh moon of Alabama . . ." From this point there is a growing eagerness, as she demands "the next whiskey bar . . . the next pretty boy . . . the next little dollar."

Just so with Lenya's straining diffidence intermingled with a strange passion, in Brecht's cynical lyrics for "Denn wie man sich bettet, so liegt man" (also from *Mahagonny*). The promise that if someone's to be hurt it won't be she, if someone's to be stepped on, she'll do the stepping, has the subtle plaint, the deft touch on the words "Ein Mensch ist kein Tier!—A human being is not an animal!" that lifts the veil behind Brecht's harsh and dour proclamation. Whereas Weill's music is everywhere appropriate—self-mocking, pliant even to a touch of the lubricious in those strings—it is Lenya's soaring delivery, sometimes strident, sometimes full of yearning, that makes the emotions palpable.

But she smiles, too. The "Bilbao Song" from *Happy End* sounds, in this version, like an emotional photo-album set to music. "Es war das schönste auf der Welt!—It was the most beautiful in the world!" she proclaims of that old Bilbao moon, and we hear her mouth widen in a grin of zany memories. As this irresistible melody continues, the honky-tonk piano seems for a moment almost indistinguishable from Lenya's voice.

"Surabaya Johnny," on the other hand, may well demonstrate the crucial difference between Lotte Lenya and a singer like Marlene Dietrich, who later claimed this was as much her own theme song as "Lilli Marlene." But Lenya's middle-aged voice has a sudden youthful urgency as she rushes—almost hissing—through the crucial words in German (which translate as "You said so much, Johnny—not a word was true, Johnny—you deceived me, Johnny—from the very first moment . . . I hate you so, and you stand there grinning"). And then the tragic self-revelation, half-whispered to herself: ". . . mein Gott, und ich liebe dich so . . . My God, and I love you so!" But by the end, the betrayed woman's recrimination pales. Lenya's voice shakes just for a moment when she complains that Johnny has no heart, for her breathless finale is really for the young woman herself, and the fatal love that drew her and draws her still to the mythic Johnny. Dietrich's live concert renditions, on the other hand, somehow always swaggered a little with self-confidence: in this song, Marlene was almost a scold, and in any case we never *really* believed that Dietrich would not recover from love's wounds.

But Lenya's voice, with its sudden vibrato and equally sudden hoarse speech or whisper, conveyed the possibility of fatal turmoil. In Lenya's artistry these songs are full of recognizable fears and longings. They are little musical narratives sprung free from a particular time by Lenya's attack to Weill's always astonishing musical line, through a voice alternately thin with the pain of aging, or thick with the hope of youth. The plain truth of her style—apparently untheatrical, evidently undaunted—releases her and the songs from the specificity of Weimar Germany. They are, as we listen to them decades later through her voice, musical odes celebrating what Lenya knew so well—the fine art of perseverance.

Eight

Reprise

1955–1957

WHEN LENYA AND GEORGE RETURNED TO AMERICA AT summer's end in 1955, they had never been in better spirits, nor closer. The distance from New York had been good for George, and the new celebrity connected with her devotion to Kurt's music had buoyed Lenya. He was gratified by her gratitude, and she was openly appreciative of his efforts. He had become, in effect, her producer and publicist—the man, as Milton Caniff had said, who made everything work. And in his efforts for *her* fulfillment, he seemed to find something that had been absent from his own life, a sense of mission and purpose very like hers for Kurt. They began to consider one another's preferences and inclinations with a new tolerance, and to compromise their schedules and leisure activities to accommodate one another. As this simple kindness deepened, it became a psychological resource they would soon need to tap.

On September 30, *The Threepenny Opera* reopened at the Theatre de Lys, with Lenya again as Jenny. "We found wonderful new people," she wrote to Mary Daniel in West Virginia, "and it is worthwhile all the effort one makes." The effort was further compensated when Lenya received the Tony award as best supporting actress in a musical from the American Theater Wing on April 1, 1956. (Between 1955 and its closing in 1961, the cast included Valerie Bettis, Grete Mosheim, Dolly Haas, Jerry Orbach, Jane Connell, Pert Kelton, Nancy Andrews, Georgia Brown, Edward Asner, Charlotte Rae, Beatrice Arthur and Estelle Parsons. In all, over seven hundred actors performed in twenty-two roles.) Jerry Tallmer, writing that autumn in the premiere edition of a new neighborhood weekly, the *Village Voice*, added that when Lenya sang "Pirate Jenny,"

> We are face to face against a kind of world and a kind of half-century no one born this side of the water can ever quite fully make, or want to make, his own. Hogarth and Gay, Goya and Lautrec, Koestler, Malraux, Traven, and even such as Remarque and George Grosz—all of it, all of them, and a hundred others, are packed into this one hot hellish instant, with the smoke still rising from the crematories and Bert Brecht's old friend Uncle Joe Stalin just sitting there, waiting, far to the north. . . . In Miss Lenya's hands a great half-truth still gets annealed nightly, after 25 years, into a weapon of blinding strength and beauty.

As the show's success continued, Lenya and George finally decided to rent a Manhattan apartment, at 994 Second Avenue—a small, one-bedroom place they never really considered home, but which would be convenient for Lenya and a social necessity for her husband. "I am so happy for George," she added in the same letter to Mary.

> He seems to have found himself, and the idea of having an apartment in town where he can have people to communicate with (which he needs more than anybody I have ever known, and which he could not find [at Brook House]). Surely we will have our ups and downs, but who hasn't? But at least we know how to cope with it and not get so frantic any more.

The renewed success of *The Threepenny Opera* delighted and exhausted Lenya. "It turned out beautifully, much better than last year," she wrote to Mary just after reopening.

> Four performances over the week-ends knocks the hell out of me, and I can't take it less seriously, otherwise it won't be good. So today was supposed to be my day off, and what did I do? I got up at ten, started washing my dirty clothes, ironed them as I took them off the line, looked at the fall leaves for a while and wished I could stay [at Brook House] a few more days. . . . Today I got the reviews from Berlin where Kurt's

last show [*Der Silbersee*] was given at the Berlin Festival. . . . It is such a tremendous success and the publisher wrote me a letter. . . . I am very happy about it, but tired, too. What a fight that was. I am laughing now, thinking back what I told them and how fresh I was. But the result is what counts and so I can't feel bad about it. Kurt would have giggled, too, if he could have seen me, running from one brass-head to the other to make them see it my way. . . . George is happy in town. . . . It takes a little while until everything settles down to normal. What am I saying—normal! With George, not a chance! . . . Columbia is bringing out a record of me singing the "Moritat" from *The Threepenny Opera*. I had more fun doing it and they all love it and George was sitting there and you should have seen his face! Beaming is not the right word for it. It's strange, Mary, how much confidence he gives me.

In October Lenya heard from Germany the news that her recording of the Weill songs ("Lenya Singt Kurt Weill," released in America as "Lotte Lenya Sings Berlin Theater Songs by Kurt Weill") had become an instant hit. "As a result," she wrote to Mary, "the biggest broadcasting company will devote a full hour to my record. When I went there, sent by Columbia, they didn't know what they were getting (neither did I at that time)."

In addition, she eagerly anticipated an imminent trip to Düsseldorf for the German premiere of *Street Scene* . . . especially since the U.S. Department of State was paying her expenses.

I would have to leave [*The Threepenny Opera*] for a few weeks [she wrote Mary from New City], but it won't hurt much. We have a good cast. . . . What fun to hear *Street Scene* again. If only Kurt would know. He would be so proud. And that George running around and working on so many things at the same time that I get dizzy listening. He really has found a new function in life. . . . [I have] a heavenly vase full of autumn leaves today. They look so beautiful. How much closer to God can one get? And a beautiful blue heron flew over the brook. Nature can make me cry faster than anything. And now I will wash my filthy hair, take a bath, try to get the greasepaint out of my nails and look human again for

tomorrow, when another week of Pirate Jenny will start. . . .
George is in town having dinner with Auden. I am glad. He
needs a little brain nourishment once in a while. He is amaz-
ingly patient in listening to the very repetitious crap about
[*Threepenny Opera*].

The trip to Germany did indeed take them away from the
show for several weeks at year's end, and as she predicted business was not adversely affected. Much as she enjoyed returning
to it at the end of December, it occurred to her that Kurt's reputation would not suffer if she left the cast.

I am even thinking of leaving the show end of March if I can
[she wrote to Mary on January 6, 1956]. And George seems to
feel, too, that by that time I will have done more than my duty,
and if they are not able to run it without me, with all the fabulous
breaks they get through all the recordings and the publicity, then
they don't deserve to have a success like that. I would love to
go then for a week to Mexico and really get a good rest. But
without George. That would be very necessary. . . . To get an
Austrian and a Scotsman [part of George's ancestral back-
ground] together is madness. [But] George is my husband and
I wish to live with him in peace and with no malice around him.
What he is doing for me and Kurt is what I want most. *Threepenny* is selling out ever since I got back. "Moritat" ["Mack
the Knife"] has been recorded by 17 different companies. You
hear it coming out of bars, jukeboxes, taxis, wherever you go.
Kurt would have loved that. A taxidriver whistling his tunes
would have pleased him more than winning the Pulitzer Prize.

Kurt would indeed have been pleased by the appearance of
"Mack the Knife" on the popular music charts. Bobby Darin
had a great hit with it, and Louis Armstrong, at his recording
session, dropped Lenya's name into the list of Mack's victims.
From that time forward, the song is often sung with a mention
of "Miss Lotte Lenya."

The mention of Kurt in her letter reminded Lenya of a recent
dream about him, she added.

He was lying in a sort of bed, and his pillows had slipped
down and I kept piling up his pillows to make him feel more

comfortable and whenever I turned, there he had slipped down again. I woke up in tears and unhappy for days, and yet happy that I had at last seen him alive. Oh, Mary! Try to live a fairly happy life with *that* in your heart, never knowing when it will hit you and how hard.

On August 14, 1956, Lenya and George returned to Hamburg, where she was contracted to record both *The Seven Deadly Sins* and *Rise and Fall of the City of Mahagonny*. Next morning, they learned that just before midnight, Bertolt Brecht had died of a heart attack in East Berlin, at the age of fifty-eight. But any confusion of sentiments was soon obliterated. Two nights later, at three o'clock, George suffered a heart attack. He was fifty years old, exactly Kurt's age at death. A frightened Lenya wrote to Mary on August 27.

It was not a serious [attack], but nevertheless the X-ray next morning showed that his heart was enlarged on one corner. I do not know what that means and how serious it can become. Unfortunately, I had only one experience and everything about the heart frightens me. He is getting ten injections. Had four already and feels real fine. It was kind of frightening at three o'clock in the morning. . . . I really have to keep my head up and not let myself get too depressed. . . . The first shock was the sudden death of Brecht here. And my darling sister in Vienna has some trouble with her abdomen and is in the hospital for a minor operation and check-up for possible cancer danger. I close my eyes and shudder by the very thought that this could happen to that darling girl. I am afraid, dear Mary, this is a rather grim letter. . . .

She added that just before his illness she and George had seen the Pabst film of *The Threepenny Opera*, a print of which was found and shown for the first time in Germany since Hitler.

It was strange to see myself some twenty-five years younger. Very slender, very softspoken. And the audience listened as attentively now as once upon a time. George grabbed my hand and was very moved by the whole thing. I wasn't. I looked at it too critically.

Lenya was not only to record *The Seven Deadly Sins* and *Mahagonny*, she was also permitted creative control over both projects, as well as approval of conductor, singers and the final cuts. Columbia Records, New York, had once again joined with their German affiliate, Philips Phonographische Industrie, to contract Lenya for both Weill-Brecht works. For *Seven Deadly Sins*, she received an advance of $416.75, but the musicians' fees were charged against her royalties, as were studio fees. For *Mahagonny*, she received $1,250.25 advance with the same conditions. Once those advances were made up, she was to receive a royalty of five percent of the list price for each set sold.

Delays in scheduling singers and conductors allowed Lenya time for George, who was told to avoid stress at all cost. She tried to be cheerful, but anxiety for him worsened her anxiety about the recordings. On September 9 she wrote to Mary that George was feeling much better, and that the day before she had finished recording *Seven Deadly Sins*,

> and everybody thinks it's beautiful. I was, as usual, deeply depressed and could not see anything good in what I did— and it needed one night's sleep to make me realize that it really is lovely. It's such a beautiful work and the four singers representing the family are excellent and Miss Lenya does a very moving and sometimes bitter job of getting her sister Anna to understand about the cruelty of this world. So this is done and I feel sort of empty until I get around to *Mahagonny*. . . . I do not like sitting around in strange places . . . I feel homesick. But dear Kurti has given me a job to do and an important one, too, so please shut up, Miss Lenya, and be happy to be a part of something so lovely. George is so comforting in a crisis like the after-effects of a week's recording. He is able to detach himself and float on what he is hearing on the record and is able afterwards to analyze in a few words, like "impeccable taste" and "harsh" and "infinitely moving performance" of mine. It helps to make me believe that it is good, what I did. And you know how severe a critic he can be and must be when it comes to things one wishes to last for a long time. We do want to go for a week to Berlin and then maybe for a week to see my darling sister in Vienna. I just have to see her. And I think George should know my birthplace too. He might understand my madness

sometimes when he sees the house I was born in—and he might then also understand my fear of poverty. And maybe I then eventually will learn, too, that one does not need too much in order to live a useful life.

George appended a handwritten note to Mary at the end of this typewritten letter from Lenya, saying he was

as above-the-battle as it will ever be permitted me in this world. The recording sessions were happy, happy hours from beginning to end. The end result strangely moving and beautiful—a tour de force for Madam, very poetic, very girlish and young. Now a rather rugged time is ahead, with *Mahagonny*. Lenya simply adores the conductor [Wilhelm Brückner-Rüggeberg] and I know he will lead her along with a great sense of security.

Lenya's recording of *The Seven Deadly Sins* is one of the glories of her recording career, as the alternately sparkling, moody, ironically nostalgic Weill score is one of his great achievements. The music had to be transposed downward to meet Lenya's vocal limitations as "Anna" (actually, the two "Annas," as she also speaks the brief responses of the narrator's twin), but the listener to this fervent, bittersweet song cycle can only marvel at Lenya's continuity.

In the prologue, for example, as she sings of her sister and of her family's home in "Lou'siana," the description of homesickness is never maudlin; there seems to be a naughty curl right round Lenya's lips as she swings into the quasi-picaresque account. Her triumphant delivery of the "Pride" section ("Als wir aber ausgestattet waren"), with its iridescent waltz, is a firm counterpoint, as Anna tells her sister to forget her pride and her art and give her cabaret patrons what they want: "Think of our little house in Lou'siana. . . ."

Lenya's voice is in fact always poised for irony in *The Seven Deadly Sins*. "Jetzt geht es vorwärts!—Now we're getting someplace!" is a deliciously parodic moment as the sisters arrive in Hollywood, where all the studios are desperate for new faces; their stardom is sabotaged, however, by Anna II's righteous anger. And the "Lust" section reveals yet another vocal subtlety, as a current of fear intersects her description of the

sister's turning over to her poor boyfriend the money she receives from a rich lover. The conclusion, however, brings all
the text's complexities into focus with one instant of Lenya's
technique'' the final protracted syllable of her ''in Lou'siana-*a-
a-a-a*''—gently spun out until she speaks the final words of the
piece, ''Nicht war, Anna?—Isn't that right, Anna?'' and the last
gentle sigh of response, ''Ja, Anna,'' as affecting as the haunt-
ing, graceful ''Ja, ja'' with which the Marschallin in *Der
Rosenkavalier* leaves the stage and her young lover.

In their separate letters to Mary, both Lenya and George referred to a ''new sense of self'' for the other, and such was
indeed the case. Perhaps never before had each of them extended
so patient and concerned an attitude toward anyone—George
encouraging his wife, doing what he could to smooth daily business by telephone between the Philips office and the recording
studio, Lenya summoning all her energy for rehearsals, for
George's sake as well as Kurt's. She was now rejuvenated by
Berlin in a way she never thought possible, having at last the big
success she had sought in Germany in the 1920s—as an exponent of Kurt's music to be sure, but now known by all as an
American and the wife of an American. And these two Americans were doing for Kurt what Germany, she felt, never had.

On Saturday, November 3, Lenya and her colleagues as-
sembled for the first day's recording session of the complete
Mahagonny, and on November 14 George wrote in triumph to
Mary that the opera had been completely recorded,

> and Lenya held up so marvellously right up to two hours
> before the end—then recovered herself at once. It is like no
> record ever made. I think it is the only experience of which I
> have been a part—so tiny a part in this—[and it] has left me
> in so exalted a state. There is nothing, nothing I would want
> changed—the conductor, the orchestra, the singers, the
> chorus, the technicians—all were inspired, and in the tenor
> who sang Jim Mahoney [Heinz Sauerbaum], Lenya at last
> met her match—a crazy, wild man of genius—and I never
> expected to use genius for a tenor! This is it now, everything
> I dreamed of—and the fulfillment has brought us closer to-
> gether than I ever dared hope. Lenya has slept for two days—
> is now lively and gay and refreshed.

George's enthusiasm was well founded, as a hearing of the recording today confirms. As the prostitute Jenny Smith, Lenya is more confident than ever. Her "Moon of Alabama" is even more urgent this time, beginning with a manic rush on "Oh, show us the way to the next whiskey bar!" and followed by an astonishing shift in the quiet blues tempo, her voice sinuous with the rising beat of one of Weill's most beguiling melodies. With the other operatic voices on the recording (Sauerbaum, Gisela Litz, Peter Markwort, Horst Günter), Lenya's voice is heard with complete differentiation: "Ach, bedenken Sie, Herr Jakob Schmidt!—Oh, think it over," if her prospective client thinks she will accept a mere thirty dollars. Less vocally "appealing" than ever now—if one judges the singing voice by any traditional standard of "beautiful singing"—Lenya's instrument united text and musical line as never before. The tone is harsher than in the "Berlin Theater Songs" album, but there is no need for audio cosmetics: singer and role are one.

This rich, throaty ambiguity is perhaps clearest in the famous "Denn wie man sich bettet, so liegt man—For as you make your bed, so you will lie," in which Lenya has gone beyond the appealingly sassy, brittle casualness of her earlier recording. When she comes to "Ein Mensch ist kein Tier!—A human being is no animal!" this time, she seems to spit the words out. There is a kind of acidic shimmer in her voice, and that voice stings the hearing.

Her "Crane Duet" with Sauerbaum, on the other hand, reveals how she could just as well accommodate herself to the lilting polyphony of one of Weill's most inventive moments. "Sieh jene Kraniche in grossen Bogen!—Look at those cranes, sweeping wide!" she says to her lover, and from there it is one seamless rise, one careful interlocking of voices until Lenya's answer to the final question: How long will the two cranes, like lovers, be together? "Seit kurzem—A short time." And when will they separate? "Bald—Soon." A presage not only of Mahoney's execution, but also of the final destruction of the city, the moment is one of the glories of her recording career, for both music and text are delivered with a ruthless tenderness that perhaps only Lotte Lenya could make credible. George was right to be so elated.

The evening she finished recording, Lenya and George dined with a new friend, Anna Krebs, who worked at the Hamburg office of Philips and with whom they would visit frequently, both in Hamburg and on Krebs's journeys to New City. Then, on December 11, the Davises went to Berlin, and from there they went on to Vienna where they stayed at a hotel and spent Christmas with Lenya's sister. After two weeks in Munich and Frankfurt, they then returned to New York on January 5, 1957.

By this time, letters and telegrams were already exchanged between Columbia and Philips and between Columbia and George, who was moving energetically on negotiations to record *Die Dreigroschenoper* with Lenya later that year. For the next two months, George wrote almost daily to this administrator in New York and to that one in Germany, making many requests through Anna Krebs. He also made detailed lists of technical and artistic requirements, textual and musical cuts as he had discussed them with Lenya, as well as comments about album cover design for all the Weill-Brecht recordings.

By March 17, 1957, Lenya was writing to Mary Daniel that she and George might return to the biography of Kurt that they had been too busy to pursue. "My problem for the moment," she confided to Mary,

> is my weight (130 lbs), just 12 too many and I can't get it down. I have not really tried yet and I sort of dread to go on a diet, so all I can do is let my seams out on my clothes, so they fit. It looks good in the face, that overweight, but the hips, dear Mary! They sure are there!

But her next letter to Mary, dated March 26, had much more serious news.

> George was rushed to the hospital last Thursday morning with a coronary thrombosis. . . . George himself is in good spirit after the first shock had passed. . . . If he pulls through he can live a very useful life. . . . He cannot have any visitors and I spent several hours with him and he is very brave. It's hell for me to find myself once more staring at an oxygen tent and it seems like yesterday that I was watching Kurt. But I am a little better now than I was then. . . . Poor Georgie, nobody really believed him when he complained about his pain. . . . Does one ever do anything right? . . . I have a

good feeling that he will pull through, though it will be a long process.

In May, Mary Daniel arrived to help, and for the next four months she was, as usual, Lenya's maid, housekeeper, cook, secretary and comforter. On July 1, Lenya signed a contract with Columbia Records for a two-record set of "American Theatre Songs of Kurt Weill." She was paid one hundred dollars for each recorded song as advance against a five percent royalty on each set sold. Also in July, George and Lenya were able to plan yet another trip to Germany, to attend a new production of *Die Bürgschaft* in October and, they hoped, for the recording of *Die Dreigroschenoper*. In spite of two heart attacks, George had made sufficient recovery that his physicians were optimistic, and by the end of September the Davises were preparing to depart New York. They had received word that in addition to their other plans for Germany, Lenya was to receive the "Freiheits-glocke"—the Berlin Freedom Bell, a decoration rather like the cultural keys to the city—in recognition of her achievements as a German-American artist. (The presentation was eventually made at a reception in Berlin on November 11. "It all sounds rather silly," George commented in a letter to Lys Symonette, "but it does do one important thing, [it gives] Lenya and with her Kurt's music an official recognition.")

The recognition was timely, bolstering Lenya's confidence and public image in Germany at a time of her ongoing battle over the performance rights to *The Threepenny Opera*. The previous year, for example, she was informed by Elisabeth Hauptmann that a London production of that work had been negotiated, since (it was wrongly claimed) Weill had ceded all rights to the work to Brecht. Lenya flatly denied this, insisted such rights were hers to share, and she defied anyone to produce a Suhrkamp contract with Weill's signature or hers.

They arrived in Berlin on Sunday, September 29, and were met by the Aufrichts, who had returned there after the war, and by Paul Moor, an American music critic and journalist who had been living and working in Europe since 1949, writing for the London *Times* and other periodicals. The Davis apartment—a small one-bedroom apartment in an elevator building—was at 10 Olivärplatz, very near the Aufrichts.

Paul Moor had been invited to hear the first tapes of the newly recorded *Mahagonny* in Hamburg, and then to attend the Berlin Festival and its new production of *Die Bürgschaft* on October 6. (He had met George briefly in 1948 through Moor's agent Elizabeth McKee, when George was teaching at Columbia University.)

George had had cosmetic surgery to restore his face after the various severe beatings [Moor recalled in an interview years later], but the scars had not really healed properly. When I was invited to their apartment, I was not at all sure it was George who opened the door. And his reaction wasn't one of joy. He was apprehensive, as if he felt, "Oh God, what does he know about me?" He gave an edgy response. Only later did I learn that George had an awful lot in his past to be apprehensive about.

After the premiere of *Die Bürgschaft* and because George was feeling unwell, Lenya went alone to Hamburg for discussions with executives there regarding the recording of *The Threepenny Opera* (which was to be recorded in a Berlin studio). George invited Paul Moor to accompany him to a second performance of *Die Bürgschaft*, as Moor remembered.

After the performance, as we were leaving the theater, George sat down in the foyer. "I think I'm having an attack," he said quietly. I asked if he needed medical help, and he said, "No, let's just sit here." He took out nitroglycerin pills and at last felt strong enough to return to his apartment. Next day, he called me and asked me to inquire about a Berlin cardiologist. I found a doctor at the Lazarus Hospital, and I went with him, as his interpreter, because although he was fluent in French he had no German. En route to the doctor, George with elaborate casualness said, "You know, Paul, Kurt Weill died of heart failure at fifty. Lenya flies into a thousand pieces when my heart disease is an issue. There are several things I've not been able to discuss with her. Should I die, Paul, I want to be cremated here in Berlin and my ashes returned to my home in Michigan."

The doctor ordered bed rest, and Paul remained in atten-
dance. On October 17, George wrote to Mary Daniel.

> Here it is, Lenya's birthday [the next day], and she is in Ham-
> burg and I am in Berlin. We were supposed to go together
> last week, but I suppose the trip plus all the emotion around
> [*Die Bürgschaft*] was too much for me. . . . At the dress
> rehearsals she was horrified by some of the cuts that had been
> made, and remains completely against the "optimistic" end-
> ing that was substituted for the original one. There was a wild
> scene—fortunately, I was here in the flat, or I think my heart
> would have stopped once and for all—with Lenya rushing out
> of the theatre, [the conductor] at once telephoning here, a
> meeting with him and Neher [the designer] that night that
> lasted for hours, with the result that many last minute changes
> were made, and *all* to the good. . . . Lenya also had to talk
> to the heads of the [German] radio, and also to the Hamburg
> Opera, where she also was going to try out the acoustics this
> morning . . . and to be photographed for *Time* magazine,
> who have ordered a big story on Lenya here.

A week later, Lenya added her own version of the premiere
in a letter to Mary.

> I saw three rehearsals, was not always too happy with the cuts
> they made, but the production and the cast and choruses could
> not have been better. After we had a few battles about the
> changed ending and meaning, the premiere took place and
> was a tremendous success by critics and audience. You see,
> Mary, all the young audience of Germany today only know
> of [*Threepenny Opera*] and nothing more. Now here they
> learn about a new work. . . . Now my battle with the Ham-
> burg Opera starts. They don't have the right choreographer
> for [*Seven Deadly Sins*], whose premiere has been announced
> for February 18 with me singing the lead. I felt like an ant
> when I was trying out on the huge stage. . . . It's easy to
> sing, but to show it at the same time is not easy and needs an
> imaginative choreographer. But we have been lucky so far
> and so I trust just a little longer that everything will turn out
> right.

In the same letter, Lenya remarked that she and George had spent an evening with David Drew, the English musicologist and critic.

He is thinking of writing a biography of Kurt, and Mary, he is a dream of a guy. Young, witty and extremely clever. . . . He was with me during the rehearsals . . . and a blessing it was to have him with me, so I could rebel musically—not reading a note, as you well know—so he helped out there with his musicologist's brain, and we had fun, too, besides just raising hell.

But on November 16, Lenya's letter to Mary was more somber.

Last Saturday I had to take [George] to the hospital after he went through a terrible week of not being able to sleep and having pains like the ones he had before his last attack. And sure there was one coming again, which was prevented by taking him to the hospital. He had two very bad days with oxygen again and today he was so weak that he could hardly speak. But the Dr. assured me it is not his heart, only a terrible tension which of course hits the weakest part of his body, which is the heart. I was called to the hospital at 6 o'clock in the morning by George in complete hysteria and when I got there he was gray as ashes. He quieted down after I sat at his bed holding his hand, and finally he fell asleep for a little while. Mary, he should not be here going through all the excitement and all the necessary and unavoidable troubles. I can take them if I have to, but he is not strong enough and I cannot make him see that. And also what adds to his tension is the language he does not speak and it must be a strain to try to understand. If I only could pack him up and go home. I am really desperate. I know if he gets out of the hospital, he will not and cannot relax. It is not in his nature. But it might kill him. Margarethe [Kaiser] is with me. She came to visit a friend in Berlin and I am glad she is here now. . . . George lies in an evangelical hospital across the Russian zone. The sisters sing every night with the patients' doors open. Sounds lovely and comforting, though. Maybe we are the poor ones. Well, dear Mary, as my song says, "How you make your bed, you lie in it," etc. Let's bear it together, we heathens. . . . This Austrian of yours seems to have unknown resources. But I would be grateful if I would not have to see a hospital again for some time to come.

Lenya also wrote to Neil Fujita, whose art work at Columbia Records was so important to the commercial success of her albums and whose friendship she prized.

George is in the hospital, terribly depressed and there is so little I can do except hold his hand to reassure him. In the meanwhile I try to keep on working and maybe some good work will come out of that pressure. George will be filled with Presbyterian hymns when he leaves the hospital. That's what the sisters are singing morning, noon and evenings. The food is lousy but in the hymns they seem to have great confidence. I do hope I can give you better news next week, and maybe George will be able to write to you himself.

But her hopes were not realized. Just before six o'clock on the morning of November 25, Paul Moor's telephone rang. "My number had been at George's bedside, and he had asked the staff to telephone me instead of Lenya in case of emergency." After a dreadful night, George had died after a massive heart attack. He was fifty-one years old.

Paul arrived at Lenya's apartment soon after, and years later he recalled what followed.

Margarethe Kaiser was with her, and it was so early that I had awakened them. Lenya asked if I was crazy coming at that hour. When I told her why, she collapsed in uncontrollable sobbing. She was utterly shattered, inconsolable. This was the man who had created her career, had carried forward what had only dimly begun with Kurt. All she could utter were choked cries of grief.

Ernst and Margot Aufricht were summoned, and they arrived within the hour.

She held onto my husband [Margot recalled in an interview many years later] and she was frantic. Ernst said to her, "Lis-

ten, Lenya, I believe that death is not the end—that we will
all meet again.'' And with that she went round to all of us,
crying and repeating almost hysterically, ''Aufricht says I'll
see him again! I'll see him again!''

She then took a photo of George and put it in a prominent
position in the room. It was an icon she never removed until she
left Berlin. ''When the recording of *Threepenny Opera* was
completed in Berlin in January,'' according to Moor, ''she went
over to the photo and addressed it aloud. 'You did it! You got it
done, George!' ''

Moor arranged for the transfer from the hospital to the cre-
matorium, and he brought back the container of George's ashes
several days later. Very quickly, he had become a devoted friend
to Lenya.

''Dearest Virgil,'' Lenya wrote in a reply to a condolence
telegram from Thomson, ''I cherish your affection. I will need
it in the future. I could not come home now. Home has lost its
meaning for me. I know it will get better as time passes, but
that passing time is hell.''

To Neil Fujita's wife, Aiko, Lenya wrote on December 10
that she felt as if she were

swimming under water, and I don't quite dare to lift my head.
But only two weeks have passed without George's gentle,
guiding hand over me. It's living hell right now and I can't
get that big lump out of my throat and still I did a retake of
the Alabama Song from the big *Mahagonny*, which was the
only thing I was deeply unhappy about, and it is now right.
The tape is on the way to Columbia.

But as always her deepest thoughts were saved for a letter to
Mary Daniel, on December 13, 1957.

My dear, dear Mary,

How I wish you could be with me to hold my aching hand,
to tell me that George knew that I loved him dearly in spite
of our quarrels. Why does one always remember the bad
things first and why do I always feel guilty? Why, why? I only
wish they would tell me to stop torturing myself. I have started

working with my actors for the [*Dreigroschenoper*] recording, which will be done between the 11th and the 16th of
January. I must work very hard in order to do a good job.
And I am grateful that I can work and have not too much time
to think. The nights are drowned out by sleeping pills, which
the doctor gave me and still I have those terrible nightmares,
where I am in the hospital, trying desperately to work the
oxygen mask and can't, and poor George looks at me with
big eyes. Oh, Mary, one should think to go through something like that once would be enough. It's lonesome without
him and to work alone without his guiding hand is not easy
and still I must try. This is what he would want me to do
most. . . . Mary dear, I cannot write more today, my back
hurts, my eyes are blurry and it's living hell right now. Let's
see what this bragging Austrian can do with her so often
mentioned courage. Does not look too good to me right now.
Good-bye, my dear Mary. Do write to me. I do need it.

All my love,

LENYA.

Nine

Concealed Weapons

1958–1965

AFTER KURT'S DEATH, HILDE HALPERN RECALLED,

> Lenya couldn't stop talking about him, and so she married
> someone with whom she could do just that. George did so
> much with her for Kurt's music, and that was her consolation
> for the fact that he was not a real marriage partner to her.

Weill had gently haunted Lenya since his death in 1950. Her
concerts and recordings of his music, her public statements and
interviews about him and his place in music history, the unfore-
seen success of *The Threepenny Opera* in Greenwich Village,
her attention to artistic and legal details surrounding his estate
and to the preservation of his music in its integrity—all these
focused her strong will. And George Davis, who gave her life
purpose by forever linking her to the art of Kurt Weill, effectively reinforced her debt to Kurt even as he enabled her to
balance it. The more she emerged on her own and the more her
own talent was refined, so much the more identified was she
with the ghost of Kurt Weill.

Then, while in Germany for work inseparable from Kurt, who
had died of heart disease at fifty, Lenya lost George—to the same
illness, at fifty-one. Now her responsibilities were compounded
once again. She had to continue—for both her lost husbands—
what George had evoked from her on Kurt's behalf.

"The only thing I can do," Lenya wrote from Berlin on January 11, 1958 to Neil Fujita, "is to turn in a hell of a good

Threepenny Opera record, and I am on the way. It is eleven p.m. now, and I just got home from the first recording session at the studio, and I have to start again at nine a.m. tomorrow.''

Five days later, the tapes were complete, and Lenya confided to Paul Moor that she felt a little peace for the first time since George's death. From her work she gathered the strength to endure her grief and her loneliness; and grief and loneliness forced her to work. And so the ebb of loss and the flow of achievement took her through the long winter days and nights in Germany.

Lenya's Jenny on the German *Dreigroschenoper* recording of 1958 is a treasure, and one quite different from the 1954 New York recording of the English Blitzstein adaptation. Her ''Pirate Jenny,'' for example, is much more threatening here. When she predicts the arrival of the pirate vessel that will bombard the town (''Und das Schiff mit acht Segeln . . . wird beschiessen die Stadt—And the ship with eight sails . . . will bombard the town''), it is almost hissed in vengeance on the final syllables. And as she builds to the third and fourth stanzas, her Jenny becomes almost deranged with maniacal glee. The vindicators will ask her which of the townsfolk should they kill: ''Welchen sollen wir töten?''—and there is a lunatic, sadistic veil over her voice. In the earlier version, ''Kill 'em now or later?'' had sounded not nearly so ominous. The rage may indeed also have expressed some of her confused feelings and her rage of grief over George.

Just so her ''Tango-Ballad'' with Macheath (Erich Schellow, on the recording): her voice is thinner now, but more insistent. Her Jenny is more than just a tart, she is a coherent portrait of hardened malevolence. Even in the portion of the ''Survival Song'' (sung by Charlotte Rae in 1954, now sung by Lenya), the reminder that spiritual needs can only be addressed after a hungry man is fed—''Erst kommt das Fressen, dann kommt die Moral''—is practically a shout of defiance. (Lenya's assumption of this song—like her frequent repositioning of Weill compositions from one work to another, her arrogation to herself of a number designed for another character or her request to have a song reorchestrated in a key more congenial for her voice—demonstrated that she exercised considerable leeway in the Weill works when her own performances were involved.)

Lenya's musicianship in this valuable recording demonstrates

not only her surer grasp of every musical and textual nuance
(not surprising by this time), it also demonstrates—when we
recall how soon she did this after George's death—that the act
of singing *Dreigroschenoper* was an act of devotion to him and
Kurt and an act of defiance, too. She would surmount grief by
a straight thrust; her art was again an act of her own will to
endure.

Soon, the young scholar David Drew (who also shared Lenya's commitment to the Weill artistic legacy) would replace
George as a professional ally and an emotional support. Drew
undertook research for the Weill biography and assisted Lenya
in her (ultimately infertile) attempt to compose an autobiography.

Not everything was onerous duty, however. Then and in the
years to come she enjoyed the fame, the social and professional
connections and the prestige of being the widow Weill. She was
indeed a living legend.

But she would also, and again, evoke her survival instinct
from a renewed watchfulness over the Weill interests. Home
from Germany for late winter and early spring, Lenya needed
her survivor's strength for the difficult negotiations over publishing, performing and film rights to *The Threepenny Opera*. On
April 13, 1958, she wrote to Karl Fromm (her attorney in Germany) about what she termed

> the first storms in Universal Edition's skies. It is all very
> mysterious, but the paths of Universal Edition were never
> smooth. . . . U.E. never lifted a finger on behalf of Kurt's
> music, and only through my efforts has this Weill Renais-
> sance occurred. That, of course, they will never admit, and
> they will blame it [the prior lack of European interest in Weill]
> on the Nazi era, during which their hands were tied. That
> seems to be their standard answer. It is also important to
> know that U.E. was totally passive when we had difficulties
> here with the local production of *Threepenny Opera*. . . .

(Lenya appreciated her own efforts, and she often reminded
others of her function as reviver of Weill's fame: "This whole
Weill Renaissance," she wrote Fromm again on September 4,
1959, "came into existence through my tireless work, and I'm

not saying that with arrogance—it's a fact, and even U.E. knows the truth of it. . . . They're old sharks and we have to treat them accordingly.''

Regarding a projected new film version, Lenya had done her homework:

> If it's true [she wrote further to Fromm on April 14, 1958] that the rights of the old contract with Nero Films, and the American distribution rights to it through Warner Brothers (which I believe they had for ten years) expired in 1940, then there is nothing in the way of including American film distribution rights with the new German rights. . . . Billy Wilder would be a first-class director, and it would really be wonderful if you could insist on having me as Jenny, especially in case of an American version. But even for Germany, my name would be of value. Of course I wouldn't make that a condition.

And in a letter of June 8, 1958, to Fromm, after he had spoken with Helene Weigel's representatives, Lenya reiterated that

> if you ask me if Brecht ever received any rights from me to negotiate on my behalf, I can answer with a very clear no. As you know, Brecht without authorization handed over rights to Suhrkamp without Weill's permission, and Weill never signed any contract. Suhrkamp also knows that. As is widely known, Brecht unscrupulously gave away rights he didn't even have. Please insist that such a contract [with Suhrkamp] signed by either Weill or me has to be produced to support his claim that Brecht has the rights. I think you'll have trouble producing such a document. . . . And what happened to the 5,000 German marks paid by [a German film company] to Weigel as an option fee? Did that issue ever come up, or did she simply pocket that money?

("I've had a call from [the agent] Robert Lantz," Lenya wrote later to Fromm, on September 26, 1960,

> that Weigel is making the worst trouble and has a clause in her contract that she has the right that, after the film is completed, to approve its release or not. If I understand this cor-

rectly, the contract says exactly the contrary. I thought we both signed the same contract. I also don't understand how she receives another 27,000 marks for her work on the text. This is totally mysterious to me, and I'd like an explanation.)

Paul Moor, who had been so attentive in Berlin, visited briefly during the spring of 1958, and then Mary Daniel was with her as companion and virtual servant during May and June. Lenya never sulked nor burdened her friends, and if tears came she excused herself and walked in the field behind Brook House.

It seems to me [she wrote to Mary later in the summer] that something in me refuses to think at the moment. I can't and I must not. I must use this time to learn and accept that George is no more. You know how I miss him, how lonesome I feel without him, what he meant in my life. And what happens now with me and around me will help me later on when I am alone again.

In May, the *Mahagonny* recording was reviewed in the American press. "Miss Lenya is a remarkable performer as Jenny," wrote Herbert Kupferberg in the *New York Herald-Tribune* Book Review, "creating with her voice a young prostitute who is sympathetic and yet unreal." And Marc Blitzstein, in the *Saturday Review of Literature*, typed her voice as "a cross between a choir-boy and Duse, [and she] can apparently do anything. . . . She emerges as a singing and acting star of the first rank."

That spring, she accepted an offer from Hayward Recordings and Dover Publications to read forty-two lyrics for an "Invitation to German Poetry," one in a series of literary records. Receiving as full and final payment the sum of five hundred dollars for her efforts, she spent four months preparing and then several days in August recording the poems (which span from the time of the minnesingers to Brecht). There is, for example, particular poignancy in her reading of "Gefunden" ("Found") by Goethe: "Ich ging im Walde/So für mich hin/Und nichts zu suchen,/Das war mein Sinn.—I walked in the forest/So all by myself,/And to search for nothing,/That was my intent." Her clarity and calmness are the keys by which she unlocks the door beyond Goethe's surface gloom and suggests that there is something in her own history that connects with the poet's. (In com-

ments published in the *Saturday Review of Literature* on the
release of the album, Victor Seroff praised Lenya's "perfect
diction, so simple and yet so moving a rendition of the varied
moods of the poems . . . all worth knowing and beautifully
delivered by Lotte Lenya.")

The sensitive readings came naturally to Lenya, who was all
her life an avid reader of poetry. "She had a craving for absorb-
ing the best in literature, the best in music," according to Lys
Symonette,

> and she reached for the highest. She read and reread Dylan
> Thomas, e.e. cummings, James Joyce, Brecht, Goethe,
> [Heinrich] Heine, [Eduard] Mörike. She also loved the [Eu-
> gene] O'Neill biography by the Gelbs, and the novels of Bal-
> zac and Stendahl.

Regarding Brecht, Lenya preferred his poetry to his plays, as
Lys Symonette also remembered. "She said once of his theatrical preachiness, 'Bis der sich wieder ausgekotzt hat,' '' which
might be rendered, "He [Brecht] puked and puked until there
was nothing more to puke!"

Lenya's serious reading did not, however, extend to philosophy or religion, and Lys Symonette also remembered her aver-
sion to psychology and psychiatry.

> Nothing about Freud or his life interested her, and Ernst
> Jones's life of Freud she couldn't get through. Poetry she
> loved, as well as Dostoevsky and Tolstoy. We talked about
> Tolstoy's longing for a simple faith. This was a very big issue
> for Lenya, for she could not believe. And that was one of the
> things that made her dying so difficult. She had no faith—she
> just couldn't believe.

But Lenya also appreciated reading other than first-rate literature and entertainment, as Symonette also recalled:

> She hated the serious newspapers because she found politics
> depressing; in fact after Roosevelt and Kennedy she lost in-
> terest in politics and didn't vote. She felt she'd been through
> enough with the Nazis. But she loved gossip of all kinds,
> political and social, and she was an avid "Jackie-watcher"

[a follower of news items concerning Jacqueline Kennedy Onassis]. Her favorite television program was *Family Feud* [a game show, known for raucous humor and much shouting, in which two families compete for prizes].

But most of her nonperforming time was still consumed with the guardianship of Weill's rights. "New difficulties with Brecht's heirs are approaching," Lenya wrote to Karl Fromm on August 19, 1958:

> in regards to the new recording of *Dreigroschenoper* which I made in January. . . . Apparently it seems that I did not have the right to record the connecting prose passages without permission of the Brecht heirs. However, the texts I used on the record are already on the old record from 1928, and the few newly added lines (since I recorded the full work, not just selections) were taken from the Suhrkamp text. We're dealing here with a minimal number of lines—sometimes only the mention of the title of the coming song. . . . It's simply bad will, and that includes Mr. Suhrkamp too, who plays the role of protector, which he's not.

Her refuge from this continuing concern was the summer visit of David Drew to New City, and he and Lenya began sorting through letters, scores and cartons of memorabilia for his planned biography of Kurt Weill. In September, they went to California to interview friends and colleagues of Weill, and Drew returned to England from New York in October.

That month Lenya learned that George Balanchine, at the New York City Ballet, wanted to stage *The Seven Deadly Sins*, with a translation by W. H. Auden, and with Lenya in her original role as Anna I and dancer Allegra Kent as Anna II. "Isn't that exciting?" Lenya asked Mary Daniel rhetorically in a letter dated October 3. "Life begins to look more cheerful now."

And so it did. Only one matter needed her attention to smooth the path to recovery. "I cannot stay a single night alone in that house [Brook House]," she wrote Mary later that month, a sentiment she often repeated. That autumn she signed a lease on apartment 7-B at 316 East 55th Street. Whenever she spent more than an afternoon in New City, she made sure friends were present. Margarethe Kaiser was a frequent visitor over the next several years, as were Mary Daniel and Anna Krebs, Lys Symonette, Victor Carl Guarneri, and David Drew.

The Seven Deadly Sins opened in repertory at the City Center on December 3, 1958, after first stagings set for Hamburg were canceled because of the so-called Widow Wars. (A New York staging could be arranged in spite of continuing dispute over German productions, however, because American copyright law permitted each joint owner of a work to license production if nothing were changed—a condition Lenya normally demanded in any case.) Among the elements disputed in those ''wars'' were the argument of who would have priority to produce—the Brecht/Weigel Berliner Ensemble or the Berlin State Opera? Which element should receive preferential treatment in the production—the text (as Brecht had insisted) or the music, or each equally?

There was also Weigel's insistence on assigning publication rights of certain works to a new publisher. ''Why,'' Lenya asked Karl Fromm in a letter dated February 3, 1959,

> are the Brecht heirs protesting so vigorously about Universal Edition? All the works with Weill were published with U.E., and Brecht never had anything against U.E. Publishers are all the same, and I see no reason why Weigel hopes for more from [the firm of] Schott. . . .

Lenya received only a total of three hundred dollars for her dozen performances of *The Seven Deadly Sins* with the New York City Ballet (commensurate with the dancers' always modest salaries), but there was handsomer compensation psychologically from critics and audiences. On opening night she was brought back for twenty-one curtain calls, and the next day she read the first critical raves.

''There has never been another singer of Weill's music to match Lenya,'' wrote John Martin in the *New York Times*.

> The quality of her voice, the exquisite purity of her diction, the vividness of her dramatic projection, the grasp of what lies under the line of her words, all unite in a performance of real artistic magnitude.

In the *Herald-Tribune*, Walter Terry agreed. He felt she performed ''with sardonic wit and husky loveliness and gave a

triumphant performance as the practical side of the heroine.''
The anonymous reviewer for *Time* reported that Lenya ''chanted
the English lyrics . . . with the shrugging mock quavers and
smoky, wistful quality that she commands as gracefully as ever.''

But perhaps the most significant personal element was located by Richard Lipsett, who wrote in *The Theatre*, ''Lotte
Lenya has become the revered interpreter of Kurt Weill's music.
But it almost seems as if the music of Kurt Weill is instrumental
in building a shrine in honor of Lotte Lenya.''

That winter she also prepared for a Kurt Weill Evening, held
at Carnegie Hall on February 15, 1959. She offered ten songs
in the first half of the program, and then sang Jenny in a concert
of the original *Dreigroschenoper*—in German, so as not to compete with the English version at the Theatre de Lys, still playing
to full houses.

Commenting on what he called ''the fabulous Lotte Lenya,''
the critic for the *New York Herald-Tribune* noted that,

> singing solo, the lights seemed to dim (they didn't) and a spot
> seemed to single out her image (no such thing happened). A
> great actress, this lady . . . it was Lenya's evening.

When Lenya departed for Germany to work with David Drew
on the critical biography of Weill (from March 2 to April 4) she
was dispatched in a swirl of celebrity publicity. But her return
to Berlin was perhaps precipitous, as she wrote to Mary on
April 18 from Brook House.

> Berlin was sad for me without George. He loved it so much
> and was happy there. I miss him more and more as time goes
> on . . . it is a struggle, no matter how one looks at it. I do
> the best I can and that's all I can do. . . . I wish I could find
> a man, too—the right one. But I am afraid George cannot be
> replaced.

That spring she was back for a few final performances in
Seven Deadly Sins at the City Center, and Margarethe Kaiser
again came to spend a few months with her. And at precisely
that time, she felt she might have found ''the right man.'' He

was, of all people, the remote, enigmatic, deeply philosophical
Dag Hammarskjöld, Secretary-General of the United Nations
and a wise, pragmatic seeker of peace. They had met at a New
York dinner party, where Lenya was impressed as much by his
erudition, his elegance and quiet dignity as she was by his crucial role in world affairs. He was unmarried and handsome, and
she was lonely for male company. With no delay she swung into
action.

She wrote to Hammarskjöld on June 15, inviting him to *Seven
Deadly Sins* and to dine with her and Margarethe afterward.
Hammarskjöld replied three days later, politely refusing and
inviting them instead to the United Nations for a private tour
and a glass of wine—but not until after he returned from a Eu-
ropean journey. When he did, Lenya sent him a first copy of the
German poetry recording and reminded him of his promise.
"Champagne was served and he personally showed us around,"
Lenya wrote to Mary on August 31. Then she got to the heart
of the matter. "I have found out," she added, "that there is no
Mrs. Hammarskjöld. Not a female, anyway. But I like him enormously and hope that I will see him again."

And so she pursued him by extending an invitation to spend
a weekend at Brook House. Apart from whatever personal hesitation Hammarskjöld might have felt there were also serious
international issues demanding his daily attention—the Tibetan
uprising against Chinese rule, the political situation in Cuba,
army revolts in Iraq and civil war in the Belgian Congo. Lenya
did, however, receive an invitation to a dinner party with forty
other guests at his New York townhouse later that year, and
afterward she jotted an impression in a notebook: "Hammarskjöld's trophies from all over the world are over his fireplace—
swords, daggers, hatchets, etc. If you want to talk about
disarmament, let's start with his room."

Hammarskjöld was adamant in preserving a cordial distance
between them despite her frequent letters and cards, her invitations and small gifts. In his replies he always addressed her as
"Mrs. Lenya," and by January 1960 she understood that there
was no hope for any kind of intimacy (much less a romance)
with him.

But with her usual vitality and optimism she began the new
year by rehearsing for another Carnegie Hall evening, held February 7, 1960, for which she was paid one thousand dollars.

(Her adjusted gross income that year, from her own performances, royalties and accrued interest, was $86,000; on it she paid a $20,038 tax.) The highlight was another concert version of the original *Dreigroschenoper*, with Lenya of course as Jenny, and before that she again sang a dozen Weill-Brecht songs—a savage demand for any voice, but especially hard for a woman past sixty who was also a heavy smoker.

"During rehearsals she worked night and day, with a voice coach and alone," recalled Tonio Selwart, who appeared with her that evening. "I was surprised, given her familiarity with the material, how nervous she was, constantly clearing her throat because of stage fright."

That spring she returned to Germany, where that country's premiere of *The Seven Deadly Sins (Die sieben Todsünden)* was at last staged in Frankfurt, on the same bill with the first postwar performances of the original German versions of *The Protagonist* and *The Czar Has His Photograph Taken*. This was Lotte Lenya's first stage appearance in Germany in almost thirty years, and the press took notice.

"The evening concluded with the expected triumph of Lotte Lenya," wrote the anonymous reviewer for the *Frankfurter Rundschau*. "The public premiere in the Frankfurt Opera House could not have received more applause." Other German notices were similar: Lenya was politely praised, but not elaborately, and the impression was that she was indeed very fine, but that it was a German work by the great German poet Brecht. Little was celebrated in the art of Weill.

British critics were there, too, and the reaction of *The Observer* was typical: Lenya was described as

> stridently expostulatory, tenderly poetic, frayed by experience into an infinite bittersweet weariness, [and she] showed us that her star-personality still glitters brightly.

On May 6, she was in Munich, where the postwar revival of Weill's music continued with a Musica Viva concert. After participating in a concert version of the *Mahagonny Songspiel*, Lenya sang six songs (from *Dreigroschenoper*, from *Mahagonny*, *Berlin Requiem* and *Happy End*), and then *The Seven Deadly Sins*.

She remained in Germany until July, recording the songs from

Happy End for Columbia/Philips in Hamburg, where she stayed with Anna Krebs. The thirty-nine-minute recording (again under the baton of Lenya's favorite conductor, Wilhelm Brückner-Rüggeberg) features Lenya's stern renditions of several characters—a decision perfectly consistent with the nature of the songs, according to Weill scholar David Drew, because they "are not essential to the development of the play, nor are they expressions of individual psychology." But they are in any case rousing examples of Lenya's confidence in 1960. The marching fervor of "Der kleine Leutnant des lieben Gottes" is perfectly balanced by the nuances of the "Bilbao Song," while the "Sailor's Tango" is full of a blazing affirmation of life.

Returning to New York, Lenya moved to a one-bedroom, rent-controlled apartment on the sixteenth floor at 404 East 55th Street, superior to her previous place nearby. She now had a fireplace, more closet space and a low monthly rent of $214.95; fifteen years later she was paying only $468.41 when comparable places were leased for much over a thousand dollars. With the help of her friend, art and antique dealer Victor Carl Guarneri, Lenya decorated in her choice of colors and styles—in this case, a red and green Chinese motif interrupted by a Chippendale cabinet, mock tapestries and green velvet upholstered chairs. *Architectural Digest* may not have sent photographers to her door to document the furnishings, but friends always felt comfortable in her immaculately clean and tidy apartment with its unpretentious warmth.

As she was directing the movers and washing new dishes, Lenya was contacted by an agent for José Quintero, who was about to direct his first motion picture—a screen version of Tennessee Williams's novel *The Roman Spring of Mrs. Stone*. Quintero had been contracted by producer Louis de Rochemont, and it was de Rochemont's colleague Lothar Wolff who suggested Lenya for the role of the wicked procuress, Contessa Magda Terribili-Gonzales. (Among others de Rochemont more or less seriously considered were Greer Garson, Lana Turner, Susan Hayward, Claudette Colbert and Barbara Stanwyck.) Lenya obtained a copy of the novel and then listened to Quintero's telephone description of the nicely augmented role she was offered. She promptly accepted.

The Roman Spring of Mrs. Stone concerns the newly widowed Karen Stone (Vivien Leigh, in the film), a fifty-year-old

American actress who settles in Rome and is both frightened and attracted by the cruel machismo of the city's gigolos. She meets the Contessa Magda Terribili-Gonzales, described in the script as "nothing but a female pimp with a stable of handsome boys she sells to the highest bidder." After some hesitation, Karen yields to one of the Contessa's studs, a particularly handsome and singularly abusive gigolo named Paolo (Warren Beatty, hilariously attempting an Italian accent).

The Contessa, however, becomes annoyed with Paolo for neglecting the great financial potential in his relationship with Karen, and she encourages him to ply his trade elsewhere. When the affair ends miserably, Karen turns to a stranger who has been following her for months, a ragged young man of the streets whom she invites to her apartment. (In the final pages of the novel, which Lenya found powerfully moving, Williams used the word "drifting" no less than twenty-three times to describe Karen's state of soul. The word forever entered Lenya's vocabulary, and she would apply it to herself later at her most desperate time.)

The film was made not in Rome (as the producers had hoped) but in London the following winter; Italian authorities—after the bad press following the premiere of Federico Fellini's then controversial film about Roman decadence, *La Dolce Vita*—withdrew their original permission to shoot there. Before she prepared for her first movie in thirty years, however, Lenya flew to California at the end of October, where she appeared in a concert version of *The Threepenny Opera* at Orange County State College, Fullerton.

On November 29, Lenya arrived in London for *The Roman Spring of Mrs. Stone*. From her suite at the Belgravia House Hotel in Halkin Place she was driven daily for rehearsals and filming, which began December 5 at the Elstree Studios. "She doesn't play evil," José Quintero said of Lenya's performance, "she is the essence of it. It becomes the atmosphere she breathes."

Lenya relished the character's nastiness. "I loved doing it," she told an interviewer. "So wicked and stark and old, this Contessa. . . . But she was not all that vicious. She split fifty-fifty with her call-boys. That's not bad for an agent."

Production proceeded smoothly, with the cast working well together and Lenya striking up an immediate friendship with the brooding, sad Vivien Leigh. The film—a depressingly sordid chronicle of human dissolution and corruption—has its most striking moments in Lenya's waspish portrait. When she notices Leigh's barely suppressed interest in Beatty, for example, she remarks to him quietly, "I could see she was a little—well, ha-ha—something—" and she ends the line with a deft little wave of her hand suggesting erotic arousal as something so common she cannot bother to elaborate. And in a classic moment, she adds grim humor to a scene. Trying to obtain the appropriate gigolos for her clients, she says to one overstuffed matron, "Signora, I have an appointment for you this evening at ten o'clock, Café Minerva." She then turns to an aging dissolute: "But, Baron," she says with mock apology and a twisted smile, "for you I need . . . a . . . little . . . bit . . . more time"—a sentence languorously protracted to insinuate the Baron's exotic request.

Gavin Lambert's luxuriantly ill-flavored screenplay was also slightly modified by Lenya with lines descriptive of her own life. "I remember when my first husband died," she says to Beatty. "I retired like Signora Stone. I had to be forced back to life." And later, she admits to Vivien Leigh, "Since I lost my husband, life has not been easy for me, and it's never been more difficult than it is now." The lines alluded severally to Kurt and George, who were never far from her thoughts or conversation even while the script was completed on the set. (In her London day-book, Lenya wrote at March 2: "Birthday, Kurti!" and at April 3, "Kurt + [the sign for death-date].") Both de Rochemont and Quintero were pleased to accommodate her small adjustments to the screenplay.

Neither the producers nor the critics were disappointed when the film was finally released on December 29, 1961, just in time to qualify for Academy Awards. Lenya was nominated soon after as best supporting actress of the year, a prize which the following spring was presented to Rita Moreno for *West Side Story*.

"She haunts and shakes the mind like a portrait by Goya," wrote Alan Dent in London's *Sunday Telegraph*. "Lotte Lenya is so incredibly good she almost steals the picture," commented critic Bryan Buckingham in *News of the World*, and David Robinson, in the *Financial Times*, felt that the role was "played with macabre comedy by the splendid Lotte Lenya, whose sharp and knowing Berlin face has changed little [since *The Three-penny Opera*, 1928]."

American reviews were equally enthusiastic. "The triumph of the film is Lotte Lenya," Arthur Knight wrote in *Saturday Review*, "every word glittering, every line in the insolent old face speaking of stratagems and threats . . . Lotte Lenya can create by herself the image of a vicious, trafficking society." *Time* praised her oddly appealing characterization of "a ludicrous old mascaraed barracuda." And Paul V. Beckley, in the *New York Herald-Tribune*, pointed out "a procuress [of] rapacious gentility, played with savage sureness by Lotte Lenya."

Photography was completed on March 10, 1961, and Lenya departed for Vienna for continuing negotiations with Universal Edition, and to visit her sister. By April 10 she had returned to New York.

On August 15 she was back in London at the Hyde Park Hotel, to work with David Drew on Kurt's biography. Together they attended performances of Weill's works, and they visited Anna Krebs in Hamburg and Margarethe Kaiser in Ammersee. There, on September 17, Lenya learned of the airplane crash in Africa that took the life of Dag Hammarskjöld.

"Not a day has gone by since the accident," she wrote to Andrew Cordier at the United Nations in December,

> that I have not thought of him. This is my daily tribute to this extraordinary, irreplaceable man I had the great fortune to know. This is a clumsy way to express my feelings, but I do hope you will understand.

Lenya returned to her New York apartment at the end of October with a gnawing loneliness and an increasing inability to remain alone at Brook House. In addition, she felt more than ever the sharpness of an emotional void. She needed, she complained to friends, a man in her life. "I am not a woman to live alone," she even told a newspaper reporter. "I am far too dependent on the company of men."

On December 17, she attended a party after the closing of *The Threepenny Opera* at the Theatre de Lys, but this coincided with another premiere for her, and at the same theater. Producer Cheryl Crawford had asked Lenya to appear with Viveca Lindfors, Dane Clark, Anne Jackson and others under Gene Frankel's direction in an evening of poems, songs, scenes and stories by Bertolt Brecht, arranged by George Tabori. *Brecht on Brecht* opened to superb notices on January 3, 1962. (It had been presented as part of the ANTA matinee series for a single performance the previous November 14, but there was such word-of-mouth that it had to be repeated the following Monday for a demanding public. Cheryl Crawford was then encouraged to produce it for a regular run.)

In *Brecht on Brecht*, Lenya read several Brecht poems, sang "Pirate Jenny" and the "Solomon Song" from *The Threepenny Opera* and Dessau's setting of the song from *Mother Courage*. Always especially chilling for audiences was, of course, "Pirate Jenny." But there was also loud applause when she concluded her selection from "On the Burning of Books," Brecht's expression of rage at *not* having his books burnt by Hitler. And in her final selection ("Last Song"), audiences felt it was she as well as Brecht whose great pleasures were "to travel, to sing, to be friendly."

"Lenya always stole the show, and the audiences adored her," according to Lys Symonette, "and she did it apparently without doing anything special." Even her wardrobe was simplicity itself: she wore a plain black jumper and a red blouse. But with a half-sad, half-smiling, vaguely rueful expression and her wistful manner and voice, she conveyed an understanding of basic human emotions without overstatement or hysteria.

The critics were ecstatic. "Miss Lenya's singing of the song of Mother Courage, with the pride of a marcher in the ranks," wrote Howard Taubman in the *New York Times*, "has a grim vitality," and regarding the same number the *Christian Science Monitor* termed Lenya "hard-bitten and fierce, yet not unmaternal: the gamin as a woman . . . using hammerlike monotony as a weapon for assault." In the *Herald-Tribune*, Joseph Morgenstern commented that Lenya sang "her brash, malicious, marvelous songs with her unflagging authority, providing a lesson in how to put an entire theater in your pocket." The unsigned *New Yorker* review called her simply "tremendous. She has only remnants of a voice left, but her fire and delivery are unimpaired [and] her whole body moves in rhythm as she stares at the audience." For Henry Hewes, writing in the *Saturday Review*,

The production's greatest asset is Lotte Lenya [who] . . . appears to have no more acting technique than a girl who gets up to sing at a party. But her capacity for zest in performance is unsurpassed in our theatre. With her songs do not seem chores, but joyous opportunities for rediscovery of wonder and truth.

And "D.H." in *Women's Wear Daily*, felt that Lenya simply sang "with the great understanding that has earned for her a worldwide reputation as the foremost interpreter of Brecht's songs."

Terry Southern, writing a feature on Lenya in *Glamour* later that year, wrote of her as

craggy-faced, throaty-voiced, passionately dedicated. [She] speaks hauntingly and directly to Americans in the sixties [and is] probably the most alive talent in the American theatre today. . . . Only a few artists of recent times—most notably Billie Holiday, Edith Piaf and Judy Garland—have achieved this state, approaching universal faultlessness.

Lenya herself took a characteristically calm approach to the fresh veneration offered to her and Brecht.

This talk about Brecht [she told John Crosby, from the *New York Herald-Tribune*]—it's all so serious and holy. It's as if he were Martin Buber. It strikes me as funny. You know there is no such thing as the Brecht theater. . . . They are always speaking of starting one here—but I don't understand what it is they will start. It had a certain style, but it was no different from classical Japanese or Greek.

For George Tabori, who had arranged the selections, there was

something very *jeune fille* about Lotte. She seems like a sixteen-year-old girl. As an artist, she's tremendous, extraordinary. There is a discipline in Brechtian tone, in Brechtian style. Lotte knows exactly how to do it. Theories are fine, but the proof of the pudding is in the eating.

She was, he felt, "more emotional than Strindberg and O'Neill put together."

Backstage, colleague Viveca Lindfors found Lenya fascinating:

> Whatever she tells you, you pay attention. One day, she said to me, "Don't lose your intensity." Another time she said, "As an actress, you go out and do your best, but remember, it's not *all* important."

And that spring, Lenya spoke to an editor from *The New Yorker* with characteristic bluntness:

> Half the audience understands us, the other half comes because Brecht is this year's playwright to know. . . . Brecht now is like a new toy.

But to the same interviewer she could go deeper:

> To be friendly is harder than to make love. When you say "to be friendly," you cover everything. "To be friendly . . ."

With the publicity surrounding the new show, she was much in demand in theatrical social circles, and acquaintances old and new appeared at her stage door. In early April she received an importunate letter from Max Ernst, who had vanished from her life for almost thirty years. He was residing temporarily in New York, and he begged to see her. Still the same bluntly rebellious Max, he drew a caricature of himself at the bottom of the letter: a young swain, naked and anatomically ready for sex.

Max's raw entreaty may have amused her, but not enough to elicit a response, for by this time Lenya had already met someone who greatly piqued her interest. At a Sunday evening dinner party in the East Village home of W. H. Auden, Lenya was introduced to a popular New York physician who cared for a number of literary and theater folk. His name was David Protetch, and he introduced himself and his friend, a gifted painter named Russell Detwiler. (David Protetch died in 1969 at the age of forty-six. In his honor, W. H. Auden wrote a memorial poem, published in *The New Yorker* of September 15 that year.) Russell seemed to Lenya a handsome, shy man, awkward in elite company. That spring of 1962, Lenya was sixty-three. He was thirty-seven.

Russell Claude Detwiler was born February 7, 1925, in Pennsylvania. He had served in the army during World War II but was stationed near home. Honorably discharged as Private First Class on March 7, 1946, he then studied painting at Philadelphia's Academy of Fine Arts and at the Art Students League, New York. He also took courses in California and Hawaii, and his paintings had found a few notable champions. Vera Stravinsky liked his heavily daubed oil paintings, with their provocatively abstract backgrounds, and contralto Jennie Tourel owned two oils and a watercolor. Through contacts provided by Stravinsky and Tourel he managed to hang several works in New York galleries and to have one-man shows in Florida and Maine.

Russ, as he was known to friends, had been married briefly just after his army discharge, but he and his wife divorced and Detwiler began his travels. By the early 1950s he had lived with a succession of male roommates, and when Lenya met him he was being supported by David Protetch, who was apparently besotted with him. There was, however, a serious problem in the painter's life: he was an alcoholic.

After their meeting at Auden's, Lenya briefly lost contact with Detwiler until Vera Stravinsky reintroduced them at a gallery opening. Shortly thereafter, he appeared at the Theatre de Lys stage door to escort Lenya to a late supper after *Brecht on Brecht*. He was sober, and she saw only his charm, clear and undiluted. He spoke knowledgeably about Berlin in the 1920s, its artistic upheavals, its vitality and its libertinism; and he spoke as well of his own background, his unhappy marriage, his dissatisfaction with a series of lovers he did not love, and his artistic aspirations. Lenya was touched by his sincerity, his unhappiness and his loneliness, and she accepted his invitation to a gallery opening the following weekend. She also accepted a pastel sketch of her he had done from his place in the audience of *Brecht on Brecht*.

By May, a courtship was in progress. Lenya was intensely flattered that a man twenty-seven years younger seemed to have fallen in love with her, for so his manner indicated. He was not merely attentive, he was ardent. But much of the time they were together he also became drunk to insensibility. Lenya—who enjoyed a cocktail but was nothing like an alcoholic—saw his drinking as the result of his unhappiness, a condition that could change if his life were more fulfilled; she did not, however, appreciate that their growing infatuation for each other would not relieve him of his problem—and that indeed the relationship could aggravate it.

Before summer, Lenya told her friend Lys Symonette that she had rejected Russ's marriage proposal. She was unwilling, however, to end the relationship. She invited him to Brook House, where during her two-day break from *Brecht on Brecht* he slept long hours after drinking heavily. Lenya washed clothes and typed letters, content simply to know there was someone in the house, someone to share breakfast coffee and household chores. "She hated to be alone," Gigi Gilpin recalled.

She had developed a real passion for Russ and his work, and she had bought several of his paintings. Frankly, I always thought she was much too young for *him*. He seemed like the old person, she the much younger. I think from the start she knew he was a heavy drinker, but it took a while for her to accept that he was an alcoholic. That didn't make him a very good companion, but as independent as she liked to consider herself, Lenya couldn't be alone at this time of her life. She wasn't married, and that meant alone for her.

Lenya later confided to Gilpin the moment that altered her refusal to marry Russell Detwiler. At the end of May she fell ill with a viral infection that forced her absence from *Brecht on Brecht* for several performances. Bedridden in her 55th Street apartment, she was feverish and depressed. "There was a knock at my door," she told Gigi, "and I had to crawl to open. I thought, 'If it's a man, I'm going to ask him to marry me!' " And there stood Russ, holding a small painting she had liked. "He looked so sweet, so caring, so boyish," she concluded in a helpless tone. And she decided on the spot to marry him.

Milton Coleman, Lenya's accountant, recalled an ancillary logic.

When she first met him, she had no intention of marrying Russell. But she did want to help him, to encourage him. She never threw money around, but she didn't mind helping

younger artists. I said to her, "Lenya, you're single and you're
in the highest tax bracket—I'm not telling you to marry him,
but if you did, do you realize what a tax savings you'd have?"
This made an impression on her.

Lonely and vulnerable, Lenya was soon introducing Detwiler
to all her friends. "We all knew she needed someone around,"
according to Milton Caniff,

> but we were afraid, when we met Russ, that here was another
> coat-holder, another dog-walker. He was very talented, but
> he was a terrible drunk. He was surely no match for Kurt or
> George, although he could be very pleasant and was obvi-
> ously well informed. But when he wasn't sober it was awfully
> difficult, and that was most of the time.

The drinking problem had in fact been of long duration, as Caniff and others soon learned, and it was part of a broadly unpredictable nature.

> He was a strange, eccentric creature [Caniff continued]. When
> he was in the army, he told me he had once had a toothache,
> and that it had made him so angry he got drunk and had all
> his teeth removed so nothing like that would ever happen
> again.

After the show one evening early that summer, Lenya invited
Russ to spend the night at her apartment. But when she got him
into bed (only after several beakers of whiskey) she was horrified to find his genitals covered with sores, the residual effects
of lingering venereal disease. She nursed him patiently and ten-
derly, and she responded completely to his childlike need of
her.

No one, in fact, had ever seemed to need her so much. No
one had seemed so deeply marred and deeply dependent on
her—and this was at the root of Lotte Lenya's attraction to Russell Detwiler. Kurt Weill had never needed Lenya's ministra-
tions, and even George Davis, in spite of his material reliance
on her, made some oblique attempts to assert his independence.
But Russell Detwiler was willingly and completely submissive
to her benevolent care.

"Lenya never understood the physical or psychological aspects of alcoholism," according to Lys Symonette. "She sat with me in the dressing room during *Brecht on Brecht* and said, 'I know he's an alcoholic, but I believe I can help him.' " That she could not never occurred to her.

"I strongly advised her, again and again, against marrying Russ," Victor Carl Guarneri said,

> for the obvious reason that he was a self-destructive gay man, steeped in alcoholism. She was furious with me, called me names, almost threw a lamp. After George's death, she said she had such terrible loneliness. She looked at Russell and thought she saw the security of a home life, someone to have around. And for him it was simple security. She said she was willing to support them both—so that he could paint. But the money she gave him went for liquor, and soon there were bottles stashed in the studio over the garage at Brook House— Scotch in the chimney, vodka in the bottle marked turpentine.

Lenya went to London with *Brecht on Brecht*, arriving on August 24. The opening, on September 11 at the Royal Court Theatre, Sloane Square, was another triumph. "We have Lotte Lenya on the stage, singing, acting, just magically *being*," wrote the critic of the *Daily Mail*. "Her range is breathtaking." And the *Times* reviewer rhapsodized:

> The programme brings back the incomparable Lotte Lenya to the London stage for the first time since the early 1930s; and on those terms it is a triumph . . . after countless performances, she sings with undimmed freshness and passion: every part of her body is bound up in the performance—the weight of emotion transforms her by turns into ravaged cripple and confident young girl; everything about her, the tortured, angular arm gestures and the hoarse, sweet voice, is uniquely her own.

But Russell Detwiler was not to be put off. He arrived in London for opening night and restricted himself to coffee, tea, and lemonade. It was Lenya he wanted, he told her, and he would do anything to prove that. On September 19 she wrote to Victor in New York:

The show is a big success and I am once more in the middle—
the toast of the town, and you know how big London is. Russ
is doing fine, goes to galleries, and all my friends like him
very much. . . . I am doing so much more in the show than
I did in New York, but the audience is nuts about me and I
think that's as it should be. . . . We are staying six weeks at
the Royal Court. . . . You would like the billing I have, pictures and notices of mine all over the place and my name in
lights above the title.

Then, until late October, no one in New York or Rockland
County heard anything from Lenya other than a few cheerfully
vapid postcards. But soon the clippings arrived, just as the wire
services reported the news. On November 2, in the Registry
Office, City of Westminster, Greater London, Russell Detwiler
("artist, 37 years old," read the certificate) married Karoline
Weill-Davis ("actress, 64 years old, otherwise known as Lotte
Lenya"). Her wedding gift to him was a single large cash payment to his ex-wife, representing a final payoff of future alimony
for which he would still otherwise be responsible.

Within days of the ceremony, they departed for Germany;
Lenya was glad the show was a limited run, for she had in mind
a real honeymoon. "When I saw them together after their marriage," said Lys Symonette, whom the Detwilers visited in Düsseldorf, "she was vibrant, she looked wonderful, in great spirits,
younger than ever. And he was sober."

Like Guarneri, many of Lenya's friends were disturbed by
news of the marriage. "She had lost George, she was lonely,
she met this young and needy artist," Neil Fujita reflected years
later.

She had a very keen sense of appreciating talent in people,
and she could be in love with an aspect of that talent, or with
some ability in someone, or even with someone's style or
individuality. She was very enthusiastic about Elvis Presley,
for example, often calling him "fantastic."

But Lys Symonette—who had known Lenya since the first
full rehearsal of *Firebrand of Florence* in 1945—understood an
added complexity in Lenya's decision:

She loved to be married. Like her mother and her sister, Lenya wanted to serve a man and she took punishment as part of it. Weill she could not baby, so he wasn't the perfect mate. But Russell Detwiler was. He needed caring, and she had an incurable need to care for a man.

Symonette is on the mark in understanding that in an important way Lenya had become "like her mother." Johanna Blamauer's patience and long-suffering with her husband had made her a kind of enabler, an unwitting accomplice to his alcoholism and brutality. Now, with Russell Detwiler, Lenya too was becoming a *de facto* supporter of his weakness.

With him, Lenya responded once again to a dependent man—like George Davis—with whom she recreated something of the painful situation of her childhood, in a repeated attempt to reverse and, finally, to change the past. Hating to be alone, she took in Detwiler a tragically inappropriate partner, continuing the pattern according to which she was basically still relating to her father, trying to win love from the alcoholic, emotionally distant man—but, as with Davis, one who would be physically unthreatening.

In Berlin, the Detwilers attended a performance of *Dreigroschenoper* at the Berliner Ensemble. "She seemed to me very edgy about the marriage," according to Paul Moor, who met them in Berlin.

She was very self-conscious and nervous when the Berlin press picked it up. She told me he had been reared by his grandmother, and I thought Lenya had become just that to him. While we visited, Russell wanted all the champagne he could get his hands on.

Moor escorted Lenya to the Berliner Ensemble and next day to business meetings with Helene Weigel. There were still in 1962—and would always be—disputes regarding performances of the Weill-Brecht works in Europe. And as Lotte Lenya and Helene Weigel represented, with equivalent and tenacious loyalty, the artistic and financial interests of their husbands' estates, the so-called War of the Widows continued. Was *The Seven Deadly Sins* a ballet or a work for the theater, and how ought it to be represented? How should the future film rights to *Drei-*

groschenoper be negotiated, and by whom, and with what apportionment of profits? Who would determine translations, publishers, foreign agents, and who would oversee adaptations? Moor remembered one such meeting.

I thought of a science experiment from my school days, a demonstration of what short waves could do. There had been two shortwave electrodes and between them a plastic container of popcorn. The container remained cool but the corn popped. And there I was, a container between those two electrodes. Lenya always referred to Helene Weigel as Anna Pauker, that formidable Communist agitator in postwar Rumania—a hell on wheels, like a Sherman tank. I'll always remember the friction of those meetings. At the law offices, because every new production of *The Threepenny Opera* demanded a new contract, all the old wounds were reopened because a new film version was to be made. So Lenya and Weigel went at it, and the meeting was hot and intense, with Weigel striking a pencil repeatedly on the desk until it flew from her fingers out the window.

The "Widow Wars" progressed unabated and hot, particularly during the period 1957 to 1960, when Weigel tried to negotiate a film contract for *Dreigroschenoper* that would allow the Weill estate only twenty-five percent royalty. By 1959, Lenya had raised that by ten percent (which was more typically the composer's royalty for a collaborated book-musical work), but years later she was still working on the problem of the 1949 Brecht contract with Suhrkamp. If she had not the security of a contract—as was the case—then she had no recourse when the Brecht heirs were making unilateral decisions such as forbidding performances in certain cities. Lenya was usually not consulted in these matters, and she rightly felt that she deserved a voice in creative and commercial decisions. As a matter of principle, too, she properly believed that Weill's importance and his stature would be diminished if she simply capitulated to the demands of the Brecht heirs and accepted their arbitrary arrangements for contracts and payments. She could not, therefore, simply be deferential to Weigel in order to avoid tedious negotiation, and so she always stood up to the actress often referred to as "the Duse of the barricades."

* * *

On November 29, Lenya and Russell returned to New York and Brook House and began to receive friends. Neil Fujita remembered that season clearly.

> I saw them once crossing 57th Street, apparently very much in love. But usually there was a great sadness in being with them, since he was constantly inebriated. Once, at a party Burgess Meredith gave, Russell fell from a deck to the gravel below, stone cold drunk. Lenya said quietly, "He'll be all right, just let him sleep it off."

Before the end of the year, Lenya prepared a will. The terms would be much modified later, as Lenya's loyalties and affections shifted, but in this first testament there is a good indication of her state of heart in 1962. To Detwiler she left her art, antiques, household goods and automobile; to the Caniffs, furs, jewelry, personal effects and books; and to David Drew she bequeathed seven original silhouettes by Lotte Reiniger dating from the 1928 *Dreigroschenoper*, and two Cocteau drawings. She also left $20,000 to her sister, $15,000 to her friend Victor Carl Guarneri, $5,000 each to three of Kurt's grandnephews, and $2,000 to the caretaker of Brook House. From whatever monies were on deposit in Germany, she left 10,000 marks to Margarethe Kaiser and twice that to Anna Krebs.

Finally, she directed that "in preparing my body for burial, no makeup should be used other than lipstick." The appointed executor of this will was her good friend Milton Caniff.

In January 1963, Lenya made a quick visit to Stratford, England, for the British premiere of *Rise and Fall of the City of Mahagonny*. Helene Weigel also attended what turned out to be a stunning musical success and the most important production of the work since the Leipzig premiere in 1930. Kurt Weill's stature as a great twentieth-century composer was becoming clear to larger international audiences, and Lenya, of course, represented his life and his life's work to an increasingly enthusiastic public.

And with that, the "Widow Wars" heightened furiously. The following month, a jealous Helene Weigel—eager to promulgate the myth of Brecht's primacy at the center of any Brecht-Weill collaboration—produced at the Berliner Ensemble a sixty-minute play with incidental music that contained portions of both the *Mahagonny Songspiel* and the complete opera (arranged for a five-piece band), offered as "a little *Mahagonny*." This version David Drew has termed "the most celebrated of those bastard-izations of Weill that owe their existence, and their spurious legitimacy, to the claim that Brecht himself fathered the music in those works where he collaborated with Weill. . . ." Lenya forbade performances of this mutilation elsewhere (she claimed that it contained not one measure of authentic Weill music) and legal files on both sides of the Atlantic grew fatter.

Russell, meanwhile, remained at home—to paint, he said, and to prepare for a scheduled gallery opening that spring. But no work for a show was done. When Lenya returned she found him trembling with alcohol poisoning. "I've married a child," she told Tonio Selwart, "and the result I've brought on myself."

She was, besides everything else, disappointed that his art was not flourishing. Her marriage was not an effort to manipu-late a man's life but rather, she thought, to facilitate his talent. Here was someone she felt she could benefit, and whose gifts she sincerely admired. That failure, as much as any other, hurt her deeply.

In February she was distracted from an accelerating domestic crisis by the offer to come to London to appear in the film *From Russia with Love*, second in a series of James Bond thrillers. In this installment of the adventures of "Agent 007," Bond (Sean Connery) goes to Istanbul in search of a secret Russian decoding machine. There, typically, he meets a lissome young blonde (Daniela Bianchi), an unwitting accomplice of the enemy. In pursuit of Bond are a lunatic killer (Robert Shaw) and a sado-masochistic lesbian assassin named Rose Klebb (Lenya). Bond survives; Klebb does not.

As it happened, Lenya's role in *From Russia with Love* intro-duced her to the widest audience of her career and forever sealed her public image for a new generation as the angular, steely, deadly female. Recruiting the espionage services of Bianchi, Lenya brandishes a stick and simultaneously caresses the blonde's knee, then her shoulder and face. "I have selected you for a most important assignment," she says provocatively. "You are very fortunate to have been chosen for a labor of love, as we say."

In another scene she delivers a fierce wallop, with brass

knuckles, to the gut of the impervious Robert Shaw. "He seems fit," she sighs, as he thus proves his ability to dispatch James Bond. And in the film's most famous sequence, Lenya is disguised as a hotel maid bent on killing Bond by jabbing him with poisoned knives that spring neatly from the tips of her sensible shoes. She does a properly graceful feint-and-parry with Connery, kicking and darting round him like a proficient picador. Her death scene is deliciously overplayed, as required by the cartoonlike tone of the Bond films.

This performance she enjoyed more than anything since the Greenwich Village revival of *The Threepenny Opera*, and into it she threw her considerable energy and all the nervous anxiety she brought from home. The character was written as a two-hundred-fifty-pound bulldozer of a woman. Lenya, at just over one hundred pounds, needed padding, the designers said. But when they presented her with a weighty costume, she objected. "Look," she told the producers, "forget the costume. I will look heavier, walk heavier." She was right. The heaviness is there in her oily malevolence.

"When I do a film that has nothing to do with Kurt Weill, then I am happy," she said at the time. "I am on my own. In a Kurt Weill work I am as nervous as a cat. A burden falls on my shoulders. I feel a crushing responsibility." But in this colorful movie caper, she could spoof everything, even her own worst image. She was delighted.

So were critics and audiences. When the film opened in New York on April 8, 1964, *Newsweek*'s review was typical:

> Lenya plays with thrilling malice [a role that recalls] our high-school principal gone bad, our mother angry at us for misbehaving. . . . She is the nightmare conversion of all that should be comforting, feminine, societal and safe.

By summer 1963 she was back in New York and New City, preparing for a thirty-college tour with *Brecht on Brecht*, undertaken at least partly to escape life with Russ, who could barely stumble through a day of work. The tour began in October, in Boston, and when it drew to a close the following year Lenya wrote to Lys Symonette:

> The Brecht tour through colleges was not as interesting as I
> thought it would be. The students were not as alert as I thought
> they would be. . . . I am also sick and tired of Brecht.

Nevertheless, reviews everywhere—from Princeton and Penn
State to Chicago and Cornell—were splendid, and student news-
papers praised her as much as local journals. The *Chicago Daily
News*, with colorful hyperbole, was fairly representative:

> When she steps into the spotlight she is the greatest lady that
> ever walked the earth, a magnetic, vital force that conquers
> through complete conviction and intensity. Here is pathos,
> defiance, outrage and beauty. Here, as Brecht wanted it, is
> humanity.

Lenya could be unusually generous and patient with students,
and in fact whenever school groups showed any interest in Weill
she hastened to help. When, for example, the German department
of New York University wanted to present a modest concert version of *The Threepenny Opera* for a hundred students in the spring
of 1964, the undergraduates could not afford the seventy-five-dollar
fee for the score and script charged by Tams-Witmark, the theatrical licensing agents. Informed of this, Lenya asked her attorney,
Charles B. Seton, to inform the university that she herself would
pay the fee so the students need not be disappointed.

One of the students who met Lenya when she played at the
Detroit Institute of Arts that November was named Ted Mitchell, and they began a friendship that was remarkable for its
warmth and freedom from constraint, and for the maternal affection he seems to have roused in her. Mitchell thenceforth
enjoyed an avid correspondence with Lenya, and her letters provide important details and comments on the last seventeen years
of her life. They also reveal her concerned and generous attitude
toward a young admirer.

The end of the college tour, in 1964, coincided with an automobile accident she described for Mitchell in a letter dated
June 11.

> A drunken teenager hit my car and I was injured. Back, ribs
> and eye. The beautiful blue of the eye has cleared up by now,
> but my back still hurts and the ribs are stubborn. But in time

everything will be fine again. . . . New York is not a pleasant town to live in right now. Nothing but crowds of people, the traffic is unbearable and thank God I can stay out in the country most of the time.

Her trips to Manhattan with her husband were, however, more frequent in 1964, partly because she hoped that by attending theater or movies Russell would be deterred from drinking. They saw Richard Burton's performance as *Hamlet*, as she wrote Ted Mitchell on July 28:

Quite an experience. He is a completely unorthodox Hamlet, humorous and tragic, with a peasant-like elegance. So very, very different from all the Hamlets I have ever seen. You would have loved it. When we left the theatre, there were thousands of people standing in line, with mounted police around them, just to see Miss [Elizabeth] Taylor and him riding by in their closed limousine.

By year's end she was preparing another Kurt Weill evening for Carnegie Hall, scheduled for January 8, 1965. She arranged a fiercely ambitious program: fourteen songs from Weill's German and American theater pieces, and then a concert version (with ten colleagues) of the original German *Dreigroschenoper*. Her usual stage fright was more acute than ever, and the evening of the concert she suffered a nightmare. She dreamed (she later wrote Ted Mitchell) that no one came to Carnegie Hall except for a group of old ladies sitting in the front row, eating from a picnic basket and talking throughout her performance.

But her fears were, as usual, baseless, and Lenya even managed to overcome her stage fright when the microphone failed at the beginning of the event. "You see?" she cried to the audience with a wide smile when it was repaired. "Alles kommt wieder, die Stimme mit!—Everything comes back, even the voice!"

Just before intermission, Lenya borrowed a handkerchief from the first violinist, wiped her brow and neck and addressed the audience: "Isn't it *hot* in here!"

"It was [hot]," wrote music critic Alan Rich, replying in the *New York Herald-Tribune* next morning, "and it was all her fault."

The incandescent surging vitality of Miss Lenya and of the
music she sang . . . turned the old auditorium into a caul-
dron, a bubbling and seething inferno of theatrical genius. It
was hot, all right, and a sold-out house underwent a scorching
that it will not soon forget. . . . She does not sing this music,
as we usually understand singing; she speaks it to musical
pitches, and in her work there is the deep, throbbing vibrancy
of the full human voice. It seizes her, sets her to dancing and
clawing the air. She is emotion in its elemental and complete
manifestation, and there is no better way to deal with this
music.

Theodore Strongin, writing the same day in the *Times*, agreed:

With no effort at all she kept the audience, the musicians on
stage and everyone in the palm of her hand. Her hair was
dyed bright orange, she was slim, she had a million gestures,
all apt, and she sang in a low, worldly wise voice steeped in
knowing artistry.

And Jerry Tallmer, in the *New York Post*, taking the audience
into account, asked,

Have you ever been where thousands of people begged re-
plenishment from one person and poured down love on that
person in return? [That happened] Friday night with Lotte
Lenya. She is a woman who happens to have been born with
the map of life in her face and voice, and four decades have
been stirred by it. She has lost nothing, except a little breath.
She stands there, head back, hands on hips, the joyous scar
of a mouth slightly grinning in recognition of a disordered
world.

For an encore, Lenya offered "September Song," reaching
out her arms for the audience on the last line ("These precious
days I'll spend with you"). "Nobody missed the implication,"
Alan Rich added in his review, "poignant almost beyond endurance." Lenya had billed the evening, after all, as a "Memorial Tribute" to Kurt Weill.

After that encore the audience demanded even more. "But I

can't!'' Lenya cried, her smile once again causing an uproar in the hall. "The orchestra's gone!"

Later that evening, she and her visitors Anna Krebs and Ted Mitchell drove round Manhattan's streets as Lenya gave a tour of all the places she and George had known together. Russell, she said, was in New City with influenza.

For the rest of the winter, Lenya tried to encourage her husband in his sad efforts to complete a few paintings. He did in fact sell a few that season to buyers outside their social circle, "so a little peace has set in to the house of the Detwilers," as she wrote to Mitchell on January 28.

But more than once, Lenya in fact arranged for friends to purchase Russell's art, as Milton Coleman, her accountant, remembered. "She told me it would build his ego to know a painting had been sold. And so I bought two of the paintings, and Lenya reimbursed me by simply paying additional accounting fees." She also regularly paid for Russell's supplies, and when there were sufficient canvases for an exhibit she telephoned friends, made contacts and did all she could to arrange for publicity and for whatever exposure might help her husband have some success.

"Perhaps she did too much for him," Neil Fujita commented years later. "Whereas he should have gone out to set up his own shows in galleries, she made the contacts for him. She very much wanted the marriage to work, and to make his career work for him."

Some days Detwiler was sober enough to work four or five hours, and when he did the result was creditable. His art, which hangs in private collections and at the Weill-Lenya Research Center in New York, reveals an eye for the telling detail and a strong sense of color. But his alcoholism prevented anything close to the full flowering of his talent. When he received offers for commissions or inquiries about prices, he let Lenya reply for him. "He just does not write letters," she confided to Mitchell on April 19. "He is just lazy, that's all."

At the same time, friends were urging Lenya to relax a bit, to indulge herself with some new clothes and luggage for an imminent European trip. But her rigid economizing had become downright stinginess by this time, with herself most of all. "She was most comfortable," Milton Caniff remembered, "being entertained, having supper at Sardi's, and not spending any money.''

In the 1960s and 1970s, Lenya quite regularly asked friends to shop for long lists of groceries when they came to visit, and she never offered to repay them—not even Lys Symonette, who tirelessly and without compensation assisted Lenya with mountains of correspondence as well as with translation details, preparation of performing editions and musical editing and transposing for concerts. "It was as if being with her was considered repayment enough," Symonette recalled, "and she became more and more like this as she got older."

Paul Moor remembered a particularly poignant moment some time later, when Margarethe Kaiser was at Brook House.

Margarethe was elderly and a little confused, and without asking Lenya she took some of Lenya's old, unused clothes from a closet and asked a handyman to pack them up and send them to the poor in Germany. When Lenya learned of it, she was furious. Reverting to early behavior, she was terrified that she would have no clothes at all if anything were given away. And on the spot Lenya ended a friendship of half a century.

Yet at the same time, if Russell Detwiler were involved, nothing was too much trouble or too expensive for Lenya. As Milton Coleman recalled:

She was very happy driving a Ford for years. She loved them, because she could drive and drive and drive and it wasn't expensive. But Russell talked her into a Jaguar. ''You're Lotte Lenya,'' he said, ''you should be driving a Jaguar.'' But he cracked it up again and again, when he was drunk, and it was always in the shop.

The trip for which friends urged her to shop was for her appearance in Brecht's play *Mother Courage*, to be performed in Recklinghausen, Germany, that summer. "I am looking forward to playing that old bag Mother Courage," she wrote to Ted Mitchell on April 19. "It's a chance for a change." It was also a chance to see if foreign travel would keep her husband sober. And it was her opportunity to perform the role that was indelibly associated with Helene Weigel.

In late May they arrived for rehearsals. Recklinghausen, in the Ruhr district, is a working-class city known for a socialist-oriented theater with a vast auditorium. Productions in this auditorium routinely employ a prompter, conveniently housed in the traditional box downstage center. "But the prompter was giving Lenya virtually every line," Lys Symonette recalled, "and Lenya found this unnerving. Finally she went up to the prompter in front of the entire cast and said in Viennese German, 'Listen, I'll gladly pay you a hundred marks if you'll keep this shit to yourself!' " The reaction of her colleagues and of bystanders was a burst of appreciative laughter.

While she rehearsed all morning, Russ kept to their rooms at the Hotel Engelsburg, where he was drunk every day before noon. Lys Symonette remembers going to the room one morning at ten o'clock and sensing a pervasive aroma of gin. During her rehearsal break that day, Lenya returned to the hotel, and they bundled him into a wheelchair, took a taxi to the train station, and sent him off to Anna Krebs, who had offered to care for him and remove the burden from Lenya while she opened the play. But Krebs could not cope either, and finally he was put on a plane for New York before Lenya was finished with the run of *Mother Courage*.

The play opened June 12, and Lenya played every performance through July 25. One of Brecht's great works, it combines strikingly strident poetic diction with a profound humanitarian message, all delivered with the bittersweet emotional restraint characteristic of Brecht's best plays.

A chronicle set during the Thirty Years War, it centers on the journeys of Mother Courage, whose living depends on following the wandering army and selling trifles to the soldiers. She is a woman of earthy strength (Brecht always insisted he wanted Mae West for the role, and once, in America, he hoped Lenya would appear in a New York revival), but she pays dearly for her economic dependence on militarism. Her three children are destroyed by war, and at the end Mother Courage is left alone, still following the infantry. The play postulates that even a simple soul like her is partly responsible for war's horror: she contributes to it by depending on business dealings with the army.

She is the worst casualty of all, for she learns nothing from her tragedy.

Lenya's reviews were cool. She was generally regarded as miscast and not up to the challenge of the role, but the prevailing tone of critical comment was that she was no match for Helene Weigel or Therese Giehse, who had been widely hailed in the role before 1965. In addition, it is hard to avoid the impression that the German press really resented Lenya because, quite simply, she had left Germany; had she remained a dutiful citizen, an attentive Berliner who had not lost touch with Germany—at whatever price—she might have been a better actress. Several critics, in a curious complaint, mentioned that Lenya's German had become heavily tinged with a Viennese-American accent.

"Lotte Lenya does not correspond to the usual idea of Mother Courage," wrote the critic of the *Düsseldorfer Nachrichten*.

> Of course she can sing, and to the songs she gives herself entirely, letting stage and theater disappear. But she's no Mother Courage. . . . Her voice lacks variations and shading . . . and her tone is always a little hesitant, her gestures oddly monotonous.

"In choosing her for the role," commented the reporter for the *Frankfurter Rundschau*, "sentiment was clearly in the foreground. But her performance reinforces the usual misperceptions of the role."

Critic Albert Schulze Vellinghausen was bluntest of all: "She's no actress. In normal prose, her voice is that of a singer who suddenly has to speak softly. Helene Weigel, Therese Giehse and Ursula von Reibnitz are far above her in their ability to convey the text."

Typical of the few gentler notices was that of Wilhelm Unger, in the *Kölner Stadtanzeiger*, who first said that casting her in the role was an "experiment that went wrong," and that "Lenya has much less stage experience than her colleagues." But then he softened:

> She did her work in an admirable way and did not step out of character in the songs, when she could have revealed herself as Lotte Lenya, the star. She was obviously moved to be celebrated again in the German theater.

But Lenya's performance, preserved on tape, is in many ways enormously complex, subtle and rewarding—German opinions to the contrary notwithstanding. Her Mother Courage is a feisty survivor with wit and grit, but she is also a woman with a deep capacity for pain. Lenya etched a credible portrait here, as when Mother Courage's dead son is carried on and she is challenged to identify him as war's victim. She strolls up to the dead boy— it is almost a saunter—gazes down unblinkingly at the body, and shakes her head. They must be mistaken. The transporters depart and Lenya, seated, then effects a faint—all the more poignant because unexpected, all the more affecting because underplayed.

A similar moment, when another child's body is returned to her, captures the character's richness perfectly. She approaches the shroud-covered remains, lifts the covering, and then, as she sees what she had feared, hides her own head under the shroud for just a moment, as if to cancel the effects of the girl's death by identifying herself with it, or even by substituting herself.

Lenya's Mother Courage is more than a woman of blind self-determination and of a steely confidence finally undone. Her portrait is a treasure, from the first scene, when she seems to have an almost adolescent optimism and energy, to the last, when the burdens of war and death have overwhelmed her and she is left to go on alone, dragging her cart and still following the troops.

But more than any critical reaction, the response of Lenya's sister Maria touched her most of all. Maria had come from Vienna for opening night, and in Lenya's dressing room afterward she bowed and kissed Lenya's hand, thanking Lenya not only for the play but also for the money she had sent. "Lenya became tense and uneasy as her sister repeatedly kissed her hand, like a servant," according to Hilde Halpern, who was present. "They could both barely refrain from crying, it was such an emotional moment. Later I asked her if she had got over that evening, and she said she was still working on it."

On July 26, Lenya arrived in Cologne, and on the thirtieth and thirty-first she sang five Weill-Brecht songs at a summer festival held in a 7,000-seat sports hall. "I wish you could have been there and heard the applause," she wrote to Ted Mitchell. "I could not leave the stage. Thank God I had only music to five songs—which I had to repeat—otherwise I would still be singing there.''

By the end of August, Lenya had returned to Brook House and to a humbled but unchanged husband. Mary Daniel arrived to provide the usual practical help and emotional solace. ''She loves to cook and take care of us,'' Lenya wrote Ted Mitchell. ''And I don't especially care for cooking; but I love to eat.'' (Albert Samuelson, a friend of both Victor Carl Guarneri and Lenya, recalled that the only time Lenya or anyone else ate well at Brook House was when Mary Daniel or Anna Krebs was there. Otherwise, Lenya boiled some frankfurters and potatoes. ''She couldn't be bothered with anything else.'')

That autumn, after Mary's departure, was a tense and painful time. Burgess Meredith visited, only to find Russell unable to emerge from his room, unable to be roused from a drunken stupor.

Lenya was humiliated and angry, and she had a hard time suppressing it—which she did only because Fritz Loewe [Alan Jay Lerner's collaborator-composer on, among other works, *My Fair Lady*] had accompanied me on the visit. It was a most embarrassing time. We were hard put to do anything to make her feel better. I always wondered what a man like that was doing in her life, but perhaps he supplied something for her.

Ted Mitchell wrote to ask about Russell's health that autumn. She replied simply, ''Russ went to the hospital on Monday [September 13, 1965] to get a complete checkup to find out what the cause is for his fainting spells, which have increased so rapidly.'' But in a letter to Lys Symonette the previous evening, she admitted that she already knew the cause perfectly well: Russell had had an alcoholic convulsion, caused (as she wrote) ''by his excessive drinking over many years.'' She also knew he needed psychiatric treatment, ''a dreadful thought. . . . It will be a long process, I am afraid, but [it] must be done. One just can't let him die. He is too good a human being not to help him. . . . I want to see him through what will be a difficult period.''

A month later she wrote to Lys:

I hope I never again have to go through a time like this. . . .
He needs all the care one can give him and he cannot be left
alone. It will take many months before he can stand on his
own two feet again.

"It was all so sad, really," according to Lys Symonette, "for
Russell was really a decent, sweet, talented man underneath all
that illness. Lenya had to cope with his alcoholic seizures, his
falls, his injuries—he even had a seizure once while he was
driving—and finally even she had to admit she reached a limit."
Lenya's compassion, her tenacity and her perseverance impressed even those friends who thought her patience was not
entirely helpful to her husband.

Released from the hospital, Russell was soon stealing money
from Lenya's purse and accusing houseguests of filching—
friends like Victor Carl Guarneri, Albert Samuelson or Mary
Daniel. More than once that season, Victor was summoned by
Lenya to rush to Brook House to tidy up after Russell had fallen
and cut himself badly. Not long after that, he seriously damaged
the new Jaguar he had forced Lenya to buy.

Ten

"What Would
You Do?"

1966–1969

ON JANUARY 19, 1966, LENYA WROTE TO LYS SYMO-
nette:

> Russ is not doing too well. Drinks again, has quit his doctor
> and does exactly as he did before he got so ill. It's a vicious
> circle. I just have to sit it out. I cannot do much more. He might
> collapse again and that would be the time to put him in a san-
> atorium. He would not go without a preceding disaster. Some
> outlook—I hope that's not all the new year has to offer me.

The new year, on the contrary, would offer her much more
than undiluted hardship, and very soon. By May she was preparing to sing and comment for a German television documentary. "Kurt Weill songs and a narration," as she had written to
Ted Mitchell in March.

> It's lots of work and I need all the little time I have right now
> to prepare it. For me it is always like starting from scratch. I
> forget the lyrics from one time to the next. It's unbelievable
> but it is the truth. I never forget the music, but the lyrics fly
> right out of my head.

Lenya sang, among other songs, "Pirate Jenny" on the television special. "Although her voice was going and she couldn't

read music,'' said Gershon Kingsley, Lenya's musical director for the film, "her personality communicated the songs. Her husky vibrato became the standard for Weill's songs. But she was very nervous: she didn't like the way she was singing during the filming.''

The anxiety is sometimes apparent, watching the show years later; her rendition of "Surabaya Johnny," for example, had little of the immediacy of a continuous concert, or of the controlled intensity of her recordings.

With the spring thaw came the professional event of the decade for Lotte Lenya, the project that brought her the most happiness and was arguably the greatest stage success of her life.

Harold Prince had been producer and/or director of a number of Broadway musicals up to 1966—most notably *The Pajama Game, Damn Yankees, West Side Story, Fiorello!, A Funny Thing Happened on the Way to the Forum, She Loves Me, Fiddler on the Roof* and, in 1965, *Flora, the Red Menace* (which marked the Broadway debut of Liza Minnelli). Both Prince and Joe Masteroff, who had written the book for *She Loves Me*, had for several years admired Christopher Isherwood's *Berlin Stories*, a lightly veiled fictionalization of his time in Germany on the eve of the Third Reich. They had also seen John van Druten's 1951 Broadway adaptation, *I Am a Camera*, and now they discussed a new version of the Isherwood stories, to be produced as a serious musical. And because Prince had so enjoyed collaborating with composer John Kander and lyricist Fred Ebb on *Flora, the Red Menace*, he and Joe Masteroff turned to them to complete a creative quartet.

In the Isherwood stories was a woman named Schneider, who managed a Berlin boarding house. "We never thought of anyone but Lenya for Fraülein Schneider," Joe Masteroff recalled in an interview years later, "and had she chosen not to play the role it would have been a great blow. Both Lenya's role and that of Jack Gilford [as the grocer Schultz] were written with the expectation that they would do them." They were the first two actors considered for what would be the great success *Cabaret*.

"I had Lenya and the sound of her voice in my head the entire time I was composing," recalled John Kander. When her songs were completed, a meeting was held with Prince, Masteroff,

Kander and Ebb and Helen Harvey of the William Morris Agency, who as agent would negotiate Lenya's contract.

"Well, Lenya, do you want to do it?" Prince asked quite directly after she heard the music—and just as directly Lenya replied, "Of course I do it!" Terms had not even been discussed, and Harvey interrupted, "Lenya, don't be so quick!"

"But she was such a straightforward person," Prince remembered, "and if you ever convoluted your questions or answers or indulged in any kind of nonsense, you'd be in deep trouble with her." She had said yes, and the matter was settled.

"A moment later," Fred Ebb added, "when we decided to have coffee, Lenya just took over making the coffee. 'This is a woman's job,' she said, and there was no argument about it."

After four years of marriage to Russell Detwiler, Lenya perhaps realized that she could not, after all, change him, could not cure him, could not make their marriage a success. So without even asking her salary, and in spite of her fears at the prospect of undertaking all the demands accompanying Broadway performances, she agreed. Acting, singing and dancing in a new musical at her age would be a major and risky enterprise, but this was her opportunity to demonstrate that she could still summon energies, still succeed at projects, still gratify an audience. Quite simply, she may have felt that she needed to succeed at something. This was a chance not only to please others, then, but to see her own talent at work. If George Davis was right, this would once again allow her gifts to have a healing power in her life. Her performance, in other words, would be a way to achieve the orderliness in art which she could not realize in life. "Of course I do it!"

No one, as the cast was assembled and rehearsals began, was more cooperative than Lenya, and few knew how delighted she was to be temporarily sprung from a private life that was dangerous and violent.

"She was so unlike many other players," according to Fred Ebb,

> those who ask for rewrites of lyrics one on top of another. She requested only one change in a line of one song, as a favor to rescue her embarrassment. She came to me one day very shyly. There was a line in "So What?" that referred to her character's abundant bosom. She whispered to me, "Dar-

ling, look!'' and she opened her blouse. "I can't sing about 'the abundance of me.' *What* abundance? Please, dear, to rewrite the verse, yes?" She hated to ask it but she felt she had to, and she was right. So I changed "the abundance of me" to "the uncorseted me," and she was thrilled and grateful.

Harold Prince recalled the astonishing first run-through of Lenya's "Pineapple Song" which captivated everyone in the production as it would the audiences. "Seeing this apparently fragile woman, at sixty-eight, was amazing," he recalled.

At the end of the first act, when she danced with Jack Gilford and the sailors, she said it was the most fun she'd had in years, and it certainly was that for the people in the theater. *From Russia with Love* and *Cabaret* came along, I think, at a moment in her life when she could easily have been forgotten, consigned to the status of a long-ago legend, emblematic as she was of a certain past period. Suddenly she was alive, on movie screens and on stage with us. Artists deserve that—to be rediscovered late in life by a young and appreciative generation, and not just become part of literature and legend. It was hard for her to spend so many years walking around on this earth representing a period, representing Weill and Brecht, always and forever. What sort of lunacy is that? She had a wider range, as her films showed and as *Cabaret* showed.

As summer rehearsals continued, Prince found Lenya the most agreeable player.

You never had to be diplomatic or fancy-talking with her, and as a director I never had to soften any comments. In fact if you weren't straight with her you got in trouble. She was exceedingly receptive to my notes, which I gave her as I gave other members of the cast. She was impatient only with herself, when she went wrong. I had been told she was difficult to work with, and that we should beware. Such warnings are usually unfounded, and the one you're warned against turns out to be the best person to work with. So it was with Lenya.

John Kander agreed.

During rehearsals she was terrifically cooperative, great fun and very encouraging to everyone. Any suggestions she had about the details of authenticity for Berlin 1930 were made just as suggestions, with no trace of a Grande Dame attitude at all. She loved preparing the show and she loved being in it—and she was wonderful to everyone connected with *Cabaret*.

But her public happiness during rehearsals always masked private pain. "She put up with an awful lot from Russell Detwiler," according to Kander, "but once the rehearsal hours began she was a delight, and you'd never know how painful her life was."

As summer ended, Lenya had two days free to film the small role of the gypsy's mother in Tennessee Williams's one-act play *Ten Blocks on the Camino Real* for public television. (Aired on October 7, the play is an early short form of Williams's full-length play *Camino Real*, staged on Broadway by Elia Kazan in 1953.) Directed by Jack Landau, the cast also included Martin Sheen as Kilroy.

As the gypsy, Lenya was asked to portray a wise-cracking phony whose daughter Esmeralda is given to Kilroy, a former boxer, now a vagrant who finds himself in a tropical town. Brash and venal, the gypsy is to be played with fine edges of both hostility and humor, and Lenya was the right choice for that. Although her Viennese accent was not entirely apt for the role, it could be ignored in this plotless dream-play that in any case freely intermingled characters American (Kilroy), French (Camille), Italian (Casanova), Spanish (Don Quixote and Sancho Panza) and Mexican peasants—all assembled in a place not clearly identified.

In "Block 7" (of the ten short scenes or "blocks"), Lenya revealed how easily she moved from stage and film to the demands of television production. In her blond pompadour wig, with long bauble earrings dangling almost to her shoulders, Lenya sits behind a dusty crystal ball. Lively and colorful as a parrot in her sequined bodice and sheer sleeves, she is a perfect cartoon of a fortune teller.

"I'll show you how to take a slug of tequila," she snaps cheerily at Sheen. "First you sprinkle salt on the back of your hand"—she does it as raffishly as a Mexican—"and then you lick it off with your tongue"—which she does still staring at Sheen. "Now then—you toss down the shot!"—and with one quick flip of her wrist and toss of her head, the drink is down and that wide smile lightens the set. "And then you bite into the lemon—that way it goes down easy, but what a bang!"

Sheen had all he could do to avoid laughing aloud and breaking character. In a special like this, television audiences (and, later, students of entertainment history) glimpsed the coincidence of character and technique in Lenya's acting. She was *Lenya*, a presence so unique as to make an understudy perplexed; but she was also whatever woman she was playing, and she was that woman as a part of herself and as a part of every woman in the genre. Perhaps no gypsy in *Camino Real* could have improved on Lenya's slick squalor, Viennese lilt or no.

That autumn, she also narrated (off-camera) another public television special—*Interregnum*, about Germany between the wars. Her voice as she read the documentary text was appropriately affectless, almost flat and detached, since the images were so powerful they needed no auditory support or acting presence.

On October 10, *Cabaret* opened at Boston's Shubert Theatre for a pre-Broadway run. From Brook House, Russell sent her a birthday greeting on October 17.

> You know of course how much I would love to be spending the day with you. I hope you have a lovely day and there are people there who love you, but only half as much, as we do here. I am getting along fine, the shoulder hurts [from a fall]. . . .

In another note he wrote that he was having trouble housekeeping, and that a part of her brain must have gone, since he could not find some housewares.

> I hope the house is in order [she replied]. You say part of my brain is gone. Wouldn't it be nice if we didn't elaborate on that. You are the most important person that has ever lived who is a little stupid, too.

Cabaret came to New York's Broadhurst Theatre on November 20, where it began a three-year run of 1,165 performances, most of them with Lenya. Harold C. Schonberg, in a feature on Lenya that appeared in the *New York Times* on opening day, wrote:

She has a rasping voice that could sandpaper sandpaper, and half the time she does not even attempt to sing, but she can put into a song an intensity that becomes almost terrifying.

But while her star was shining, Russell felt himself a failure.

As she became the darling of critics and audiences, Lenya once again found it hard to understand the reason for her celebrity. "She never understood why some people found what she did difficult," according to Hesper Anderson.

"What is so hard?" she used to ask me rhetorically. "You stand perfectly still, you open your mouth, and you feel the song—that is all there is to it!"

Only one performer in *Cabaret* received poor notices.

Lenya was absolutely wonderful with Jill Haworth [Harold Prince said], who was so mercilessly treated by the New York critics, and which was deeply unfair. When the *Times* singled out Jill for its wrath, Lenya was terrific. She was angry and went out of her way to be compassionate and concerned. She knew as we all did that the role of Sally Bowles as written for the stage was a girl who was *not* supposed to sing and dance well—as Liza Minnelli did in the film, which changed it somewhat.

Lenya's defense of Jill in fact touched everyone in the company. "She was very supportive," according to Fred Ebb.

Lenya rushed to Jill when she got this bad review. She told Jill that she, too, had had unfavorable notices, and she was full of solace and caring for Jill's feelings. It was almost noble, really, the way she took Jill under her wing during that show.

Joe Masteroff frequently met Lenya between the matinee and evening performances on Wednesday or Saturday and took her to supper at Sardi's, the famous theater restaurant a few steps from the Broadhurst.

She always spoke her mind about everything and never put on airs with waiters or demanded special seating or special food. She was very easy to be with, and there was no pretense about her. Whatever her dinner companion suggested was fine with her. Here she was, a legend and now a Broadway star at last, but she never gave that impression. She enjoyed a drink and a cigarette and defended her smoking by insisting that if she stopped she'd probably lose the unique voice!

The creators of *Cabaret* were all surprised by its enormous success, as Masteroff remembered:

> Hal [Prince] and John and Fred and I would have been very happy had it run a year and done fairly good business. We were always aware that it was a show about Nazis, abortions, deceit, crime—a show in which the chorus girls were intentionally not very attractive, and in which virtually every character ended unhappy. We hardly thought it would be a giant commercial success. But we didn't compromise.

And Lenya's personal success—because she, too, never compromised her professionalism—was just as great.

Fred Ebb also dined frequently with Lenya during that first year of *Cabaret*. He recalled that she enjoyed being treated like a date, waiting for a restaurant door or a taxicab to be opened for her, and telling a man what she wanted from a menu, so that he could inform the waiter. On the other hand, along with this ladylike propriety she loved to go to the more sordid Lower East Side and Greenwich Village dives, and to places which, in New York in the late 1960s, recalled the earlier Berlin whose facsimile she helped create at the Broadhurst Theatre. Transvestite shows, drag queens and stripteases by both sexes delighted her, and as Ebb recalled, everyone at such places seemed to know her.

> She took me to strange places all over town, and all these characters would come off the stages to greet her. It was clear they were virtually old friends. And without condescension she was very kind to them all. I think her own cult confounded her, and when people approached her with deference she froze and turned them off. Once, when [German actor] Helmut Berger was very courtly on meeting her, she rejected him flatly. And to [actor-director] Otto Preminger, who acted similarly, she said, "Oh, go away—you were nothing but a waiter!"

Cab drivers, waiters, struggling performers—she was considerate to everyone. Milton Caniff agreed with Kander, Ebb and Masteroff that Lenya never acted grandly at the time of her greatest fame:

> Often when we went to Sardi's, people stood to applaud her entrance, and she was very gracious. A number of the waiters were middle Europeans, and she may have represented the triumph every immigrant longs for. They did homage to this queen of Broadway with a courtly bow, and although it seemed to embarrass her she accepted it with great grace and charm.

And her humor sparkled with this success. "Bombay gin!" she cried when a dinner companion specified a brand. "I've never heard of it! If only we'd known of it back in Berlin—what a title for a Brecht-Weill song—'Bombay Gin'!" And so, twenty-two years after the failure of *The Firebrand of Florence*, Lenya had her Broadway hit.

"I have the same awkwardness," she told an interviewer in March 1967, "the crooked teeth and smile. My voice is just an instrument that happens to function. But I am the eternal optimist. I love life and I believe in survival." And for a visitor from the *New York Times* she summed up her feelings about the past and about *Cabaret*. "For sixteen years I've been the widow of Kurt Weill. Now I'm *me*!"

But domestic life continued to dilute her professional happiness. Lenya had formed a fast friendship with Harriet Pinover, a generous and congenial woman to whom she was introduced during the early months of *Cabaret*. "There were such horrible scenes with Lenya and Russ by 1967," Pinover remembered, "and it was very sad, because in her own way she loved him and really wanted to care for him. I think she thought of him, in a sense, as the son she never had. But his life was so wasteful, and he was so self-destructive."

Paul Moor, visiting New York and lunching with Lenya and Russell, was concerned too. "Russell used the word 'zombie' to describe himself, and that's just what he seemed to be. He was dopey from drink and tranquilizers. Privately Lenya admitted to me, 'I'm sick and tired of him.' She was very calm about this, but she meant it."

The crisis Lenya and everyone else had foreseen finally came. In early March 1967, Russell and Lenya were walking their German shepherd on East 55th Street, and in his inebriated state he started to argue with his wife. He lunged out at her and she tripped over the dog's leash, falling to the sidewalk. Taken to French Hospital with a broken shoulder, she had to miss several performances of *Cabaret*.

Three days later, still hospitalized, Lenya asked Lys Symonette to have Russell admitted to the same hospital. But once there, he was not confined to a secure ward, and in a fit of alcoholic paranoia he shouted that enemies were after him. He rushed from the hospital, the police were sent in pursuit, and he was removed to the psychiatric unit at the Bellevue Medical Center. In the violence of this transfer, he sustained a broken leg.

Two physicians from the New York State Department of Mental Hygiene then signed papers committing Russell Detwiler to confinement at Bellevue, to which Lenya agreed. He was admitted as case number 03-33-22 on March 9, 1967, a man suffering the severest effects of alcohol addiction, with episodes of paranoid schizophrenic behavior and hallucinations that made him dangerous to himself and others. A few days later, Lenya mentioned to a reporter from the *New York Daily News* that she was married to "a nice nut."

On March 26, Russell wrote from his hospital ward to his wife.

You just got to get me out of here. Send me to jail or any damn place you like but I can't stand being locked up with these crazy men. There is nothing wrong with me mentally but if I have to take much more of this there will be. . . . There's 30 of them and only 4 in help and they can't tie them all up. I just try and sit up and smoke all night and sleep in the daytime. . . . They have a place for drunks in [Long Island] but I can't go there until my leg is better, 12 to 18 weeks. There's no medical care for the drunks there except getting them off the drink. So this means I have to [go] into a medical ward [here] with more serious mental cases. If they do send me out there I have a record the rest of my life as a mental case. Any wrong move I make they could commit me to a mental home—auto accident, etc.—I don't think I could live or want to with that over my head. . . . God I miss you.

On April 2, he wrote again, after Lenya visited. "You sure
don't look good, you're so pale and weak, and you can see the
pain you're in. You're just like a poor little sick bird with a
broken wing." He then added that if anyone was coming to visit
him he would love some black pepper. "Most of the food is so
bad anything will help it. Only one wild thing—the coffee is
great. I had three cups for breakfast." The following day (the
anniversary of Kurt's death), Lenya was informed that Russell
needed intensive treatment and would not be released from
Bellevue for an indeterminate period.

By the end of April, officials at Bellevue were proposing to
transfer him to an alcoholic sanatorium in Connecticut. Lenya,
exhausted and in physical pain from the broken shoulder but
back in *Cabaret*, was on the verge of physical collapse. Then,
while Mary Daniel was helping her, Lenya was forced to withdraw from the show for several performances in May. She wrote
undramatically to Ted Mitchell:

> I am in pretty poor shape at the moment. I had to cancel a
> few performances out of sheer exhaustion. But it will get
> better as time goes on. My spirit is not the best with this
> everlasting pain in my shoulder. But a slight improvement is
> visible and that gives me hope it will eventually disappear.
> Russ has been moved out of the psychiatric ward to the reg-
> ular surgical one, which of course is much better for his mo-
> rale. He will be at the hospital for many months to come,
> which will give him a good chance to recover also from his
> drinking problems. And it will give me a chance to recover
> from that last year of nightmare of living under that constant
> fear of what I would find when I got home from work.

In June, Russell was transferred to High Watch Farm in Kent,
Connecticut—a clinic for alcoholics that gave them some hope
that he might yet be cured of his disease.

> They know all about me here [he wrote her on June 5] but I
> don't seem to mind so much. Even when one gal asked me if
> I broke your shoulder, I just said yes and didn't get mad or
> hurt or even bother to explain. They have some very fine
> proof of how well A.A. works but as yet I still have a lot of
> things to learn and to figure out just what will work for

me. . . . At times they talk of something other than A.A. but always get back to it. I'm sorry to say that they lose me when they blame everything that ever happened in their adult life on drink.

Detwiler was unable to admit first of all to himself that he had a disease that could be treated only by permanent abstinence. Because of this inability or unwillingness, he neither fully accepted help nor cooperated with the programs at High Watch.

I know you're saying it's me [he wrote to Lenya early that summer] and I'm just finding fault, but I'd like to see you sit through a meeting [of Alcoholics Anonymous] and [try to think] good, clean, godly thoughts. . . . But now I'm in a spot and if I'm to live through this I'll have to play along. . . . It's much too soon to say I know anything about A.A. but I do know why I'm here and what I want from them. All I want is to live a good life, a life I can live with, on my terms and thinking *sober*. I want to be a good man, husband, painter. I want love in my life but I'm not going to go out to find someone to hate just so I know the difference. . . . Even though I hit bottom I still have enough self-respect to expect respect from others.

He concluded the letter with a statement of his understanding of Lenya: "When you married me it wasn't so much that you loved me as it was that you would have someone in times like these, when you're sick and alone. True? You know it." Even he understood, it seems, that there was a desperate need for companionship in Lenya's life.

On July 7, Russell was discharged from High Watch Farm and returned to Brook House—just at the time when Lenya had a brief vacation from *Cabaret*.

You would not recognize him [she wrote to Ted Mitchell on July 13]. He is a different person now. He goes to his AA meetings, has made new friends, which is good, and feels wonderful. Has not touched a drop of liquor for five months. If he stays with this, then I will feel better too. Those last six months, from the beginning of the year, really got me down to a point where I could not see straight anymore.

On November 8, 1967, Lenya signed a contract with MGM to appear with Omar Sharif in a film called *The Appointment*, to be produced by Martin Poll and directed by Sidney Lumet in Rome the following spring. "Another procuress," Lenya wrote to Ted Mitchell about the role of Emma Valadier.

The contract for her role had been sent directly to Lenya, but she asked agent Helen Harvey to read it and advise her. "I was practically moved to tears," Harvey recalled years later, "for when she was paid she sent me the standard agent's commission. She also enclosed a little note of appreciation. Perhaps she knew that money was very welcome to me just then, but whatever the reason, it was extremely considerate and totally unrequired."

At the same time, Lenya was unsure she wanted to return to *Cabaret* the following year, but she quickly recommitted when she totaled her earnings from the show for that year—$73,264, with an increment scheduled.

That winter, Lenya's optimism for Russell's return to health kept her in good spirits. "She could be absolutely enchanting at that time," recalled actress Dolores Sutton, a neighbor in Lenya's apartment building who had appeared in part of the road tour of *Brecht on Brecht*.

> She had the spontaneity of a child, and she loved a good time. She and Bertha* and a few others played poker or canasta endlessly. It was a great tension-reliever for her, and of course there was a lot of tension during the Russell Detwiler years.

In February 1968, Lenya flew to Rome for ten days of costume fittings and meetings with the production staff on *The Appointment*. (Harold Prince had generously given her leave to withdraw temporarily from *Cabaret*.) Russell, precariously sober, would go at the same time to Bridge House, a retreat for alcoholics in the Bronx, for three weeks of psychological treatment.

She returned to New York and to *Cabaret*, and later Prince again granted Lenya free time from the show for the filming. On April 21, she and Russell departed New York for Rome. She was to be handsomely compensated for her participation: $10,000 a week for two weeks of work, first-class airfare for herself and

---

* Lenya had met and been befriended by theatrical and literary agent Bertha Case.

her husband, and five hundred dollars a week for hotel and food expenses. Her services for rehearsals, shooting, retakes and voice-dubbing actually totaled only eight days of work.

In the film, Sharif portrays a lawyer who woos Anouk Aimée away from her fiancé and marries her. But he begins to doubt her fidelity when he suspects that she may be a high-priced prostitute, one of a group managed by Lenya—in a role impossible to assess because the film was dubbed and edited so confusingly.

Screened at the Cannes Film Festival in May 1969, *The Appointment*, was, as *Variety* reported, "a tepid romantic suspenser that fails to convince, [and was] jeered so vociferously that the director [Sidney Lumet] said he would never return to Cannes." Even desperate months of additional editing could not redeem what *Variety* called a narrative that "makes no sense. Characters appear and disappear, plot elements emerge, then are dropped— it's ridiculous." (But not too ridiculous, as it turned out, to be an enormous financial success when it was released in Japan, Thailand and Argentina.) After a sneak preview in Los Angeles in 1970 (but without any regular booking thereafter), the film remained unseen in America until a late-night television broadcast—again heavily edited—in July 1972. Thereafter it virtually vanished into oblivion, to the dismay of no one, including Lenya.

In the custom of Italian productions, however, there were (even with Lenya's whirlwind working schedule) many free hours, and she and Russell enjoyed the usual tourist and gastronomic pleasures of the city. His strongest beverage was Italian espresso.

"Everything is going well," Lenya wrote to Victor Carl Guarneri on a postcard dated April 27, 1968. "I wish I could stay here for a while, but *Cabaret* is waiting. See you around the 5th of May. Weather is gorgeous and so am I." The next day, they visited the Colosseum, which delighted her: "Wonderful!" she wrote to Guarneri. "It makes one feel so young, looking at *this*!" And after visiting the Sistine Chapel she wrote to the Fujitas:

> This city is so beautiful that we dread the moment when we will have to leave. I am enjoying my work. People are so friendly and there is no pressure and the food is so good. I feel like one big spaghetti—and Russ looks it. Hope to see you before our summer retirement. Love to everybody in the cast of the Fujitas.

The *Cabaret* company welcomed her back in May. "It's very good that she did come back," according to Harold Prince, "even though she said she was exhausted and drained and didn't want to. It was good for her." But her return was brief, for she had already contracted for a long summer holiday, from June 2 to the Labor Day matinee on September 2. The schedule was nothing if not unpredictable, however. She had to return for a week of performances on June 10, when the actress Despo, her summer substitute, was sent to Los Angeles to replace Signe Hasso, who was playing Lenya's role there and had fallen ill. After a week Hasso returned to the show, Despo flew back to New York, and Lenya resumed her vacation.

> Thank God I have left *Cabaret* for a while [she wrote to Ted Mitchell on June 24] . . . and now, being out there in the country, I feel like a new person. I really don't like big cities and N.Y. has become unbearable with all that noise and that rotten air. . . . And now Russ has given up drinking, everything has become so much easier in my life. . . . I wish I could not have to go back to *Cabaret*. But the producer has been so nice to me, when he let me do the movie, which he did not have to, so I could not say no, when he asked me to come back after Labor Day. It's such an anticlimax to go back to a show, when you have said good-bye to everybody. . . . The Detwiler household is richer by a little gray kitten called Teeko. A wild little thing, but we love him and the dogs get along fine with him. Otherwise nothing has changed here.

Her husband's abstinence, however, was soon broken. After sixteen months of sobriety, he was by midsummer drinking heavily again. On August 5 Lenya again wrote to Ted.

> I was a little too optimistic when I wrote you that Russ has given up drinking. He went back to it [and] when drunk he gets completely irrational and then life becomes unbearable for me. But I still have hopes that he will wake up some day and see what this unfortunate habit is doing to his health and figure.

With the retirement of her longtime handyman, Lenya pitched herself into the summer distractions of cleaning the house and garage and repainting, with occasional help from Russell. When she returned in September to *Cabaret* (then transferred to the Broadway Theatre), she was neither relaxed nor refreshed, and a virulent case of the Hong Kong strain of influenza (as it was called that year) weakened her for the rest of 1968. She did not, however, miss more than a total of four performances—far fewer than almost everyone else in the cast. They all gathered in October to celebrate her seventieth birthday, which everyone said was incredible. She thought so, too.

Another celebration, for the thousandth performance of *Cabaret* on April 13, 1969, was not as joyous for Lenya as for her colleagues, for life with Russell was now insupportable. Drunken rages alternated with stuporous days and nights and blind, irrational fights. "I will never get out of this vicious circle I am in," she wrote in despair to Lys Symonette. "Sometimes I feel somebody is strangling me but not enough to kill me." Friends noticed her vacant response even when she was presented with West Germany's highest award. At a luncheon on September 9 at the Park Avenue residence of German Consul-General Klaus Curtius, Lenya was given the Federal Republic's Great Service Cross "for her merits in the German and American theater and for furthering cultural relations between Germany and America."

For the first time, not even the possibility of another Broadway role interested her when she left the cast of *Cabaret* in 1969. Alan Jay Lerner met with Lenya to discuss her appearing as the lengendary Coco Chanel in his forthcoming musical. "But by this time," as Milton Caniff recalled, "it was well known that she'd become lazy, that she just didn't want to crank herself up and go to work, which is what George Davis had been able to overcome." More than ever she felt no obligation to force herself to work. (The role of Coco was finally undertaken by Katharine Hepburn.)

By this time, however, she was already working quietly with friends to see how she might remove Russell Detwiler from her life. She told Victor Carl Guarneri that she would not file for divorce and would not pay alimony, but that she could no longer live with him. And so she asked Guarneri to help find a New York apartment for him. That she would pay for; it would be the price of her peace and safety.

"She just couldn't take it anymore," Lys Symonette recalled. "She rented an apartment for him on the West Side, a good place with lots of light and high ceilings for his painting. She felt terribly guilty about it, and in fact she delayed telling him."

Lenya never had to break the news.

At the end of October, she was in New York rehearsing for an imminent Lincoln Center appearance, and Lys Symonette was staying with Russell at Brook House. He grew more depressed than ever, a condition aggravated by the failure of a recent show of his paintings, which had aroused no interest and produced no sale.

After breakfast the morning of Thursday, October 30, Russell spoke sadly to Lys Symonette about his idol Judy Garland, whose recordings he had been playing day and night, and whose life and tragic death in a drug and alcohol overdose that year had become an obsession for him. "Judy knew what to do," he said quietly, and then he complained about the futility of all life.

He left the house and headed for the studio, and not long after that a call came with the message that his canvases would be delivered to Brook House from the art show within a few hours. Lys went to find him. He was lying dead in the driveway near the garage and studio, his skull split open from the impact of a fall. When the police arrived they found empty liquor bottles hidden in spare auto tires. An autopsy later confirmed that he had collapsed in a seizure caused by alcohol and narcotics, and that death resulted when his head struck the cement driveway. He was forty-four years old.

On November 2, 1969, the Detwilers' seventh wedding anniversary, Lenya buried Russell in Mount Repose Cemetery, in a plot near Kurt's. After the brief graveside service, she stood by his coffin for several minutes, clutching a single red rose in her hand and shaking as she tried to choke back her sobs. "She told me," Lys Symonette remembered, "that of her husbands she loved Russi the most, because, as she said, 'He needed me the most.' "

Eleven

Distances

1970–1981

WHEN KURT WEILL DIED, LOTTE LENYA HAD FOUND relief from her remorse and loneliness by overcoming her stage fright and singing his music before an audience gathered in tribute. After the death of George Davis, she kept her promise to him and recorded *The Threepenny Opera*. Now in 1969, she coped with sudden widowhood a third time by keeping an obligation to sing Kurt's songs. One week after Russell Detwiler's burial, she appeared at New York's Lincoln Center.

"Lenya had only to take ten steps out onto the stage," according to Harriet Pinover.

She hadn't done or said or sung anything yet, but with her body language and her extraordinary presence she had the audience in the palm of her hand. She had a lilt to her step, she kicked up her feet and picked up her body like a young colt—and the audience was grabbed from that moment.

"What a trooper she was," Lys Symonette recalled.

A Weill evening had been scheduled, and she didn't disappoint them. Amid all the glittering stars singing that night, with their finery and exaggerated mannerisms, Lenya came on in a simple black and purple dress with a ribbon round her neck, and when she stood still and sang the "Bilbao Song" she brought down the house.

271

Very soon, however, Lenya's life began to alter dramatically. "After Russ's death, her friendships changed," as Neil Fujita remembered.

There were many women friends, strong women friends—an agent [Bertha Case] and others—and occasionally Lenya called me to join them, saying, "I think you'll be a good balance." Frequently, I went, although I was cool to the whole thing. About that time she began to draw a new group, and unhappily some of her old friends, like Victor Carl [Guarneri] were dropped for long periods of time when the new hangers-on surrounded Lenya and got what they wanted, materialistically and personally. Many of her old friends then began to stay away, not wanting to interfere with this new group and new part of her life.

Some of these women were drawn to Lenya for her wealth, others for the erotic attraction fame bestows; few of them, however, offered true affection or unselfish companionship. Loneliness and a sense of failure about Russell's fate made Lenya susceptible to their persuasion and diminished her ego, and blandishment dulled her judgment. The new group often acted like an elite team of social directors, urging her to spend a weekend with this admiring woman fan or a night with that one. As Lys Symonette recalled, "Because of Lenya's insecurity, she always hoped someone would come along who was very strong and would take over the tasks of life, and often she made poor judgments when it came to selecting those to whom she handed over decisions."

Some women in Lenya's new social group could be helpful and sometimes enjoyable—like agent Bertha Case, whom she had known since the time of *Brecht on Brecht*, and who represented the American interests of Brecht's son Stefan and occasionally acted on Lenya's behalf. A tough and able negotiator, Case was affable and engaging when sober, but otherwise (which was increasingly often in her later years) she could be a tiresome bully. In New York's literary-theatrical life, Case was also firmly near the center of a famous (if discreet) circle of lesbians. Whether any of these gay women ever succeeded in bedding Lotte Lenya may never be known for certain, since in those less free times most who kissed did not tell. We do know, however, that several women friends outside that special circle with whom Lenya felt comfortable discussing intimate matters—longtime confidantes like Hesper Anderson, for example—are convinced that Lenya had several overtly sexual lesbian experiences during her later years.

A frequent social companion in Lenya's later years was the controversial Margo Harris. A talented European-born sculptor, the twice-married Harris was a fan of a number of New York celebrities, and to none of them had she ever been more attached than to Lotte Lenya. In the 1970s especially, Lenya often went to Harris's apartment on East 74th Street and to her country home in Maine—sometimes gladly, at other times because she had nothing else to do and was glad of the companionship and a few days' diversion.

The relationship between Harris and Lenya was an uneven and unpredictable one, with periods of warm alliance alternating with chilly distances, and with Harris alternately included and excluded from various versions and codicils of Lenya's wills. Lenya often referred to her as "The Pest," and as Lys Symonette, Milton Coleman, Harriet Pinover, Victor Carl Guarneri and others clearly remembered, she would often urge her friends to "tell her I'm not home" if a telephone call came from Margo Harris. And Lenya made no secret to these friends that Harris's strong, directive presence often made her feel singularly uncomfortable.

But Lenya held no ambiguous feelings about others—Harriet Pinover, for example, who was introduced to Lenya during *Cabaret*. Pinover often helped Lenya when she was ill, accompanied her to concerts and theatrical premieres, and welcomed her to her New York apartment and to her Long Island country home. This was a friendship without pressure or pretense.

Ken Andorn, who lived in the adjacent apartment on the sixteenth floor at 404 East 55th Street, also became a caring, friendly neighbor in Lenya's last years. "My bathroom abutted her fireplace wall," he recalled, "and one day I was singing in the shower when my telephone rang. She announced herself and said cheerily, 'Okay, darling, you passed the audition. When you're dry, come in for a drink.' "

From that day, Lenya and Andorn frequently shared supper or watched television together.

She was just the little lady next door who liked to visit. She didn't have to live up to being the legendary Lotte Lenya. Ethel Merman was a good friend of mine, and once I invited them both for a simple supper. Lenya was very deferential, very respectful of Merman, and so Merman liked her at once. They met at my apartment several times, and Lenya always allowed Merman center-stage to tell stories and never tried to top her or compete with her.

Lenya felt secure when Andorn was at home; often at the sound of his key in the door she peeked out to greet him, and frequently she left a note asking if she might visit. "I have the impression there were many lonely times for her in the last ten years of her life," he said.

We just sat and talked, and I welcomed this fragile little old lady, wrapped in her nightgown, robe and carpet slippers. She curled up in a corner of my couch and we'd have a quiet visit. But if my doorbell rang, if another neighbor or visitor arrived, this wizened little lady suddenly transformed into a bright alert companion, bouncing around, telling stories like a twenty-year-old.

Andorn's evenings with Lenya and Merman were quite different, however, from that which was innocently arranged by Harold Prince not long after Detwiler's death, as Prince himself remembered.

I introduced Lenya to Helene Kazantzakis, the widow of the great Greek writer [Nikos Kazantzakis] and a writer herself. The two women couldn't bear each other from the first moment! Here were these two apparently fragile widows, keeping flames alive and trying to develop their own talents too. They couldn't wait to get out the door, and they were each preparing to leave by nine o'clock, just after dinner. I thought they were mirror images of each other. Each had had a tough life earlier and each represented an epic man.

During the winter after Russell's death, Paul Moor visited New York and spent time with a downcast Lenya. When he asked if there were anything he could do to lift her spirits, she quickly and seriously replied, "Find me another husband."

To a fan named Ann Fall (who since the Carnegie Hall recital of 1965 had become a kind of pen-pal and whom she also occasionally invited to lunch or tea), Lenya wrote during the spring after Russell's death:

> I have been drifting now for the last six months, and don't really know yet how I will survive the death of my beloved husband. It's a terrible loss (for the third time in my life) and I feel so lost and lonesome and there is nobody who can help. One has to find oneself again and that's it. But dear God, it is a struggle. . . . I try to keep busy . . . but my heart is not in it. I know from my past experience that time eventually will help and that's what I am waiting for. . . . I try my best to find a reason to go on living.

That same season, in response to Ann Fall's offer of prayers, Lenya wrote:

> No, dear Ann, you don't have to pray for me. I don't believe in that escape either, and [I'd] rather face whatever my fate has lined up for me. I admit the other way is easier, I have seen it work, but why try to escape pain and despair for someone I loved so dearly? . . . I don't know from one day to the next what I feel and therefore I have to let things drift until I am steady on my feet again. . . . But I look out the window and see the seasons change and know, since we are part of nature, that I too will change and will find a purpose again for existence.

And in a similar spirit she later wrote to Hesper Anderson:

> Once in a while I go to the cemetery and stand there, looking down to the Hudson, and I cry and feel better after. I am glad they [Kurt and Russell] are together there. No, darling, one never really gets over these losses, and why should one? One learns to live with them, but one does *not* want to forget. They are part of living and they also hold lovely memories. Hold on to them. They are in times comforting.

In early 1970, Lenya learned that Mary Daniel—who had suffered heart trouble in recent years—was now gravely ill. It was Lenya's turn to help with chores in West Virginia, which she gladly did. To Ted Mitchell Lenya wrote on her return to Brook House:

> We stayed quietly in the house, watched TV, played Scrabble and the time passed much too fast. I hope her doctor will allow her to come up here sometime in July. It would be a nice change for her and would be wonderful for me not to be alone and have someone around me who does not mind my moodiness, which overcomes me suddenly and I cannot stop it.

And in the same letter she confided her sadness:

> You ask how I am. Well, dear Ted, it's not the best life I am leading. It's a lonesome life in spite of all my friends trying to help. How I wish *Cabaret* would open tomorrow instead of three years ago. It would help a great deal to work. After all that taking care of Russi I feel so empty-handed. It's seven months now, and I feel that time just creeps along. Also, South Mountain Road is so deserted. All my friends have moved away, mostly to California [e.g., Hesper Anderson and the Caniffs]. Nobody wants to hang around New York any more.

In spite of her black periods, however, her vigilance over Weill's interests never slackened. In April she instructed the Theodore Presser Company, an American agent for Universal Edition, that his "Ballad of a Drowned Maiden" must not be in any way edited or revised for a projected recording: "I am not agreeable . . . to any performance in any other form than the original Weill scoring."

Such protests were as frequent as ever during Lenya's last years. In March 1975, for example, she asked Bertha Case to contact the Italian agents of director Giorgio Strehler, who planned to use a reduced score of *The Threepenny Opera* at a production he was planning for the Piccolo Teatro, Milan. "There is only one score written by the late Kurt Weill," Case wrote directly from Lenya's own handwritten note, "and there can be no deviation nor interpolations in such score. If Mr. Strehler wishes to see the original score, he can secure a copy from Weill's German publishers, Universal Edition. . . .''

But by September 1970, Lenya was at her lowest point of depression, and she wrote to Lys on the seventh of that month:

> I am smoking much too much and don't seem to be able to settle down one way or the other. I hate that feeling of drifting without any sort of energy. Just moping around. It's awful. In two months it will be already a year since Russi died and I still can't believe it. . . . Before I get too maudlin, I better stop and pay a few bills. That'll sober me up.

On the twenty-third she was still miserable. "As October approaches," she wrote Ted Mitchell, "my spirit (what's left of it) seems to go downhill. Oh, will I ever get out of this hole?"

But by the anniversary of Russell's death she in fact began to feel better. When broadcast journalist Edwin Newman requested an interview for NBC's television program *Speaking Freely*, Lenya invited him to come to Brook House on October 14 with a small crew. At the end of the conversation (aired ten days later), Newman asked "a personal question, if I may. You have been married and widowed three times. What does that do to somebody?"

Her reply:

> Look at me and tell me what it does. You cannot explain what it does to you. I am sure there are many women who went through the same thing. There are many young women with children right now, with the war in Vietnam, who go through the same thing. You just take it. There are many beautiful things still in life which you can enjoy and you should enjoy. I am sure each one of my three husbands, whom I loved very dearly, would not want me to sit here and put on my mourning clothes and never get out of it. I don't think that's the idea. They wouldn't like that at all. I think they would like what I'm doing now—that I keep working, that I keep alive. Keep alive, that's it. Sometimes it's difficult to be alone, especially for me. I'm a person who loves to share, whether it's good or bad, but I love to share my life with somebody, and if that

somebody is taken from you, it takes time to adjust yourself
to the loneliness again. But you learn. I've learned it, and
now I'm learning it again for the third time. So that's the only
answer I can give you.

On October 21, Lenya wrote to Lys Symonette, "I think the
interview went awfully well." She could not have been more
right. As such things will frequently do, it in fact relaxed and
refreshed her to "speak freely," as Edwin Newman hoped she
would. Once again, here was evidence of her extraordinary will
to endure rather than just survive, to persevere, to triumph after
heartbreak.

That same day, she wrote to her fan Ann Fall about the reissue
of her albums "Berlin Theatre Songs" and "American Theatre
Songs," "with a new photograph by [Richard] Avedon. I was
surprised to see myself in the windows [of stores] again." By
Christmas she was writing letters full of more news and making
cheerful inquiries about friends' lives. Even the death of Rex,
her German shepherd, "hit by a car driven by one of those crazy
hippy girls" (as she wrote to Ann Fall on December 20), did
not pitch her back to the same depression, saddened by it as she
was.

She was also reading more than ever. Always interested in
poetry, a good biography, serious fiction and first-rate essays,
Lenya was eclectic but her taste in serious literature was unas-
sailable. She had developed a habit of reading the classics ever
since her time in Zurich with Richard Révy, who had introduced
her to the great European and Russian novelists, and she had
progressed to moderns like Koestler and Cocteau while she was
on tour with *Candle in the Wind*. Now she was reading Truman
Capote's *In Cold Blood* and also, as she wrote to Ted Mitchell
on December 20, 1970, "a very interesting book about King
Ludwig of Bavaria and his strange—or not so strange—
relationship with Wagner."

The subtleties and elaboration of literary biography always
appealed to her in a way that a television version of a life—with
its tendency to glamorize and simplify—did not. During a
broadcast dramatization of Beethoven's life, the composer was
presented as annoyingly hesitant to pursue his romantic intentions for a young woman. Irritated by the contrived, soap-opera
style, Lenya suddenly indulged an uncharacteristic vulgarity.

"For God's sake!" she shouted at her television screen, to the actor portraying Beethoven: "Fuck her and get it over with!"

By early 1971, Lenya had met a documentary filmmaker named Richard Siemanowski. "Chandler Cowles was a producer I knew," according to Lys Symonette,

> and when I mentioned to him that I knew Lenya was interested in having a documentary made about herself and Weill, Chandler showed me Richard's film on Rembrandt [*In Search of Rembrandt*] and we agreed that they should meet. I called Siemanowski and he jumped at the chance to meet her, which they finally did in New York.

Richard Siemanowski was born May 25, 1926, in Chicago. After serving in the army during World War II as a sergeant, he became a newspaper reporter, first for the *Daytona Beach News-Journal* and then for the *Chattanooga Times*. In 1953 he joined the public affairs department of CBS, and after that he began a career in film and television production. By the time he met Lenya he was a forty-four-year-old filmmaker and writer who had produced more than two hundred television shows on religion and on culture. His four-hour special on Africa for ABC-TV (part of the *Saga of Western Man* series) had won the Emmy as outstanding television documentary for 1964–1965, and his 1970 special *In Search of Rembrandt* for National Educational Television had been critically acclaimed and frequently rebroadcast—as well as distributed independently as a featurette.

Siemanowski was a witty, genial and cultured man who wore his education modestly (he had a master's degree from the University of Chicago) and he was a pleasant companion in any social gathering. After several evenings as a card partner with Lenya, Bertha Case and the film editor Hans Dudelheim (who had worked with Siemanowski on the *Saga of Western Man*), Richard announced that he and Lenya were busy on a movie treatment of Lenya's fascinating life story, which he hoped to render as a documentary called *Lenya—and a Girl Named Jenny*.

Throughout that spring, Siemanowski spent more and more time with Lenya—sometimes discussing the planned film, but mostly playing cards, dining, talking about art and literature.

He had ideas for a number of projects, but not the ability to finance them.

"He had a money problem," according to Hans Dudelheim. "There was always the wolf at the door and terrific pressure on him. And for a time he didn't get any work at all in spite of his awards. But that isn't unusual in this business." When Richard Siemanowski asked Lenya for a loan, she wrote a check and he signed a note. "But he never repaid her," as Milton Coleman attested, "and of course she never undertook legal proceedings."

Not that Lenya was suffering because of the loss. Her financial situation had never been more impressive, and although she always believed that she was on the edge of poverty, a list of her assets in 1971 indicates the truth of the matter. In nine savings accounts she had $155,000 cash; in five checking accounts, $143,115; four foreign accounts held more than $40,000 and she had an additional $552,103 in securities. Brook House had been valued at more than $40,000 and the land at 116 South Mountain Road at $60,000. Her ownership of municipal bonds (for the cities of Syracuse, Islip, Massapequa, Oswego, for the Port of New York and for the territory of Puerto Rico) were that year valued at $512,000 and produced a tax-free income of $31,501. In addition, she held two hundred shares of Food Fair stock, one hundred of Avco, two hundred eight of Allied Chemical, one hundred eighty of Texas Gulf Sulphur and five hundred of International Nickel, which together yielded $30,103 that year. Her copyrights, jewelry, two mink coats and personal effects brought the full value of her net worth that year to over $2,000,000.

In May, Siemanowski told Hans Dudelheim that he had fallen in love with Lotte Lenya. That month, she took him to dinner at the Fujitas' and also invited the Caniffs (then visiting New York from their California home) to attend a private screening of one of his films.

Milton Caniff recalled wondering about her choice of male company, and well he might have. For although Richard could be an interesting conversationalist and an attractive dinner or card partner, he was an alcoholic homosexual. He was often optimistic and creative, but his heavy drinking made his energies erratic. At that time he was living with his male lover in

New Jersey, and he had apparently no intention of breaking the relationship.

Richard may well have made Lenya think of Russell, and this was the core of her attraction as well as its danger. But she was repeating the pattern of her childhood, trying to win love from an impossible source. Once again, she was becoming an enabler to a dependent alcoholic; once again, she was becoming like her mother, a woman who perhaps felt secure only in caring for a crippled and emotionally distant man. Sexually unthreatening, gifted, artistic, capable of great charm, Richard found her company delightful, he admired her, he was willing to be her escort and companion. And again (as with Davis and Detwiler) she could make herself materially indispensable, offering security once again instead of sexual favors. At forty-four, Richard was exactly the age of Russell at the time of his death. It was as if she were being given a kind of second chance to cancel the tragic outcome of her former marriage.

"He was well read and highly intelligent," according to Lys Symonette,

> and she respected him. Also, he looked a little bit like George, and he was more than a little bit like Russell. But they had some fun together, and then one day she said to me, "I'm going to get him, I'm going to marry him." She liked to conquer men. That gave her satisfaction, when she conquered someone. Then, like a child with a toy, she got tired of the conquered. And although she claimed she could be alone, she really couldn't.

On June 9, 1971, the seventy-two-year-old Lenya married the forty-five-year-old Siemanowski in Goshen, New York. "The truth is," as Lys Symonette clearly remembered, "they were both drunk when they got married, and she didn't spend the wedding night with him."

Nor, it seems, did they ever live together. Only Symonette and two or three of Lenya's oldest friends were ever told of the marriage, and Lenya never used his name as hers. She continued as Lotte Lenya Weill-Detwiler.

Like Russell, Richard was young enough to be her son and he placed no sexual demands on her. "It's so nice to be dependent on a man," she told a reporter from the *Long Island Press* later that year, without mentioning her recent marriage. "I can't think of anything nicer."

But in fact almost anything might have been "nicer," and she must have suspected that the marriage was without meaning, for she confided the fact to so few she knew. Not even Hans Dudelheim knew of it until after her death:

> The only time I ever saw them together was when we played cards, which wasn't that often. Occasionally he mentioned that he had been to or was about to go to New City, which he really loved, but there was never any mention of a marriage.

When friends like Harriet Pinover, Victor Carl Guarneri, Hesper Anderson, the Fujitas and the Caniffs learned about the marriage—but only after Lenya's death—they expressed a common belief that it was contracted out of her desperate need for companionship.

"I think," Dudelheim added, "that for him it was equally a desperate act for money. And Lenya seemed to have a need for some kind of crippled person, an invalid she could take in hand."

But her goal must have seemed unreasonable and unreal even to her, for she went ahead with her plans to travel alone that month to narrate and sing in a concert version of *Der Silbersee* at The Hague's Holland Festival on June 25, and to attend the world premiere in Utrecht of Weill's recently discovered *Recordare* (for four-part mixed chorus and children's chorus, set to a text from the Lamentations of Jeremiah). Richard Siemanowski, meanwhile, was heading for Cairo to work on a film project.

Throughout a summer of separation, he sent postcards describing his itinerary. More interesting than the content, however, is the way he wrote her address on cards and envelopes: from Cairo to "Mrs. Linnerl Detweiller [*sic*], The Short Broad with the Orange Hair" or to "Mrs. Karoline Detwiller [*sic*], She's Very Small and Wears Sneakers" or to "Lotte Lenya, The One Who Stamps Her Sneaker in Anger." He also addressed her in the letters (from Beirut, Milan, Florence, Amboise and Paris) as his "Austrian Twit" and signed himself "The Polack."

On her return to New City that summer, Lenya received a professional invitation from stage director Herbert Machiz. He had an appointment to teach and direct drama at the University of California at Irvine that autumn, and he invited Lenya to appear in an English-language student production of Brecht's *Mother Courage*. She accepted without hesitation, perhaps in much the same spirit of creative desperation with which she had accepted the role in *Cabaret* at a time of stasis and depression in her previous marriage.

In early October Lenya arrived at Irvine for rehearsals. (She received $6,500 plus expenses for two previews and nine performances between November 15 and 28.) Ernest Hood, a 1971 graduate of Irvine's drama department, was then Machiz's assistant. He recalled that Lenya was the first star to act with the university's students.

Set on rolling plains sixty miles south of downtown Los Angeles and just east of Newport Beach, Irvine's campus was developing a first-rate arts center. Clayton Garrison, former chairman of drama at the University of California at Riverside, was imported to direct the fine arts division at Irvine, and attempts were made to invite major writers and directors on a continuing basis. William Inge, for example, taught playwriting about the same time, and Machiz had already staged an impressive production of Tennessee Williams's *Camino Real*, which was followed by *Cabaret*. He then decided on *Mother Courage*.

> The rehearsals are going very well indeed [Lenya wrote to Lys Symonette on October 29] and Herbert Machiz does a terrific job. I am still struggling with the enormity of the dialog. It's a tapeworm and just to handle all the props is a job in itself. The students are wonderful and needless to say I am getting along with them beautifully. They gave me a surprise birthday party onstage and it could not have been sweeter. It's really lovely out here and the daily drive along the ocean to the university (about 25 minutes) is a sheer delight. God, I wish I could have had the opportunity to learn under such ideal circumstances. It's just staggering, the luxury of instruments, rehearsal halls and God knows what. No wonder most of them delay their graduation. I would too. . . . This trip has done me a world of good. To work is what I like most and I am happy doing it. . . . The ocean sweeps all the [annoyances] away.

In the same letter to Symonette she added that Richard was still trying to raise money for the Lenya-Jenny project, but that she had invited him to join her in Irvine instead:

> It would do him good to get away. . . . He won't do it, I know, but at least I made the gesture. He also has money problems, it seems. No wonder, with his generosity [to his lover]. I am glad I am not there.

Otherwise, her communications to friends in New York were cheerful accounts of her California life. To the Fujitas she wrote on November 8 that she was having a wonderful time doing *Mother Courage* with students.

> Most modern stage and no money problems. Should make Broadway producers envious. I am living right on the ocean and the daily drive to the college along the Pacific is lovely. It's easy living out here and people are friendlier than in New York. I wonder what is so fascinating about New York that one can't leave it? Must be something.

"Everyone was very reverential to her," Ernest Hood recalled,

> but she never acted the Grande Dame. Herbert and I drove her back to her bungalow on the beach after evening rehearsals. The place faced the ocean and was cluttered and dark, but she had made it her own, had brought her two cats along, and the house was as unpretentious as herself.

But although Lenya was enjoying life in Southern California, the production was not as smooth as she would have her friends believe.

> She was having trouble with her lines [Hood continued], and although she was always cooperative and cordial, it was clear that this problem preoccupied her. The production was rather heavy and self-conscious, too, and even after the opening she was still having trouble with dialogue. But after all she was seventy-three, and more than fifty years older than the rest of the cast, so there was some awkwardness. Although it was clearly an effort for her, she had some wonderful moments.

Her silent scream when her dead son is brought onstage—
Helene Weigel's famous silent scream—was unforgettably
moving, an astonishing look of pain.

(The "silent scream" had not been used by Lenya in the 1965
Recklinghausen production [or at least not for the filming of it];
it seems to have been introduced here at Herbert Machiz's suggestion. In any case, it is hard to imagine Lenya consciously
affecting a "homage" to Weigel or deliberately imitating any of
Weigel's technique.)

The ambiguities of Lenya's valiant performance and impressive energies were noted by the drama critic of the *Los Angeles
Times*, Dan Sullivan, who wrote a major review:

> Lotte Lenya grows plainer and more beautiful as the years go
> by. . . . And yet it is not the definitive performance you'd
> hoped for, principally because there is not enough of the old
> Lenya in it. . . . [She] doesn't do or say anything that makes
> us feel uncomfortable, that suggests she might be a war crim-
> inal of a sort, too. Morally, she's clean, a sharp-tongued but
> basically delightful old gal who is trying to get by. It is a
> comfortable rather than a challenging characterization and it
> results in a performance perilously lacking in dynamics. . . .
> But it is a chance to warm yourself in Miss Lenya's authen-
> tically human presence and one is grateful for that.

Sullivan's reaction was on the mark. Lenya's performance
(preserved on tape) had more warmth than the character of
Mother Courage usually conveys. Perhaps in an attempt to overcome stage fright and her difficulty with the lines, she developed
an approach to the role that was indeed more appealing than
challenging—certainly less fiery than Anne Bancroft's acclaimed 1963 Broadway portrait and less fierce than Helene
Weigel's. Lenya enjoyed working with the students, and she
seems to have caught their rather gentler approach to the play
and the role than Brecht intended.

Lenya's only expressed disappointment was a typically par-
adoxical one. She was hurt when Richard Siemanowski did not
come to Irvine for opening night, for that meant she had no
"date" to escort her afterward. On November 22 he wrote an

apology, pleading work and adding a protestation of love. A few days after that he was in Europe and she was back in New York.

A batch of legal papers relative to Weill's copyrights had accumulated in her absence. "Oh, Kurti!" the visiting Hesper Anderson recalled her crying in exasperation that season, "I'm getting so *bored* with you!" And Dolores Sutton also saw Lenya with music and legal briefs scattered round the apartment. "Why did he leave me with all this?" Lenya asked rhetorically. "Why do I have to devote myself to all this?" And then she answered her own question: "Well, I am responsible." And so she continued to be.

Her sense of responsibility took her in December to London, where she attended rehearsals of *The Threepenny Opera*, directed by Tony Richardson, at the Prince of Wales Theatre. The auditorium itself, she told a reporter from the London *Times*, was ideal for the play—"not snazzy and elegant, but a bit seedy." She then flew to Hamburg for a Christmas holiday with Anna Krebs, and after a brief return to New York she went in January to West Virginia to visit Mary Daniel, whose health was now more precarious than ever. On February 7, 1972, she was back in London for the premiere of the Richardson production, and when she returned to East 55th Street she prepared for a March departure to the Florida State University at Tallahassee, where she was to play Jenny in nine April performances of *The Threepenny Opera*, "I hope for the last time," as she wrote to Ted Mitchell.

During all this fast-paced traveling over great distances, however, there was the issue of Richard, whose alcoholism had landed him in a New York clinic. The parallels to her marriage to Russell must have occurred to her when, after visiting him in Columbia-Presbyterian Hospital, she wrote to Lys on February 23:

I found Richard sitting at the window of the solarium. . . . He was in a much better mood and ready to leave the hospital by the end of next week. His "roommate" has invited me for dinner, but I did not go. I do not want to get involved in that setup family. In a way it's good for him. He needs somebody to take care of him, cook for him, do all his finances, take the dogs out for him, etc. It's a babysitting job for a spoiled man. No thanks.

Soon after, Lenya realized fully just how empty the marriage had always been—and, indeed, that it had not even been much of a friendship. Visiting Richard again at the hospital, Lenya noted that he had listed his lover as next of kin for hospital records. "That," Lys Symonette said, "was when Lenya realized it was all over for good."

There was not much contact between Lenya and Siemanowski for the next several months, as Richard returned to his lover and at the same time Lenya helped to publicize the imminent opening of *Berlin to Broadway with Kurt Weill*, a review with five singing actors. The opening, on October 1, 1972, was appropriately at the Theatre de Lys, and there were one hundred fifty-two performances over the next nineteen weeks. During the run, Lenya frequently gave interviews; she also appeared on Dick Cavett's television show, and she was a mystery guest on *What's My Line?* (where panelist Arlene Francis guessed her identity within a minute).

Once again, then, she was involved in activities that focused on the name and fame of Kurt Weill. For the rest of her life, events and business affairs relative to his work would be her great concern. Her life, she felt, would have been unremarkable but for him: "There is no Lenya story without the complete Kurt story," she wrote on May 17, 1977, to Hesper Anderson, who had proposed a teleplay on Lenya's life. "I am not famous enough that people would get interested in my life without Kurt."

That season, some of Russell's remaining paintings were stolen while en route from an art exhibit. "Two of my most beloved paintings," Lenya wrote to Ted Mitchell on August 22,

> *The Seven Deadly Sins* and *Surabaya Johnny* [the names of the paintings] were missing. The driver parked his truck on 123rd Street and 3rd Avenue and when he returned from his dinner, the truck was broken into. . . . I put out a reward of a thousand dollars for their return. Since they were stolen evidently by some drug addict, the police are very doubtful.

On the anniversary of Detwiler's death, Lenya was lonely and reflective. "I still miss him very much," she wrote to Ted Mitchell.

It's lonesome without him, difficult as he was sometimes. I
visited his parents a few months ago. They are doing all right.
I looked at his father's hands, which are so very like Russi's.
I wonder how much damage was done to Russi by him. He
surely did not understand that complicated creature.

In November she flew to the John F. Kennedy Center for the
Opera Society of Washington's production of *Rise and Fall of
the City of Mahagonny*, which delighted her, according to critic
Alan Rich, her escort. He recalled that she "seemed a somewhat
nervous person,

> despite the fact that she had by this time been receiving enormous
> adulation for years. . . . Either through her own choice or
> through the advice of friends, she was being frozen into a per-
> sona, made into a waxworks figure, paraded around as the keeper
> of the Weill flame. On the other hand, of course, she loved the
> music. But maybe she could have enjoyed a bit more tranquillity.

As for the production, Lenya wrote on a Christmas card to Hesper Anderson that "it was lovely, and I am exhausted."
But friends also noticed that she was nervous—and understandably so. Telephone calls from Siemanowski—for money,
for forgiveness, for reconciliation—bothered her everywhere.
On the advice of friends, Lenya subsequently asked her attorneys to draw papers by which both she and Richard released
one another from any claim on their respective properties. In
exchange for the legally fixed sum of one dollar (and without a
personal meeting), Mr. and Mrs. Richard Siemanowski signed
those documents on January 18, 1973.
Her busy travel schedule then resumed: a trip to Frankfurt for
a Brecht seventy-fifth birthday festival, at which she sang three
Weill-Brecht songs; a visit with her sister in Vienna and then
with Anna Krebs in Hamburg; and a week with David Drew in
London, where she discussed the still active contracts for two
books he was to write—Kurt's biography and Lenya's (ghosted)
autobiography. In a letter to Milton Caniff she described her
inconstant progress on these books:

> [David Drew] made me write my first episode. He told me,
> just write five lines and I will tell you whether you should go

on or not. Well, I got so mad at myself, stalling for so many
years now, that I just sat down and wrote two pages. He was
very happy with the result and now here I sit and try to get
the promised two pages every week ready to send to him. I
think the more I write, the easier it will get. Maybe not,
maybe it gets more difficult when you discover the danger of
trying to make up stories. But I am already fully aware of
that, so "schtick to the truth, kid—it's bad enough."

Back home she learned from her attorney that she could file
for divorce on grounds of desertion. She took appropriate legal
measures, and on May 7 she wrote to Lys Symonette, "My
divorce is coming up in June. I will be glad [when] that is out
of the way." On June 6, it was. New York State Supreme Court
Justice W. Vincent Grady decreed that the marriage was dissolved "by reason of the abandonment of the plaintiff by the
defendant." The crucial finding of fact was that Richard Siemanowski had maintained a legal residence in New Jersey during the time of the marriage, "with intent not to return and
without any cause or justification . . . [whereas] plaintiff has
always conducted herself as a faithful and obedient wife."

After several weeks in Europe, Lenya returned to Brook
House to find a letter from Siemanowski, who was in Beirut and
had been shocked to learn of the summary divorce action. He
insisted he had no apologies to make, that he knew no reason
why she should be offended and that he thought their relationship had proceeded exactly as they had previously agreed. He
added that he never liked being Mr. Lotte Lenya, and that he
would remain his own person. He did not have the genius of
Kurt, he wrote (which was true enough), but neither did he have
the dependencies of George or Russell (which was not entirely
true). On October 17 she replied:

Dear Richard,
    I wish I could say that I am angry. It would at least mean
that I feel something—but I do not—no anger, no love, no
dislike, just no feeling at all. Try not to feel badly.
                                        Lenya

She then departed, flying to Berlin, Vienna, Zurich, Hamburg and then to London—"to get out of that daily routine of

shining the copper in the kitchen, picking up leaves and pine-cones,'' as she wrote to Hesper Anderson on November 3.

At the beginning of 1974, Lenya began to experience al-most constant gastrointestinal distress. Her physician diag-nosed a sliding hiatus hernia, a protrusion of the stomach above the diaphragm—a common condition found in almost half the adult population at some time or another, and which usually responds to self-care and dietary adjustments. She avoided the restricted foods, but as the year advanced so did her discomfort.

''I have no talent for being sick,'' she wrote to Hesper An-derson on July 18. In November, this was aggravated by painful arthritis, which attacked her back, arms and the once broken shoulder. ''I cannot write long letters any more,'' she wrote Ted Mitchell on November 11, 1974, thanking him for remembering her birthday (''which I make the greatest effort to forget'').

Even at seventy-six, Lenya was never a complainer about health problems, and she maintained a cheerfully optimistic at-titude that she was quite indestructible, that her ailments would pass. ''Everybody has some sort of trouble,'' she wrote Mitchell on March 16, 1975. ''Mine is not too serious.''

By this time, however, her life had become severely restricted with the pain—''It was a hard winter for me,'' she wrote without detail to Bunny Caniff on May 3, 1975. A seventy-fifth birthday celebration for Kurt was scheduled for Berlin during the late summer and she intended to be the major guest, but she canceled after an auto accident on South Mountain Road in June, which left her badly shaken, but with only bruised ribs.

All Lenya's old friends—the Caniffs, the Fujitas, Ted Mitch-ell, Hesper Anderson, Victor Carl Guarneri—recognized that Lenya's age and illnesses would necessarily begin to restrict her social life somewhat. But they did not expect her gradual with-drawal from their frequent companionship, which began in 1976 and continued until her death. She was not often confined to her home and she did, after all, continue to travel when she felt well, spending weeks at a time in Europe and at Margo Harris's country home in Maine. According to those who maintained fairly regular contact with her—Lys Symonette, Milton Cole-man, Harriet Pinover and a few others—Margo Harris contin-ually tried to manage much in Lenya's life during the last few years. And because it was often simply easier to have someone supervise travel plans, arrange transportation, see to details large and small regarding social and professional life, Lenya—perhaps unwisely—yielded more and more decision-making to Margo Harris.

Sometimes, however, Lenya tried to assert her independence. "Often," according to Lys Symonette, "especially when she and Margo had had bad words, she drove out to New City. In fact she preferred to stay there most of the time, even though that meant being alone." All the while, Margo Harris seems to have remained devoted—indeed, frankly obsessed—with Lotte Lenya.

How much Lenya enjoyed Brook House, even when alone, is clear from a letter to Hesper Anderson dated January 11, 1976, which is one of the most felicitous and touching she wrote:

> It's so beautiful. Snowed in. Quiet, no cars passing. Real wintery Sunday. Grandma Moses had a flair for this kind of landscape. Xmas passed without much excitement. To hang a wreath on the door and light a few candles does not mean much if there is no one one loves. New Year's Eve I spent with my neighbors—nice, with the butler playing the mouth harmonica, trying to sing like Chevalier. He is French, but that alone does not do it. So another year has started and one always hopes for something good to happen. Maybe it will. . . . I never forget that winter night when you were about ten and stood outside on the little terrace and sang Xmas carols. It was a cold night and you all had red noses. That was Xmas for me. Now it's all gone and one wraps those few packages rather listlessly. One should not look back and if one does one should be able to smile and remember all the lovely things. Today I am just drenched in nostalgia. It's the snow.

On January 14, 1976, the *New York Times* reported that Lenya donated several acres of her land in New City to Rockland County. "It feels wonderful to give the land away," she told reporter James Feron. "If the gift will help preserve the area, it is well worth it." Her donation contributed to two preserves being assembled in the rustic central portion of the county, a

three-hundred-acre park and a seventy-eight-acre town bird and
animal sanctuary.

Another and more demanding task occupied her for most of
1976. With the cooperation of Goethe House (the German-
American cultural center in New York), an exhibit of Weill-
Lenya memorabilia was to be mounted at Lincoln Center's
Library for the Performing Arts in November. To its preparations she gave herself dutifully throughout 1976, collecting and
identifying photos, posters, programs and musical manuscripts,
a sampling of letters to and from their most famous friends over
the years, and compiling a chronology of her life and Kurt's (not
always accurate, as it turned out) for use in a commemorative
pamphlet. She was not so enthusiastic, however, about a Lincoln Center revival of *The Threepenny Opera* that year, which
she thought had "no humor. I grew up with it. I know what
Kurt Weill and Brecht meant."

One ugly event tainted her early summer, however. "I was
trimming some ivy leaves off the window-sill," Lenya wrote
Ted Mitchell,

> not noticing the hornet's nest underneath. I was stung several
> times and had a terrible reaction, was rushed to the hospital
> and given all kinds of injections and oxygen but could not get
> any breath from the internal swelling. Well, I survived it, but
> I still have strange reactions to flowers, fruits, etc.

Margo Harris took Lenya to recuperate at her country home in
Maine.

> It's lovely here [Lenya wrote to Hesper Anderson on July 9],
> luscious green trees, icy blue waters and lovely clean air. And
> I guess that's all one can expect of a 10-day vacation, so well
> deserved after three vicious wasp bites.

By the time of the opening of the Lincoln Center exhibit,
Lenya had signed for her fifth motion picture role. The first
week of September, director Michael Ritchie invited her to lunch
at the Russian Tea Room to discuss a small but hilarious role in
a satire on professional sports. Titled *Semi-Tough* and starring
Burt Reynolds, Kris Kristofferson, Jill Clayburgh, Robert Preston and Bert Convy (her costar in *Cabaret*), the film called for

Lenya to play a cameo as Clara Pelf, the originator of a slightly
sadistic muscular therapy called "pelfing" (an allusion to the
"rolfing" technique and its originator, Ida Rolfe). For working
on one brief scene in Miami the following March, Lenya received five thousand dollars and a new and younger audience.

"It's only one scene," she wrote Hesper Anderson on October 11, 1976,

> but funny—an old masseuse digging in to Reynolds—in what
> part of his body I don't know yet. Let's hope it's above his
> waistline and not bigger than a breadbox, to use one of those
> unforgettable lines of "What's My Line, Please?" [*sic*].

When *Semi-Tough* was released in 1977, Lenya's five-minute
scene with Reynolds was a savagely amusing highlight. "You
have sexual problems?" she asks him, and when he denies it
she counters, "*All* American men have sexual problems!" Then,
when he shrieks in pain on her massage table, she drives a prob-
ing finger into his ribs and shrieks right back—"*Aha!!!* You hate
your mother! No? Your *father*?" Those who saw Ritchie's film
invariably remember Lenya's satirically sinister scene.

Working in the warmth of Florida reinvigorated Lenya. "Just
got back from Florida," she wrote Ted Mitchell on April 2,
"massaging Burt Reynolds in *Semi-Tough*. It was fun and he is
a darling to work with."

Refreshed by the work and eager to capitalize on her energy,
she agreed to coach the young soprano Joy Bogen, who was
about to give several recitals of Kurt Weill's songs. "Her smallest motion had meaning," Bogen recalled. "But she never approached a song intellectually. She was also a terribly sexy
woman, even at seventy-nine. She wasn't beautiful, but she had
a terrifically strong personality, and the Austrian propriety was
sometimes mixed with a little innuendo of flirtatiousness. When
she came to my home for parties, she was great fun. She exuded
a kind of animal sex appeal along with her charm."

On April 4, 1977, Lenya presented Kurt Weill's autograph
orchestral score for *The Seven Deadly Sins* to the Music and
Dance Divisions of the Lincoln Center Library, and her friends
were invited to a brunch at the library that day. She also continued her critical hovering over all the Weill productions she could
attend. After the premiere of a disappointing revival of *Knick-*

erbocker Holiday (planned for three weeks that season) she wrote
to Hesper Anderson on April 21, "The Knickerbocker evening
was rather dreadful. The director could not make up his mind
between a concert version and a stage production. A real misch-
masch. . . . I am glad nobody taped it. It's agony to sit there
with the sound of the original score in your ears. . . ."

By November 7, however, she was in agonizing abdominal
pain, and she knew it was neither indigestion nor a simple hernia. Margo Harris recommended a surgeon she knew, Dr. Ernest W. Kulka, and Lenya underwent tests. The pathologist
reported widely spread cancer. Lys Symonette recalled Lenya's
early reactions.

Lenya thought her problem was something minor and cura-
ble. She thought she was immortal, that nothing would touch
her. And she never listened to anything about sickness or
cancer, couldn't stand it, and never went to see people if they
were in the hospital—not her relatives, not even friends like
myself. She couldn't stand being around sickness.

On December 1, 1977, Lenya entered Doctors Hospital in
Manhattan, and next day Dr. Kulka performed a hysterectomy.
To her friends, however—like Ted Mitchell, to whom she soon
wrote—Lenya simply reported surgery for "a benign tumor in
my abdomen."

"However, it turned out to be a very serious form of cancer,"
Lys Symonette said. "But she could take pain. She never complained, never cringed."

When she departed the hospital, Lenya went to Margo Harris's apartment to recuperate. "She believed she was going
to be all right," Harris remembered. "She had a tremendous
will power and nothing would stand in her way. Not even
death."

But soon Lenya found living with Harris difficult, and Lys
Symonette received a frantic telephone call: "I can't stand it
here!" Lenya cried. "You've got to come and take me to my
own place!"

Harris insisted on accompanying them to Lenya's East 55th
Street apartment, and she would not leave when Lenya was settled. "It was raining heavily," Symonette recalled,

and Margo said she'd have to stay, that she couldn't get a taxi in the rain. That was the only time I ever heard Lenya holler with real vulgarity—she threw Margo out with incredible language, just had to get rid of her. She then told me, very calmly, that she had had cancer but that she was going to get better, that she was cured of it. And she was well for about a half a year.

Lenya's attitude toward Margo Harris was nothing if not volatile. She could be infuriated by what she called Harris's exaggerated attention and control, but she was often grateful for her ministering. She might call Harris "The Pest" to others, she might often ask Harris to leave her alone, and Harris might be ignored on the telephone. But in two letters to Ted Mitchell, Lenya praised

> my friend Margo who helps more than I can say. I would not have the patience. Sometimes when I can't do things as fast as I would like to, I am irritable and cranky. That's where her patience comes in. . . . Margo is a great help to me. She nursed her late husband for five years and knows how to treat me when I get impatient.

With the holidays came the news that Mary Daniel had died in West Virginia on Christmas Day 1977. "I had just talked to her the day before and she sounded as nice as always," Lenya wrote Ted Mitchell. "She died in her sleep. It's a miracle she lived that long with that damaged heart of hers. I would have loved to see her once more." And as for herself: "I will be, so my doctor tells me, my old self in about two months."

That winter there was exceptionally heavy snowfall in the Northeast. "I am looking out the window where fourteen inches of snow are lying on the field," Lenya added in the same letter to Mitchell. "It's lovely and I hope it won't melt too soon. It's so peaceful to look at." And to Bunny Caniff, after a blizzard in early February 1978, she wrote,

> I could not open my kitchen door on account of the snow. About four inches are still there, waiting to be kissed by the sun. You know my passion for winter, so I enjoyed every minute of it. . . . I have to do my shopping. It's very cold

and wonderfully sunny. I will take a walk through the snow
on my return, and I see you [in Southern California] shivering
at that report.

On April 4, the Rockland County Center for the Arts sponsored a dinner in Lenya's honor at the Rockland Country Club
in Sparkill. Helen Hayes joined Alan Jay Lerner, Jack Gilford,
Jo Sullivan (the actress-singer who had appeared with Lenya in
the Theatre de Lys *Threepenny Opera*, and the widow of composer Frank Loesser) and others in celebrating Lenya's life and
career. Joan Mondale, wife of the vice-president of the United
States, was hostess.

When Lenya learned from Ted Mitchell that his brother David
had died of leukemia, she offered what comfort she could, in a
letter dated April 11:

> I am not very good in consoling you. I wish I could. I have
> had my share of sorrow in my life and I know time will help
> you to learn to live without him. I hope you will find some
> joy again and remember dear David for the good days I am
> sure you had with him. Those are the things one tries to hold
> on to. I hope I will see you during the summer. Right now I
> am not in the best of health but improving slowly.

But she was not, indeed, improving slowly, nor at all. She
began to have abdominal discomfort and bladder problems that
spring, as Lys Symonette recalled,

> but she was given nothing but pain-killers. Eventually they
> didn't help and her pain got worse, and although she could
> tolerate pain this was beyond her endurance. I encouraged
> her to go to a well-known and highly respected internist, Dr.
> [Hugh] Davidson. He sent her to a urologist, a Dr. Marshall,
> who diagnosed cancer of the bladder.

Before she underwent treatment, however, Lenya drew up a
new will, in which she bequeathed Weill's Steinway upright piano to Margo Harris; a weaving of a clown to Milton Coleman;
a gold watch Kurt had given her to Alfred Rice (an attorney);
$10,000 to Lys Symonette; and $5,000 and some furniture and
furnishings to Victor Carl Guarneri. She also left royalties from

ASCAP and its German equivalent, together with all royalty income due her in perpetuity, as well as Weill memorabilia, manuscripts and compositions to the Kurt Weill Foundation for Music, which she had founded "for the purpose of providing funds for musical activities and/or musical education projects dedicated to immortalizing the music of Kurt Weill." There were also provisions for the interest from a trust to be given to her sister, to Anna Krebs and to Margo Harris.

And so on June 6 Lenya entered New York Hospital, where she underwent bladder surgery. "All the nurses loved her," Symonette said, "she was so sweet and courageous and uncomplaining."

Anna Krebs visited from Hamburg to be with Lenya daily at the hospital, and then to help when Lenya was released the first week of July. "Anna was marvelously helpful when those of us who had families and jobs couldn't be there all the time that summer," according to Lys Symonette,

> and Lenya required a lot of care, even though she tried to be cheerful and independent. She had a catheter which was attached to a bag, which she just slipped into a shopping bag, and walked around with it as if it were the most normal thing in the world. She made light of the whole situation. She didn't know and didn't want to know how serious it was.

Although she continued to be plagued with urinary incontinence, Lenya made a quick recovery and was for a while pain-free. At the end of July, Anna Krebs returned to Germany, and Margo Harris took Lenya to Maine for several weeks.

On September 17, Lenya wrote to Ted Mitchell: "I am spending most of my time at [Brook House] since I am still pretty shaky and have to take it easy. . . . I can't write letters for the time being. My back hurts too quickly." Her general discomfort was aggravated by a broken left wrist, suffered when she slipped at home and requiring a day's stay at Nyack Hospital in September. This, too, she endured in good spirits. (In her last years, the frequent fractures from minor falls were due to osteoporosis, a common malady afflicting the elderly—especially women who are slightly built and heavy smokers.)

Her eightieth birthday, in October, was marked by a concert of Kurt's symphonic music by the Greenwich Philharmonic at

Avery Fisher Hall, Lincoln Center. "With her arm in a sling,"
Lys Symonette remembered, "Lenya put on a red morning gown
that she'd inherited as a hand-me-down from the late wife of an
acquaintance, and she looked fabulous." (Milton Caniff always
insisted that Lenya was "the only red-head I ever knew who
could wear red and get away with it.") Lenya thoroughly enjoyed the evening, which included performances of Weill's first
symphony; of the *Quodlibet*, an orchestral suite from the children's pantomime *Die Zaubernacht*, the original 1922 preparation of which had been the setting of her first encounter with
Weill; the New York premiere of Weill's *The New Orpheus* (a
1925 cantata for soprano, violin and orchestra); and a suite from
The Threepenny Opera.

She returned to Fisher Hall on November 12, when a concert
of musical works by John Kander and Fred Ebb was held to
benefit the American Musical and Dramatic Academy. To everyone's delight, Lenya walked onstage with Jack Gilford and,
smiling broadly, sang "So What?" and the "Pineapple Song"
from *Cabaret*.

Then, before departing for a Christmas visit to Anna Krebs
in Hamburg, Lenya summoned her attorneys and drew up a
codicil to the will she had signed in May. Now, the Steinway
piano in her apartment was left to the Kurt Weill Foundation;
and the sums of money and property bequeathed to Lys Symonette and Victor Carl Guarneri were altered, with Symonette
now to receive $5,000, and Guarneri $40,000. In addition, there
were now bequests to Kurt's grandnephews and grandnieces,
and to her own nephew, niece and grandnephews ($2,000 to
each of ten people). There were then provisions for apportionment of a trust fund among her sister, Anna Krebs and the Kurt
Weill Foundation for Music. There was no provision at all for
Margo Harris.

From Hamburg, Lenya wrote to Victor Carl Guarneri on December 30:

> From yesterday to today fell about five inches of snow which
> didn't stop us from taking a long walk to a wonderful mu-
> seum. Yesterday we went to a music shop like Schirmer's [a
> New York store] where my appearance caused a little riot.
> Needless to say I had to sign all kinds of programs, records,
> etc. It was all great fun.

And to Hesper Anderson she wrote on January 2, 1979, "I am having a lovely time here with Anna. It was a good idea to get away for a while." Returning home the following week she wrote another card to Anderson: "It's depressing after having such a good time to return to an empty house, [but] I will love it again."

In January, Lenya sat for an interview with Schuyler Chapin, for public television's *Skyline* series (broadcast January 30) and then she tackled a pile of correspondence. In cards and notes that were sometimes handwritten, Lenya's calm and cheerful tone prevailed, despite penmanship indicating a progressive weakness. In March, she was back in Nyack Hospital, this time to treat a fractured shoulder, sustained when she slipped on ice near Brook House in February. "I am still marching to the hospital out here in Nyack three times a week [for physical therapy on the fractured shoulder]," she wrote to Ted Mitchell on May 2. "Such a bore but very important not to be left with a stiff arm." Her vitality amazed and edified everyone who knew her.

"A few times, when she was very ill at home [in her New York apartment]," recalled her neighbor Ken Andorn,

> she asked me to come fix something in the apartment, or to see if I could improve her television reception by fiddling with the antenna. But it was really the company she wanted. The request was an excuse. Then she was afraid that a leak in her bedroom ceiling would cause the plaster to collapse on her bed—a penthouse terrace was directly above. So she had a bed set up at the far end of her living room, and there she slept.

"I am now trying acupuncture [she wrote Ted Mitchell on May 27]. Luckily we have here in New City a Chinese doctor who is very good. I hope by the end of summer I will be my old self again, with a few wrinkles added." Anna Krebs came for the summer, performing household chores and generally assuming the duties that were once Mary Daniel's.

That autumn, Lenya attended meetings regarding the imminent production of *Rise and Fall of the City of Mahagonny* at the Metropolitan Opera, which had its premiere on November 16. During rehearsals, she met the soprano Teresa Stratas, who would sing the role of Jenny and soon become an interpreter of

Weill's songs. Lenya also attended the dress rehearsal, where she made only one rejected suggestion to conductor James Levine, regarding the tempo of the "Alabama Song."

"During *Mahagonny* rehearsals [Stratas recalled in an interview], she would say nothing, only sit watchfully. When I would ask for help and whether or not I was doing it right, all she would tell me was, 'Just keep doing what you're doing.' "

Despite Stratas's initial uneasiness, Lenya in fact liked her and admired her thoughtful approach to the role.

> At first [Stratas continued] I had wondered, is Lenya going to try to control me? I resented her. I wouldn't talk on the phone when she called. I'd make excuses to avoid getting together. It was the way a child resists a parent. But she was so patient with me. . . . You can imagine the privilege of being given the Weill songs, but simultaneously I feared being compromised by the burden. . . . She felt resentment, too. I was taking what had been hers. But she must have loved Kurt so much to do all she did to keep his music alive, and to relinquish her hold.

On Sunday, November 18, the same weekend of the *Mahagonny* premiere, Cheryl Crawford, Alan Jay Lerner, Elmer Rice, José Quintero, Tennessee Williams and Lotte Lenya were inducted into the Theater Hall of Fame after an election by the nation's drama critics.

On January 4, 1980, she attended a musical celebration at New York's Whitney Museum, where Lenya heard Teresa Stratas, Mabel Mercer and the Gregg Smith Singers. Then, for a Weill eightieth birthday tribute, she flew to Wayne State University in Detroit on February 29, where she was also awarded the university's citation "for humanity in the arts." Cheerful and vivacious in a simple black suit, and with the orange hair and ubiquitous cigarette, her trademarks by this time, she greeted the press and charmed the students.

"I'm not so remarkable, really," she said to a reporter, deflecting praise about her appearance and energy: "It's just that so many other people are lazy! I never cared about age. I think it's better to live to 81 than die beautifully at 25, don't you think?" And then she answered a question about her professional plans:

No more recordings. I have done my job. All those records are a guide for young singers. Now I work in the background. I'm as free as a bird. I will go on for however many years I have left.

Lenya kept her usual sharp eye over performances and productions of Kurt's work. When Universal Edition informed her of a proposal to reduce the orchestration for a new production, she fired back: "Under no circumstances will I allow this major work Mahagonny played on two pianos with singing actors!" And when Paul Moor sent a tape of a German broadcast of *Die Bürgschaft*, she commented in her reply:

What in heaven's sake had the conductor in mind cutting two bars here, four there, etc. Terrible tempi . . . and so many cuts for no reason. The singers—well, they depend on the conductor. I can't say I liked any of them.

She concluded with an equally candid political comment:

With the elections coming up, time seems to stand still. What the big excitement is for I don't know. . . . There are two possibilities: Carter, Reagan—ugh!

Her correspondence, especially to the children of old friends, never wavered in its genial tone and cheerful encouragement. To Burgess Meredith's son Jonathan, who had sent Lenya a recording of his guitar-playing, she replied with a note of gratitude, adding that "a few of my young generation friends have enjoyed the music. . . . It took me some time to dig it, but I like it too," and she wished him well.

Margo Harris often accompanied Lenya to social events, but a ride home from one ended disastrously. On April 6, they had been to a neighbor's dinner party, where the wine had flowed freely. Against advice, Lenya insisted on driving, lost control of her car, struck a telephone pole and she and Margo landed in a ditch off Congers Road, New City. When they were rescued, Lenya and Harris had not suffered so much as the car, but bruises and the general shock to her already weakened system (and to the recently fractured shoulder) put Lenya in Nyack Hospital.

The accident caused rancor when Lenya refused to pay what

she considered Harris's exorbitant medical claims. Harris's insurance company then brought suit against the ailing Lenya. A begrudging settlement was finally reached (and Lenya agreed to pay part of the claim) after it was suggested that the Department of Motor Vehicles would be displeased to learn that Lenya had been drinking.

She recovered in time for the Atlanta visit of the Metropolitan Opera's spring tour of *Mahagonny*. This she attended with Ronald Freed, president of European American Music and the representative, on behalf of Universal Edition in North America, of a major selection of Weill's work. Before they departed New York, however, Lenya asked Freed not to tell Margo Harris they were going to Atlanta; she was afraid Harris would insist on accompanying them.

> It was a very exciting time for her [Freed recalled] and she was quite wonderful. I hate flying, and she had a special something to cure fear of flying—a container of martinis. It was a trip I'll never remember. That season, and on our other visits during the last years of her life, she liked to discuss things that made her laugh. She was also hungry for news of young composers we were publishing.

Back in New City, Lenya's old friend Anna Krebs again arrived to help throughout the summer, for Lenya now had constant back pain—but also constant optimism, as indicated in a July 28 note to painter Richard Ely, for whom she had sat. "Come Labor Day it [the back pain] will change—everybody changes at that time. No white slacks any more, no more straw hats, no bikini." She continued to distract herself from discomfort by reading widely and seriously. Anna Krebs had sent her Klaus Mann's *Mephisto*, which (she wrote to Paul Moor) she thought "well written, [but] I don't think it would go well here. One has to have lived in Berlin to know the secrets. Why it was forbidden in 1968 is beyond me. Don't the Germans like to be reminded of their glorious times?"

Frail though she was, she insisted on attending another Kurt Weill concert in Washington in November, as she had insisted on attending a performance of *Silverlake* (as it was called) at the New York City Opera earlier that year. She responded graciously when asked to pose for publicity photographs and answer questions from reporters. As it had been so often, no one guessed her pains. Harriet Pinover accompanied her to the Washington concert at the Kennedy Center. "She was in failing health at this time, and I quickly realized why she had arranged for us to share a bedroom at the hotel—she simply hadn't the energy to dress herself, she needed help with the simplest chores."

Lenya's Christmas card that year to Hilde Halpern, then living in London, was full of memories:

> I don't like holidays, not here—it's a giant supermarket, and I'm thinking with nostalgia of my childhood with a tiny Christmas tree and a doll with a porcelain head which I smashed the same evening, showing it to my little friend one flight up the stone steps, and fell. Still, it was Christmas.

Before the year was over, she expanded her financial portfolio by purchasing tax-exempt securities in the amount of $206,858. At the same time, Kurt's nephew by marriage, Vlasek Holesovsky, wrote that he was suffering from cancer and beginning chemotherapy. She replied with details of her own illness:

> You only just started your chemotherapy and may very well be one of the lucky ones on which it may work. . . . You may or may not know that I have been undergoing two severe cancer operations myself, whereby one of my surgeons told me to my face that I would never make it. However, my strong desire to be a survivor pulled me through—and so far, so good. After that I suffered a broken shoulder, a broken wrist and finally a car accident, which left me with a constant backache, which I simply ignore.

This was a preface to her refusal of Holesovsky's request for money to help himself and then his wife in case of his probable death:

> When you write me that you don't know how Hanne [his wife, daughter of Kurt's brother] could cope emotionally and financially, should she be left alone, I can only remind you that I have been made a widow three times and none of my husbands—including Kurt—left me as a "rich widow." I had

to start my career from scratch at an age about the same as
Hanne, and I have been working until this very day to support
myself. Contrary to common belief, Kurt's affairs were in a
mess at the time of his death, and I believe I can say in all
truthfulness that the legal fees I paid to bring them in order
came very close to the income I derived. . . . I am truly sorry
that I cannot help you in your unhappy situation. But I am
sure you will understand that at my age I cannot *possibly* take
on any kind of financial obligations.

The letter, uncharacteristically sanctimonious and more than
a little disingenuous, does not reveal Lenya at her best. Perhaps
her lifelong fear of poverty, which now led her beyond frugality
into downright stinginess, blinded her to the moral claim Kurt's
relatives could surely make to some modest share of his estate—
particularly under these circumstances. And perhaps she still
resented the Weill family's opposition to the marriage with Kurt,
and their condescension toward her. Whatever the conscious or
unconscious grounds for this reply, Kurt's art (as she was first
to recognize) had made her what she was, and in his honor she
surely could have helped his family.

But quite apart from her attitude about donations, Lenya's
letter reveals a strong sense of self and of accomplishment at
the end of her life. She would not have stated it so formally, but
in fact she had been both catalyst and casualty of many roles a
woman could play in relation to a man in the twentieth century.

Lenya had been a frightened and abused child, a teenage
prostitute, and a hopeful young apprentice in a variety of demanding crafts. She had become the freewheeling wife of a
musical genius and had supported him at every step of his career, in spite of her occasionally strong feelings of resentment
that he preferred his art to her. She had become a recognized
exponent of that art, and she had proven her talents independently as well.

She was both divorcée and remarried woman, and she never
put anyone's life or career ahead of the man who was always her
best friend. She had become a kind of surrogate mother *man-
quée* to several young men, some of them her lovers, others her
husbands. She had become the keeper of her first husband's
flame and, in midlife, she had become a living legend with a

revived career. She had become a screen personality, a concert and recording artist and a cultural idol completely *sui generis*.

It is difficult to mention many other women who passed through so many cultural epochs and personal phases, and who like her maintained her integrity, her simplicity and her blunt refusal to aggrandize, advertise or apologize for herself. She could be ruthless, withdrawn and suspicious, but she could also be deeply compassionate. She had an insatiable thirst for knowledge, and she never capitalized on her pain or misfortune to win sympathy. For more than eighty years, she unwaveringly embraced life with all its pleasures and all its problems.

Defiant at some times and sometimes vulnerable, she had become, onstage and off, a digest of much that a woman can be, fears to be and longs to be in contemporary society. But perhaps most impressive of all her traits: she had evoked from within herself a mysterious mechanism by which she transformed the meanings of courage and of survival from clichés of praise to inner habits, and from inner habits to a tangible stance toward the world. Forbearance had become endurance, endurance had become her honor.

Lenya's condition deteriorated further in the early weeks of 1981, and she asked Paul Moor's forgiveness for a "sloppily written letter" she wrote to him in Berlin on February 11. "I have neuralgia in my back, hips, elbows, toes, knees. There is not much left to be hurt." Her humor, however, never flagged: "When you left [after a recent visit] I found a string of brown beads. Are they yours? Looks like a rosary of some strange country. . . . They are too short for me to wear, otherwise you never would get them back."

But contrary to what she had told Moor about "not much left to be hurt," unfortunately there was, and the hurt came at her own insistence. On February 22 she signed herself into Doctors Hospital, and next day an unnecessary surgical procedure was performed. Her entire body was by this time laced with metastatic disease—cancer had spread to her bones, liver and lungs, and the "neuralgia" was, as she well knew, the sign of its virulent spread even to her extremities. Nevertheless, in a move that shocked everyone who cared for her, she demanded cosmetic surgery for breast beautification.

Among those who tried to dissuade her was Harriet Pinover.

When she insisted on having this done I objected strenuously, and told her so. "Lenya," I asked, "what do you want to do—sing 'Mack the Knife' in a topless bar?" But she replied, "I just can't stand my body, I can't stand seeing myself when I take a bath." So I took her to the hospital, and she introduced me as her daughter and told them I was to be contacted in case of emergency. She was very sick with cancer by this time, and she knew it, although she never discussed it. When the surgeon came in to mark her for the cosmetic surgery, I told her it wasn't too late for her to back out and leave the hospital. But she was determined, and she went ahead with it.

Three weeks after her discharge from the hospital, she again fell at home and fractured two vertebrae. In March, she signed another codicil to her will, leaving everything in her possession relative to Kurt Weill—manuscripts, memorabilia, photographs, letters, personal articles—to the Yale University Library.

She was hospitalized three more times over the next three months—at Lenox Hill and New York hospitals—for tests and therapies, but in spite of great fatigue and discomfort when fluid accumulation caused abdominal distention, she cheerfully summoned the strength to honor her friends Fred Ebb and John Kander. On March 29 their new musical *Woman of the Year* opened on Broadway, and Lenya rose from her bed to gather with them and a small group to await the first notices.

"Of course those were the television reviews," Ebb remembered. "One of them came on, and to say the least he didn't like the show. When he gave his unflattering comment, Lenya shrieked, 'You son of a bitch! Stupid!' We had nobody more loyal than Lenya."

With equally undiminished passion, her loyalty to Kurt Weill's legacy also continued. In March she fired off a stern letter to Alfred Schlee at Universal Edition after she learned that a production of *The Threepenny Opera* at the Berliner Ensemble in East Berlin was to be reorchestrated for a rock band:

I never gave nor will I ever give authorization to anyone to alter the instrumentation, nor to make any music changes for performances of *Threepenny Opera* in East Berlin.

By this time she was weary of the long battles on behalf of Kurt's work, but nothing undermined the commitment that had sustained her for over thirty years—ever since she had first articulated, in the letter to Manfred George, what would become the fundamental goal of her life: "to fight for this music, to keep it alive, to do everything in my power to make it known."

That summer, after a prolonged stay in her New York apartment (to be closer to her physicians and surgeons) she was able to return to Brook House, but she required daily nursing care. Burgess Meredith's daughter Tala visited, and the two sat gazing out over the back field. "I knew you before you were born," Lenya said. She then pointed to the field. "Your mother walked over to visit me this way when she was eight months pregnant with you," she said, holding her stomach in imitation of a woman large with child. She patted herself gently and smiled. But then she became very quiet and her smile faded.

"They found something here, inside me," she whispered to Tala, her hand still on her abdomen. She took the younger woman's hand and held it, saying nothing, only wiping the perspiration of the summer heat and of her fever and pain from her face and mouth. Tala never forgot that some of Lenya's pink lipstick rubbed on the tissue. Lenya noticed that too, and smiled. She then pointed to pink flowers on Tala's dress, the same color as her own lipstick. "Now *this* would be a good color lipstick for *you*!" Lenya said, patting the girl's hand and then closing her eyes. It was the last time they met.

Ted Mitchell also visited that season. "The last time we had a long talk at Brook House," he recalled,

> she turned to me—as if to set the record straight once and for all—and as we were discussing Russell Detwiler, she said, "Of all my husbands I loved Russi the most." She said it in such a heartbreaking tone of voice.

In September, Lenya read of the death of Richard Siemanowski, at age fifty-five, from heart failure hastened by alcoholism. Enshrouded in her own pain, and requiring constant nursing care, she still expressed pity that this man should die so young. Like Russell, she may have thought. Like George. Like Kurt. Like Howard Schwartz, her young lover during the war who had gone down in a fiery crash.

In late September, Lenya (accompanied by Margo Harris) asked her physician about the future, about nursing care, home services, all the details of debilitating illness. But there would be no need for that, she was told, and when Lenya quietly asked if the end was near, he nodded yes. Lenya's face showed no sign of emotion or expression; she had, after all, known the truth for a long while.

A few days later, Harris urged Lenya to enter Memorial Sloan-Kettering Cancer Center where, she insisted, curative treatment could be applied: Lenya was going to improve, she said, Lenya would soon be on the path to recovery. Proper treatment was all she required, and the correct diet. "Lenya had no resistance by this time," Lys Symonette said.

> She was in great pain, she was unsteady, and now she was beginning to have the problem of fluid [accumulation, which caused abdominal swelling]. Lenya was simply glad that someone took over. But she was greatly angered by Margo's insistence that her illness was all mental, and that Lenya should see a psychiatrist!

In the hospital, many of her old friends tried to visit or call, but they were prevented by Harris, who had drawn up a list of those who could have access to Lenya and those who should be barred. Only a few celebrities or those who forced their way managed to gain entry, and Harris continually encouraged Lenya to discourage people from contacting her.

"There was a list of approved people for hospital visits when Lenya was dying," Fred Ebb recalled. "I was on the list, and I visited her, but even Hal Prince was shut out. There she was, frail and sick, but she smiled weakly and whispered, 'Oh, I'm so tired,' and our visit was short."

"I remember," Harold Prince added, "that my feelings were somewhat hurt that I was not permitted to visit her in the hospital, or at the home of her friend later. But an unfortunate conflict around her prevented that."

On Lenya's eighty-third birthday, October 18, Harris arranged a celebration in the hospital room, complete with balloons. Then Lys Symonette arrived and suddenly Lenya thrust out her hand. "Look what Margo gave me!" she whispered.

"And there," Symonette said, "was a ring on her finger! I

had the feeling that Lenya was saying to me, 'I'm going to explain this before you ask me what it is and how I got it!' " Lenya was simply too weak to fight the gesture. Margo Harris then said proudly, "Oh yes, it's been in my family for generations!" Later, when other friends arrived, Lenya, embarrassed by it, removed the ring so as not to invite questions about it—an action which, friends observed, caused Harris considerable dismay.

After a (futile) surgical procedure and unrealized plans for yet another operation in October, physicians at Memorial Sloan-Kettering Cancer Center finally admitted there was nothing more to be done for Lenya in the hospital, and Harris replied at once that she would care for Lenya at her own home. And so, on October 28, she was transferred to her friend's thirty-third-floor apartment at 300 East 74th Street, where a hospital bed was installed in a small second bedroom Harris normally used as her sculpture studio. She encouraged Lenya to walk, to eat, to have psychiatric counseling. Remarkably, a psychic was brought in, but Lenya was too weak to respond. She was declining rapidly by the end of October, and had little energy, even for brief conversation.

Teresa Stratas arrived one afternoon, and generously stayed for several weeks. "That meant so much to Lenya," according to Lys Symonette. "Stratas literally slept on the floor of Lenya's room [in Harris's apartment] to be with her until she had to begin rehearsals for *La Bohème* [at the Metropolitan Opera]."

As the days grew short that autumn, Lenya was conscious only for a few moments each day. On a dark and rainy afternoon, while Stratas was visiting, Lenya suddenly awoke. "Teresa, what are you thinking?"

"I'm thinking how I don't like the fall, Lenya, and how I hate the winter."

"Which seasons *do* you like then?"

"I like the summer a lot, and I love the spring." And then Stratas asked Lenya, "Which seasons do *you* like?"

There was the hint of a smile, and Lenya tried to lift her hand. "I love them all," she whispered.

A few friends were eventually permitted to visit, but many were not. "When I called to ask if I might come," Ken Andorn said, "Lenya whispered, 'I don't think, Ken, that you'll be coming.' "

"When I visited her at the apartment," Fred Ebb remembered, "she was full of tubes. Her lungs were filling up frequently, and she had to be drained. She was in great misery, but she endured without complaining."

Neil Fujita also arrived.

Toward the end, there was no way many of her old friends could draw near her. She was well guarded. Reasons and excuses were given: she was incapable, she was too frail. Only a very few people were permitted to see her, and for me this was sadness. All the old friends were excluded. One day, however, I was invited. I took her hand. She was listless and pale and unable to speak. I looked around at the little room, a small guest room, with a nurse sitting there. Lenya didn't even know who she was, I'm sure. It became ugly. Some people became more concerned with her will, with all the material things.

Lawyers were indeed summoned, and on November 6 Lenya's signature, an entirely illegible scrawl, was put to a new will.

Her piano was now bequeathed to the Kurt Weill Foundation for Music; the weaving of a clown to Milton Coleman; and the gold watch to Alfred Rice. Lys Symonette was still to receive $5,000; Victor Carl Guarneri's inheritance was now to be $30,000 and the items of furniture specified earlier by her. The ten bequests of two thousand dollars each to her relatives and Kurt's remained as before, and paintings by Russell Detwiler were left to Teresa Stratas and a friend of Lenya, Alfred Andriola. Royalties from Kurt Weill's music would go to the Foundation, whose trustees, at her request, elected Kim Kowalke as president and Lys Symonette as artistic executive.

But also in the last will it was stipulated that Margo Harris was to receive the complete contents of Brook House, and the income from a trust from the residue of her estate would be distributed among Lenya's sister, Anna Krebs and Margo Harris. As executors and trustees she appointed Alfred Rice and Alfred Andriola (the latter died shortly thereafter).

Late one afternoon the first week of November, Ted Mitchell arrived. Lenya was so heavily medicated that she needed time to recognize him. Neither he nor anyone had ever seen her hair completely white and down on her shoulders, but her face appeared astonishingly lineless, as if pain had refined every wrinkle. Her fingernails were freshly painted bright red, and she tried to make her visitor feel comfortable in so distressing a situation. He watched as she seemed to sleep, and then he could not restrain his tears. But in the angular autumn twilight he then heard her whisper, "Don't cry—the doctor says I might recover." Almost as if she believed that, she then seemed to rally, to exert a last powerful effort to beat the illness she always said was just a nuisance—only one obstacle among many that she could overcome, as she had so many others.

"The last weeks were very difficult," according to Margo Harris, who—whatever the complexities of her relationship with Lenya—must be credited for her attentive care and constant vigilance at the end.

She often said good-bye [Harris recalled], but she couldn't believe she was going to die. She hoped against hope always. She did not die easily. She did not have much pain, and she did not want drugs because she wanted to be alive—to be alert was terribly important to her. She never gave in, and she wasn't a complainer.

Toward Thanksgiving, Hesper Anderson arrived, who had been not only a loyal friend but was also like a daughter. "I knew how much she loved life, and how she seemed to be clinging, just clinging with all her might. I sat with her and told her yes, it was all right to let go."

During the last two weeks of November, less alert but also less restless, she seemed to "see" people from her past, in dreams and hallucinations. Her visitors—among them Ted Mitchell, Neil Fujita, Ronald Freed, Teresa Stratas, Victor Carl Guarneri—often heard a gentle litany of those she had known and loved and lost, from the grimy alleys of Penzing to the clear air of Zurich; from Berlin, with its dusty stages, to Paris and London, with their crowded music halls; from New York, with its cramped dressing rooms, to the private homes and professional studios she had known all over the world.

"Kurt," the visitors heard her whisper, and "Schwarzi." She whispered of Pasetti, and of the smiling Tilly Losch, who had died not long after their last visit in 1975. "George," Lenya

said more than once, and even more often, "Russi . . . Russi."
Mary Daniel's name was on her lips, too. She even spoke the
old Viennese nicknames for "Mother" and "Father," and there
were some names that were unclear. It seemed as if she were
drawing toward them all, and drawing them to herself now,
when everything bitter and shallow and extraneous was fading
with the autumn light. Now at last, as Hesper Anderson had
said, she could let go.

During early afternoon on Friday, November 27, 1981, the
names were heard no more. Lenya became very still, her breathing slow and irregular. Then, at five-thirty, there was the flicker
of a smile, her lips moved silently, and with one long sigh she
joined them.

NOTES

For brevity, details of *interviews* conducted for this book are supplied only at the first citation; unless otherwise stated, subsequent quotations from the same source derive from the identical interview with that source. It should also be remarked that bibliographical detail on several German newspaper reviews (beyond the name of the journal and the reviewer) has been lost over the decades. Thus there is often no more information than what is stated in the text.

CHAPTER ONE

1 "*Cabaret* has" Kevin Kelly, *Boston Globe*, Oct. 11, 1966, p. 13.
4 "the central" *Ibid*.
4 "are gifted" Elliot Norton, *Record American*, Oct. 11, 1966, p. 26.
4 "an acute" Samuel Hirsch, *Boston Herald*, Oct. 11, 1966, p. 16.
4 "Lotte Lenya" Alta Maloney, *Boston Traveler*, Oct. 12, 1966, p.4.
5 "Miss Lenya" Walter Kerr, *New York Times*, Nov. 21, 1966, p. 49.
5 "patented brand" Julius Novick, *Village Voice*, Dec. 1, 1966, p. 22.

CHAPTER TWO

11 "Imperial Vienna" Salka Viertel, *The Kindness of Strangers* (New York: Holt, Rinehart, Winston, 1969), pp. 35–36.
12 "The gentleman" quoted in S. C. Burchell, "The Last Waltz in Vienna," *Horizon*, vol. 10, no. 1 (Winter 1968), p. 95.
12 "These were" Bernard Holland, "Through Vienna's Glass, Darkly," *New York Times*, Sept. 18, 1986, C27.
13 "The people" quoted in Burchell, art. cit., p. 86.
13 "a testing-lab" quoted in Kirk Varnedoe, *Vienna 1900: Art, Architecture and Design* (New York: The Museum of Modern Art, 1986), pp. 15–16.
19 "She said" Hilde Halpern to DS, Nov. 25, 1986.
20 "Some parts" Margot Aufricht to DS, Mar. 24, 1986.
21 "This part" Paul Moor to DS, Mar. 24, 1986.

28 "Karoline herself had an abortion" This fact was confided by Lenya to Lys Symonette.

30 "Cabaret Voltaire" Lisa Appignanesi, *Cabaret: The First Hundred Years* (New York: Grove Press, 1984), p. 76.

31 "His long" Lenya, in Charles Osborne, "Berlin in the Twenties: Conversations with Otto Klemperer and Lotte Lenya," *London Magazine*, vol. 1, no. 2 (May 1961), p. 47.

31 "She was" Elisabeth Bergner, *Bewundert viel und viel gescholten . . . Unordentliche Erinnerungen* (München: Goldmann, 1978), pp. 76–77; trans. by Prof. Jon Zimmermann.

35 "She told" Harriet Pinover to DS, Nov. 12, 1985.

CHAPTER THREE

36 "We thought" Lenya to Alan Rich, oral history, KWF-WLRC.

36 "a wonderful" Brecht, cited in Werner Frisch and K. W. Obermeyer, *Brecht in Augsburg* (Frankfurt, 1976), translated in Ronald Hayman, *Brecht* (New York: Oxford University Press, 1983), p. 53.

37 "swept in" Hans Heinsheimer, *Best Regards to Aida* (New York: Knopf, 1968), p. 17.

37 "There was" Lenya, in *Playbill*, Apr. 16, 1962, pp. 7–8, 10–11.

38 "what this" quoted in Percy Knauth, "Are We as Nude, Even as Lewd, as Brazen Old Berlin?" *New York Times*, Oct. 27, 1974, sec. 2, pp. 1, 15.

39 "a place" Gershon Kingsley to DS, Apr. 14, 1986.

39 "Boys" Stefan Zweig, *Die Welt von Gestern* (Stockholm, 1947), pp. 286–287, trans. and cited in Hayman, p. 53.

41 "Frequently" Julius Cohn, cited in Eberhard Roters et al., *Berlin, 1910–1933* (New York: Rizzoli, 1982), p. 34.

41 "It was" Nora Hodges, trans., *George Grosz: An Autobiography* (New York: Imago/Macmillan, 1983), p. 149.

42 "In such" Knauth, art. cit., p. 15.

42 "in a strange" *Ibid*.

48 "He exuded" Heinsheimer, p. 109.

50 "There were" Dimitri Mitropoulos, quoted in notes compiled by George Davis for the (unrealized) biography of KW.

51 "Weill had" Claudio Arrau, *ibid*.

51 "the most important" Maurice Abravanel to DS, Sept. 25, 1985.

51 "There had been" Osborne, art cit., p. 47.

53 "She had" Gigi Gilpin to DS, Dec. 9, 1985.

53 "There was" Lys Symonette to DS, Nov. 18, 1985.

58 "People have" Lenya to Edwin Newman, NBC television program, *Speaking Freely*, interview, Oct. 14, 1970.

CHAPTER FOUR

62 "the most powerful" Weill, quoted in Hayman, p. 122.

62 "From that" Lenya, *Ibid.*

64 "When Brecht and I" Kurt Weill, "Notes to My Opera Mahagonny," in Bertolt Brecht, *Rise and Fall of the City of Mahagonny and The Seven Deadly Sins*, trans. W. H. Auden and Chester Kallman; ed. John Willett and Ralph Manheim (London: Eyre Methuen, 1979), p. 91.

68 "It's just" Hanne Weill Holesovsky, oral history, KWF-WLRC, Dec. 16, 1983.

71 "she looked" quoted in Hayman, p. 132.

72 "Four actresses" Alfred Kerr, *Berliner Tageblatt*, Sept. 1, 1928.

72 "proclaims a new" Herbert Ihering, *Berliner Bösen-Courier*, Sept. 1, 1928.

72 "Weigel and" Bergner, p. 77; trans. Prof. Jon Zimmermann.

73 "When the checks" Heinsheimer, p. 126.

73 "We liked" Weill, on the NBC radio network show, "I'm an American!" Mar. 9, 1941.

74 "Weill with Brecht" Ned Rorem, "Notes on Weill," *Opera News*, Jan. 21, 1984, p. 16.

77 "For the female characters" review by critic Monty Jacobs (newspaper source unknown, as for the contemporaneous review excerpts cited in the text), Nov. 30, 1928; trans. Ute Claus.

81 "[Lenya] is the" David Drew, *Kurt Weill: A Handbook* (Berkeley and Los Angeles: University of California Press, 1987), p. 375.

83 "Two men" Weill, "Introduction to the prompt book of the opera *Mahagonny*," in Brecht, trans. Auden and Kallman, p. 92.

83 "*Mahagonny* isn't" Lenya in interview with David Beams, 1961; supplied to DS by the interviewer.

84 "Even at" Alfred Polgar, "Krach in Leipzig," in his later collection, *Ja und Nein: Darstellungen von Darstellungen* (Hamburg, 1956), pp. 298ff; trans. from Ronald Sanders, *The Days Grow Short: The Life and Music of Kurt Weill* (New York: Holt, Rinehart and Winston, 1980), p. 149.

84 "fist fights" Herbert F. Peyser, "Berlin Hears Mahagonny," *New York Times*, Oct. 1, 1932.

84 "Kurt's parents and I" *Philips Music Herald*, vol. 4, no. 1 (Spring 1959), p. 9.

84 "It was" Heinsheimer, pp. 132–133.

84 "It won" Maurice Abravanel to Alan Rich, oral history, KWF-WLRC.

85 "We had" Dolly Haas to DS, Oct. 17, 1987.

89 "We sat" Lenya to Edwin Newman, Oct. 14, 1970.

90 "I was somehow" Lenya, in Stephen Wadsworth, "Zeitgeist," *Opera News*, vol. 44, no. 6 (Dec. 1, 1979), p. 43.

90 "the bourgeois world" Theodor W. Adorno, cited in Sanders, p. 156.

91 "You couldn't" Elfriede Fischinger to DS, Mar. 23, 1986.

91 "Kurt Weill" *Völkischer Beobachter*, Mar. 9, 1932.

92 "Lenya fitted herself" Heinsheimer, p. 136.

92 "She took one" Heinsheimer to DS, Mar. 12, 1986.

95 "along with the" Marcel Moré, quoted in *Philips Music Herald*, no. 3 (Autumn 1956), p. 23.

98 "It's not so" Edouard Bourlet, in *Marianne*, June 14, 1933, trans. by DS.

99 "Madame Lenya" Virgil Thomson, in Herbert G. Luft, "As We See It," *New York Post*, Nov. 11, 1960.

101 "a choreographic" Arnold L. Haskell, "Les Ballets 1933 at The Savoy," *The New English Weekly*, July 13, 1933, p. 303.

101 "a singer" *Yorkshire Post*, June 29, 1933.

101 "rather bitter" *London Sunday Express*, July 2, 1933.

102 "incomparable" Constant Lambert, "Matters Musical," *London Sunday Express*, Aug. 13, 1933.

105 "fiery, prodigal" Maria Ley Piscator to DS, Nov. 10, 1987.

CHAPTER FIVE

107 "Kurt had" Lenya to David Beams, 1961.

108 "We made" Kurt Weill on NBC radio network show, "I'm an American!" Mar. 9, 1941.

108 "Rape it" Lenya to Schuyler Chapin, PBS television program *Skyline*, interview Jan. 17, 1970 (broadcast Jan. 30).

109 "His English" Douglas Gilbert, "German Refuge [sic] Discovers Romantic America," *New York World-Telegram and Sun*, Oct. 17, 1935.

111 "The hand-picked" Marc Blitzstein in *Modern Music* 13 (Jan.–Feb. 1936): 36–37.

113 "The material" Cheryl Crawford to DS, Oct. 6, 1985.

114 "*Johnny Johnson* was" Lenya to Schuyler Chapin, Jan. 17, 1970.

116 "We spent" Lenya to Hans Dudelheim, quoted to DS, Nov. 13, 1985.

118 "deeply moved" Kurt Weill to Maxwell Anderson, Oct. 13, 1937.

118 "I had had" Burgess Meredith to DS, Feb. 7, 1986.

119 "He looked like" John F. Wharton, *Life Among the Playwrights* (New York: Quadrangle/New York Times, 1974), p. 6.

121 "My husband" Lenya to Alfred Shivers, May 15, 1978.

124 "incurably" Irving Drutman, *Good Company* (Boston: Little, Brown, 1976), p. 98.

124 "George told" Paul Moor to DS, Aug. 19, 1986.

130 "all that was" Denis de Rougemont, quoted in Virginia Spencer

Carr, *The Lonely Hunter: A Biography of Carson McCullers* (New York: Doubleday, 1975), pp. 124–125.

132 "I adored her" Hesper Anderson to DS, Mar. 22, 1986.

132 "Long before" Quentin Anderson to DS, Feb. 11, 1986.

133 "Lenya was" Milton Caniff to DS, Oct. 15, 1985.

CHAPTER SIX

135 "Miss Lenya is" Arthur Pollock, "Maxwell Anderson Writes About Love and Germans," *Brooklyn Eagle*, Oct. 23, 1941, p. 8.

135 "She comes" *Houston Press*, Apr. 25, 1942.

136 "an excellent performance" *Variety*, Sept. 16, 1941, p. 60.

136 "A rather remarkable" Russell McLauchlin, *Detroit News*, Apr. 3, 1942.

136 "Lotte Lenya's conversational" Cecil Smith, *Chicago Tribune*, Mar. 17, 1942.

136 "There is a Lotte Lenya" Ardis Smith, *Buffalo Evening News*, Feb. 6, 1942, p. 30.

136 "pedestrian" *New York Herald-Tribune*, Oct. 23, 1941.

136 "She admitted" Ken Andorn to DS, Feb. 6, 1986.

147 "I'm lucky" quoted by Dolores Sutton to DS, Jan. 20, 1986.

152 "Unfortunately" *Boston Post*, Mar. 4, 1945.

152 "lacks sparkle" Lewis Nichols, *New York Times*, Mar. 23, 1945.

155 "the most important" Olin Downes, *New York Times*, Jan. 26, 1947.

158 "it had" Cheryl Crawford, *One Naked Individual* (Indianapolis: Bobbs-Merrill, 1977), p. 171.

158 "He was thoroughly" George Jenkins to DS, Sept. 15, 1987.

161 "There was always" Lenya to Peter Adam of the BBC-TV, 1980.

CHAPTER SEVEN

165 "Don't write" Lenya, in Guy Stern, "Woman With a Mission," *The Theatre*, July 1959, pp. 12–13.

166 "I scarcely" George Davis, *ibid.*

167 "Somehow it makes" This and the preceding anecdote are recorded in Drutman, p. 95.

167 "He could help" Victor Carl Guarneri to DS, Oct. 20, 1985.

168 "But I'm not stingy" quoted by Guarneri.

169 "She was always," Milton Coleman to DS, Jan. 22, 1988.

170 "I don't remember" Lenya, in David Beams, "Lotte Lenya," *Theatre Arts*, vol. 46, no. 6 (June 1962), p. 12.

171 "the impeccable" Virgil Thomson, in *New York Herald-Tribune*, Feb. 5, 1951.

172 "George married me" Lenya to Schuyler Chapin, Jan. 17, 1979; also to Virginia Spencer Carr, May 24, 1972, cited *op. cit.*, p. 541, n. 8.

174 "I was one" Marguerite Young to DS, Sept. 15, 1986.

174 "The play wasn't" Alan Anderson to DS, Feb. 3, 1987.

174 "The playing is" Jerry Gaghan, "Barefoot in Athens," *Philadelphia Daily News*, Oct. 16, 1951, p. 34.

174 "The much maligned" Henry T. Murdock, " 'Barefoot' at Locust," *Philadelphia Inquirer*, Oct. 16, 1951.

175 "Lotte Lenya is" John Chapman, "Anderson's 'Barefoot in Athens,' " *New York Daily News*, Nov. 1, 1951.

175 "just the right" Walter Kerr, *New York Herald-Tribune*, Nov. 1, 1951, p. 22.

175 "excellent performance" Brooks Atkinson, "At the Theatre," *New York Times*, Nov. 1, 1951.

175 "Lenya knew" Paul Moor to DS, Aug. 19, 1986.

179 "Lenya took care" Virgil Thomson to Alan Rich, oral history, KWF-WLRC.

180 "Without stopping" Lenya to Alfred Shivers, May 15, 1978.

181 "On first meeting" Stanley Chase to DS, Mar. 24, 1987.

182 "She was also" Carmen Capalbo to DS, Mar. 7, 1986.

182 "the strategist" Drew, p. 8.

183 "Eighteen hours" Capalbo, in John Allen, "A Five-Year Hit for only $10,000," *New York Herald-Tribune*, Sept. 20, 1959.

184 "I remember" Julius Rudel to DS, Jan. 28, 1986.

185 "One of the" Lewis Funke, *New York Times*, Mar. 11, 1954.

185 "Lotte Lenya helps" Brooks Atkinson, *New York Times*, Mar. 21, 1954, sec. 2, p. 1.

185 "Lotte Lenya stepped" Jay Harrison, *New York Herald-Tribune*, Mar. 12, 1954, p. 12.

185 "hard to believe" Virgil Thomson, "Music and Musicians," *New York Herald-Tribune*, Mar. 21, 1954.

185 "She was really" Alan Rich to DS, Feb. 3, 1986.

191 "I had never" Andreas Meyer-Hanno, "Lenya's Return to Berlin," *Kurt Weill Newsletter*, vol. 3, no. 1 (Spring 1985), p. 9.

191 "I showed him" Lenya to Peter Adam, BBC-TV, 1980; also to Schuyler Chapin on PBS program *Skyline*, interview Jan. 17, 1979.

192 "I have completely" in Guy Stern, 44.

194 "You don't know" Lenya, quoted by Tonio Selwart to DS, Nov. 11, 1985.

CHAPTER EIGHT

200 "We are face" Jerry Tallmer, *Village Voice*, vol. 1, no. 1 (Oct. 26, 1955).

210 "George had had" Paul Moor to DS, Aug. 19, 1986.

CHAPTER NINE

220 "Miss Lenya is" Herbert Kupferberg, "The Record World: Kurt Weill's Unheard Opera," *New York Herald-Tribune* Book Review, May 4, 1958, p. 11.

220 "a cross between" Marc Blitzstein, "On Mahagonny," *Saturday Review of Literature*, May 31, 1958, p. 47.

221 "perfect diction" Victor Seroff, "Readings by Lenya," *Saturday Review of Literature*, Dec. 3, 1960, p. 57.

223 "There has never" John Martin, *New York Times*, Dec. 5, 1958, p. 38.

223 "with sardonic wit" Walter Terry, *New York Herald-Tribune*, Dec. 4, 1958.

224 "chanted" *Time*, Dec. 29, 1958, pp. 42–43.

224 "Lotte Lenya has become" Richard Lipsett, quoted in Stern, p. 45.

224 "singing solo" W.F., *New York Herald-Tribune*, Feb. 16, 1959.

226 "stridently" Edmund Tracy, "Seven Lively Sins," *The Observer*, Apr. 17, 1960.

227 "are not essential" David Drew, cover notes for the American release of the recording *Happy End* (Columbia Records, 1973: COS 2032).

228 "She doesn't play" José Quintero, *New York Post*, Jan. 8, 1962, p. 36.

228 "I loved" Lenya in station WPAT *Gaslight Revue Program Guide*, vol. 7, no. 1 (September 1961), p. 59.

229 "She haunts" Alan Dent, "Two American Tragedies," *London Sunday Telegraph*, Feb. 18, 1962.

229 "Lotte Lenya is so" Bryan Buckingham, "Spring Comes a Little Late for Mrs. Stone," *News of the World*, Feb. 18, 1962.

229 "played with" David Robinson, *Financial Times*, Feb. 16, 1962.

230 "The triumph" Arthur Knight, "Romans in the Gloamin'," *Saturday Review of Literature*, Dec. 9. 1961.

230 "a ludicrous" *Time*, Dec. 29, 1961.

230 "a procuress" Paul V. Beckley, *New York Herald-Tribune*, Dec. 29, 1961.

230 "I am not" Lenya, in Robert Wahls, "Footlights," *New York Daily News*, Mar. 19, 1962.

231 "Miss Lenya's singing" Howard Taubman, "Theatre," *New York Times*, Jan. 4, 1962.

231 "hard-bitten" *Christian Science Monitor*, Jan. 6, 1962.

231 "her brash" Joseph Morgenstern, "First Night Report: Brecht on Brecht," *New York Herald-Tribune*, Jan. 4, 1962.

231 "tremendous" *New Yorker*, Jan. 8, 1962.

232 "The production's" Henry Hewes, "The On-Brechtian Theatre," *Saturday Review of Literature*, Mar. 24, 1962.

232 "with the great" D.H., *Women's Wear Daily*, Jan. 4, 1962, sec. 1.

232 "craggy-faced" Terry Southern, "The Beautiful Art of Lotte Lenya," *Glamour*, September 1962.

232 "This talk" Lenya, in John Crosby, "Brecht Warning: Don't Catch Cult," *New York Herald-Tribune*, Mar. 11, 1962, p. 14.

232 "something very" "On Brecht on Brecht," *New Yorker*, June 6, 1962, pp. 26–27.

233 "Whatever she" *Ibid.*

233 "Half the audience" *Ibid.*

235 "When she first" Milton Coleman to DS, Jan. 22, 1988.

237 "We have" Peter Lewis, "Well, Was This Man a Saint?" *Daily Mail*, Sept. 12, 1962.

237 "The programme" "Our Century's Lunacies Confronted," *The Times* (London), Sept. 12, 1962.

238 "She had" Neil Fujita to DS, Jan. 16, 1986.

242 "the most celebrated" Drew, p. 175.

243 "Look, forget" Lenya, quoted in *New York Post*, Oct. 1, 1966.

243 "When I do" Lenya, quoted in John Rockwell, "Lotte Lenya, 83, Star of Stage and Motion Pictures, Is Dead," *New York Times*, Nov. 28, 1981, p. 21; also, Bernard Weinraub, "Lenya on Weill: The Memory Lingers On," *New York Times*, Oct. 25, 1964.

243 "Lenya plays" *Newsweek*, Apr. 13, 1964, p. 93.

244 "When she steps" Richard Christiansen, "Lotte Lenya Magnificent in 'Brecht,' " *Chicago Daily News*, Nov. 14, 1963.

245 "It was [hot]" Alan Rich, "The Unforgettable Night That Lotte Lenya Scorched Carnegie Hall," *New York Herald-Tribune*, Jan. 9, 1965, p. 8.

246 "With no effort" Theodore Strongin, "Miss Lenya Stars in Weill Tribute," *New York Times*, Jan. 9, 1965.

246 "Have you ever" Jerry Talmer, "Miss Lenya at Carnegie," *New York Post*, Jan. 10, 1965.

250 "Lotte Lenya does not" *Düsseldorfer Nachrichten*, June 14, 1965; trans. Prof. Jon Zimmermann.

250 "In choosing" *Frankfurter Rundschau*, June 15, 1965, trans. Prof. Jon Zimmermann.

250 "She's no" *Ibid.*, trans. Prof. Jon Zimmermann.

250 "experiment that" *Kölner Stadtanzeiger*, June 16, 1965, trans. Prof. Jon Zimmermann.

252 "She couldn't" Albert Samuelson to DS, Oct. 20, 1985.

CHAPTER TEN

254 "Although her voice" Gershon Kingsley to DS, April 14, 1986.

255 "We never thought" Joe Masteroff to DS, Mar. 10, 1986.

255 "I had Lenya" John Kander to DS, Feb. 5, 1986.

256 "But she was" Harold Prince to DS, Nov. 19, 1985.

256 "A moment later" Fred Ebb to DS, Feb. 5, 1986.

260 "She has" Harold C. Schonberg, *New York Times*, Nov. 20, 1966, p. 44.

262 "I have the same" Lenya to Robert Wahls, *New York Daily News*, Mar. 19, 1967.

262 "For sixteen years" Rex Reed, "The Lady Known as Lenya," *New York Times Magazine*, Nov. 20, 1966, p. 128.

267 "a tepid" *Variety*, July 19, 1972.

CHAPTER ELEVEN

280 "He had a" Hans Dudelheim to DS, Nov. 13, 1985.

281 "It's so nice" Lenya to Linda Deutsch, "Lotte Lenya Shuns Thoughts of Retiring," *Long Island Press*, Nov. 29, 1971.

284 "Everyone was very" Ernest Hood to DS, Apr. 7, 1986.

285 "Lotte Lenya grows" Dan Sullivan, "Lotte Lenya in 'Courage,' " *Los Angeles Times*, Nov. 19, 1971, part IV, p. 23.

286 "not snazzy" *The Times* (London), Feb. 11, 1972.

291 "It feels wonderful" Lenya, in James Feron, "Residents of Rockland County Donate Land for Park," *New York Times*, Jan. 14, 1976, p. 37.

292 "no humor" *New York Times*, Nov. 12, 1976.

293 "Her smallest" Joy Bogen to DS, Jan. 6, 1986.

300 "During *Mahagonny*" Teresa Stratas, in Louis Morra, "The Personal Pilgrimage of Teresa Stratas," *Ovation*, vol. 3, no. 10 (November 1982), p. 14.

302 "It was a" Ronald Freed to DS, April 24, 1988.

307 "I knew you" quoted by Tala Meredith to DS, Feb. 10, 1986.

309 "Teresa, what" quoted on the record jacket for *Stratas Sings Weill* (1986, Nonesuch 9-79131-1).

LOTTE LENYA

SELECTED DISCOGRAPHY

Aufstieg und Fall der Stadt Mahagonny. Wilhelm Brückner-Rüggeberg, conductor. CBS M2K 77341 (all formats).
Berlin and American Theater Songs. CBS MK 42658 (CD); Columbia MG 30087 (LP).
Brecht on Brecht. Columbia O2L 278.
Cabaret. Original Cast Album. Columbia CK 3040 (CD); KOL 6640 (LP).
Die Dreigroschenoper. Wilhelm Brückner-Rüggeberg, conductor. CBS MK 42637 (all formats).
Die Dreigroschenoper. Excerpts recorded in 1930. Dokumente 6.41911.
Happy End. Wilhelm Brückner-Rüggeberg, conductor. Columbia Special Products 2032 (LP); CBS 88 028 (LP).
Johnny Johnson. Samuel Matlowsky, conductor. PolyGram Polydor 831 384 (all formats).
The Lotte Lenya Album. Columbia Masterworks M6 30087.
Seven Deadly Sins. Wilhelm Brückner-Rüggeberg, conductor. Columbia AKL 5175 (LP); CBS 88 028 (LP).
Threepenny Opera. English adaptation by Marc Blitzstein. Samuel Matlowsky, conductor. Polydor 820 260-2 (CD).

SPOKEN WORD RECORDINGS
Invitation to German Poetry. Selected by Gustave Mathieu and Guy Stern. New York: Dover, 1959.
The Stories of Kafka. In English. Caedmon TC 1114.

FILM APPEARANCES AVAILABLE ON VIDEOCASSETTE
The Threepenny Opera [*Die Dreigroschenoper*]: German, 1931. Embassy Home Entertainment.
The Roman Spring of Mrs. Stone, 1961. Warner Home Video.
From Russia with Love, 1963. MGM/UA Home Video.
Semi-Tough, 1976. CBS/Fox Video.

INDEX

About the Author

DONALD SPOTO is the author of THE DARK SIDE OF GE-
NIUS: *The Life of Alfred Hitchcock*; FALLING IN LOVE
AGAIN: *Marlene Dietrich*; THE KINDNESS OF
STRANGERS: *The Life of Tennessee Williams*; CAMER-
ADO: *Hollywood and the American Man*; STANLEY
KRAMER: *Film Maker*; and THE ART OF ALFRED
HITCHCOCK: *Fifty Years of His Motion Pictures*. He lives
in California, where he is working on biographies of Preston
Sturges and Marlene Dietrich.

FORMIDABLE
BIOGRAPHIES
OF SOME OF SOCIETY'S
GREATEST AND
MOST INTERESTING
TALENTS, BY:
DONALD SPOTO

Available at your bookstore or use this coupon.

___**Kindness of Stangers**   32618 $4.95
The first complete, critical biography of America's finest playwright, Tennessee Williams.

___**Dark Side of Genius: The Life of**   31462 $4.95
Alfred Hitchcock
A definitive biography of Alfred Hitchcock, from boyhood to the apex of his career to his eventual demise.

___**Lenya: A Life**   36542 $5.95
A extraordinary biography of the legendary singer/actress, Lotte Lenya.

BB   **BALLANTINE MAIL SALES**
       Dept. TA, 201 E. 50th St., New York, N.Y. 10022

Please send me the BALLANTINE or DEL REY BOOKS I have checked above. I am enclosing $...............(add $2.00 to cover postage and handling for the first book and 50¢ each additional book). Send check or money order—no cash or C.O.D.'s please. Prices are subject to change without notice. Valid in U.S. only. All orders are subject to availability of books.

Name_____

Address_____

City_____State_____Zip Code_____

05   Allow at least 4 weeks for delivery.   **TA-263**